Scripture Commentary Sampler

*Anthology of Scripture Commentaries
Selected and Supplemented by a Layman*

DAVE MARTIN

Scripture Commentary Sampler: Anthology of Scripture Commentaries Selected and Supplemented by a Layman

This book is written to provide information and motivation to readers. Its purpose is not to render any type of psychological, legal, or professional advice of any kind. The content is the sole opinion and expression of the author, and not necessarily that of the publisher.

Unless otherwise specified, Scripture Quotations are from
THE HOLY BIBLE, NEW INTERNATIONAL VERSION®, NIV® Copyright © 1973, 1978, 1984, 2011 by Biblica, Inc.® Used by permission. All rights reserved worldwide.

Scripture quotations other than NIV

KJV: King James Version (1611)

ESV: English Standard Version: The Holy Bible, Copyright 2001 by Crossway Bibles, division of Good News Publications.

NASB: New American Standard Bible Copyright © 1960,1962, 1963, 1968, 1971, 1972, 1973,1975,1977,1995 by The Lockman Foundation.

NKJV: The Holy Bible, New King James Version®. Copyright © 1982 by Thomas Nelson, Inc. All rights reserved.

Copyright © 2021 by Dave Martin.

All rights reserved. No part of this book may be reproduced, transmitted, or distributed in any form by any means, including, but not limited to, recording, photocopying, or taking screenshots of parts of the book, without prior written permission from the author or the publisher. Brief quotations for noncommercial purposes, such as book reviews, permitted by Fair Use of the U.S. Copyright Law, are allowed without written permissions, as long as such quotations do not cause damage to the book's commercial value. For permissions, write to the publisher, whose address is stated below.

Printed in the United States of America.

ISBN   978-1-953150-96-7   (Paperback)
ISBN   978-1-953150-97-4   (Digital)

Lettra Press books may be ordered through booksellers or by contacting:

Lettra Press LLC
30 N Gould St. Suite 4753
Sheridan, WY 82801
1 307-200-3414 | info@lettrapress.com
www.lettrapress.com

Contents

Acknowledgments v
Note about Copyrights vii
Hymn and Worship Song List ix
Bibliography xi
Preface xix
Introduction xxi
Old Testament (Genesis) 1
New Testament (Matthew) 253

Epilogue: What God's Word Says to Me 431
Quotations 453
Author Index 455

Acknowledgments

How can I repay the Lord for all his goodness to me? (Psalm 116:12)

This book is the culmination of a twenty-five-year journey of faith in which God's word has greatly enriched my life (and continues to do so). This book would obviously have not been possible without the excellent resources available through two main publishers: InterVarsity Press (the *Bible Speaks Today* or BST series) and Thomas Nelson (*The Preacher's Commentary*). I've also drawn on Matthew Henry's 18th century classic commentary and on Charles Haddon Spurgeon's *Treasury of David* commentary on the Psalms, which I consider among of the finest masterpieces in all of English literature. In addition, the *Doubleday Christian Quotation Collection* edited by Hannah Ward and Jennifer Wild is an absolute treasure chest of gems that add sparkle to this Sampler.

I also want to thank my dear brothers and sisters in Christ in the three churches I attended during the compilation of this book: Cedar Springs Presbyterian Church in Knoxville, Tennessee; Evangelical Presbyterian Church in Newark, Delaware; and my current church home of Chestnut Mountain Presbyterian Church in Flowery Branch, GA. All three of these congregations have greatly enriched my knowledge of God's word and my life in general.

Finally, I thank my dear wife Laurie for her advice, support and encouragement during this study. Of her, I can truly say: "Many women do noble things, but you surpass them all." (Prov 31:29)

Dave Martin, Gwinnett County, Georgia, USA   Published July 2019, Revised March 2021

Note about Copyrights

Most of this book is comprised of excerpts from the works of others. In all, I've quoted seventy authors of over a hundred different commentary books. A major objective of this anthology is to shine a spotlight on these learned scholars. Their books represent an impressive life work that I want to share with others in hopes that they will buy and read the originals.

Ten of the seventy authors deserve special mention. The following works were especially crucial to this volume, and I urge others to purchase and read these extraordinary commentaries:

Dunnam, Maxie D.
    The Preacher's Commentary NT vol 31, Thomas Nelson, 1982. (*Gal, Eph, Phil, Col*)

Edwards, James R.
    Romans, Grand Rapids, MI: Baker Books, 1992.
    The Gospel According to Mark, Grand Rapids, MI: Eerdmans, 2002
    The Gospel According to Luke, Grand Rapids, MI: Eerdmans, 2015

Green, Michael
    The Message of Matthew Leicester, England: Inter-Varsity Press, 1988.

Kitchen, John A.
    Proverbs: A Mentor Commentary, Fearn, Ross-Shire UK: Christian Focus Publ, 2006.

Milne, Bruce
    The Message of John Leicester, England: Inter-Varsity Press, 1993.

McKenna, David L.
    Job: The Preacher's Commentary, OT vol 12. Nashvlle: Thomas Nelson, 1982.

Oswalt, John N.,
  The Book of Isaiah: Chapters 1–39, Grand Rapids, MI: Eerdmans, 1986.
  The Book of Isaiah: Chapters 40–66, Grand Rapids, MI: Eerdmans, 1998.

Wilcock, Michael,
  The Message of Psalms 1–72 Leicester, England: Inter-Varsity Press, 2001.
  The Message of Psalms 73–150 Leicester, England: Inter-Varsity Press, 1992.

Wright, Christopher J.H.,
  The Message of Lamentations Downers Grove IL: Inter-Varsity Press, 2015.
  The Message of Jeremiah Downers Grove, IL: Inter-Varsity Press, 2014.

Hymn and Worship Song List

Title	Author	Year	Verse
Come Ye Thankful People Come	Alford, Henry	1844	Deut 11:14
This Is My Father's World	Babcock, Maltbie	1901	Ps 19:1
Let All Things Now Living	Davis, Katherine K.	1939	Ps 95:2
O Worship the King	Grant, Robert	1833	Ps 104:1
Joyful Joyful We Adore Thee	Van Dyke, Henry	1907	Isa 35:10
Christ is Made the Sure Foundation	Neale, John Mason, tr.	1861	Mt 28:19
How Deep the Father's Love for Us	Townend, Stuart	1995	Mk 15:30
Hark the Herald Angels Sing	Wesley, Charles	1739	Lk 2:13
See What a Morning	Getty, Keith; Townend, Stuart	2003	Lk 24:5
Spirit of God, Descend upon my Heart	George Croly	1854	Rom 8:5-6
When I Survey the Wondrous Cross	Watts, Isaac	1707	Phil 3:8
Fairest Lord Jesus	Seiss, Joseph A (tr.)	1873	Col 1:15
Love Divine, All Loves Excelling	Wesley, Charles	1747	1 John 4:9
Crown Him with Many Crowns	Bridges, Matthew	1851	Rev 22:20

Bibliography

Adam, Peter, *The Message of Malachi*, Leicester, England: Inter–Varsity Press, 2013.

Allen, Leslie C., *The Books of Joel, Obadiah, Jonah, and Micah* Grand Rapids, MI: Eerdmans, 1976.

1 & 2 Chronicles, The Preacher's Commentary, OT Vol 10., Nashville: Thomas Nelson, 1987

Atkinson, David, *The Message of Genesis 1–11*, Leicester, England: Inter-Varsity Press, 1990

Augsburger, Myron S., The Preacher's Commentary, NT Vol 24, Nashville, TN: Thomas Nelson, 1982.

Baldwin, Joyce, *The Message of Genesis 12-50*, Leicester, England: Inter-Varsity Press, 1986

Baker, William, Cornerstone Biblical Commentary, Vol 15, Carol Stream, IL: Tyndale, 2009

Barnett, Paul, The *Second Epistle to the Corinthians* Grand Rapids, MI: Eerdmans, 1997.

Boice, James Montgomery, *Genesis, Volume 1*, Grand Rapids, MI: Baker Books, 1982.

Briscoe, D. Stuart, *Genesis, OT Vol 1., The Preacher's Commentary*, Copyright © by Word, Inc 1987

Romans, NT Vol 29, The Preacher's Commentary, Copyright © by Word, Inc 1982.

Bridger, Gordon *The Message of Obadiah, Nahum & Zephaniah* Leicester, England: Inter-Varsity Press, 2010

Brown, Raymond, *The Message of Numbers*, Leicester, England: Inter-Varsity Press, 2002

The Message of Deuteronomy, Leicester, England: Inter-Varsity Press, 1993.

The Message of Nehemiah, Leicester, England: Inter-Varsity Press, 1998.

The Message of Hebrews, Leicester, England: Inter-Varsity Press, 1982

Bruckner, James K., *Exodus*, Grand Rapids, MI, Baker Books, 2008

Cedar, Paul A., *The Preacher's Commentary*, NT Vol 34 *(James / 1 & 2 Peter / Jude)*, Nashville: Thomas Nelson, 1984.

Chafin, Kenneth L., *The Preacher's Commentary*, OT Vol 8, Nashville, TN: Thomas Nelson, 1989

Clowney, Edmund, *The Message of 1 Peter* Leicester, England: Inter-Varsity Press, 1988

Davis, Dale Ralph, *Joshua: No Falling Words*, Fearn, Ross-Shire UK: Christian Focus Publ, 2000.

1 Samuel: Looking on the Heart, Fearn, Ross-Shire UK: Christian Focus Publ, 2000

2 Samuel: Out of Every Adversity Fearn, Ross-Shire UK: Christian Focus Publ, 2002

1 Kings: The Wisdom and the Folly, Fearn, Ross-Shire UK: Christian Focus Publ, 2002

2 Kings: The Power and the Fury, Fearn, Ross-Shire UK: Christian Focus Publ, 2005

Demarest, Gary W., *The Preacher's Commentary OT vol 3*, Thomas Nelson, 1990. (Leviticus)

The Preacher's Commentary NT vol 32 (1 and 2 Thes, Timothy, Titus), Thomas Nelson, 1984

Diehl, Judith A., *The Story of God Bible Commentary:2 Corinthians*, Grand Rapids, MI: Zondervan, 2020

Dilday, Russel H., *The Preachers Commentary*, OT Vol 9 (1 & 2 Kings) Nashville: Thomas Nelson, 1987

Dunnam, Maxie D., *The Preacher's Commentary OT vol 2*, (Exodus) Nashville: Thomas Nelson, 1987.

The Preacher's Commentary NT vol 31, Thomas Nelson, 1982. (Gal, Eph, Philippians, Col)

Edwards, James R. *Romans*, Grand Rapids, MI: Baker Books, 1992.

The *Gospel According to Mark*, Grand Rapids, MI: Eerdmans, 2002.

The Gospel According to Luke, Grand Rapids, MI: Eerdmans, 2015.

Evans, Louis H., *The Preacher's Commentary: Hebrews (NT Vol 33)* Thomas Nelson, 1985.

Evans, Mary J., *The Message of Samuel*, Leicester, England: Inter-Varsity Press, 2004

Firth, David G., *The Message of Esther*, Leicester, England: Inter-Varsity Press, 2010.

Fredrikson, Roger L., *John, The Preacher's Commentary*, Nashville: Thomas Nelson, 1985.

Ferguson, Sinclair B.,*The Preacher's Commentary*, OT vol 21 Nashville: Thomas Nelson, 1988

Fyall, Robert, *The Message of Ezra and Haggai*, Leicester, England: Inter-Varsity Press, 2010.

Gledhill, Tom *The Message of Song of Songs* Leicester, England: Inter-Varsity Press, 1994.

Green, Christopher, *The Message of 2 Peter and Jude* Leicester, England: Inter-Varsity Press, 1995.

Green, Gene L., *Thessalonians* (Pillar NT Commentary), Grand Rapids, MI: Eerdmans, 2002.

Green, Michael *The Message of Matthew* Leicester, England: Inter-Varsity Press, 1988.

Grogan, Geoffrey, *Mark: Good News from Jerusalem* Fearn, Ross-Shire UK: Christian Focus Publ, 1995

Guest, John, *Jeremiah / Lamentations, The Preacher's Commentary*, Nashville: Thomas Nelson, 1988.

Hartley, John E., *Genesis*, Grand Rapids, MI: Baker Books, 2000

Henry, Matthew Commentary (1710) on line at www.BlueletterBible.com

Hillyer, Norman *1 and 2 Peter, Jude*, Grand Rapids: Baker Books,1992.

Hubbard, David A., *Proverbs, The Preacher's Commentary OT Vol 15*, Thomas Nelson, 1989.

Ecclesiastes/Song of Solomon, The Preacher's Commentary OT Vol. 16, Thomas Nelson, 1991.

Hubbard, Jr, Robert L., *The Book of Ruth* Grand Rapids, MI: Eerdmans, 1988.

Huffman, Jr., John A., *Joshua: The Preacher's Commentary (OT Vol 6)* Nashville, Thomas Nelson, 1986

Jackman, David, *The Preacher's Commentary, OT Vol 7, Judges / Ruth*, Nashville: Thomas Nelson, 1991.

The Message of John's Letters Leicester, England: Inter-Varsity Press, 1988.

Jacobson, Rolf A., *The Book of Psalms* (NICOT), Grand Rapids, MI: Eerdmans, 2014

Jennings, Frederick Charles, *Studies in Isaiah* Neptune, NJ: Loizeaux Brothers, 1935.

Kaiser, Walter C., *The Preacher's Commentary, OT Vol 23, (Micah, Nahum, Habakkuk, Zephaniah, Haggai, Zechariah, Malachi)*. Nashville, Thomas Nelson, 1992

Keller, Timothy, *The Prodigal God*, Dutton, 2008.

Kidner, Derek, *The Message of Ecclesiastes* Leicester, England: Inter-Varsity Press, 1976.

Kitchen, John A. *Proverbs: A Mentor Commentary*, Fearn, Ross-Shire UK: Christian Focus Publ, 2006.

Colossians and Philemon for Pastors, The Woodlands, TX: Kress Biblical Resources, 2012

Konkel, August H, *Cornerstone Biblical Commentary*, Vol. 6, Carol Stream, IL: Tyndale, 2006

Laansma, Jon C., *Cornerstone Biblical Commentary*, Vol 17, Carol Stream, IL: Tyndale, 2009

Larkin, William J., *Cornerstone Biblical Commentary*, Vol 12, Carol Stream, IL: Tyndale, 2006

Larniac, Timothy S., *Ezra, Nehemiahm, Esther*, Grand Rapids, MI: Baker Books, 2003

Larson, Bruce, The Preacher's Commentary, NT Vol 26, Luke, Nashville: Thomas Nelson, 1983.

Lucas, Dick, *The Message of 2 Peter and Jude* Leicester, England: Inter-Varsity Press, 1995

The Message of Colossians and Philemon, Leicester, England: Inter-Varsity Press, 1980.

MacArthur, John, *1 Corinthians*, Chicago: Moody Press, 1984.

Mackay, John L., *Haggai, Zechariah, & Malachi: God's Restored People,* Fearn, Ross-Shire UK: Christian Focus Publ, 2003.

Maxwell, John C. *The Preacher's Commentary*, OT Vol 5, Nashville, TN: Thomas Nelson, 1987

McKenna, David L., *Job: The Preacher's Commentary, OT vol 12*. Nashvlle: Thomas Nelson, 1982.

Mark: The Preacher's Commentary, NT vol 25. Nashville: Thomas Nelson, 1982.

Millar, J. Gary. *ESV Expository Commentary*, Vol 3, Wheaton, IL: Crossway 2019

Milne, Bruce, *The Message of John* Leicester, England: Inter-Varsity Press, 1993.

Motyer, J. Alec, *The Message of Exodus*, Leicester, England: Inter-Varsity Press, 2005.

The Message of Amos Leicester, England: Inter-Varsity Press, 1974.

The Message of James Leicester, England: Inter-Varsity Press, 1985.

The Message of Philippians Leicester, England: Inter-Varsity Press, 1984.

The Prophecy of Isaiah, Downers Grove IL: Intervarsity Press, 1993.

Mulholland, Jr, M. Robert, *Cornerstone Biblical Commentary*, Vol. 18, Carol Stream IL: Tyndale, 2011

Nixon, Rosemary, *The Message of Jonah* Leicester, England: Inter-Varsity Press, 2003.

Nouwen, Henri J.M., *The Return of the Prodigal Son*, New York: Doubleday, 1992.

Ogilvie, Lloyd J., *Hosea/Joel/Amos/Obadiah/Jonah: The Preacher's Commentary, OT vol 22*, 1990.

Acts: The Preacher's Commentary, NT Vol 28, Nashville: Thomas Nelson, 1983.

Olley, John W., *The Message of Kings*, Leicester, England: Inter-Varsity Press, 2011
Oswalt, John N., *The Book of Isaiah: Chapters 1–39*, Grand Rapids, MI: Eerdmans, 1986.
  The Book of Isaiah: Chapters 40–66, Grand Rapids, MI: Eerdmans, 1998.
  Cornerstone Biblical Commentary, Vol 1, Carol Stream, IL: Tyndale 2008
Palmer, Earl F. *The Preacher's Commentary, NT Vol 35*: Thomas Nelson, 1982
Patterson, Richard D., *Cornerstone Biblical Commentary, Vol 10*, Carol Stream IL: Tyndale, 2008
Peterson, Eugene H., *Reversed Thunder: The Revelation of John & Praying Imagination*, San Francisco: Harper Collins, 1988
  A Long Obedience in the Same Direction: Discipleship in an Instant Society, Downers Grove, IL: InterVarsity Press, 2000.
  The Message: The Bible in Contemporary Language, NavPress, 2002.
  First and Second Samuel, Louisville: Westminster John Knox Press, 1999.
James Philip, The Preacher's Commentary, OT Vol 4, Nashville: Thomas Nelson, 1987
Phillips, John, *Exploring Genesis*, Grand Rapids, MI: Kregel Publications, 2001.
Phillips, Robert D., *Zechariah*, Phillipsburg NJ: P&R Publishing, 2007.
Prior, David, *The Message of 1 Corinthians* Leicester, England: Inter-Varsity Press, 1985.
  The Message of Joel, Micah, & Habakkuk, Leicester, England: Inter-Varsity Press, 1998
Roberts, Mark D., *Ezra/Nehemiah/Esther (The Preacher's Commentary – Vol 11)*, Nashville: Thomas Nelson, 1993.
Robertson, O. Palmer, *The Books of Nahum, Habakkuk, and Zephaniah*, Grand Rapids, MI: Eerdman's, 1990.
Scott, James M., *2 Corinthians*, Grand Rapids, MI: Baker Books (1998)
Smith, Chuck, *The Book of Acts*, Costa Mesa, CA: The Word for Today, 2013.
Spurgeon, Charles Haddon, (1834-1892, *The Gospel of Matthew*, Reprinted 1987, Fleming H. Revell Co.
  The Treasury of David (1885)
  The Golden Alphabet (1887) www.gospelweb.net/Spurgeon
  Sermons on line http://www.romans45.org/spurgeon/spsrmns.htm
Stott, John R.W., *The Message of Acts* Leicester, England: Inter-Varsity Press, 1990
  The Message of Romans Leicester, England: Inter-Varsity Press, 1994.
  The Message of Galatians Leicester, England: Inter-Varsity Press, 1968.
  The Message of Ephesians Leicester, England: Inter-Varsity Press, 1979.
  The Message of 1 and 2 Thessalonians Leicester, England: Inter-Varsity Press, 1991.
  The Message of 1 Timothy and Titus Leicester, England: Inter-Varsity Press, 1996.
  The Message of 2 Timothy Leicester, England: Inter-Varsity Press, 1973.

Storms, Sam, *ESV Expository Commentary* (1 Peter), Vol. XII, Wheaton, IL: Crossway, 2018

Stuart, Douglas, *The Preacher's Commentary*, OT Vol 20, Nashville: Thomas Nelson, 1989

Swindoll, Charles *Insights on Luke*, Grand Rapids, MI: Zondervan, 2012
    Living Insights, Vol 1a (Matt 1-15), Carol Stream, IL: Tyndale, 2020
    Living Insights, Vol 4, Carol Stream, IL: Tyndale, 2014
    Living Insights, Vol 5, (Acts) Carol Stream, IL: Tyndale, 2016
    Insights on James and 1 & 2 Peter, Carol Stream, IL: Tyndale House, 2014.
    Insights on Galatians / Ephesians, Carol Stream, IL: Tyndale, 2015
    Living Insights, Vol 14, Carol Stream, IL: Tyndale, 2018
    Job: A Man of Heroic Endurance, Nashville, TN: Thomas Nelson (2004)

Tanner, Beth LaNeel, *The Book of Psalms* (NICOT), Grand Rapids, MI: Eerdmans, 2014

Thompson, David L., *Cornerstone Biblical Commentary*, Vol 9, Carol Stream, IL: Tyndale, 2010

Thompson, J.A., *The Book of Jeremiah*, Grand Rapids, MI: Eerdmans, 1980.

Tidball, Derek, *The Message of Leviticus*, Leicester, England: Inter-Varsity Press, 2005.

Trites, Allison A., *Cornerstone Biblical Commentary*, Vol. 12, Carol Stream, IL: Tyndale, 2006

Wallace, Ronald S., *The Message of Daniel* Leicester, England: Inter-Varsity Press, (Date not specified)

Waltke, Bruce, *The Book of Proverbs 1–15* Grand Rapids, MI: Eerdmans, 2004.
    Genesis, A Commentary (with Cathi J. Fredricks), Grand Rapids, MI: Zondervan, 2001

Ward, Hannah and Wild, Jennifer, *The Doubleday Christian Quotation Collection*, New York: Doubleday, 1998.
<u>Note</u>: As an anthology, quotation sources are cited in Acknowledgements section of Ward and Wild's collection.

Webb, Barry G., *The Message of Zechariah* Leicester, England: Inter-Varsity Press, 2003.

Widder, Wendy L.,*The Story of God Bible Commentary*, *Daniel*, Grand Rapids, MI: Zondervan,2016

Williams, David J., *1 and 2 Thessalonians*, Grand Rapids, MI: Baker Books, 1992.

Williams, Donald M., *Psalms 1–72: The Preacher's Commentary (OT Vol 13)*, Nashville: Thomas Nelson, 1986

Wilcock, Michael, *The Message of Judges* Leicester, England: Inter-Varsity Press, 1992.
  The Message of Chronicles Leicester, England: Inter-Varsity Press, 1987.
  The Message of Psalms 1–72 Leicester, England: Inter-Varsity Press, 2001.
  The Message of Psalms 73–150 Leicester, England: Inter-Varsity Press, 1992.
  The Message of Revelation Leicester, England: Inter-Varsity Press, 1975.
Woodhouse, John *So Walk in Him (Colossians and Philemon)*,Fearn, Ross-Shire UK: Christian Focus Publ, 2011.
Wright, Christopher J.H., *Deuteronomy*, Grand Rapids, MI: Baker Books, 1996.
  The Message of Ezekiel Leicester, England: Inter-Varsity Press, 2001.
  The Message of Jeremiah Downers Grove, IL: Inter-Varsity Press, 2014.
  The Message of Lamentations Downers Grove IL: Inter-Varsity Press, 2015.
  Hearing the Message of Daniel, Grand Rapids, MI: Zondervan, 2017
  The Story of God Bible Commentary, *Exodus*, Grand Rapids, MI: Zondervan, 2021

Preface

Over the centuries, The Holy Bible has inspired scholars to write commentaries on its profound truths. This selection of scripture verses and commentaries is intended to provide a small taste of this rich but often neglected literary genre. Most of the words presented here were penned by others and not myself. I attempt to give credit where credit is due, but I urge readers to respect copyrights and to buy the commentaries and read them first hand. Here is a brief overview:

Sources

- Bibles

    - NIV (Main source): Scripture References are NIV unless otherwise cited.
    - ESV, NASB, KJV, NKJV
    - www.blueletterbible.com Bible translations including all those above plus Greek and Hebrew
- Bible Commentaries
    - *The Bible Speaks Today* (Intervarsity Press)
    - *The Preacher's Commentary* (Thomas Nelson Publishers)
    - *Understanding the Bible* (Baker Books)
    - *Cornerstone Biblical Commentary* (Tyndale)
    - *NICOT / NICNT* (New International Commentary OT and NT)
    - *Focus on the Bible / Mentor* Commentaries (Christian Focus)
    - Matthew Henry Commentary (18th Century)
- *Treasury of David* by Charles Haddon Spurgeon

- *Doubleday Christian Quotation Collection* (Hannah Ward and Jennifer Wild)
- Hymns and Worship Songs
- Christian Books (authors include Philip Yancey, Eugene Peterson, and Henri Nouwen)
- Proclamations by American leaders
  - Washington's proclamation on the first Thanksgiving
  - Lincoln's proclamation of National Fast Day
- Sermons
- Anecdotes from SS Class, Men's Prayer Group, Christian Mentors

Conventions and Caveats

- This is a *Sampler*, and makes no attempt to be comprehensive.
- To put the *Sampler* in context, go back to the originals (both Scripture and Commentary). I urge readers to get a fuller picture by reading the originals.
- For brevity, as I transcribed the commentator's text, I made small edits to make context more clear. I apologize if I inadvertently mangled the commentator's work!
- Verse references in square brackets [] are not in original commentator's text but were added
- I am not a seminary trained Bible Scholar and so I may make some 'amateur's mistakes.'

Introduction

The Bible is like a telescope. If a man looks through his telescope, then he sees worlds beyond; but if he looks at his telescope, then he does not see anything but that. The Bible is a thing to be looked through, to see that which is beyond; but most people only look at it; and so they see only a dead letter.
Phillips Brooks (1835–18903), Bishop of Massachusetts
(Quoted in Ward and Wild)

When we look at all the significant people and documents in human history, the Bible stands alone. It has outlasted philosophers, empires, and potentates and continues to influence hundreds of millions of people in every time zone on the planet. No other document has had such a powerful impact on people's lives for so long and over so much territory as the Bible. It stands above history and time to proclaim that life on earth has meaning. If we would just look around us and tap a wisdom that is higher than ourselves, we would begin to see rich patterns emerge from the apparent cacophony of our existence. We would see that life is a gift from our Creator. We were made in his image and given dominion over the earth. And a magnificent destiny awaits us as we conclude our journey on this earth thanks to his glorious grace.

The Bible has not only inspired people in their daily lives, it has been a foundation stone of the arts. Many of the greatest works of Art, Literature, and Music spring from the wisdom contained in scripture. In particular, a literature of commentaries on the Bible began in ancient times and continues to this day. This summary compilation of mainly modern works in the genre of Bible Commentaries is intended to give a small sampling of the rich wisdom that rewards diligent study of the scriptures and commentaries.

I began my personal study of the Bible in 1994. Pastor John Wood of Cedar Springs Presbyterian Church (Knoxville TN) delivered a sermon centered on 2 Timothy 3:16. He cited surveys that found that about seventy percent of the U.S. public considers themselves to be Christian, but only eleven percent read their Bible every day. Pastor Wood then made the caveat that this may be misleading since a lot of people call themselves 'Christian' but may not be strongly committed to the faith. So another survey was conducted only among those who considered themselves to be 'born again.' One would expect the percentage to be much higher among that group. But the survey found that only eighteen percent of born again Christians read their Bible every day and more than half admitted they never read it at all.

Pastor Wood issued a challenge. He stated that one could read the entire Bible in one year easily simply by reading about four pages a day. No matter how busy a person might be, surely he or she can find time to read four pages each day! His challenge resonated with me and I immediately began reading the entire Bible. As I read, I found many "verse nuggets" and jotted them down. The more I read, the more I was captivated.

Since that time, I have read the entire Bible at least a dozen times (and counting) and have read and studied parts of it numerous times. In 2005, I decided to not only read the Bible, but also read and study a Christian commentary for every book of the Bible. At each study session, I chose the most salient points the commentary made and wrote them down in a journal. In parallel, I read Christian quotations from the excellent compilation by Hannah Ward and Jennifer Wild and occasionally interspersed some of the more compelling quotes into my journal. In all, I filled several spiral bound journals with my notes, which formed the nucleus of this *Bible Commentary Sampler*. The journals were later supplemented with a selection of famous hymns (which are in themselves a kind of scripture commentary) and other sources such as books, sermons, and studies I have encountered.

The dozen or so hymns, worship songs, and choral anthems contained in this book are only a small representative sample of the rich heritage of hymn writing through the ages. Even well-known hymns have verses that are not as familiar but are nonetheless artistically magnificent. As I sang many of these songs in church, I recognized that most of the lines echo Scripture, and this inspired me to look up a verse reference for each line.

In the year 2017, I began to consider whether others would like to read the *Sampler*, but by that time it had swelled to over 1,500 pages. So I decided to compile a succinct, concise selection of only the best highlights. The result is this book.

While most of the words in this document are not my own I occasionally add my remarks as a layman (marked by <u>Personal Note</u>, or <u>My Comment</u>). In some cases, I cite a particularly memorable excerpt from a sermon (eg, Pastor John Batusic applying the words of a rock song called 'Bohemian Rhapsody' to Gen 4). In others, I add observations I have gleaned from my studies (e.g., the discussion on joy overtaking us after Isa 35:10). In other cases, I add little anecdotes I've picked up along the way in my study groups. In spite of years of diligent study, however, I confess I still find some Bible concepts baffling and occasionally I just express my own ignorance and uneasiness (for example, on Josh 11:20 on the issue of leaving no survivors).

I must emphasize that I am not a professional Bible scholar and have had no seminary education. I'm just an engineer reading the Bible in my daily devotions. But I record the observations of those who *are* experts and *are* Bible Scholars in hopes that those who read may receive just a small taste of a new world that awaits discovery. The Scripture commentators have revealed a fascinating kaleidoscope of wisdom that has greatly enriched my understanding of the sacred text. In addition to providing insight into Scripture, these authors present an abundant cornucopia of just plain good writing.

I hope that this *Sampler* may inspire others to explore the Bible more deeply. A few caveats are in order, however. First, there is a danger in distilling down vast and complex passages of scripture to a few sentences. This book highlights about seven hundred verses out of a total of over 31,000. It thus represents a two percent sample. By lifting verses from their context, we may obscure their message. The same is true of the Scripture commentaries. This book of about 260 pages represents over a hundred books totaling over 35,000 pages, less than one percent. Many of the points recorded in this *Sampler* reflect the culmination of a thorough discussion over many pages of a commentary. The antidote to the error of missing context is to go back and read the original (both the Scripture and the commentary). The aim of this sampler is to whet the appetite, not to satisfy it.

The second caveat is that while Christians believe Scripture is the inerrant revelation of God's word, the same cannot be said of the commentaries. While the Bible scholars are very learned and thorough, they can and do make mistakes and so do I. But I believe that most of the points these commentators make are on target and helpful to those who seek wisdom from God's Word.

With these caveats in mind, I hope the reader may glean even a small fraction of the joy I have gained in this study of God's word. The Bible can be read on many levels and the points I have recorded cover some of these levels. It can be read as a literary masterpiece with intricate poetic devices such as *chiasm* (Lk 15, Jonah 1, Isa 55), *inclusio* (Psalm 84), and strategic word repetition (Isa 53). It can be read as a fascinating story of the lives of people from ancient times who show us that we are in many ways just like them. It can also be used as a guide to life: an unabashed display of the foibles of man to warn and correct him as well as a divinely lit path (Ps 16:11, 119:105) to true joy and contentment (Isa 35:10).

There are, however, no pat answers in the pages of Scripture. While some of the guidance found in the text is fairly straightforward (ie, "thou shalt not bear false witness"), the Bible often contains passages that baffle even the most industrious scholar. A world which seeks answers to such questions as "how could an almighty and all-loving God permit such suffering and violence?" will not find a satisfactory answer in a verse or two (however, see David McKenna's brilliant treatment of this in his commentary on the book of Job). Those who ask complex questions often expect simple answers. Experience and scripture teach us that this expectation is unrealistic.

Another point that must be made is that while Scripture provides a guide for my life, it does not provide a platform to force others to accept my judgments of right and wrong. All too many Christians have done damage to the faith by getting on their moral high horse, trying to dictate how others should live. One of the commentators, John Stott, summed it up well in his commentary on Thessalonians: "we have become known as people who preach the gospel rather than as people who live and adorn it." A message that is reiterated over and over in Scripture is that God seeks to change people from the inside out (eg Phil 2:13, Eph 3:16). Only he knows the thoughts and motives (1 Sam 16:7, 1 Cor 4:5), so only he can correct behavior. This does not rule out all judgment of our fellows, but it does place a clear constraint on our attempts to force a lifestyle on others who have not been touched by the Holy Spirit (1 Cor 5:12).

I hope and pray that anyone who reads what I have compiled may experience a fraction of the joy I have received in producing this work. May God's word enlighten and inspire you!

Special Note to Technical Types: I have heard some objections to faith from scientists and technical types. They may object that faith is not based on hard scientific evidence and sometimes even ridicule faith as weakness and fairytales. As an engineer, I have experienced the tension between faith and science. If this topic interests you, you might want to read the short excursus on Scripture from an Engineer's perspective, found following Hebrews 11:1.

Note on March 2021 Revision: In this second edition of the Sampler, I have added a couple dozen new commentaries that I had not read when the Sampler was first published in 2019. I've also added a few personal notes in an attempt to pull some insight from Scripture that may have relevance to the turbulent history we've all been through in the years 2020 and 2021.

Genesis

Commentaries:
- *Exploring Genesis*, John Phillips Series, by John Phillips (2001)
- *The Message of Genesis 1–11*, by David Atkinson (1990)
- *The Preacher's Commentary*, OT Vol. 1, by D. Stuart Briscoe (1987)
- *The Message of Genesis 12-50*, by Joyce Baldwin (1986)
- *Genesis*, Volume 1, by James Montgomery Boice (1982)
- *Genesis*, by John E. Harley (2000)
- *Genesis, a Commentary*, by Bruce K. Waltke and Cathi J. Fredricks (2001)
- *Matthew Henry Commentary* at BlueLetterBible.org (1710)

Gen 1:1: *In the beginning God created the heavens and the earth.*
בְּרֵאשִׁית בָּרָא אֱלֹהִים אֵת הַשָּׁמַיִם וְאֵת הָאָֽרֶץ׃ (Westminster Leningrad Codex) The world is a great house, consisting of upper and lower stories, the structure stately and magnificent, uniform and convenient, and every room well and wisely furnished. It is the visible part of the creation that Moses here designs to account for; therefore he mentions not the creation of angels. But as the earth has not only its surface adorned with grass and flowers, but also its bowels enriched with metals and precious stones, so the heavens are not only beautified to our eye with glorious lamps which garnish its outside, of whose creation we here read, but they are within replenished with glorious beings, out of our sight, more celestial, and more surpassing them in worth and excellency than the gold or sapphires surpass the lilies of the field. In the visible world it is easy to observe, [1.] Great variety, several sorts of beings vastly differing in their nature and constitution from each other. *Lord, how manifold are thy works* [Ps 104:24, KJV], and all good! [2.] Great beauty. The azure sky and verdant earth are

charming to the eye of the curious spectator, much more the ornaments of both. How transcendent then must the beauty of the Creator be! [3.] Great exactness and accuracy. To those that, with the help of microscopes, narrowly look into the works of nature, they appear far more fine than any of the works of art. [4.] Great power. It is not a lump of dead and inactive matter, but there is virtue, more or less, in every creature: the earth itself has a magnetic power. [5.] Great order, a mutual dependence of beings, an exact harmony of motions, and an admirable chain and connection of causes. [6.] Great mystery. There are phenomena in nature which cannot be solved, secrets which cannot be fathomed nor accounted for. But from what we see of heaven and earth we may easily enough infer the eternal power and Godhead of the great Creator [Rom 1:19], and may furnish ourselves with abundant matter for his praises. And let our position as men remind us of our duty as Christians, which is always to keep heaven in our eye and the earth under our feet.
Matthew Henry Commentary (1710)

"That the universe was formed by a fortuitous concourse of atoms, I will no more believe than that the accidental jumbling of the alphabet would fall into a most ingenious treatise of philosophy".
Jonathan Swift (1667–1745)   Quoted in Ward and Wild

He is the first subject mentioned: "In the beginning God created the heavens and the earth." Science can take us back to the big bang, to the moment of creation. But if that original, colossal explosion obliterated anything that came before it, as science suggests, then nothing before that point can be known scientifically, including the cause of the explosion. The Bible comes forward at this point to tell us simply, "In the beginning, God…". We may want to bring God down into our little microscope where we can examine him and subject him to the laws of matter, of cause and effect, which we can understand. But fret as we might, God does not conform to our desires. He confronts us as the One who was in existence *before* anything we can even imagine and who will be there *after* anything we can imagine [Ps 102:25–27].   Boice, p. 17

"Atheism is so senseless. When I look at the solar system. I see the earth at the right distance from the sun to receive the proper amounts of heat and light. This did not happen by chance."
Sir Isaac Newton (1642–1727)

Personal Note on Creation

"The Bible shows the way to go to heaven, not the way the heavens go."
(Galileo Galilei, 1564–1642)

The doctrine of Creation has spawned heated discussions both between believers and non-believers and within the believing community. The literature on this subject is rich and I make no attempt to present a comprehensive survey of it, but I hope that the few points I raise here will cause others to explore this subject more deeply. I also want to emphasize that as a Christian, I firmly believe that God created the heavens and the earth. No question about it.

Within the Christian community, there are two main schools of thought on Creation. One view, popularly known as 'Young Earth' holds that the Biblical account must be taken literally. The earth was created in six consecutive twenty-four-hour days around 4004 BC or so. This camp criticizes scientists as being every bit as dogmatic as the Young Earthers in making assumptions that cannot be proven due to lack of empirical experimental evidence. They posit the claim that we really don't know that the speed of light c has always been constant, that the correlation between spectral red shift and distance in space cannot be proven (no one has a long enough tape measure to verify it), and that linear relationships between carbon decay and the age of an object are only theories. They point to inerrant Scripture as a superior source of truth.

Another Christian camp which gets less media attention may be called the 'day-age' group. The day-agers claim that the one can read Genesis 1 and not take the Hebrew word יוֹם *Youm* to mean a literal twenty-four-hour day, but descriptive of a non-determinate period of time. Even in modern English we speak of "the day of the dinosaurs" or "in George Washington's day." In fact, Psalm 90 (written by Moses, the author of Genesis) states:

"For a thousand years in your sight are like a day that has just gone by, or like a watch in the night." (Ps 90:4)

While I lean toward the Day-Age theory, I don't buy it entirely. One needs to remember the genre of Scripture. The Bible is not an astronomy or geology textbook, but a revelation from God about his plans for the universe and for humanity. Just as we don't read Shakespeare to learn about nuclear physics, we may be mistaken if we expect to find the whole truth about the origin of the universe in the Bible. The brevity of the creation account in Genesis should be the first clue. Many many details were obviously left out of this story.

When we don't try to force the creation account into either strait-jacket of literal interpretation (eg Young Earth) or conformity with science (eg Day / Age), what emerges is a powerful revelation of God's character and a magnificent hymn to Him, not to mention an extraordinary piece of Hebrew poetry. The Genesis account shows the orderliness of the Lord's creation plan. He gives order to three dimensions in turn. First he gives order to time (dimension four) by separating light from darkness and setting the stars and planets in place with their periodic dance of precise clockwork. Then he separates sea from sky and thus gives order to space (dimension three). Next, he gives order to the earth's surface (dimension two) by separating land from sea and creating a place for inhabitants of those realms. Finally, he gives order to dimension 1 by focusing man's eyes upwards to God as he hallows the Sabbath day.

Mr. John M. Wood, senior pastor of Cedar Springs Presbyterian Church in Knoxville Tennessee, has pointed out the intricate poetic structure of the Genesis creation account. He notes that the creation days are paired through the first six with the seventh day as a pinnacle to a "pyramid." The creation days pair what was created on one day with the "lords" of those realms on a corresponding day:

Days	What	Lords	Gives Order to	Dimension
1,4	Light	Sun, moon, stars	Time	4
2,5	Sea, Sky	Fish and Birds	Space	3
3,6	Land	Animals, humanity	Surface	2
7	Rest	The Lord	Direction	1

While the Biblical creation account is remarkably consistent with science in terms of the beginning with light and the order of appearance of the various animals, its consistency or lack thereof may not be the point. The Bible aims to point us back to the creator in adoration and praise, not to explain every detail of science. As Matthew Henry put it: "the scriptures were written, not to describe to us the works of nature, a general view of which is sufficient to lead us to the knowledge and service of the Creator, but to acquaint us with the methods of grace, and those things which are purely matters of divine revelation." (Comment on Ex 25:9)

While neither camp (Young Earth or Day/Age) can be pronounced correct this side of glory, neither camp's position is vital to salvation. The Lord saves whom he chooses regardless of their view on points of doctrine. Both Young Earther's and Day/Agers may be in for a surprise when they meet their maker. It's possible that neither is right. But both owe praise to the Lord as their creator, redeemer, sanctifier, and sustainer.

Gen 1:27–28: *So God created man in his own image, in the image of God he created him; male and female he created them. God blessed them and said to them, 'Be fruitful and increase in number; fill the earth and subdue it.'* [cf Gen 5:1–2] Whenever mankind tries to figure out God, the result is God made in the image of man. When mankind is open to a divine initiative in which God reveals Himself, the result is rewarding in the extreme.   Briscoe, p. 25

Gen 2:16–17 *You are free to eat from any tree in the garden; but you must not eat from the tree of the knowledge of good and evil, for when you eat of it you will surely die.*
The one negative command is set in the context of divine care and provision. It is not a harsh restriction, but rather a symbol of the fact that crossing God-given limits diminishes rather than enhances human well-being. Freedom without bounds can all too quickly become a destructive license which binds instead of liberates. True liberty is only found within bounds [cf Joel 2:13–14, Rom 6:23].   Atkinson, p. 65

Gen 2:18: *The LORD God said, "It is not good for the man to be alone. I will make a helper suitable for him."*

Gen 2:23: *The man said, "This is now bone of my bones and flesh of my flesh; she shall be called 'woman,' for she was taken out of man."*
"Not made out of his head to top him, not out of his feet to be trampled on, but out of his side to be equal with him, under his arm to be protected, and near his heart to be beloved."
Matthew Henry Commentary (1710)

Gen 3:6: *When the woman saw that the fruit of the tree was good for food and pleasing to the eye, and also desirable for gaining wisdom, she took some and ate it. She also gave some to her husband, who was with her, and he ate it.*
Our first parents, who knew so much, did not know this—that they knew enough. In the heavenly paradise, the tree of knowledge will not be a forbidden tree; for there we shall know as we are known [1 Cor 13:12]. Let us therefore long to be there, and, in the mean time, not exercise ourselves in things too high or too deep for us [Ps 139:6], nor covet to be wise above what is written. ... The steps of the transgression, not steps upward, but downward towards the pit. 1. *She saw.* She should have turned away her eyes from beholding vanity; but she enters into temptation, by looking with pleasure on the forbidden fruit [1 Jn 2:16]. 2. *She took.* It was her own act and deed. The devil did not take it, and put it into her mouth, whether she would or no; but she herself took it. Satan may tempt, but he cannot force; may persuade us to cast ourselves down, but he cannot cast us down, Mt. 4:6. 3. *She did eat.* Perhaps she did not intend, when she looked, to take, nor, when she took, to eat; but this was the result. The way of sin is downhill; a man cannot stop himself when he will [Prov 22:3]. The beginning of it is as the breaking forth of water, to which it is hard to say, "Hitherto thou shalt come and no further." [Prov 8:29] Therefore it is our wisdom to suppress the first emotions of sin, and to leave it off before it be meddled with. *Obsta principiis*—Nip mischief in the bud. Matthew Henry Commentary

Gen 4:7: *If you do what is right, will you not be accepted? But if you do not do what is right, sin is crouching at your door; it desires to have you, but you must master it."*
Sin is always crouching at our door; indeed, it is sometimes even across the threshold and entrenched on the hearth [Rom 7:21]. It desires to master us

and in many cases has. We must master it. But How? We are inadequate for such things. If we would master sin, we must first be mastered by him who mastered it [Heb 4:15]. We must be the Master's.   Boice, p.253

Personal Note: Pastor John Batusic of CMPC in Georgia preached on Gen 4–11 on Sep 11, 2016. Genesis 4 depicts the "City of Man" whose mayor appears to be Cain. Abel brings his best to God, but the fact that the text doesn't mention Cain bringing his best implies by contrast that he did not. The Lord gives Cain several chances to repent. Sin is crouching at Cain's door but instead of mastering it, he invites it in and commits one of the worst sins, murder. Batusic surprisingly applied the *Queen* rock band's song *Bohemian Rhapsody* to the situation: Cain might have sung "Life had just begun, but now I've gone and thrown it all away." Cain is sentenced to wander (v 12), but Cain rejects the Lord's sentence by building a city and naming after his son. Cain is essentially saying, "Oh no I'm not going to be a wanderer. I'm going to build a city. I don't need God to make it in this world." Chapter 4 continues the sordid story of the City of Man. Lamech has perhaps the first example of "gangsta rap" in v 23 where he establishes his "street creds." Basically absent in the activities in most of chapter 4 is any mention of God's blessing. Even when culture progresses, morality regresses apart from God. We see it in Genesis 4 and we see it in the 21st century world in which morality has become a caricature of itself (Isa 5:20–24). People are still trying to build a tower to reach heaven and make a name for themselves (Gen 11:4) instead of bringing glory to God. So the question we face is this: do we want to live for our pleasure or God's glory? The stakes are cosmic and our choice matters.

Genesis 5 Genealogy
Bible Scholar Chuck Missler has noticed an interesting pattern in this Genealogy when we look at the Hebrew names alongside their English translation:

Hebrew	Heb Transliterated	English
אָדָם	Adam	Man
שֵׁת	Seth	Appointed
אֱנוֹשׁ	Enosh	Mortal
קֵינָן	Kenan	Sorrow
מַהֲלַלְאֵל׃	Mahalalel	The Blessed God
יֶרֶד	Jared	Shall come down
חֲנוֹךְ׃	Enoch	Teaching
מְתוּשֶׁלַח׃	Methuselah	His death shall bring
לֶמֶךְ׃	Lamech	The despairing
נֹחַ	Noah	Comfort, or Rest

So putting it all together, the genealogy says "Man is appointed mortal sorrow; (but) the Blessed God shall come down teaching (that) His death shall bring (the) despairing rest."

Here's the "gospel" hidden within a genealogy in Genesis! "It is hard to imagine the Jewish Rabbis conspiring to hide the Christian Gospel right here in the Torah!", says Missler.

Gen 6–8 The Flood: Overview

Waltke shows the elaborate chiastic structure of the flood narrative, citing B.W. Anderson, "From Analysis to Synthesis: The Interpretation of Genesis 1–11", JBL 97 (1978):

Transitional Introduction (6:9a)
   Noah and the world at the time of the flood (6:9b–12)
      Provision for the flood with divine monologue (6:13–22)
         Embarkation (7:1–5)
            Beginning of Flood (7:6–16)
               The triumphant flood (7:17–24)
                  God Remembers Noah (8:1a)
               The waning flood (8:1b–5)
            Ending of Flood (8:6–14)
         Disembarkation (8:15–19)
      Provision for post flood world with divine monologue (8:20–22)
   Noah and the world conditions after the flood (9:1–17)
Transitional introduction (9:18–19)

Waltke also notes the chiastic arrangement of the number of days:

>   7 days of waiting for the Flood (7:4)
>   7 days of waiting for the Flood (7:10)
>   40 days of flooding (7:17a)
>   150 days of water triumphing (7:24)
>   150 days of water waning (8:3)
>   40 days of waiting (8:6)
>   7 days of waiting (8:10)
>   7 days of waiting (8:12)

Gen 6:9: *Noah was a righteous man, blameless among the people of his time, and he walked with God.*
Noah's righteousness was the product of his having found favor and is therefore the proof of that favor, not its ground. This is a great biblical principle, namely, that the grace of God always comes before anything (6:8). We imagine in our unsanctified state that God loves us for what we are intrinsically or for what we have done or can become. But God does not love us because of that, nor is he gracious to us because of that. He is gracious to us only because he is [Deut 7:7–8]. What kind of logic is that: I love you because I love you? Well, it may not be the logic of Aristotle, but it is the logic of grace. Grace is grace. If grace were based on anything in us, it would not be grace [Rom 11:6]. In fact, it would not operate even as something less than grace, for there is nothing in us that can possibly draw forth God's favor. Yet grace does go forth to us and to others, who are undeserving. Boice, p. 321

"If the ways of the Almighty are not humanly logical, it is not the fault of the Almighty but of the limitations of human logic."
Maria Montessori (1870–1952)

Gen 9:13: *I have set my rainbow in the clouds, and it will be the sign of the covenant between me and the earth.*
The thicker the cloud the brighter the bow in the cloud. The rainbow appears when one part of the sky is clear, which intimates mercy remembered in the midst of wrath; and the clouds are hemmed as it were with the rainbow, that they may not overspread the heavens, for the bow is coloured rain or

the edges of a cloud gilded. The rainbow is the reflection of the beams of the sun, which intimates that all the glory and significance of the seals of the covenant are derived from Christ the Sun of righteousness, who is also described with a rainbow about his throne (Rev. 4:3), and a rainbow upon his head (Rev. 10:1). The rainbow has fiery colours in it, to signify that though God will not again drown the world, yet, when the mystery of God shall be finished, the world shall be consumed by fire. A bow bespeaks terror, but this bow has neither string nor arrow, as the bow ordained against the persecutors has (Ps. 7:12, 13), and a bow alone will do little execution. It is a bow, but it is directed upwards, not towards the earth; for the seals of the covenant were intended to comfort, not to terrify. As God looks upon the bow, that he may remember the covenant, so should we, that we also may be ever mindful of the covenant, with faith and thankfulness.   Matthew Henry Commentary

Gen 11:7: *Come, let us go down and confuse their language so they will not understand each other.*
Waltke (p 176) notes a chiastic structure (below) which exposes the theme of reversal around the pivot "the Lord came down." The plot moves from humanity's construction of a city and a tower to God's deconstruction of them:

>All the earth one language (vs 1)
>>People settle together there (vs 2)
>>>Said to each other (vs 3a)
>>>>Come now, let us make bricks (vs 3b)
>>>>>A city and tower (vs 4)
>>>>>>And the Lord came down (vs 5)
>>>>>The city and the tower (vs 5)
>>>>Come now…let us confuse (vs 7a)
>>>Not understand each other (vs 7b)
>>People disperse from there (vs 8a)
>Language of the whole earth (vs 9)

Gen 12:2: *"I will make you into a great nation and I will bless you; I will make your name great, and you will be a blessing."*
The first promise was that God would make him into a great nation. God's second promise was to bless Abram. Blessing, which corresponds

to the English word 'success,' encompasses the well-being of a person or a people: good health, long life, numerous offspring, fertile fields and flocks, harmony within the clan, and freedom from oppression. Emphasis falls on this word *blessing*, which occurs five times. By its very nature a blessing is a process that takes considerable time for its realization. Thus in calling Abram, God was looking far into the future. The third promise is that God would make his name great. In this promise, God addressed the human search for recognition and respect and thus provided the proper way to fame, in bold contrast to the misguided search for fame that inspired the building of the tower of Babel (11:4). The noblest reputation comes from a life directed by God for the good of others. ... Then God stated the highest goal for Abram's calling: all peoples on earth will be blessed through him. God's primary way of working among the nations is through Abram's seed. Thus, to experience God's blessing, the various peoples must interact with Abram's offspring. Having selected one family, God in a sense shows favoritism, but his design is not parochial. God was and is working through one family for the benefit of all families. Through Abram's seed he is achieving his goal in creating the earth, namely people worshiping only him. That this program is just rests on God's wise sovereignty.

Hartley, pp. 132–133

Gen 13:12: *Abram lived in the land of Canaan, while Lot lived among the cities of the plain and pitched his tents near Sodom.*
Gen 13:12: *Abram lived in the land of Canaan, while Lot lived among the cities of the plain and pitched his tents near Sodom.*
Lot had visions of the good life as he had witnessed it in Egypt, with all the latest in artistic and technological development, and time and leisure to enjoy it. He would be a fool to miss the opportunity of self-advancement and assured prosperity! He pitched his tent near Sodom, undeterred by its foul reputation [13:13], and when next he is mentioned he is living in Sodom (14:12). What he did not reckon was the downward pull of evil around him, and the enervating effect of prosperous ease on a self-centered life. He had made his choice, and it would soon become apparent whether Lot found the advantages he was hoping for in his new surroundings.
Meanwhile Abram, looking intentionally in every direction from a vantage point in the hills, was musing upon his nephew's opportunism and his own

way of life. It was after he had parted with one of the most desirable areas of the land promised to him that he was reassured by a word from the Lord. Abram, unlike Lot, had not chosen for himself, but far from losing out, he had the word of the Lord.

Baldwin, Joyce, *The Message of Genesis 12-50*, Leicester, England: Inter-Varsity Press, 1986, p. 41

Gen 19:12-13: *The two men said to Lot, "Do you have anyone else here--sons-in-law, sons or daughters, or anyone else in the city who belongs to you? Get them out of here, because we are going to destroy this place."*

Throughout the whole sordid mess of Sodom and Gomorrah, we see God's grace shining through. First, he spares Lot (Gen 19:29). Then he offers grace to a wide net—anyone Lot can convince it is time to leave. Then in 19:21, he spares the entire town of Zoar. God is a God of compassion and grace. Baldwin p.78

Gen 22:1: *Some time later God tested Abraham. He said to him, "Abraham!" "Here I am," he replied.*

Modern man, if he believes in God, has a tendency to think of the God in whom he believes as a benevolent figure whose main concern is to make man feel good about himself. This God is regarded as something like the recreational director on a cruise ship whose task is to give everyone a good time with no expense spared. The idea that God might initiate a test is therefore foreign to many people both outside and inside the kingdom. ... Faith is matured through the experience of stressful testing in much the same way that the cardiovascular system is strengthened through exercise and the muscles are developed by pumping iron. Faith is not lived out in a vacuum. It operates in the tensions of life and often demonstrates itself more fully by its responses to the furnace of affliction than the warm shallow waters of ease and prosperity. For faith to become visible it has to perform, or, as James said, 'Show me your faith without your works, and I will show you my faith by my works' (James 2:18). Briscoe, p. 183

Gen 22:9: *Abraham built an altar there and arranged the wood on it. He bound his son Isaac and laid him on the altar, on top of the wood.*

The great sacrifice, which in the fullness of time was to be offered up, must be bound, and therefore so must Isaac. But with what heart could tender Abraham tie those guiltless hands, which perhaps had often been lifted up to ask his blessing, and stretched out to embrace him, and were now the more straitly bound with the cords of love and duty! However, it must be done. Having bound him, he lays him upon the altar, and his hand upon the head of his sacrifice; and now, we may suppose, with floods of tears, he gives, and takes, the final farewell of a parting kiss. With a fixed heart, and an eye lifted up to heaven, he takes the knife, and stretches out his hand to give a fatal cut to Isaac's throat. Be astonished, O heavens! at this; and wonder, O earth! Here is an act of faith and obedience, which deserves to be a spectacle to God, angels, and men. Abraham's darling, Sarah's laughter, the church's hope, the heir of promise, lies ready to bleed and die by his own father's hand, who never shrinks at the doing of it. ... God, by his word, calls us to part with all for Christ,—all our sins, though they have been as a right hand [Mt 18:8], or a right eye [Mt 18:9], or an Isaac—all those things that are competitors and rivals with Christ for the sovereignty of the heart (Lu. 14:26); and we must cheerfully let them all go. God, by his providence, which is truly the voice of God, calls us to part with an Isaac sometimes, and we must do it with a cheerful resignation and submission to his holy will, 1 Sa. 3:18.
Matthew Henry Commentary

Gen 25:12: *This is the account of Abraham's son Ishmael, whom Sarah's maidservant, Hagar the Egyptian, bore to Abraham.*
Ishmael was rebellious. He resented the birth of Isaac and all that his birth meant for the future. He grew up to be a rebellious teenager, 'turned off' as we would say, to spiritual things. He wanted no part of any blessing that had come though Isaac. Yet the Lord loved Ishmael as much as He loved Isaac and His heart yearned over the rebellious young man. Again and again he picks up his name, writes it into His Book, then, seemingly sadly, puts it back down again. Ishmael, in spite of all the advantages of his birth and training, wanted no part of any Messiah the coming of whom would mean that he must acknowledge Isaac. ... Names! Towns! Powers! Princes! Nations! These were the five triumphs of Ishmael. They are all carnal, worldly triumphs. History shows how Ishmael has enjoyed in full

measure all that God pledged to him [17:20]. The Spirit of God, however, jots down Ishmael's triumphs in the barest fashion possible. He spends no time on them, does not elaborate on them at all. We are not particularly impressed by them. Phillips, excerpts, pp 202–205

Gen 32:24: *So Jacob was left alone, and a man wrestled with him till daybreak.*
One night stands out in the eventful life of Jacob. It was the night he added wrestling to his other accomplishments. The bout in which he was involved was no minor incident for he wrestled with the Lord Himself—an exercise in futility if ever there was one and yet one of the most common pursuits known to mankind. The finality of the subtle but powerful touch of God on Jacob's life must have been unnerving. Suddenly he realized that his wrestlings were puny and that when God chose to reveal the true nature and extent of his power he was powerless to withstand. This lesson would be taught and learned and forgotten by the children of Israel for centuries to come, despite the fact that their father had learned it the hard way. Their striving and wrestlings with their God would be evidence of their imagined self-sufficiency and arrogant waywardness which would always end in chaos and exile. Donald Grey Barnhouse used to say 'the way up is down. And the way down is up.' By that he meant that God is committed to bringing down those who exalt themselves but is equally committed to exalting those who will humble themselves under his hand [Mt 23:12, James 4:10, 1 Pet 5:6]. Jacob was busy learning what everybody who is earnest about spiritual life must learn either the hard way or the easy way. Briscoe, p. 259–261

Gen 41:40: *You shall be in charge of my palace, and all my people are to submit to your orders. Only with respect to the throne will I be greater than you.*
His chariot was of gold, his home a mansion in the gilded suburbs, his life one of opulence and power. This was the position for which God, through twelve long years of suffering and silence, had been preparing Joseph. Truly God's schools are not like ours. To prepare a man for such a position we would send him to Princeton; God sent Joseph to prison. Joseph had passed through some stiff tests, but he graduated at last with flying colors, having won honors in every difficult trial that came his way. And now the

moment had come when he was pulled from prison, hastily shaved, made presentable, thrust before Pharaoh, and then promoted to the lofty post of grand vizier of Egypt. All in the space of an hour! Little did Joseph dream that morning as he took the keys of the cells and began his daily, tedious rounds, that the sufferings were over and the glories were to begin. The years of adversity were finished, the years of advancement had come.... The 18th century poet and hymnist William Cowper wrote:

> *God moves in a mysterious way, his wonders to perform;*
> *He plants His footsteps in the sea and rides upon the storm.*
> *Deep in unfathomable mines of never failing skill,*
> *He treasures up His bright designs and works His sovereign will.*

Phillips, excerpts, pp 316–321

Gen 45:7: *But God sent me ahead of you to preserve for you a remnant on earth and to save your lives by a great deliverance.*

How admirable are the projects of providence! How remote its tendencies! What wheels are there within wheels, and yet all directed by the eyes in the wheels [Ezek 10:9–10, 13]! Let us therefore judge nothing before the time [1 Cor 4:5]. God often works by contraries [1 Cor 1:27]. The envy and contention of brethren threaten the ruin of families, yet, in this instance, they prove the occasion of preserving Jacob's family. Joseph could never have been the shepherd and stone of Israel if his brethren had not shot at him, and hated him; even those that had wickedly sold Joseph into Egypt yet themselves reaped the benefit of the good God brought out of it; as those that put Christ to death were many of them saved by his death. God must have all the glory of the seasonable preservations of his people, by what way soever they are effected. *It was not you that sent me hither, but God*, v. 8. As, on the one hand, they must not fret at it, because it ended so well, so on the other hand they must not be proud of it, because it was God's doing, and not theirs. They designed, by selling him into Egypt, to defeat his dreams, but God thereby designed to accomplish them. Matthew Henry Commentary

Exodus

Commentaries:
- *The Message of Exodus*, by J. Alec Motyer (2005)
- *Exodus*, by James K. Bruckner (2008)
- *The Story of God Bible Commentary, Exodus*, by Christopher J.H. Wright (2021)
- *Cornerstone Biblical Commentary*, Vol 1 by John N. Oswalt (2008)
- *The Preacher's Commentary*, OT Vol 2, by Maxie Dunnam (1987)

Ex 1:11: *So they put slave masters over them to oppress them with forced labor, and they built Pithom and Rameses as store cities for Pharaoh.*
Like them (the Israelites) we find ourselves exposed to days of darkness, and we ask, why? We would like some 'spelling out' of the situation which would satisfy our need for logic. But God does not come down to explain himself. The biblical account provides us with no pat answers to our questions, but it does provide us with a framework and context within which we can begin to make sense of the days of darkness which have ever been the lot of God's people throughout history. God is at work from beginning to end. We see him working out his own schemes in his own way on his own time plan according to his own wisdom, and we find the assurance that, although the days were dark, it was all right, it was all planned and it will all be well. Motyer, p. 31

Motyer, J. Alec, *The Message of Exodus*, Taken from *The Bible Speaks* Today Series edited by J. Alec Motyer; John Stott. Copyright ©1983 edited by J. Alec Motyer; John Stott. Used by permission of InterVarsity Press, P.O. Box 1400, Downers Grove, IL 60515, USA. www.ivpress.com

"Experience is the best of schoolmasters, only the school fees are heavy."
Tomas Carlyle (1795–1881) Quoted in Ward and Wild

Ex 2:24–25: *God heard their groaning and he remembered his covenant with Abraham, with Isaac and with Jacob. So God looked on the Israelites and was concerned about them.*

The Israelites in Egypt had no pubic declaration from God that their prayer had been heard, they were still walking in darkness and seeing no light (Isa 50:10). We, however, see a different picture because the Lord uses his Word to lift the corner of the curtain for us. We are able to see what they could not, that when prayer was made, the prayer was heard; the grim realities of the situation were registered, and God entered into fellowship with his people in their need and came down to deliver them (3:8). This is a straightforward demonstration of the effectiveness of prayer as echoed in Daniel 9:23, 'As soon as you began to pray, an answer was given' (cf Jer 33:1–3). It was prayer that made all the difference. Our prayers are so effective and so delightful to his ears, that God condescends to accommodate his eternal, sovereign, providential working to what we can understand, as though to say 'Oh, thank you for reminding me!'

Motyer, p. 44, 66

Motyer, J. Alec, *The Message of Exodus*, Taken from *The Bible Speaks Today* Series edited by J. Alec Motyer; John Stott. Copyright ©2005 edited by J. Alec Motyer; John Stott. Used by permission of InterVarsity Press, P.O. Box 1400, Downers Grove, IL 60515, USA. www.ivpress.com

"A teardrop on earth summons the King of heaven."
Charles R. Swindoll (1934 –)

Ex 3:2: *There the angel of the Lord appeared to him in flames of fire from within a bush. Moses saw that though the bush was on fire it did not burn up.*
The opening scene of this drama is freighted with significance. Moses was gifted with a vision that was to provide the foundation of his thinking for the rest of his life. It seems to have been designed by God to touch Moses on every level. First, there was the affective level. Moses saw something that captured his whole attention. He also heard something that moved him. But there was also the cognitive aspect. The old shepherd was not simply transported into a mystical experience. He wanted to see why the fire did not consume the bush. That is, he had a reasonable question. … The significance of the imagery used in this experience is not explained by the Bible and that should promote caution in our giving a

too-easy explanation. ... "Fire" is used not only elsewhere in Exodus, but throughout the rest of the Bible as an expression of the character of God. He is energizing [Isa 40:31]; he is awe-inspiring [Ps 65:8]; he is a wonderful [Isa 9:6] blessing [Num 6:24]; he is potentially destructive [Gen 6:17]; he is never easily contained [1 Kings 8:27]; he is light [1 John 1:5]; he is purifying [Zp 3:9, 1 John 1:9]. He is all this and more. But there was something remarkable about the fire Moses saw. Everywhere else a fixed characteristic of fire is that it consumes its fuel and turns mass into energy. That did not happen here, and it caught Moses attention. This was not a normal fire. ... Here Moses is given a vision of a fire that enlightens and and enlivens but does not destroy. I cannot help but feel this is a visual statement of what God communicated to Moses verbally in the rest of this encounter.
John N. Oswalt, *Cornerstone Biblical Commentary*, Vol 1, Carol Stream, IL: Tyndale 2008, pp. 307-308

Ex 3:11: *But Moses said to God, "Who am I, that I should go to Pharaoh and bring the Israelites out of Egypt?"*
If Moses lives in our memories as the towering leader of Israel in deliverance and pilgrimage, it is well to remember where he started—insecure, uncertain, unprepared, unworthy, and un-almost-everything-else! It is also well to remember how patiently the Lord took him at point after point and ministered reassurance to him. In reply to Moses' qualms, the Lord, in effect said to him (3:11–4:17): 'But what about me? Are you taking me into account? Where are your eyes fixed?' [Heb 12:2]. When Moses was faced with his vocation to bring my people out of Egypt (3:10), his reaction was, 'I can't, therefore I won't'. The Lord sought to bring him to the point where he could say 'I can't but HE can, therefore I will.' That is the obedience of faith—doing the will of God because he will always do what he has willed; trusting the promises of God because he will always keep his word; acting on the assumption of divine provision because he will never fail to provide. ... This is so important that it is worth trying to put it another way. Moses' position was, 'Look, I'm not up to the job. You shouldn't have picked me.' The Lord's reply was, 'Of course you are not up to the job. I knew that when I chose you for it. The point is not your ability, but mine!' Moses' 'I' of incapacity is balanced by the Lord's 'I' of

ability. In a nutshell, that is how matters stand—and not just for Moses but for always and in every situation of divine choice and call.

Motyer, Excerpts pp 60, 61, 62 65–66

Motyer, J. Alec, *The Message of Exodus*, Taken from *The Bible Speaks Today* Series edited by J. Alec Motyer; John Stott. Copyright ©2005 edited by J. Alec Motyer; John Stott. Used by permission of InterVarsity Press, P.O. Box 1400, Downers Grove, IL 60515, USA. www.ivpress.com

Ex 9:27–28: *Then Pharaoh summoned Moses and Aaron. "This time I have sinned," he said to them. "The LORD is in the right, and I and my people are in the wrong. Pray to the LORD, for we have had enough thunder and hail. I will let you go; you don't have to stay any longer."*

A lesson from the plagues has to do with the tendency of all humankind to make vows to God in the midst of affliction, but not to keep them when the affliction is over. Pharaoh is the personification of that tendency. In the midst of the havoc wrought by the hail, he called for Moses and Aaron and made what must have been for him an extremely difficult confession: 'I have sinned and I and my people are wicked.' He appealed to Moses to stop the hail with the promise that he would let the Israelites go immediately. Even as Moses expected, when the hail ceased, Pharaoh returned to his hardened heart position against the Exodus of Israel. How much of Pharaoh is in us? 'Lord, if You'll get me out of this situation, I'll serve you the rest of my life.' How quickly do we make vows in the midst of darkness and difficulty, only to go back on those vows when the sun begins to shine and the roads of our lives smooth out!

Dunnam, pp. 120–121

Ex 19:4 *You yourselves have seen what I did to Egypt, and how I carried you on eagles' wings and brought you to myself.*

God's first words point to God's own historic action: "You yourselves have seen what I did…"

And they had. It was a fresh memory. A mere two or three months before this, they were being whipped and beaten, forced to make bricks without straw, subject to horrendous oppression and the slaughter of baby boys. Now they are free, through a miraculous series of events climaxing in the destruction of the oppressor's army in the sea and their complete escape. And God says, "I did all that." God had acted out of faithfulness

to his covenant promise (2:24), out of compassion (2:25, 3:7-9), and out of redemptive justice (6:6). The exodus was the great initiative of God's saving grace, the historic foundation of all that will follow.
This opening affirmation, like the opening words of the Decalogue to follow (20:2) grounds the covenant relationship and all its laws on the prior historical fact of God's redeeming work. The structure of Exodus expresses its fundamental theology in these verses: gospel precedes law and provides the only valid foundation and motivation for obedient response.
Christopher J.H. Wright, *The Story of God Bible Commentary, Exodus*, Grand Rapids, MI: Zondervan, 2021, p. 338

Ex 19:5: *Now if you obey me fully and keep my covenant, then out of all nations you will be my treasured possession.*
God's law is not a 'ladder of merit' by which we try to climb, by grim obedience, into his 'good books'; it is a way of life revealed to those who are already by redemption in his 'good books.' The grace of God precedes the Law of God. Motyer, p. 191
Election is always a secret, hidden in the divine nature. Deut 7:7 says 'The Lord did not set his affection on you and choose you because you were more numerous than other peoples…But it was because the Lord loved you and kept the oath he swore to your forefathers.' In other words, the Lord loved you because he loved you (cf Gen 6:9)! Thus, the deciding factor in the choice was not one, like poverty, which might appeal to human logic, but the hidden reason of love. This means, of course, a reason that satisfied the wisdom, justice, and every other attribute of God, but which remained hidden within the divine heart and mind. Our God is a speaking God who communicates his word to us; we are to be characterized by obedience to what he says. The hallmark of the genuineness of the people of God is that they possess, listen to, and obey the word of God. Motyer, p. 198, 200
Motyer, J. Alec, *The Message of Exodus*, Taken from *The Bible Speaks Today* Series edited by J. Alec Motyer; John Stott. Copyright ©2005 edited by J. Alec Motyer; John Stott. Used by permission of InterVarsity Press, P.O. Box 1400, Downers Grove, IL 60515, USA. www.ivpress.com

Ex 20:1: *And God spoke all these words*
Through the Psalms we look, as through a great window, right into the church of the Old Testament and find at its center a delighted, exuberant love of the Lord's word of commandment. We need to recover this for ourselves, to remind ourselves of the grace and goodness of possessing the Law of God. We have not been left to fumble around in mist and darkness [Isa 50:10–11], we have been given directions. As the Lord's redeemed, it should be our delight to give pleasure to God our Savior, and he has told us how. This is the way we are to think of the Ten Commandments—not as cramping restrictions on a fullness of life that we might otherwise have enjoyed, but as the very gateway to the fullness we seek.   Motyer, p. 214
Motyer notes the following pattern in the Decalogue:

A	God			
	a	Thoughts		(commandments 1–2)
		b	Words	(commandment 3)
			c Deeds	(commandment 4)
B	Society			
			c Deeds	(commandments 6–8)
		b	Words	(commandment 9)
	a	Thoughts		(commandment 10)

The Decalogue begins and ends with the interior aspect of our obedience—how we are required to think about God and about our relationships with other people.   Motyer, p. 216

Motyer, J. Alec, *The Message of Exodus*, Taken from *The Bible Speaks Today* Series edited by J. Alec Motyer; John Stott. Copyright ©2005 edited by J. Alec Motyer; John Stott. Used by permission of InterVarsity Press, P.O. Box 1400, Downers Grove, IL 60515, USA. www.ivpress.com

Ex 20:17: *"You shall not covet your neighbor's house. You shall not covet your neighbor's wife, or his manservant or maidservant, his ox or donkey, or anything that belongs to your neighbor."*
Most of us are guilty of coveting than any of the other sins condemned in the Ten Commandments. We look at others, compare ourselves to them, and see ourselves come out on the short end. How often do we convince ourselves that other people always get the breaks and not us? We look

at our peers and see where they are in life, and we're plagued with the notion that they had far more opportunity than we did. ... We convince ourselves that we have some sort of cosmic right to an equal share of the good things of life. That's a fallacious idea, and it plays folly in our lives. There's no equality in talents, abilities, opportunities. There is no cosmic right that is ours to have an equal share of what everybody else has. If you're prone to leaning in that direction, consider how you would feel if you were averaged out with the world's two billion starving people. You see, we always want to be averaged up and not down. ... Happiness is an inside job. It comes from the inner citadel of freedom which belongs to all of us, the inner place where we make our choices. Our problem is that we usually end up coveting that which can never make us happy, failing to realize that what matters most is not what becomes of us, but what we become; we determine that. Dunnam, excerpts, pp. 250–252

Ex 34:6 *And he passed in front of Moses, proclaiming, "The LORD, the LORD, the compassionate and gracious God, slow to anger, abounding in love and faithfulness, maintaining love to thousands, and forgiving wickedness, rebellion and sin."*

These verses are the heart of the chapter that is at the theological core of Exodus. They function as a confession of faith in God and in God's redeeming work throughout the OT. Throughout their history, Israel frequently repeated this credo, or portions of it, in a wide variety of formats and contexts.

God is **compassionate**. The Hebrew word for 'compassionate' םוּחַר *rachuwm* is from the same root word as 'womb.' The word means 'to be soft like a womb.' It is illustrated by the soft compassion of a mother for her child in the womb. The relationship of compassion is based on the Creator-created relationship. The Creator bases his compassion on an original love for creation (Gen 1:31). The NT uses the corresponding Greek word, σπλαγχνίζομαι *splagchnizomai*, to describe how Jesus was moved to compassion when healing the crowds (Mk 1:41).

God is **gracious** חַנּוּן *channuwn*. God's grace means that the Lord often acts generously, giving gifts freely, without asking for anything in return. The Lord is **slow to anger**. The Hebrew idiom 'burn with anger' is, literally, 'nostrils burn' אַף. Slow to anger is literally 'lengthened nostrils', indicating that God's anger cools before dealing with the peoples' sin. God's anger is always in response to human sin, riled when people destroy God's beloved creation, especially when it involves self-destructive, sinful actions.

The Lord is **abounding in love** רַב חֶסֶד (*rab hesed*). *Hesed* is more than generic love for which Hebrew has another word. 'Steadfast love' is a better translation but, *hesed* is even stronger than that. 'Unrelenting love' or 'pursuing love' is closest to its meaning when God is the one loving. Technically the word means 'tenacious fidelity in a relationship, readiness and resolve to continue to be loyal to those to whom one is bound.'

Bruckner, excerpts, pp. 301–303

<u>Personal Note</u>: This verse is so important that it is repeated seven more times in the Old Testament (besides here, it appears in Num 14:18, Neh 9:17, Ps 86:15, 103:8, 145:8, Joel 2:13, Jonah 4:2). Although God's wrath is also a reality (next verse), his grace is something we can bank on. This eight-fold statement of his grace in the OT is an emphatic reminder that though we sin and continue to do so, he forgives and will continue to do so.

Ex 40:34: *Then the cloud covered the Tent of Meeting, and the glory of the LORD filled the tabernacle.*
With these five verses (40:34–38), Exodus reaches a fitting and indeed beautiful climax. The form and language is virtually poetic, as if the grandeur of the theme lifted the literary presentation to its own sublime level. The theme is made plain by the repetition of key words. The *cloud* is mentioned in each verse. J.I. Durham notes the sense of promptness, to say the least, maybe even of impatience and urgency with which verse 33 is followed by verse 34. 'Moses finished the work, and the cloud covered the tent'. It is as though the Lord 'can't wait' to come and live with his people. Motyer, p. 320

Motyer, J. Alec, *The Message of Exodus,*. Copyright ©2005 edited by J. Alec Motyer; John Stott. Used by permission of InterVarsity Press, P.O. Box 1400, Downers Grove, IL 60515, USA. www.ivpress.com

Leviticus

Commentaries:
- *The Message of Leviticus*, by Derek Tidball (2005)
- *The Preacher's Commentary*, OT Vol 3, by Gary W. Demarest (1990)

Lev 1:4: *He is to lay his hand on the head of the burnt offering, and it will be accepted on his behalf to make atonement for him.*
The idea of atoning for sin is central to the message of the Bible. The history of theology and biblical interpretation abounds with efforts to develop a theory of atonement, especially with regard to the meaning of Christ's sacrificial death on the Cross. One of the most debated questions in theories of the atonement revolves around the concept of Christ's death as a ransom for sin. The most simplistic theories begin with the idea that some price must be paid in order to satisfy the wrath of God. ... To say that the death of Jesus was the price that had to be paid for our sins is to say that His love for us was so great that nothing would hold Him back from living out that love for our benefit. Let us affirm the mystery of Christ's atoning death. Let us celebrate the costly sacrifice made for us. Let us proclaim the mystery that it took the life of Jesus to bring us back from our sin and rebellion into fellowship with God [Rom 5:1]. Demarest, p. 38

Lev 11:2: *Say to the Israelites: 'Of all the animals that live on land, these are the ones you may eat'*
The obsessive style of these chapters has led one commentator to voice what many may probably silently believe: these chapters 'are perhaps the least attractive in the whole Bible. To the modern reader there is much in them that is meaningless or repulsive.' But if all Scripture is inspired and useful (2 Tim 3:17), we must not dismiss these chapters so easily. Nor need we do so. A God whose presence was felt in the kitchen was not a God

you could marginalize, keep confined to a compartment of life marked 'spiritual', or serve only at special times designated for worship. He was a God who reigned over the totality of life and was to be served at all times and in all places. Though, at first sight, the purity laws seem to usher us into an altogether foreign, unfamiliar world, a moment's reflection suggests that the territory is not as alien as it seems. Our own world operates along similar lines, as all cultures up to the present time have done. There are certain foods we will eat and others we regard as unfit to eat. Our society is riddled with regulations over how food is to be stored and preserved— just think of sell-by dates, stipulations about freezer temperatures, and the need to separate cooked from uncooked meat in a butcher's shop—which we account for in terms of hygienic necessity. ...We may draw the line in different places from where the ancient Israelites did, but we draw the line nonetheless. We may account for attitudes from a scientific or hygienic perspective, but we hold as strongly to concepts of 'clean' and 'unclean' as they did. Tidball, pp. 141–142

Lev 11:44: *I am the LORD your God; consecrate yourselves and be holy, because I am holy.*
Before we leave this section we must ask ourselves again, 'what does all of this have to do with us?' The casual reader might wish to move on quickly with the assumption that this is only of antiquarian interest. But now we know better. We must always return to the idea on which all of these laws were based, the idea of holiness. God is holy! This means that God is the 'wholly other.' God is perfect in wisdom, power, goodness, purity, justice and truth. And the Holy God calls the people of God to be holy because God is holy [Hebrew שׁוֹקָד or *kadosh*]. ... Only as we begin to enter into this understanding of the holiness of God can we begin to comprehend the seriousness with which these ancient Hebrews approached the worship of God. Every single detail—clothing, cleanliness, attitude—had to be right. Approaching God was a serious and awesome matter in which nothing was treated lightly or left to chance. Demarest, p. 152

Lev 19:18 *Do not seek revenge or bear a grudge against one of your people, but love your neighbor as yourself. I am the LORD.*

Holiness is more than just abstaining from doing wrong [Jas 4:17]. It is even more than doing right since there are people who, in Mark Twain's reported words, are 'good in the worst sense of the word.' Unless doing right is accompanied by right attitudes and dispositions it can be pharisaical rather than godly. This positive summons to love one's neighbor releases us from understanding holiness as legalistic and negative and sets us free to fulfill its generous and constructive spirit. Samuel Ballentine comments, 'If the summons to holiness in 19:2 constitutes the keynote message of Leviticus and the command to love in 19:18 brings us to the epicenter of the book.' How different our communities would be if we lived by this simple, yet demanding rule. Indeed, shock waves would radiate from us and begin to transform the wider communities we belong to for good…. The call to integrity, impartiality, mutual correction, forgiveness, trust in God's provision, and, above all, to love is the royal law [Jas 2:8] that is still binding on Christian believers. New Testament holiness is riddled with the spirit of Leviticus 19. Tidball, p. 241

Personal Note: The second half of the verse is its most famous part. The Lord Jesus put this command to love your neighbor as yourself alongside the *Shema* (Deut 6:5-6) as the most important commandment of all (Mt 22:36-40). Sometimes, the first part of the verse is overlooked. It tells us to not seek revenge. When we seek revenge we are attempting to usurp the Lord's authority (Deut 32:35) and to "play god" in his place. Revenge is a statement that we don't believe the Lord of perfect justice will set things right (Ps 73:2-5, 16-19).

Our verse also commands us to not bear a grudge. This wording implies that a grudge is like a burden we bear, like rolling the stone of Sisyphus up a never ending hill. Pastor John Wood of Cedar Springs Presbyterian Church once mentioned an incident where he was hiking in the woods with some friends. One of them was carrying a large bag of trash as they were returning from their mountain top destination. All of a sudden, the bag broke and the trash went all over the trail. Pastor Wood commented "this was a sermon that almost wrote itself." When we bear a grudge, we are carrying a load of trash instead of just giving it to the Lord and letting him fix the situation using his perfectly righteous justice. The Lord will remove the burden and set our hands free from the basket we are carrying (Ps 81:6) if we would just surrender the task of vengeance to him. Christ invites all who are weary and heavy laden (even with a grudge!) to come to him and find rest for their souls (Mt 11:28-29). May we accept this gracious invitation!

"It costs more to revenge injuries than to bear them."
Thomas Wilson (1663–1755)   Quoted in Ward and Wild

Numbers

Commentaries
- *The Message of Numbers*, by Raymond Brown (2002)
- *The Preacher's Commentary*, OT Vol 4, by James Philip (1987)

Num 6:24–26: *The LORD bless you and keep you; the LORD make His face shine upon you,*
And be gracious to you; the LORD lift up His countenance upon you, and give you peace. NKJV
[cf Ps 31:16, 80:3]

ס ׃יִבָרְכַ֖דְ יִהיִ֥וְ ויִ֛שְׁמֹתְרַ֑׃
ס ׃יֵאִ֥ר יִהיִ֖וְ ףַ֥נָיְו אָ֛לֵיּדְ ויִ֧נֲחֵנּֽוְ׃
ס ׃יִ֥אֲשׂ יִהיִ֖וְ ףַ֥נָיְו אָ֛לֵיּדְ ויִ֧שֶּׁמִ לֶ֛הָ֖שְׂוֹמ׃

Its Artistry
This tersely expressed prayer is perfectly fashioned. Its three lines are presented within a beautifully phrased framework that introduces it (22–23) and then amplifies and concludes it. The three lines in the Hebrew contain an increasing number of words: 3, 5, and 7. There is a natural expansion of the use of syllables (12, 14, and 16) conveyed also by the increasing number of consonants (15, 20, and 25)—building up to heightening awareness of divine generosity. This gradual escalation conveys in literary form the sense of God's multiplying and expanding gifts.
Brown, p. 55

Taken from The Message of Numbers by Raymond Brown. Copyright (c) 2002 by Raymond Brown. Used by permission of InterVarsity Press, P.O. Box 1400, Downers Grove, IL 60515, USA. www.ivpress.com

Its Message
The words express confident proclamation. Rather than vocalize what they want, they expound what God gives. Giving eloquent voice to the people's longings, they confirm the Lord's benevolence. This divine declaration expounds the facets of divine blessing these people need as they leave for their journey across a vast, inhospitable wilderness. Spectacular dimensions of the divine nature are itemized in this memorable benediction, assuring the travelers of their spiritual wealth [Eph 1:3]. Scripture asserts that God alone is the source of our lasting satisfaction and fulfillment (Isa 55:1–2, James 1:17). Alluring substitutes are flimsy commodities [cf 1 Kings 14:25–27], doomed to disappoint the millions who clutch at them.

Brown, p. 55, 56

Brown, Raymond, *The Message of Numbers,* Taken from *The Bible Speaks Today* Series edited by J. Alec Motyer; John Stott. Copyright ©2002 edited by J. Alec Motyer; John Stott. Used by permission of InterVarsity Press, P.O. Box 1400, Downers Grove, IL 60515, USA. www.ivpress.com

His multichrome gifts are innumerable and assured
To the Hebrew mind, 'blessing' בִּרְכֹתַי was certain and specific, a vast store of priceless gifts money could never buy [cf Isa 33:6]. It included such treasures as human love, the gift of children [Ps 127:3–5], the joys of family life, the delight of home and the security of abundant harvests [cf Ps 65:9–11, Isa 30:23, 32:20, Joel 3:18]. They [and we] did not merit the immeasurable expansiveness of the divine bounty, but their needs were supplied on the basis of his matchless generosity, not as reward for their unswerving devotion.

Brown, p. 57

Brown, Raymond, *The Message of Numbers,* Taken from *The Bible Speaks Today* Series edited by J. Alec Motyer; John Stott. Copyright ©2002 edited by J. Alec Motyer; John Stott. Used by permission of InterVarsity Press, P.O. Box 1400, Downers Grove, IL 60515, USA. www.ivpress.com

and give you peace
ialôm שָׁלוֹם: meant "wholeness"; it embraced a wide range of countless gifts and rich provisions. Thousands of our contemporaries have material benefits and financial security, but their unfulfilled hands reach out for more; they lack contentment, fulfillment, and *ialôm* [Phil 4:7]
Brown, p. 59

Brown, Raymond, *The Message of Numbers,* Taken from *The Bible Speaks Today* Series edited by J. Alec Motyer; John Stott. Copyright ©2002 edited by J. Alec Motyer; John Stott. Used by permission of InterVarsity Press, P.O. Box 1400, Downers Grove, IL 60515, USA. www.ivpress.com

Num 9:17: *Whenever the cloud lifted from above the Tent, the Israelites set out; wherever the cloud settled, the Israelites encamped.*
The picture of Israel's dependence on the divine guidance is a beautiful one. Their guidance came by the supernatural pillar; ours comes by the reality of which that pillar was nothing but a picture. This statement is a pointer to the kind of spiritual lessons that flow from the symbol of the pillar. They are many and rich. For one thing, it was a token of God's abiding presence with the people. He went before them until the day they entered the land. This is an eloquent reminder, in New Testament terms, that the Christian life is not the acceptance of a system, but the entrance into fellowship, into a relationship of companionship with Christ. ... The Lord led them unerringly where they were to go and when (in spiritual life when is quite as importance as where; to move before God's time always leads to trouble). Commenting on Israel's wilderness journeys, the psalmist says 'He led them forth by the right way' (Ps 107:7), not always the expected way or even the shortest way, but with God in the lead the longest way round is the shortest way home. There is plan and purpose in all He does [Phil 2:13], and all He does is for the best [Rom 8:28]. He guides [Ps 43:3] ! This is the overruling consideration. We are not left to walk alone. He knows the way through the wilderness [Isa 40:3].   Philip, pp 111-112

Num 11:1: *Now the people complained about their hardships*
This murmuring became a continuing characteristic and had a cumulative effect. It was not merely that the people murmured once or twice. They developed a murmuring, complaining spirit, and it was this that came to a climax. This complaining, critical spirit got into them and did something to them, rendering them progressively incapable of rising to their divine calling. ... God had bestowed on Israel the dignity and privilege of a spiritual calling and destiny; He had made bare His holy arm on their behalf, shown them the bright and glorious prospect that faced them if they were prepared to walk in His ways—and they sneered at it, reacted against it, lightly esteemed it, and turned their backs on their destiny,

in sheer carnal worldliness. Discontent with a spiritual calling—this is the theme and its relevance and importance are surely obvious for us, in relation to how He dealt with them for their sins.   Philip, pp 124-125

"I find the doing of the will of God leaves me no time for disputing about his plans."
George MacDonald (1824-1905)   Quoted in Ward and Wild

Num 20:5: *Why did you bring us up out of Egypt to this terrible place? It has no grain or figs, grapevines or pomegranates.*
The people despised God's generosity. Obsessed by what had been denied, they forgot what they had been given. Longing for what we want, we ignore what we have received. They forgot his majestic acts of deliverance. They ignored the daily evidence of his presence and the nightly assurance of his protection [cf 10:10]. They despised his unfailing gift of nourishing food, the ready supply of necessary water and restful locations where they enjoyed shelter. They marginalized his immense kindness in keeping them free from sickness and disease, even protecting their feet from discomfort and their clothes from wearing out [Deut 8:4].   Brown, p. 177
Brown, Raymond, *The Message of Numbers,* Taken from *The Bible Speaks Today* Series edited by J. Alec Motyer; John Stott. Copyright ©2002 edited by J. Alec Motyer; John Stott. Used by permission of InterVarsity Press, P.O. Box 1400, Downers Grove, IL 60515, USA. www.ivpress.com

"We write our blessings in the sand, and we engrave our complaints in the marble."
Charles Haddon Spurgeon (1834–1892)

Num 21:7: *The people came to Moses and said, "We sinned when we spoke against the LORD and against you. Pray that the LORD will take the snakes away from us."*
Only hours before they had spoken against him (v 5); now they could not wait to reach him. They hurried to a man of God who would listen to their troubles and identify with their grief. Adversity sifts our priorities—they were no longer interested in culinary provisions. They knew that Moses was a friend of God, and pleaded earnestly for something that now mattered more than food and drink. P.T. Forsyth in *The Soul of Prayer* states that

God's final purpose in trouble is to drive us closer to himself. 'The joiner, when he glues together two boards, keeps them tightly clamped till the cement sets. So with calamities, depressions, and disappointments that crush us into closer contact with God. The pressure on us is kept up till the soul's union with God is set.' Brown. p. 189

Brown, Raymond, *The Message of Numbers,* Taken from *The Bible Speaks Today* Series edited by J. Alec Motyer; John Stott. Copyright ©2002 edited by J. Alec Motyer; John Stott. Used by permission of InterVarsity Press, P.O. Box 1400, Downers Grove, IL 60515, USA. www.ivpress.com

Num 24:17: *"I see him, but not now; I behold him, but not near. A star will come out of Jacob;*
a scepter will rise out of Israel."

The message lit a flame of hope in the life of the Israelite people that was treasured by millions: Their Messiah would come. 'Hope is the positive as anxiety is the negative mode of awaiting the future. What oxygen is for the lungs, such is hope for the meaning of life. Take away hope and humanity is constricted for lack of breath. We wheeze; we cannot survive without hope.' Emil Brunner quoted in Brown, p. 223

Brown, Raymond, *The Message of Numbers,* Taken from *The Bible Speaks Today* Series edited by J. Alec Motyer; John Stott. Copyright ©2002 edited by J. Alec Motyer; John Stott. Used by permission of InterVarsity Press, P.O. Box 1400, Downers Grove, IL 60515, USA. www.ivpress.com

Like the taunt songs of the later prophets, the closing lines of Balaam's oracles give voice to one of Scripture's cardinal truths—God is sovereign. He is not simply in control of Israel's destiny; he has the whole world in his hands. Teaching of this kind is scarcely popular in a postmodern culture like our own. Instead of looking to a sovereign God and a saving Christ for help, our contemporaries are encouraged to achieve their own goals, utilize their own resources and fulfill their own dreams. Patterns of self-salvation are more acceptable than theologies of hope. The idea of looking to Christ for immediate or ultimate salvation is considered outdated, irrelevant, even distasteful. Contrary to all such popular forms of self-salvation, biblically convinced Christians declare that in Jesus, the unique Son of God, the Messiah has come, to effect for humankind the salvation we cannot possibly achieve for ourselves. They are also persuaded that one day he will come back to this world as its only redeemer, Lord, and king. Christians anticipate with incomparable gratitude this promised return of Christ, their *star* [Rev 22:16], their *scepter* [Gen 49:10, Rev 19:15], and their *ruler* (17, 19) [cf Rev 11:15]. Brown, p. 225–226

Brown, Raymond, *The Message of Numbers,* Taken from *The Bible Speaks Today* Series edited by J. Alec Motyer; John Stott. Copyright ©2002 edited by J. Alec Motyer; John Stott. Used by permission of InterVarsity Press, P.O. Box 1400, Downers Grove, IL 60515, USA. www.ivpress.com

Personal Note: This verse inspired an excellent choral anthem named *There Shall A Star From Jacob Come Forth* by Felix Bartholdy Mendelssohn. This is a beautiful piece for the Christmas season.

Num 36:13: *These are the commands and regulations the LORD gave through Moses to the Israelites on the plains of Moab by the Jordan across from Jericho.* With the aid of this brief geographical detail (Moab, Jordan, Jericho) the conclusion of Numbers offers fresh hope and renewed confidence, a new land and a better future. In God's time, we too may cross a river and, by grace alone, enter a city (Heb 13:14, Rev 21:2, 10, Rev 22:1–3).
Brown, p. 308

Brown, Raymond, *The Message of Numbers,* Taken from *The Bible Speaks Today* Series edited by J. Alec Motyer; John Stott. Copyright ©2002 edited by J. Alec Motyer; John Stott. Used by permission of InterVarsity Press, P.O. Box 1400, Downers Grove, IL 60515, USA. www.ivpress.com

Deuteronomy

Commentaries:
- *Deuteronomy*, by Christopher J.H. Wright (1996)
- *The Preacher's Commentary*, OT Vol 5, by John C. Maxwell (1987)
- *The Message of Deuteronomy*, by Raymond Brown (1993)

Deut 1:28: *Where can we go? Our brothers have made us lose heart. They say, 'The people are stronger and taller than we are; the cities are large, with walls up to the sky. We even saw the Anakites there.'*

[Context: 10 of 12 spies advised against going into the Promised Land] Problems are the easiest things to see. The sad truth is that many of us look for problems, then use them as an excuse to stay right where we are. God wants men and women who see beyond the difficulties, and who give encouragement to those facing challenges. ... Ten saw barriers; two saw blessings. Ten saw giants; two saw God. Ten saw fortified cities and their faith crumbled; two possessed faith and saw the fortified cities crumble. Two said 'The best is yet to come'; ten said 'The best is not to come.' ... It is significant that in the detailed Numbers 13 account of the spies' report, there is no mention of God. They had allowed their problems to get between them and their God. He was no longer in their field of vision. Facts without faith and goals without God can be very intimidating.
Maxwell, excerpts, pp 38, 41, 44

Deut 4:2: *Do not add to what I command you and do not subtract from it, but keep the commands of the LORD your God that I give you.*
Too many Christians use the 'dip and skip' method of Christian living. They dip into His promises and skip His commands. This type of living did not please God in the day of Moses and does not please Him now.
Maxwell, p. 83

Deut 4:28-29 *There you will worship man-made gods of wood and stone, which cannot see or hear or eat or smell. But if from there you seek the LORD your God, you will find him if you look for him with all your heart and with all your soul.*

God knows that in their prosperity, they will quickly forget him; only adversity will bring them to their senses [Lk 15:17]. When they have everything they ignore God [8:17] who has filled their hand with innumerable blessings [Ps 116:12]. Only when they have nothing will they value what they have lost. Despite the warnings, they will forget God; yet, despite their sins, he will not forget them. The triple testimony of scripture, history, and experience is that those who seek have always found [cf Jer 29:13, 2 Chr 7:14, Mt 7:7]. Brown, p. 71

Deut 6:4–5: *Hear, O Israel: The LORD our God, the LORD is one. Love the LORD your God with all your heart and with all your soul and with all your strength.*

דְחָא הָוֹהִי וּנֵיהֹלֶא הָוֹהִי לֵאָרְשִׂי עַמְשׁ:
וָהֲבַהֵת אָת הָוֹהִי דְיֶהֹלֶא לָכְבִּ דְבָבְל־לָכְבִּ דְשְׁפְנ־לָכְבִּ דְאֹמ־לָכְבִּ

The *Shema* is both an affirmation about God and a call to commitment to God. It's Jewish name, *Shema* is the first Hebrew word of the summons, *Hear O Israel*, a favorite form of address in Deuteronomy. It is also a constant reminder that Israel was a people summoned by God to hear God's word. They were not merely spectators at a divine 'show', but the recipients of divine revelation in words. They were to *hear* the truth and respond to it.

Yahweh is not the brand name of a cosmic corporation. He is one God, our God, and Yahweh is his personal name. ... The idea here would be the same as we would say of a particular individual, 'There is only one John.' We imply he is not two-faced or inconsistent; you can rely on John to be the same whatever happens. Likewise, to say 'Yahweh is one' is to affirm unchangeableness and consistency. There is no divine schizophrenia. The harmony of God's purpose for the world and its people is grounded in the ultimate unity of God's own being. ... The sharp precision of the *Shema* cannot be evaporated into a philosophical abstraction or relegated to a penultimate level of truth. ... To love God then, with all your heart and with all your soul, means with your whole self, including your rationality, mental capacity, moral choices and will, inner feelings and desires, at the deepest roots of your life. To this profound pair, the *Shema* adds a third remarkable item, literally: 'and with all your very-muchness.' ... 'Love the Lord your God with total commitment (heart), with your total self (soul), to total excess!' Loving God should be 'over the top.'

Wright, excerpts, pp. 94–99

Excerpt from Deuteronomy by Christopher Wright, copyright © 1996. Used by permission of Baker Books, a division of Baker Publishing Group.

Deut 8:17–18: *You may say to yourself, "My power and the strength of my hands have produced this wealth for me." But remember the LORD your God, for it is he who gives you the ability to produce wealth, and so confirms his covenant, which he swore to your forefathers, as it is today.*

"O Lord, thou hast set me on high. My flesh is frail and weak. If I therefore at any time forget thee, touch my heart, O Lord, that I may again remember thee. If I swell against thee, pluck me down in my own conceit."
Queen Elizabeth I of England (1533–1603)   Quoted in Ward and Wild

Deut 10:12–13: *And now, O Israel, what does the LORD your God ask of you but to fear the LORD your God, to walk in all his ways, to love him, to serve the LORD your God with all your heart and with all your soul, and to observe the LORD's commands and decrees that I am giving*

Deuteronomy 10:12–22 is unquestionably one of the richest texts in the Hebrew Bible, exalted and poetic in its language, comprehensive and challenging in its message. It purposely tries to 'boil down' the whole theological and ethical content of the book into memorable phraseology, packed and pregnant, rich and resonant of the surrounding preaching. Indeed there are not many dimensions of OT theology that are not directly expressed or indirectly echoed in this min-symphony of faith and life. ... The intention is to get down to basics and show that the claim of God upon the covenant people is not complicated and esoteric but fundamentally simple. Not simple as in 'easy'—if obedience were easy, there would be little need for these chapters full of encouragement, warnings, and promise.

The substance of obedience is relatively straightforward (a) because there is only one God to whom obedience is owed, so moral confusion of polytheism is avoided, and (b) because Yahweh has made his moral will known with unmistakable clarity (30:11–13). ... This sentence (v 12 f.) is like a five note musical chord. Each note has its own distinct tone. ... The five phrases function as a kind of text for the remainder of the preaching in chapters 10 and 11, which are essentially a twisting kaleidoscope of all the colors and patterns that flow from the central commandment—to love God (which naturally stands central to the list of five). As Moses has already pointed out (4:6–8), observing the law is wisdom—it not only pleases the giver of the law, but benefits the keeper of the law. 'Obedience is good for you,' may not sparkle as an advertising slogan, but it captures the human perspective of OT ethics.

Wright, excerpts, pp. 144–145 Excerpt from Deuteronomy by Christopher Wright, copyright © 1996. Used by permission of Baker Books, a division of Baker Publishing Group.

Deut 11:14–15: *then I will send rain on your land in its season, both autumn and spring rains, so that you may gather in your grain, new wine and oil. I will provide grass in the fields for your cattle, and you will eat and be satisfied.*

[Ezek 34:26–27]

Hymn: *Come, Ye Thankful People, Come* (1844), Text: Henry Alford, 1810–1871, Tune George J. Elvey

Come, ye thankful people, come, raise the song of harvest home;	[Ex 23:16a, Dt 28:11]
All is safely gathered in, ere the winter storms begin.	[Isa 4: 6]
God our Maker doth provide for our wants to be supplied;	[Joel 2:24, Phil 4:19]
Come to God's own temple, come, raise the song of harvest home.	[Isa 2:3, Dt 8:10]
All the world is God's own field, fruit as praise to God we yield;	[Jn 4:35, Heb 13:15]
Wheat and tares together sown are to joy or sorrow grown;	[Mt 13:26]
First the blade and then the ear, then the full corn shall appear;	[Mk 4:28]
Lord of harvest, grant that we wholesome grain and pure may be.	[Mt 13:8]
For the Lord our God shall come, and shall take the harvest home;	[Ps 121:1,2, Mt 21:34]
From the field shall in that day all offenses purge away,	[Isa 44:22, Ps 103:12]
Giving angels charge at last in the fire the tares to cast	[Mt 13:41–42]
But the fruitful ears to store in the garner evermore.	[Mt 25:34]

Even so, Lord, quickly come, bring thy final harvest home;   [Rev 22:20,22:2b]
Gather thou thy people in, free from sorrow, free from sin,   [Mt 24:31, Rev 21:4,27]
There, forever purified, in thy presence to abide;   [Eph 1:4, Rev 21:3]
Come, with all thine angels, come, raise the glorious harvest home.   [Ps 103:20, Lv 26:5]

Thanksgiving Proclamation by George Washington in 1789 (Excerpt):

Whereas it is the duty of all nations to acknowledge the providence of Almighty God, to obey His will, to be grateful for His benefits, and humbly to implore His protection and favor; and Whereas both Houses of Congress have, by their joint committee, requested me to "recommend to the people of the United States a day of public thanksgiving and prayer, to be observed by acknowledging with grateful hearts the many and signal favors of Almighty God, especially by affording them an opportunity peaceably to establish a form of government for their safety and happiness:"

Now, therefore, I do recommend and assign Thursday, the 26th day of November next, to be devoted by the people of these States to the service of that great and glorious Being who is the beneficent author of all the good that was, that is, or that will be; that we may then all unite in rendering unto Him our sincere and humble thanks for His kind care and protection of the people of this country previous to their becoming a nation; for the signal and manifold mercies and the favorable interpositions of His providence in the course and conclusion of the late war; for the great degree of tranquility, union, and plenty which we have since enjoyed; for the peaceable and rational manner in which we have been enable to establish constitutions of government for our safety and happiness, and particularly the national one now lately instituted for the civil and religious liberty with which we are blessed, and the means we have of acquiring and diffusing useful knowledge; and, in general, for all the great and various favors which He has been pleased to confer upon us.

Given under my hand, at the city of New York, the 3d day of October, A.D. 1789.

Deut 30:19–20: *This day I call heaven and earth as witnesses against you that I have set before you life and death, blessings and curses. Now choose life,*

so that you and your children may live and that you may love the LORD your God, listen to his voice, and hold fast to him.
This powerful summary of the whole book reaches its climax charged with evangelistic energy and urgency (Ezek 18:30–32). All the points expressed here have been made before, but combining them in this fashion increases their intensity. The issue is a matter of life and death. The context shows that the whole nation and its continuing prosperity on the land are in view. Yet the passage, so typically of Deuteronomy, is expressed in the second person singular; thus presenting the whole matter as an intensely personal choice—a choice that matters more than any other in life. ... The previous generation of the exodus had the land set before them, refused it, and 'chose' death and destruction as a consequence. This generation, even when they enter the land, must still go on choosing life through obedience, love, and loyalty to their covenant Lord God (Josh 24:15). This is the framework for understanding the whole of the inner contents of Deuteronomy with its detailed outworking of the choice. Wright, pp. 291–292
Excerpt from Deuteronomy by Christopher Wright, copyright © 1996. Used by permission of Baker Books, a division of Baker Publishing Group.

Personal Note: Notice that the Lord does not say "I will force you", but instead pleads with us to choose the right way. Like the father of the Prodigal Son, he does not veto our choices (Lk 15:12) even though he knows the pain bad choices will bring us. He warns, he woos (Job 36:16), he begs us to choose the right way. He lights the divine path (Ps 43:3, Ps 119:105, Isa 2:5) and whispers in our ears (Deut 30:14, Isa 30:21). But we must choose. The more bad choices we make, the harder it will be to get back to the right path. We know the blessings that result when we are on the right path, and we know the curses from the wrong path. May we resist the tinsel attractions of the world's siren song that promises blessing but ends in grief. Instead, may we *choose life* and make our journey to the glorious destination the Lord has prepared for us (Isa 35:10, John 14:2, Rev 21:3–5)!

Joshua

Commentaries:
- *Joshua: No Falling Words*, by Dale Ralph Davis (Focus on the Bible) (2000)
- *The Preacher's Commentary*, OT Vol 6, by John A. Huffman, Jr. (1986)

Josh 3:1: *Early in the morning Joshua and all the Israelites set out from Shittim and went to the Jordan, where they camped before crossing over.*
Every life has its *crossover* times. Some people call them peak experiences, but they are times of transition—often fraught with potential disaster. They are the times in life so familiar to those of the people of Israel capsuled in the phrase '*for you have not passed this way before*' (v 4). ... The word '*ābar*—meaning to 'cross over'—is used twenty-one times in the story of the crossing (3:1–5:1). This verb emphasizes the decisive nature of this moment in the history of the Hebrew people and distinguishes it from everything that had gone before. ... One of the most exciting experiences I've ever had as a pastor was to preach on this text, challenging my congregation as a community and as individuals to be a crossover people. I challenged them to be willing not just to 'set out' each day in a regular routine, but instead to face those dangerous moments of a new beginning, willing to cross over into whatever new faith experience and faith 'land' God has in store.   Huffman, p. 66

Josh 5:12: *The manna stopped the day after they ate this food from the land; there was no longer any manna for the Israelites, but that year they ate of the produce of Canaan.*
The manna was God's special supply for an exceptional need. But now that the need becomes normal his provision comes by ordinary means.

But it is still his provision, whether it is manna that falls from heaven in the wilderness or grain that grows in the ground of Canaan. ...So we must beware of thinking that God is only in the earthquake, wind, and fire [1 Kings 19:11-13]; of thinking that manna but not grain is God's food. Most of God's gifts to his people are not dazzling and gaudy but wrapped in simple brown paper. Quiet provisions of safety on the highway, health of children, picking up a paycheck, supper with the family—all in an ordinary day's work for our God. Davis, p. 49

Josh 11:20: *For it was the LORD himself who hardened their hearts to wage war against Israel, so that he might destroy them totally, exterminating them without mercy, as the LORD had commanded Moses.*
Let us react to the sheer audacity of this text. Do we not find that disturbing, offensive, outrageous? Who gave God the right to be that sovereign? But our verdict had better remain stuck in our throat. Don't try to evade the clarity of the text. It is a fearful thing to fall into the hands of the living God [Heb 10:31]. Don't think you can escape this God by running to the New Testament; you will meet the same God there (Heb 3:12-13). You will do better to tremble—and worship. Davis, p. 99

Personal Note: Davis gives another answer to our uneasiness at the violence of some OT accounts. I confess that in spite of the explanations of these learned men, I still am puzzled, perplexed, and uneasy when I see God orchestrating such violence. My main takeaway is that sin is serious business, and the sovereign Lord hates sin and deals with it harshly. I may not like it, but that's the way it is.

Josh 21:44-45: *The LORD gave them rest on every side, just as he had sworn to their forefathers. Not one of their enemies withstood them; the LORD handed all their enemies over to them. Not one of all the LORD's good promises to the house of Israel failed; every one was fulfilled.* [Ps 119:140]
This passage is the theological heart of the book of Joshua. The writer uses what I would call sledgehammer theology—he simply keeps pounding his point home. By emphatic repetition he pummels Yahweh's fidelity into our senses. In every case Yahweh gave what he swore, not a word fell [1 Sam 3:19], everything came about. There were no falling words [Isa 55:10-11]. ...Yahweh gave Israel rest when he defeated their enemies. This

is the biblical pattern. It serves, then, as a foreshadowing of Jesus victory (2 Thes 1:7–10) and our rest.　　　　　　　　　　　Davis, p. 156, 158

Josh 24:19: *Joshua said to the people, "You are not able to serve the LORD. He is a holy God; he is a jealous God. He will not forgive your rebellion and your sins."*

Don't lightly mouth your profession of faith, Joshua is saying. Don't you realize the sort of God you are dealing with? He is a holy, jealous God. You don't dare come to him thinking "though it makes him sad to see the way we live, he'll always say 'I forgive.'" Yahweh is not a soft, cuddly Santa in the sky who drools over easy decisions during invitation hymns. Joshua seeks to put down that blathering self-confidence that makes emotional commitments rather than shutting its mouth and counting the cost. The church should note this. Too frequently, the Jesus we present is some variety of prepackaged joy, peace, and provision that works twice as fast as aspirin. He is our cellophane Christ.... We must retain Joshua's paradox, must constantly stand between his 'serve Yahweh' (v 14) and his 'you cannot serve Yahweh' (v. 19). His purpose is not to drive us from Yahweh but to him. Only we must not make our commitment easily, lightly, flippantly, casually, but cautiously and fearfully (vv 21, 24).

　　　　　　　　　　　　　　　　　　　　　　　Davis, p 195,96

Judges

Commentaries:
- *The Preacher's Commentary*, OT Vol 7, by David Jackman (1991)
- *The Message of Judges*, (BST Series) by Michael Wilcock (1992)

Judg 3:15: *Again the Israelites cried out to the LORD, and he gave them a deliverer-Ehud, a left-handed man, the son of Gera the Benjamite.*
Instead of a five-star general, God chooses a left-handed assassin. Why? God *does* move in mysterious ways, 'His wonders to perform.' William Cowper went on to write, 'Blind unbelief is sure to err and scan His work in vain; God is His own interpreter, and He will make it plain.' The first three judges whose stories are related in this chapter are each in their way illustrations of this truth, that God is not bound by human restrictions or limitations. We are just as prone to domesticate the awesome power and majestic authority of God to fit into our little minds and pockets. We still want to control the omnipotent, to predict the infinite. But any god who can be encompassed by our puny finite minds and accommodated within our feeble systems is not worthy of the name. Unless we recover a healthy fear and awe of the inscrutable power and sovereignty of God, we shall end up as idolatrous as everyone else. That is why God is constantly surprising us. No situation, however desperate, is beyond His retrieval. No individual can every be written off in God's providence, or written out of God's script. God has not finished with any of us yet and He is still a specialist in the most unlikely interventions of deliverance. Let us make sure we are worshiping the real, the living God, and not being duped by all the substitutes offered in the religious supermarkets of our culture and generation. Jackman, excerpts, pp 61–73
Taken from The Preacher's Commentary Series Volume 7: Judges, Ruth by David Jackman. Copyright © 1991 by Word, Inc. Used by permission of Thomas Nelson. www.thomasnelson.com

Judg 16:16: *With such nagging she prodded him day after day until he was tired to death.*

We now begin the last episode of Samson's life, the tragic fall of the man who promised so much, but who produced so little. Each act of the drama increases the pressure and each time Samson yields a little more and slips a little nearer to revealing the secret of his Nazirite vow. The irony is that he seems blind to what is happening [before he loses his eyes, v 21]. What he does not see is how Delilah's persistent pressure on him is gradually wearing him down [Prov 27:15]. It all seems a game that the strong man can easily control, but actually he is being morally tied up and thereby weakened and softened up, made ready for the kill. ... Christians need to realize that sin which is regarded as harmless self-indulgence is doubly lethal, just because its killing power is unrecognized. A thought becomes an action, an action becomes a habit, a habit shapes a character, and a character reaps a destiny. Samson's defeat did not happen overnight. There was a hidden movement of the heart, by stages, long before the public denouement. We all need the warning because, while we tend to be very observant and critical of the sins of others, we are all inclined to be indulgent of our own 'little weaknesses,' [cf Rom 2:1, Rom 2:21] with often frightening results.

Jackman, p. 240–241

Taken from The Preacher's Commentary Series Volume 7: Judges, Ruth by David Jackman. Copyright © 1991 by Word, Inc. Used by permission of Thomas Nelson. www.thomasnelson.com

"The drop of rain maketh a hole in the stone, not by violence, but by oft falling." Hugh Latimer (1485–1555)   Quoted in Ward and Wild

Judg 17:13: *And Micah said, "Now I know that the LORD will be good to me, since this Levite has become my priest."*

<u>**Sermon Note**</u>: Rev Joshua Knott of Evangelical Presbyterian Church of Newark Delaware summed up Judges 17 with this alliterative statement: "It was a perverted private priesthood in pursuit of prosperity." Knott elaborated further. The people (Micah and his "customers") were worshiping money and calling it Yahweh. They were making an investment in spiritual stock and expecting a huge return. In verses 17:6 and 18:1, we are reminded that Israel had no king. In fact, each individual was "kinging himself" and attempting to *use* God instead of *serving* him. We sometimes do the same

things Micah and his contemporaries did. But Jesus comes into our lives to topple our idols and help us to see that he alone is sufficient (2 Cor 12:9).

Judg 19:25: *But the men would not listen to him. So the man took his concubine and sent her outside to them, and they raped her and abused her throughout the night, and at dawn they let her go.*
<u>Sermon Note</u>: The Rev Joshua Knott of Evangelical Presbyterian Church of Newark, Delaware summed up this chapter of Judges succinctly. The chapter begins with the refrain *in those days Israel had no king* (v 1). Therein lies the problem. The Lord has removed his restraining grace and sin has been let off the leash. Ironically, the Levite declines to sleep in a city of foreigners in v 12, thinking the people of God will treat him better. But we find in verse 22 that the people of God are no different than the people of Sodom and Gomorrah. As we read the horror of verses 22-25, we should begin to feel the disgust our Father feels about sin. Unless we can hate sin like the Father does, we can't appreciate the sacrifice of Christ. Without the grace and redemption of our Lord, we would be as hopeless as these wicked Benjamites. Just like these ancient people, we too need the King of Kings to rule over our lives.

Judg 21:25: *In those days Israel had no king; everyone did as he saw fit.*
[Deut 12:8]
Chapters 19–21 show progressive deterioration. Each chapter tells how a particular set of rules was discarded, and how each abandonment led to another. The pulling of the first loose end results in the unraveling of the whole. Moral life of God's people was not as it should have been, but as it all too easily can be: under the surface, a shambles of wrongness, all the wrong attitudes, with the Lord appealed to only in extremity, and then answering your prayer in a way you don't like. Decisions are reached but not by the Lord's direction. 'They said' the questions and 'they said' the answers (21:16–19)—the decisions are made by Israel talking to herself. Under a brisk coat of paint, the house rots and crumbles.
Wilcock, p. 166, 173
It looks so attractive to cast off the creaturely role of obedience to God [Ps 2:3] and to make up our own ground rules. But what offers to be freedom ends up as slavery [Jn 8:34, Rom 7:14], to our own passions and ultimately

to our own selves. The tragedy of contemporary atheistic thought is its impeccable logic. Once God is denied, then we really are on the road to the abyss of despair, where life is ultimately only a sick joke, a hollow delusion, and where human beings are nothing but a few cents worth of chemicals. If anything goes, then in the end everything goes.

Judges ends with a great longing for a better order, which depends upon a fundamental change of heart [John 3:3]. It looks for a king who will reign to bring about justice and peace. Thank God the longing was finally met when Jesus came into Galilee proclaiming the Gospel of God (Mk 1:15). There is a king in Israel, whose government and peace will increase forever, and who reigns on David's throne and over his kingdom, establishing and upholding it with justice and righteousness eternally (Isa 9:6).

Thank God that there is a day still to come when it will finally be revealed that 'the kingdoms of this world have become the kingdoms of our Lord and of His Christ, and He shall reign forever and ever' (Rev 11:15). That is the only ultimate answer to the problems of the Book of Judges, which are the problems of our sinful hearts. Once we have read ourselves into the book, as Israel, we shall never be able to forget its poignant and powerful lessons.
Jackman, excerpts, pp. 296–298

Taken from The Preacher's Commentary Series Volume 7: Judges, Ruth by David Jackman. Copyright © 1991 by Word, Inc. Used by permission of Thomas Nelson. www.thomasnelson.com

Ruth

Commentaries:
- *The Book of Ruth*, by Robert Hubbard (NICOT series) (1988)
- *The Preacher's Commentary*, OT Vol 7 by David Jackman (1991)

Ruth 1:11–12: *But Naomi said, "Return home, my daughters. Why would you come with me? Am I going to have any more sons, who could become your husbands?"*
Naomi's argument is carefully crafted to be irrefutable and is stated with brutal emotional force. Each succeeding line raised the scene's emotional intensity a notch. Ostensibly, the soliloquy is a passionate plea addressed to the women. In fact, however, it amounts to a lament accusing God of cruelly botching up her life. Its effect is to affirm his direct involvement in the story and hence his accountability for her awful situation. By holding the Lord responsible for her losses (1:13), Naomi affirmed his participation in the events. Thus, despite appearances, things were not out of control; if he is at least involved, the Lord might well straighten things out. In sum, bitter complaint cloaked firm faith.   Hubbard, pp 108, 113

Ruth 1:15–16: *"Look," said Naomi, "your sister-in-law is going back to her people and her gods. Go back with her." But Ruth replied, "Don't urge me to leave you or to turn back from you. Where you go I will go, and where you stay I will stay. Where you die I will die, and there I will be buried."*
With the ring of poetry, the now familiar words—Ruth's first in the story—soar on the wings of rhythm. They still tower as a majestic monument of faithfulness above the biblical landscape. How surprising is Ruth's embrace of the Lord in view of Naomi's bitter indictment of her God in verse 13!
            Hubbard, pp 117–118

Ruth 2:3: *As it turned out, she found herself working in a field belonging to Boaz, who was from the clan of Elimelech.*
The timing was perfect, because it was God's. He is the chief actor in the unfolding drama, but His actions are concealed. This is not a story of direct revelations, angelic visitors, or visible miracles as in the story of Gideon, for example, in Judges. No judge, no prophet, or priest is involved in these events, but the hand of God is just as discernable to the eye of faith as if it had been literally visible. And yet the wonder of His providence is that each of the protagonists is able to make his or her choices without there being even the slightest sense of them being mechanized or programmed. In these small details we see the pale reflection of the greatest of all biblical miracles—the miracle of God's grace. When we enter the narrow gate of Christ's kingdom, we are conscious of a decision of the will by which we turn from sin and trust Christ, as an expression of our free choice. Yet no sooner have we entered the door than we look back, as it were, and see inscribed over the entrance 'You did not choose Me, but I chose you' (John 15:16). The blend of divine sovereignty and human responsibility runs throughout all the comparatively insignificant details of our lives, as it did through the lives of Boaz and Ruth. It is a conviction we need to see restored running through our contemporary Christianity.

Jackman, p. 319

Taken from The Preacher's Commentary Series Volume 7: Judges, Ruth by David Jackman. Copyright © 1991 by Word, Inc. Used by permission of Thomas Nelson. www.thomasnelson.com

Ruth 3:1–2: *One day Naomi her mother-in-law said to her, "My daughter, should I not try to find a home for you, where you will be well provided for?"*
Naomi's reasoning is not difficult to follow as we see her trying to discern God's signposts. She has come home 'empty', but she realizes in her present condition the hand of El Shaddai, the Almighty, who is able to change situations. She does the sensible thing, the one thing she could do to provide for herself and her daughter-in-law, by sending Ruth to glean amid the alien corn. On the very first day, Ruth is noticed by Boaz, and not only noticed, but singled out by him for special marks of compassion and favor. Is that not an answer to prayer? Naomi, at any rate, sees it as Yahweh's provision (2:20), and begins to follow the signposts. Naomi was

not passive. She did not sit back, become a fatalist, and say 'whatever will be will be', and call that faith. There is a false piety which is an excuse for laziness and lethargy. Naomi took the initiative, but she followed the direction which she believed God was already pointing out. It is still an important ingredient of guidance to discern God's direction and then follow where he is leading and moving, whether in our personal lives or in the life of God's Church. Jackman, p. 334–335

Taken from The Preacher's Commentary Series Volume 7: Judges, Ruth by David Jackman. Copyright © 1991 by Word, Inc. Used by permission of Thomas Nelson. www.thomasnelson.com

"A possibility is a hint from God" Soren Kierkegaard (1813–1855)

Ruth 4:17: *and they named him Obed. He was the father of Jesse, the father of David.*
In sum, Naomi's needs have been marvelously met. The narrator is not finished, however. Just as the reader savored Naomi's sweet success, the narrator suddenly steps forward with a surprise—a kind of final exclamation point. Suddenly, the simple, clever human story of two struggling widows takes on a startling new dimension. It becomes a bright, radiant thread woven into the fabric of Israel's larger national history. Hubbard, p. 277

The book of Ruth's major significance remains to remind us that in the days of the judges, when the national life of Israel was under such constant threat and when at times it seemed as though the very covenant itself might be dismantled, Yahweh was preserving His people and developing His purposes, taking fresh initiatives and demonstrating covenant-love in His continuing work of redemption. The story of Ruth and Naomi provides a microcosm of the whole. Surrounded by the Lord's covenant love, they experienced His redemptive grace, not only in establishing and developing their personal relationships, but in those relationships reflecting what He was doing on the macroscale, in preparing his people for their coming King. "The Book of Ruth thus operates as a counter-point to the book of Judges, indicating the type of kingship which was to operate as a result of covenantal fidelity, and the tranquility that a true faith communicates", notes Dumbrell. That is a message which is as relevant today as it was to those who first heard its captivating story. Jackman, p. 352-353

Taken from The Preacher's Commentary Series Volume 7: Judges, Ruth by David Jackman. Copyright © 1991 by Word, Inc. Used by permission of Thomas Nelson. www.thomasnelson.com

1 Samuel

Commentaries:
- *1 Samuel: Looking on the Heart*, by Dale Ralph Davis (2000)
- *The Message of Samuel,* by Mary J. Evans (BST Series) (2004)
- *The Preacher's Commentary*, OT Vol 8, By Kenneth L. Chafin (1989)

1 Sam 4:3: *Let us bring the ark of the LORD's covenant from Shiloh, so that it may go with us and save us from the hand of our enemies.*
Their assumption is: if we bring the ark to the battle, Yahweh will be forced to deliver us to protect his honor. To have God's furniture is to have God's power. The ark is their religious ace in the hole. Here was a pressure tactic, a way of—if you'll pardon the expression—twisting God's arm. That is not faith but superstition. It is what I call rabbit-foot theology. When we, whether Israelites or Christians, operate this way, our concern is not to seek God but to control him, not to submit to God but to use him. So we prefer religious magic to spiritual holiness; we are interested in success, not repentance….Whenever the church stops confessing 'Thou art worthy' and begins chanting 'Thou art useful'—well, then you know the ark of God has been captured again. Davis, pp. 54, 55

Dale Ralph Davis, *1 Samuel: Looking on the Heart*, Copyright © 2000, by Christian Focus Publications, Fearn, Ross-Shire, Scotland. Used by Permission.

1 Sam 14:1-2: *One day Jonathan son of Saul said to the young man bearing his armor, "Come, let's go over to the Philistine outpost on the other side." But he did not tell his father. Saul was staying on the outskirts of Gibeah under a pomegranate tree*
The picture of Jonathan is consistent throughout the accounts. He was brave and daring, an impatient activist with a great capacity for commitment to God, to Israel, and to people. He inspired great loyalty in his troops and

his own armor-bearer was willing to follow him anywhere. Once he had a particular course of action in mind, Jonathan set about carrying it through immediately. The thought of following protocol and seeking his father's approval never occurred to him. The contrast with Saul is marked. There was no room in Jonathan's mind for long and anguished debates as to what might be God's precise will in this situation nor for holding back until he was completely sure that his action would be successful. That the task needed doing was already abundantly clear. As far as he was concerned, Saul was already commissioned and equipped by God to do it. What possible reason could there be for further delay? Sometimes the apparently spiritual decision to seek further guidance can simply be an excuse to procrastinate. Jonathan's active faith has much to teach us in this regard. Evans, Mary J., *The Message of Samuel*, Leicester, England: Inter-Varsity Press, 2004, p. 91

1 Sam 16:7: *But the LORD said to Samuel, "Do not consider his appearance or his height, for I have rejected him. The LORD does not look at the things man looks at. Man looks at the outward appearance, but the LORD looks at the heart."* [Jer 17:10]

One can understand Samuel's thinking. Eliab was doubtless an impressive hunk of manhood. Samuel was not alone in his estimate of Eliab. Many thought 'future' was Eliab's middle name. If we are mesmerized, Yahweh is not. He can see clearly....Only Yahweh's 'I have rejected him' saves Israel from ruin. In 16:6–7 we face another Saul situation; Eliab is created in Saul's image, after his likeness [1 Sam 9:2]. If Yahweh had not chosen the king, Israel would have suffered Saul—Act II. Yet 16:7 reaches forward as well as backward. This text, which I would call the key verse of 1 and 2 Samuel, sets itself not only against the likes of Saul and Eliab but also, in later pages against everyone's ideal Mr. Israel, Absalom (2 Sam 14:25–27). The text then contains a warning to prophets and others among God's people; it provides a revelation of our need; it shows us the discernment we lack. Only Yahweh's wisdom is adequate for directing his kingdom [1 Cor 4:5]. There is at least one thing we can seek to do: beware of impressiveness of external appearances [Gal 2:6]. We stumble here, for example, when congregations or denominations select pastors. What we seem to want are the movers and shakers, the aggressive extroverts, the pushers who meet people well and sell the church, who are smooth in the pulpit. One cannot study 1 Samuel 16 without sensing he or she is in the presence of Jesus Christ. Verse 7 dominates the chapter with its emphatic '*Man* looks on the outward appearance, but *Yahweh* looks on the heart [cf Isa 55:8, Lk 16:15].' What is this but an Old Testament rendition of John 2:25: 'For he himself knew what was in a man.' Who then is this before whom we stand? Or have we failed to see him because we put so much stock in appearances (Isa 53:2–3)? Davis, p 170-177

Dale Ralph Davis, *1 Samuel: Looking on the Heart*, Copyright © 2000, by Christian Focus Publications, Fearn, Ross-Shire, Scotland. Used by Permission.

1 Sam 20:31–32: *As long as the son of Jesse lives on this earth, neither you nor your kingdom will be established. Now send and bring him to me, for he must die!" "Why should he be put to death? What has he done?" Jonathan asked his father.*

The 'you and your kingdom' did not move Jonathan. He was bound and committed by covenant to David. He would remain faithful to the covenant even if it cost him the good will of his father....What does he teach us? This: that true life does not consist in securing 'you and your kingdom' but in reflecting Yahweh's faithfulness in covenant relationships. There is something liberating about that! Jonathan had acknowledged that the kingdom was Yahweh's and therefore David's, so his life did not need to be centered in his ambition (what can I get) but in God's providence (what Yahweh has given). Even as a believer and not as a crown prince my reigning passion is not to make my way, my living, or my mark; not to gain my place or to get ahead [1 Cor 9:15]. That may be costly; but it is certainly liberating. Life does not consist in achieving your goals but in fulfilling your promises. That (previous) sentence is only cold print. But watch it; it's dynamite. Handle with care. Davis, p. 212

Dale Ralph Davis, *1 Samuel: Looking on the Heart*, Copyright © 2000, by Christian Focus Publications, Fearn, Ross-Shire, Scotland. Used by Permission.

1 Sam 22:17: *Then the king ordered the guards at his side: "Turn and kill the priests of the LORD, because they too have sided with David. They knew he was fleeing, yet they did not tell me."*

Saul becomes one of the legion of antichrists who have always vented their spleen on the Lord's servants. There is one fact, however, that gives God's people some consolation: antichrists tend to be fragile. At least that is the case in 1 Samuel 22. True, Saul can have priests butchered by mere royal order (provided he orders the right stoolie). But that is just his problem. As Walter Brueggemann observed: 'Saul has nothing left but raw power.' Saul is increasingly isolating himself, divesting himself of whatever true support he could have had. He has pushed away his own son (20:30–42), exterminated Yahweh's priests, and repulsed his closest servants (22:17). Saul has had all but is in the process of losing everything. Now he can only say 'Doeg is for me' [contrast Ps 56:9]. When only Doeg is for me, I am in trouble. Make no mistake, the picture of Saul is tragic and sad. Nevertheless to see the weakness of his power is consoling to God's people.

Davis, p. 230

Dale Ralph Davis, *1 Samuel: Looking on the Heart*, Copyright © 2000, by Christian Focus Publications, Fearn, Ross-Shire, Scotland. Used by Permission.

1 Sam 24:4: *The men said, "This is the day the LORD spoke of when he said to you, 'I will give your enemy into your hands for you to deal with as you wish.'" Then David crept up unnoticed and cut off a corner of Saul's robe.*

There sits helpless Saul. David squats down on his haunches watching him. Words flow through David's mind. 'See! I am giving your enemy into your hand.' Was this providence or temptation? And how does one discern the difference? It was a searching test for Yahweh's servant. Yahweh's will must be achieved in Yahweh's way; the end that God has ordained must be reached by the means that God approves. David's men do not see this. To them, it was so obvious, so clear! This kind of test is not confined to David and Jesus; it comes up again and again to most all Yahweh's servants. It is the temptation to take a short cut. How we yearn for a short cut around the arduous, wearying, time-consuming labor of sanctification. What discernment we need! No wonder the Apostle left us his prayer 'That your love may abound more and more in knowledge and depth of insight, so that you may discern what is best.' (Phil 1:9–10).   Davis, p. 247–248

Dale Ralph Davis, *1 Samuel: Looking on the Heart*, Copyright © 2000, by Christian Focus Publications, Fearn, Ross-Shire, Scotland. Used by Permission.

"Wickedness is always easier than virtue, for it takes the short cut to everything."

Samuel Johnson (1709–1786)   Quoted in Ward and Wild

1 Sam 25:11: *Why should I take my bread and water, and the meat I have slaughtered for my shearers, and give it to men coming from who knows where?* Nabal said 'No' but not so simply. He called David a no-count runaway slave and his men a bunch of nobodies who have no right to *my* bread, *my* water, and *my* meat (emphasis mine and probably Nabal's). There is only one way, as conventional wisdom has it, to deal with such obnoxious muleheads. In a word 'sword'. This problem can be handled quickly. And we are apt to think that Nabal now has a problem. But of course, we are wrong. David has the problem. He has just now created it—and he does not yet know it. Davis, p. 256

Dale Ralph Davis, *1 Samuel: Looking on the Heart*, Copyright © 2000, by Christian Focus Publications, Fearn, Ross-Shire, Scotland. Used by Permission.

1 Sam 25:32–33: *David said to Abigail, "Praise be to the LORD, the God of Israel, who has sent you today to meet me. May you be blessed for your good judgment and for keeping me from bloodshed this day and from avenging myself with my own hands."*
Abigail's intervention kept David from walking in Saul's sandals, kept him from turning Nabal's Carmel into another Nob (22:11–19). The rejected king may practice sheer butchery but that is not the way for the chosen king….The text teaches us how Yahweh rescues his servants from their own stupidity, how he restrains them from executing their sinful purposes, how sometimes he graciously and firmly intercepts us on the road to folly. What loving hands construct the roadblocks to our foolishness! [Prov 14:12, 22:3] … In Chapter 24, David saw clearly what he must, or rather, must not do; in Chapter 25 he does not see it at all. He does not make the connection between the situations with Saul and Nabal. Such failure is not unique to David among all the Lord's servants. Have we not been caught in the same net? Can we recall times in which we saw God's way quite clearly in some dilemma but missed it completely in a fresh situation where the same principles applied? How multi-faceted Christian wisdom must be. How often our gracious God must stoop down to show us our inconsistency. How we need the instruction of his providence.

Davis, pp 259–261

Dale Ralph Davis, *1 Samuel: Looking on the Heart*, Copyright © 2000, by Christian Focus Publications, Fearn, Ross-Shire, Scotland. Used by Permission.

1 Sam 28:15: *"I am in great distress," Saul said. "The Philistines are fighting against me, and God has turned away from me. He no longer answers me, either by prophets or by dreams. So I have called on you to tell me what to do."*
This story is a classic example of a person who has rejected God's guidance. When he suffers the consequences of his action, he is without resource or help. Saul had 'made his bed' but now he didn't want to 'sleep in it.' We live in a society that does not see the relationship between our decisions and what happens to us. Even the religious community seems to feel that no matter what we do with God's instruction for our lives, at any moment we can repent and turn to God. Naturally He will not only forgive us but relieve us of the consequences of our actions. God does forgive graciously, and grace causes our relationship to be restored, but that does not mean that we can start afresh without having to live with the consequences of our action [2 Sam 12:14]. For Saul to be forced to go into battle alone was nothing more than the natural results of his decisions and actions.
Chafin, Kenneth L., *The Preacher's Commentary*, OT Vol 8, Nashville, TN: Thomas Nelson, 1989, p. 199

1 Sam 30:3: *When David and his men came to Ziklag, they found it destroyed by fire and their wives and sons and daughters taken captive.*
Here is a sobering and disturbing picture for God's people. Are there not times when you think it cannot get any worse? And 1 Samuel says, yes, it can. There are times when you conclude that your present trouble is the last straw; you simply cannot take any more. Then comes Ziklag, the last straw after the last straw. Sometimes you are tempted to add another line to Psalm 30:5: "Weeping may endure for a night, but joy comes in the morning"—and disaster strikes next afternoon. … We have a disturbing text. God's special servant, David, is overwhelmed with trouble. By implication we understand that this could be so for any of God's servants. The text says that your distresses and troubles could intensify. Even this, however, does not leave us comfortless. For here is the realism of the Bible. Here is no hiding of truth and preaching of half-truths. Here is no false advertising. As the Lord's servant you may be overwhelmed with troubles. You may receive more than you think you can even handle. But God in his word tells you this. You can trust a God like that; you can depend on a Scripture that tells you this. When Jesus said, "In the world you have

tribulation" [Jn 16:33], he didn't reduce it to small print or hide it in a footnote. Davis, p. 310–312

Dale Ralph Davis, *1 Samuel: Looking on the Heart*, Copyright © 2000, by Christian Focus Publications, Fearn, Ross-Shire, Scotland. Used by Permission.

1 Sam 30:18: *David recovered everything the Amalekites had taken, including his two wives.*

Note how the general structure of 1 Samuel 30 places David's victory at the heart of the narrative:

Ziklag—Destruction	1–6a
Seeking Yahweh's guidance	6b–8
Division of troops	9–10
Discovery	11–15
Victory	16–17
Recovery	18–20
Reunion of troops	21
Appreciating Yahweh's grace	22–25
Ziklag—distribution	26–31

First Samuel 30 is a long chapter and covers a lot of turf. It begins in tragedy and ends in triumph. Yahweh has a way of doing that. Davis, p. 320–321

Dale Ralph Davis, *1 Samuel: Looking on the Heart*, Copyright © 2000, by Christian Focus Publications, Fearn, Ross-Shire, Scotland. Used by Permission.

2 Samuel

Commentaries:
- *2 Samuel: Out of Every Adversity*, by Dale Ralph Davis (2002)
- *First and Second Samuel*, by Eugene H. Peterson (1999)
- *The Message of Samuel*, by Mary J. Evans (BST Series) (2004)

2 Sam 2:4: *Then the men of Judah came to Hebron and there they anointed David king over the house of Judah.*
The passage should have a 'historical marker' sign in the margin of your Bible. Here, for the first time, Yahweh's chosen king visibly rules on earth. At Hebron, in the provincial backwater. Only one tribe. This was no bump-along piece of maybe-stance; it was under Yahweh's guidance at every point (v 1). It is a small beginning, but it is the kingdom of God—concrete, visible, earthy. The kingdom of God has for a moment tucked itself away in the hills of Judah. The kingdom of God *is* like a mustard seed (Mt 13:31–32). Davis, p. 32–33

Dale Ralph Davis, *2 Samuel: Out of Every Adversity*, Copyright © 2002, by Christian Focus Publications, Fearn, Ross-Shire, Scotland. Used by Permission.

2 Sam 3:14: *Then David sent messengers to Ish-Bosheth son of Saul, demanding, "Give me my wife Michal, whom I betrothed to myself for the price of a hundred Philistine foreskins."*
It was clear as far as both David and Abner were concerned, that political expediency was more important than the personal feelings of either Michal or Paltiel. David's high-handed treatment of Michal here may go some way to explaining her reactions at a later stage (2 Sam 6). We, as readers, are again left to make the judgment as to whether or not callous disregard for the feelings of individuals is acceptable in the service of a 'higher' cause.

Evans, p. 181

2 Sam 4:8: *This day the LORD has avenged my lord the king against Saul and his offspring.*
They claimed to be channels to whom David owed the debt of posh government jobs. They came with blood on their hands but theology on their lips, expecting that the latter will magically bleach the former. Murder always seems more pleasant when wrapped in religious considerations. Baanahs and Rechabs are still extant; some are in our churches. Their methodology is unchallenged; use theology to cover sin and folly. For them theology is not truth that lures us to worship God but technique that enables us to justify ourselves. We may recognize them in the self-appointed defender of doctrinal precision, who is eager to explain, correct and inform with all harshness and severity. We must beware; when we explain things theologically we may simply be using God, using him as an argument, manipulating him for our convenience to keep from submitting to his grace or to his law [cf Titus 3:9–11].   Davis, p. 53
Dale Ralph Davis, *2 Samuel: Out of Every Adversity*, Copyright © 2002, by Christian Focus Publications, Fearn, Ross-Shire, Scotland. Used by Permission

2 Sam 6:6–7: *When they came to the threshing floor of Nacon, Uzzah reached out and took hold of the ark of God, because the oxen stumbled. The LORD's anger burned against Uzzah because of his irreverent act; therefore God struck him down and he died there beside the ark of God.*
It was fun. It was loud. It was religious. Dancing and singing and the likes of lyres, tambourines, cymbals, and so on. Kiriath-Jearim was rocking. But a strange thing happened near the threshing floor of Nacon. It took a moment for everyone to realize it. The dancing stopped. The music stopped. All eyes turned on Uzzah, on the ground, writhing, twitching. Then still. Someone called 911. The party was over. Why doesn't Yahweh cut him some slack? Why so severe? Why so arbitrary? For me, passages like this are evidence of the supernatural origin and trustworthiness of the Bible. This Uzzah story goes so against the grain of human preferences. We would never have 'invented' a God like this—not if we want to win converts and influence people. This God is not very marketable. Anyone who says the God of the Bible is merely a projection of our wish fulfillment has not read the Bible.   Davis, p. 74–75

As the Christian imagination over the centuries has reflected on Uzzah's death, one insight appears over and over: It was fatal to take charge of God. When the oxen stumble and Uzzah reflexively reaches out to keep the ark from sliding off, it is not an isolated act; it is Uzzah's habit to manage the ark, and supposedly along with it is God-in-the-ark. The eventual consequence of this obsessional management of God is death, whether slow or sudden. God will not be put and kept in a box, whether the box is constructed of crafted wood or hewn stone or brilliant ideas or fine feelings. We do not take care of God; God takes care of us. Uzzah is the person who, instead of losing himself in the worship of God, has God in a box and officiously assumes responsibility for keeping God safe from the mud and dust of the world. Men and women keep showing up in religious precincts who take upon themselves the task of protecting God from the vulgarity of sinners and the ignorance of commoners. ... God arrives, but in his own way. His action is not always congenial to our expectations or desires. God is on David's side but not 'in his pocket.'

Peterson, excerpts, pp. 163–164

2 Sam 7:22: *How great you are, O Sovereign LORD! There is no one like you, and there is no God but you*
There is a strong sense of the 'Wow!' that David felt at this time and there is no reason why any of it should not have been spoken by David. He begins 'Wow, just look at what God has done for me and my family!', and concludes 'Wow, just think about who God is and what he has done for his people!'. The 'Wow' element of prayer is perhaps something that God's people need to recapture today [2 Sam 22:47, Ps 66:16, Rom 11:33].

Evans, p. 200

2 Sam 12:7: *Then Nathan said to David, "You are the man!"*
2 Sam 12:13: *Then David said to Nathan, "I have sinned against the LORD."*
Let me state what is both obvious and significant: 'You are the man' is the punchline and not the introduction. That may disappoint some readers. They may prefer more of a John-the-Baptist approach (Mk 6:18). But Nathan knew what stout defenses mind and mouth can muster against a frontal assault. So instead of sitting down and calling David a filthy womanizer and a cruel murderer, he began with a story. Nathan's strategy

is nothing but the ingenuity of grace. His technique is the godly scheming of grace that goes around the end of our resistance and causes us to switch the floodlights on our own darkness. Nathan did not accuse or harangue. He simply upped David's blood pressure over that ruthless rich fellow and David accused himself. Alexander Whyte was right: Nathan's sword was within an inch of David's conscience before David knew that Nathan had a sword. That is the holy craftiness of grace. If God determines to bring you back to repentance, what chance do you have against grace like that? Grace is far more than amazing: it's smart.   Davis, p. 151, 152

Dale Ralph Davis, *2 Samuel: Out of Every Adversity*, Copyright © 2002, by Christian Focus Publications, Fearn, Ross-Shire, Scotland. Used by Permission

The word of God is not about somebody else. It is never a general, abstract truth, but always personal address. The biblical revelation is never a commentary on ideas or culture or conditions; it is always about actual persons, actual pain, actual trouble, actual sin: you, me; who you are and what you have done; who I am and what I have done.

It is both easy and common to lose this personal focus and let the biblical story blur into generalized pronouncements, fuzzy cosmic opinions, and religious indignation. That is, in fact, what David does. He listens to Nathan preach a sermon about (he thinks) someone else and gets all worked up over this unnamed person's terrible sin. This is the religion of the dormitory bull session, the TV spectacular, the talk-show gossip. It is the religion of moral judgmentalism, self-righteous finger-pointing, the religion of accusation and blame.

With each additional word in Nathan's sermon, David becomes more and more religious—he feels sorry for the poor man who lost his poet lamb, he seethes with indignation over the rich man who stole the lamb. Pitying and judging are religious sentiments that can be indulged endlessly, making us feel vastly superior to everyone around us, pitying and judging, becoming more religious by the minute, absorbed in a huge blur of moral sentimentality.

And then the sudden, clear focus: You are the one—you!

Nathan is the patron of all who break through the barriers of detachment and sentiment and address the person. The task of all Christian discourse, whether in word or music or image, is to get around third-person defenses

and compel a second-person recognition, which enables a first person response. Peterson, pp 184–185
Personal Note: Nathan's "You are the man!" speaks to me across the centuries. Although I haven't committed murder and adultery, I have fallen far short of the Lord's plan for me. Christ calls us to higher standards that I have failed to live up to. John reminds us in 1 John 1:9 that if we confess our sins he is faithful and just to forgive us our sins and cleanse us from all unrighteousness. May I be as ready as David to acknowledge my guilt, receive God's grace, and turn to a new life of joyful obedience. May we all acknowledge Nathan's rebuke.

2 Sam 17:14: *For the LORD had determined to frustrate the good advice of Ahithophel in order to bring disaster on Absalom.*
This is the explanation for the whole story, for all this which has occurred so naturally, so humanly, so freely. Yahweh had ordained it. That may raise some questions for you. But remember: Yahweh's sovereignty is not meant to give you philosophical problems but spiritual comfort. And the primary characteristic of his sovereignty in this passage is its hiddenness. There are no trumpets, no turmoil, no billboards or bumper stickers. No glitzy, frenetic commercials like car dealers blast out on television. Only this quiet text, this discrete aside. More often than not that is the manner of God's work. His scepter is unseen, his sovereignty hidden behind the conversations and decisions and activities and crises of our lives. We see only grocery lines and diaper changes and school assignments; but through and over and behind it all, Yahweh rules [Eph 4:6]. He is not absent but neither is he obvious. Sometimes we must be told that lest we become too enamored with our Hushais. Davis, p. 215–216
Dale Ralph Davis, *2 Samuel: Out of Every Adversity*, Copyright © 2002, by Christian Focus Publications, Fearn, Ross-Shire, Scotland. Used by Permission

2 Sam 20:3: *When David returned to his palace in Jerusalem, he took the ten concubines he had left to take care of the palace and put them in a house under guard. He provided for them, but did not lie with them. They were kept in confinement till the day of their death, living as widows.*
Personal Note: The swath of David's sin with Bathsheba continues to engulf everyone around him. It paralyzed him in dealing with Amnon

and Absalom, causing a major rebellion and the use of the concubines by Absalom as pawns in his power play. It may also have indirectly caused Ziba's brazen scheme to get Mephibosheth's property. Now it dooms the concubines to a dreary existence. How many innocent victims have been left in the wake of David's walk on the wall? I suspect that many, like David, never foresee the scope of their "one little sin." Here we learn that the consequences of sin are not always confined to the individual sinner, but often cause substantial collateral damage. In Scripture there are other examples of one sin radiating out to damage the lives of innocent victims (eg, Judges 19:25, where the Levite presents his concubine to a mob who kills her; this ultimately results in over 60,000 battle deaths in chapter 20). These examples may be among the ones the Apostle Paul identified as warnings to us (1 Cor 10:11). We may think that we can put a retaining wall around our sin to confine it in a small area. But sin has a way of seeping out and contaminating others around us. Before we sin, do we consider the impact the sin *may* have on innocent people around us? Because if it *may* impact others, it probably will.

Life of David
Personal Note, March 2006

As I conclude my study of the books of Samuel, I take time to reflect on the life of David. I confess that I struggle with the idea that David was a man after God's own heart, since he obviously did much to grieve the Lord and often had a negative impact on those around him. Consider the following negatives in David's ledger:

- Bathsheba and Uriah the Hittite incident (adultery and murder) (2 Sam 11)
- Nearly killing all of Nabal's men (1 Sam 25:13)
- Killing innocent women in his raids (1 Sam 27:11)
- Taking many wives and concubines in direct violation of Deut 17:17 (2 Sam 5:13)

- Forcibly taking Michal from her husband Paltiel for purely political reasons (2 Sam 3:15–16)
- Failing to deal with the blood-thirsty Joab on many occasions (eg, 2 Sam 3:29) and leaving him to his son Solomon to deal with (1 Kings 2:5–6).
- Failing to consult God on the first attempt to bring the ark into Jerusalem (1 Chr 13:7)
- Confining his concubines after they had been compromised by Absalom (2 Sam 20:3)
- Extremely poor parenting skills in the Amnon/Tamar affair. He was furious and yet did nothing, allowing Absalom's anger to seethe (2 Sam 13:1)
- Unjust judgment on Mephibosheth on the evidence of one witness (Ziba) (2 Sam 16:4). This was compounded by the fact that even when David learned the truth, he still let Ziba off with half of Mephibosheth's property, apparently breaking his oath to Jonathan (1 Sam 20:42)
- Turning over seven innocent men to the Gibeonites (2 Sam 21:6)
- Calling for a census against his advisor's counsel and causing many deaths (2 Sam 24:1, 10)

But there were also many positives as well:
- Sparing Saul's life twice and not lifting a hand against the Lord's anointed (eg,1 Sam 24:6)
- Excellent leader and motivator (1 Sam 22:1–2)
- Did what was "just and right" in ruling Israel (2 Samuel 8:15)
- Listening to Abigail and avoiding a serious mistake (1 Sam 25:32)
- Immediately acknowledging his guilt in the Bathsheba affair when confronted by Nathan (2 Sam 12:13)
- Kindness to Mephibosheth (at least initially) (2 Sam 9:9–13)
- Not gloating in the death of Saul (2 Sam 1:19)
- Joyful exuberance for the Lord when bringing the ark into Jerusalem (2 Sam 6:16)
- not using the ark as a good luck charm while fleeing from Absalom (2 Sam 15:25)

- Writing excellent, inspiring psalms (eg, Ps 18, 19, 23, 30, 32, 37, 40, 51, 103)
- Realizing his guilt in the census affair and confessing his sin to the Lord (2 Sam 24:10)

In short, while David had many endearing qualities, was an inspiring psalmist and great military leader, he also had some glaring deficiencies. We can learn both from his successes and his failures as we examine his life from our vantage point across the centuries. The amount of space Scripture devotes to him (his name is mentioned over a thousand times) is itself a testimony to his pivotal role in the Lord's plan of salvation. His life is a constant reminder not only of God's grace, but of his covenant of love and promised Messiah, who had all of David's strengths but was without sin (Heb 4:15). David points to the root and offspring of our faith (Rev 22:16).

1 Kings

Commentaries:
- *1 Kings: The Wisdom and the Folly*, by Dale Ralph Davis (2002)
- *The Preacher's Commentary*, OT Vol 9, by Russell Dilday (1987)
- *ESV Expository Commentary*, Vol 3, by J. Gary Millar (2019)
- *The Message of Kings*, by John. W. Olley (2011)

1 Kings 3:3 *Solomon showed his love for the LORD by walking according to the instructions given him by his father David, except that he offered sacrifices and burned incense on the high places.*
Robert Louis Stevenson's Strange Case of Dr. Jekyll and Mr. Hyde illustrates the insidious encroachment of sin in a person's life. The magic potion that turned the respected Dr. Jekyll into the wicked Mr. Hyde provided the noble physician a convenient way to enjoy sinful pleasure without losing his reputation. When he had his fill of wickedness, he needed only one sip of the antidote to become Dr. Jekyll again, all without a hint of scandal. One day, however, Dr. Jekyll awakened to discover that in his sleep, without the help of the potion, he had become Mr. Hyde. He went into the laboratory to take the antidote, but nothing happened. Try as he would no formula he concocted would restore his identity as the genial gracious gentleman he had been. The evil he had voluntarily unleashed in his life had become dominant, supreme, uncontrollable.
This was Stevenson's literary technique to illustrate the superhuman power of evil. If you give sin an inch in your life, it will take a mile. Give it a tiny foothold, and it runs rampant, getting the upper hand and destroying the quality of your life. Dilday, p 61.

1 Kings 4:20: *The people of Judah and Israel were as numerous as the sand on the seashore; they ate, they drank and they were happy.* [Gen 22:17]

First Kings 4 continues the roller-coaster ride that is the biblical account of Solomon. On the one hand, there are considerable reasons for optimism and hope. God's grand "Eden restoration project" has hit its high point. The borders of Israel have expanded. The land of milk and honey finally feels like that. The economy is booming and the civil administration is running smoothly. A godly king is flourishing, and the demands on the people are kept in check. The reputation of Israel among the nations will never be so high, largely because of the efforts of their anointed king. This truly is the golden age of Israel, and it is evident that all of this is the case because of the generosity of their God–the God who has gifted Solomon, a new Adam, with unparalleled wisdom, honor, and power [3:13]. This is a kingdom worth defending and maintaining.

And yet, the writer does not hesitate to remind us that all is not quite as it seems. Even as these chapters awaken hope of a new creation taking shape before us, discordant notes sound with increasing regularity. Yes, Yahweh has kept his promises. Yes, the land has been secured and subdued and is enjoying rest. But at what cost? God's king is looking remarkably like the kings who rule all the other nations [1 Sam 8:19-20]. He has many horses, an eviable diet. The nation is being run in a way that is more efficient than before, but is it more godly? The nations are flocking to the people of God, as was promised–but what blessing are they seeking? It seems that they come to hear the wisdom of Solomon. Do they also find the blessing of the God who has made the heavens and the earth, as Solomon, his regent on earth, speaks of the only wisdom that really counts, which is fearing Yahweh? [Prov 1:7]

Millar, J. Gary. *ESV Expository Commentary*, Vol 3, Wheaton, IL: Crossway 2019, p. 549

1 Kings 4:32–33: *He spoke three thousand proverbs and his songs numbered a thousand and five. He described plant life, from the cedar of Lebanon to the hyssop that grows out of walls. He also taught about animals and birds, reptiles and fish.*

How liberating wisdom can be! Wisdom, Solomon shows us, is incurably and rightly curious—it ranges over the whole domain of God's realm, joyfully investigating and describing all God's works [Prov 8:30–31]. Nothing is hid from the sun's heat (Ps 19:6)—nor from wisdom's interest.

Since God has left the fingerprints of his wisdom everywhere, since there is no place where God does not furnish us with raw materials for godly thinking, Christians should be seized with a rambunctious curiosity to ponder his works, both the majestic and the mundane. The task of wisdom is joyfully to describe [Gen 2:19–20] and investigate all God's works [Prov 8:30–31]. We may not have Solomon's insight, but we can gratefully examine the same data. Davis, p. 49

Dale Ralph Davis, *1 Kings: The Wisdom and the Folly*, Copyright © 2002, by Christian Focus Publications, Fearn, Ross-Shire, Scotland. Used by Permission

1 Kings 8:27: *But will God really dwell on earth? The heavens, even the highest heaven, cannot contain you. How much less this temple I have built!* Here is the God who bursts all our categories and frustrates all our attempts to surround his majesty. Here is the immensity of God…. The words drip with our happy failure to get a grip on the massive majesty of God. But conjunctions provide some of the most astounding theology. Follow Solomon's verbal tracks. No sooner does he confess God's immensity in wonder and praise than he walks right into verse 28: 'But you must turn to the prayer of your servant and listen to his plea.' What an audacious assumption! The true God is as described in verse 27, but you can talk to him with prayers, pleas for grace, and cries. Solomon teaches us that transcendence does not destroy intimacy. The Lord is transcendent yet available [Isa 57:15]. Here is reason for both trembling and joy. Yahweh's people can never comprehend him in all the fullness of his being, but they can approach him in the place of prayer. I cannot encompass God in his grandeur [Ps 145:3] but I can engage him in his grace (Isa 66:1–2). His majesty dwarfs our universe yet his ear receives our prayers [2 Chr 6:18–19].

Davis, p. 86, 87

Dale Ralph Davis, *1 Kings: The Wisdom and the Folly*, Copyright © 2002, by Christian Focus Publications, Fearn, Ross-Shire, Scotland. Used by Permission

"This morning my soul is greater than the world, since it possesses you, whom heaven and earth cannot contain." Margaret of Cortona (1247–1297)

Quoted in Ward and Wild

1 Kings 11:4: *As Solomon grew old, his wives turned his heart after other gods, and his heart was not fully devoted to the LORD his God, as the heart of David his father had been.*

The problem is not wealth or luxury or high-handedness or wisdom or popularity or renown or splendor or achievement but *other gods*. First commandment stuff. Now we can notice the subtlety of sin. How is it so subtle? Because it is internal; it is, to use the key word of our passage, a matter of the 'heart' [Prov 4:23]. This term occurs five times in verses 2–4. Long before you see a new Chemosh chapel going up outside Jerusalem (11:7) a royal heart had taken a turn. This infidelity was also subtle because it was gradual…It was not some sudden attack or irresistible assault that explains Solomon's plunge into pagan ecumenism. No, it took years— the result of the creeping pace of accumulated compromises, the fruit of a conscience de-sensitized by repeated permissiveness. So there is the tragedy: a story that begins with 'Solomon loved Yahweh' (3:3) and ends with 'King Solomon loved many foreign women' (11:1). How these 'book end' texts should sober us [cf Eph 6:24, Rev 2:4]. Where are my affections? Has an imperceptible drift taken place in them over the years? Am I headed for tragedy because I have left my first love (Rev 2:4)?   Davis, pp 112, 113, 114

Dale Ralph Davis, *1 Kings: The Wisdom and the Folly*, Copyright © 2002, by Christian Focus Publications, Fearn, Ross-Shire, Scotland. Used by Permission

Another lesson comes to light in this passage, namely, the gradual degradation of Solomon's commitment as a warning that sin's victory in our lives most often occurs not by sudden satanic assaults but by slow moral erosion. Romans 5 tells us how tribulation produces patience and patience produces character and character, hope. But in this story we are reminded that power produces pride, and pride produces arrogance, and arrogance, forgetfulness of God. Solomon's failure seems to have resulted from a gradual loosening of his firm grip on God's will.
Dilday, pp. 124–125

"The safest road to hell is the gradual one – the gentle slope, soft underfoot, without sudden turnings, without milestones, without signposts."
                                                C. S. Lewis (1898–1963)

1 Kings 16:23: *In the thirty-first year of Asa king of Judah, Omri became king of Israel, and he reigned twelve years, six of them in Tirzah.*
Our writer is not overly impressed with the great Omri. Omri bought the hill and Omri did evil. Here is a king who packs significant historical weight and the Bible assumes practically the whole story can be told in the usual formulas. He reigned, he did evil, he was buried. You want to know more? Go to the local library and punch in 'royalchronicles.com' (v 27). The Bible's account is as scintillating as an obituary. And with good reason: Omri did evil; he was more evil than all who preceded him; he walked in the ways of Jeroboam. You've heard it all before. The writer is not saying he is ignorant of Omri's accomplishments—he is saying they don't matter.... Isn't this a sobering text? Isn't this what Jesus is teaching us, but in a different mode, in Matthew 13:44–46? Are there, among the preoccupations of your life, any that are not ultimately trivial? Do the passions that drive your living and doing only elicit a yawn from heaven?

Davis, p. 191

Dale Ralph Davis, *1 Kings:The Wisdom and the Folly*, Copyright © 2002, by Christian Focus Publications, Fearn, Ross-Shire, Scotland. Used by Permission

1 Kings 18:21: *Elijah went before the people and said, "How long will you waver between two opinions? If the LORD is God, follow him; but if Baal is God, follow him." But the people said nothing.*
This is no mere academic question. Elijah's formulation assumes that theology leads to discipleship. Elijah will not allow you to attend a 'God contest' simply so you can conclude 'Well, now we know that Yahweh is the real God. What movie do you want to see?' Elijah, the Bible, Yahweh himself, will not allow you the comfort of such detachment.... The God of the Bible refuses to be the topic of your rap session. He is not an idea you play with but a King to whom you submit. You'd better understand up front all that is involved. If I am God, he says, follow me. Here is no tame God; he—we might say—keeps slopping over into my life claiming it, invading it, refusing to allow me to put him in his religion box. We may prefer a god we have domesticated—we show him his deity litter and keep him in his place. But that is not the real God. You hear him in 1 Kings 18:21, and if you transpose that text into New Testament theology, you will realize it does not permit nonsense like

having-Jesus-as-your-Savior-but-not-as-your-Lord. He doesn't give you that option. Davis, pp. 233,234

Dale Ralph Davis, *1 Kings:The Wisdom and the Folly,* Copyright © 2002, by Christian Focus Publications, Fearn, Ross-Shire, Scotland. Used by Permission

Life of Solomon
Personal Note (April 2006)

As I did with David, I now pause to reflect on the life of his son Solomon. This great king of Israel, while not quite as prominent as David, is nevertheless a formidable biblical figure. He authored three canonical books and appeared in many chapters of two different books (Kings and Chronicles). He appears in or authored over seventy biblical chapters and his name is mentioned 289 times in the NIV. His wisdom, collected in the books of Proverbs and Ecclesiastes, has become (pardon the pun) "proverbial", and has given rich insight to millions over the centuries. His reign represented the pinnacle of civilization for Israel. The apocryphal book the Wisdom of Solomon states: *Therefore I prayed, and understanding was given me; I called on God, and the spirit of wisdom came to me. I preferred her to scepters and thrones, and I accounted wealth as nothing in comparison with her. Neither did I liken to her any priceless gem, because all gold is but a little sand in her sight, and silver will be accounted as clay before her. I loved her more than health and beauty, and I chose to have her rather than light, because her radiance never ceases. All good things came to me along with her, and in her hands uncounted wealth* (Wisdom 7:7–11).

Solomon may have been the richest man in history (see the enormous quantities of gold especially 1Kings 10:14=2 Chr 9:13, which specifies the ominous number of 666 talents (compare to the mark of the beast Rev 13:18). But while he achieved much, he did not finish well. Matthew Henry sums it up: "Solomon was master of a great deal of knowledge, but to what purpose, when he had no better a government of his appetites?"

When I taught a brief 4 lesson series on his life in Sunday School, I noticed that his life could be encapsulated by several words beginning with "W":

- **Well-being** (nation enjoys rest on every side) (1 K 4:25)
- **Wisdom** (author of Proverbs, people came from far and wide to hear him) (1 K 4:32)
- **Worship** (the prayer at the dedication of the temple is a masterpiece) (1 K 8:15–53)
- **Wealth** (cargos of silver, gold, ivory, spices, and baboons) (1 K 10:22)
- **Wives** (1000 of them led him astray) (1 K 11:3)
- **Waste** (though great, he finished poorly, squandering his gifts from God and setting up the chaos of the divided kingdom) (1 K 11:9)

Though Solomon's proverbs repeatedly tell us that the fear of the Lord is the beginning of wisdom, he failed to listen to his own advice (Eccl 4:13). We moderns also do some pretty stupid things in spite of advanced education levels. His faults are eloquently outlined in Deuteronomy 17:14–20 which lays out guidelines for a successful king. He seems to have violated nearly every one of these divine boundaries.

Solomon stands as a warning beacon to all who let their pride get the better of them (see also Isa 14, Deut 8:17, 2 Chr 26:16). He focused on accumulating wealth and wives but forgot that worship and wisdom were the only lasting values. Well-being comes from the fount of every blessing, not from our paltry and self-aggrandizing efforts. We ignore Solomon's story at our peril.

2 Kings

Commentaries:
- *2 Kings: The Power and the Fury*, by Dale Ralph Davis (2005)
- *ESV Expository Commentary,* Vol 3, by J. Gary Millar (2019)
- *The Preacher's Commentary,* OT Vol 9, by Russell H. Dilday (1987)

2 Kings 1:3: *But the angel of the LORD said to Elijah the Tishbite, "Go up and meet the messengers of the king of Samaria and ask them, 'Is it because there is no God in Israel that you are going off to consult Baal-Zebub, the god of Ekron?'"*

What do we meet in this section of the story? Above all, an intolerant God. The suave, self-appointed connoisseurs of religious taste in our times will be aghast if ever they happen on this story. How can Yahweh in his wild, untamed holiness sentence a man to death simply for exercising his religious preferences in the critical hour of his life? Yahweh here is not the democratic sort of God people crave, according to the polls… In the Bible we meet Yahweh and keep bashing ourselves against the first commandment (Ex 20:3). … Again we see our uncomfortable God: Yahweh is furious, not tolerant; holy, not reassuring; loving, not nice. But there is love in his fury. He won't let you walk the path of idolatry easily; his mercy litters the way with roadblocks. That is a wonder considering he so detests our idols. Davis, p. 16, 19

2 Kings 4:5b *They brought the jars to her and she kept pouring.*

Certainly one lesson is that God keeps giving Himself to us as long as we bring to Him that into which He can pour Himself. When we stop bringing, He stops giving. Of course God can give many things whether we want them or not, but His best gift can only be given if we desire it. That gift is Himself, His saving presence within us. God will not force

Himself on anyone who will not in earnest faith open his heart like an empty vessel to Him. So the lesson here is that we have as much of God as we are willing to take in. He will not make us wise or holy or powerful unless we really desire these gifts and bring Him our empty lives for His filling. 'You do not have because you do not ask' (James 4:2). Feeble wishing for things is one thing, but the intense, steadfast desire of faith is another. Wish for anything else and you may or may not get it, but come to God with empty vessels of expectant faith, earnestly desiring His gifts [1 Cor 12:31], and He will fill them [Mt 5:6, Eph 3:19].

Dilday, pp 273–274

2 Kings 16:10 *Then King Ahaz went to Damascus to meet Tiglath-Pileser king of Assyria. He saw an altar in Damascus and sent to Uriah the priest a sketch of the altar, with detailed plans for its construction.*
After a quick tour of the Syrian religious sites, and with as much gravity and theological thought as on an episode of a home-renovation show, Ahaz decides to reconfigure everything in the Jerusalem temple. This is the ultimate triumph of style over substance. ... Ahaz loves the world. He trusts the world. If worldliness is starting to think, talk, act, and dream like everyone else, getting sucked into the anti-God patterns and rhythms of life on earth, then Ahaz is a prime example of what it means to be worldly. *ESV Expository Commentary,* Vol 3, by J. Gary Millar (2019), excerpts, pp. 832, 833, 834

Personal Note: As I read Millar's comments in December 2020, I am struck by how it seems to characterize contemporary America. Many pundits applaud Europe as the paragon of what is good and practical. But Europe seems to have gone the way of Ahaz—just go with the flow and do not consult God. Do we really want to be, as Millar states, "sucked into the anti-God patterns and rhythms of life on earth?"

2 Kings 17:33: *They worshiped the LORD, but they also served their own gods in accordance with the customs of the nations from which they had been brought.*
Pagan religion creates what it likes; biblical faith receives what is revealed. Pagans worship based on what they prefer; biblicists must worship based

on what God declares. The biblical worshiper must submit; the pagan worshiper may concoct. Davis, p 251

2 Kings 19:15: *And Hezekiah prayed to the LORD: "O LORD, God of Israel, enthroned between the cherubim, you alone are God over all the kingdoms of the earth. You have made heaven and earth."*
Hezekiah confesses that he approaches a God who is near [Deut 30:14, Ps 145:18, Phil 4:5], vast [Job 9:4, Ps 139:17], and mighty [Deut 3:24, Ps 50:1]. One who is accessible [Isa 57:15], sovereign [Ps 71:16], and able [1 Tim 1:12, Rev 5:5]. He packs a three-point sermon into the opening lines of his prayer! And the twist is that it's not only true but helpful. Is this not precisely what Hezekiah needs to remember in the present distress? What better way for Hezekiah to encourage Hezekiah than to rehearse God's majesty as he requests God's help? Speaking truth about God to God may stir up assurance in God. Is this a cue for us to take more care about our address to God, about the way we begin our prayers? Davis, p. 279–280

2 Kings 25:27–29 *In the thirty-seventh year of the exile of Jehoiachin king of Judah, in the year Evil-Merodach became king of Babylon, he released Jehoiachin from prison on the twenty-seventh day of the twelfth month. He spoke kindly to him and gave him a seat of honor higher than those of the other kings who were with him in Babylon. So Jehoiachin put aside his prison clothes and for the rest of his life ate regularly at the king's table.*
Who would think that any sure hope from God could be hidden under this failed, dilapidated, and captive people? At this point (=Mt 1:12) Israel has lost the land (Abraham promise) and the kingship (the David promise). As for the tone of the times in Mt 1:12–16, well, read Haggai, Nehemiah, and Malachi. Judah stays under foreign domination; life is hard. In those books the earth is mostly brown, the sky is gray, the leaves are pale, the wind is cold. But precisely in this time, this darkest, bleakest segment of Israel's history, the Messiah is given! It was when this people was trampled, beaten down, and teetering between faith and compromise, that the Sun of righteousness began to blaze [Isa 60:1, Lk 1:78–79]. It is not your righteousness but Yahweh's stubbornness that brings redemption. The God of power and fury turns from his fury in Jehoiachin's Descendant. And we should have more than a whisper of hope.
Davis, p. 344

1 Chronicles

Commentaries:
- *The Message of Chronicles*, by Michael Wilcock. (BST Series) (1987)
- *The Preacher's Commentary*, OT Vol 10, by Leslie C. Allen (1987)

1 Chr 10:13–14: *Saul died because he was unfaithful to the Lord; he did not keep the word of the Lord and even consulted a medium for guidance, and did not inquire of the Lord.*
In the end there will be only two classes of people, those who have said to God 'Your will be done' and those to whom God has regretfully to say 'Your will be done' [Ps 81:11–12, 2 Pet 2:10]. The message of these chapters is the same decisive choice. The Chronicler intended these narratives about Saul and David to be read together as a contrast which, transcending time, confronted readers of his own day. In turn we have been brought within the circle of his readers and are meant to hear his implicit appeal to decide for God, for our own good. Behind the specifics of the Saul obituary lies a message for the people of God in every generation. This is the broad way that leads to destruction [Mt 7:13], and for every traveler on the highway of life Saul's experience is God's road sign *DO NOT ENTER*. This is the house built on sand, and great was its fall [Mt 7:26–27]. Allen, pp 69, 73
Taken from The Preacher's Commentary Series Volume 10: 1 & 2 Chronicles by Leslie C. Allen. Copyright © 1991 by Word, Inc. Used by permission of Thomas Nelson. www.thomasnelson.com

1 Chr 16:36: *Praise be to the Lord, the God of Israel, from everlasting to everlasting. Then all the people said "Amen" and "Praise the Lord."*
In the midst of praise divine truths are taking firmer root in the hearts of God's people. Theology functions as encouragement, giving new strength to the weary and fresh hope to the disheartened. Hold on, runs the message: '*The Lord is great*' and '*the Lord is coming*' (vv 25, 33). The church is also a

community marked by joy, not because its members are blind to the facts but because they look beyond bare facts to see God at work, preparing for them a glorious destiny. They feel the rain, but see the rainbow. God's electing loves lies around them, embracing them in its strong grip. It is as strong as death and many waters cannot quench it, nor can the floods drown it [Song 8:6–7]. That love brings an assurance of victory, even now enjoyed in spirit. Come wind, come weather, they are to remain valiant in the faith, conscious of God's preserving grace. Soon the tide will turn, and then Christians will be revealed in their true colors as sons and daughters of God. This hope is a vital ingredient of their initial salvation and means that future salvation [v35] will be theirs.   Allen, pp. 106–107

Taken from The Preacher's Commentary Series Volume 10: 1 & 2 Chronicles by Leslie C. Allen. Copyright © 1991 by Word, Inc. Used by permission of Thomas Nelson. www.thomasnelson.com

1 Chr 29:10–13 *Praise be to you, O LORD, God of our father Israel, from everlasting to everlasting. Yours, O LORD, is the greatness and the power and the glory and the majesty and the splendor, for everything in heaven and earth is yours. Yours, O LORD, is the kingdom;*
you are exalted as head over all. Wealth and honor come from you; you are the ruler of all things. In your hands are strength and power to exalt and give strength to all. Now, our God, we give you thanks, and praise your glorious name.   [cf Isa 26:12]

"Praise is the honey of life, which a devout heart sucks from every bloom of providence and grace. We may as well be dead as be without praise; it is the crown of life."
Charles Haddon Spurgeon (1834–1892)

1 Chr 29:14: *But who am I, and who are my people, that we should be able to give as generously as this? Everything comes from you, and we have given you only what comes from your hand.*
In a passage more memorable than the mere description of the festival, he gives us David's prayer at the climax of its opening ceremony. It is David's words here which pinpoint the cause of this next 'great continuity', the perennial joy that God's people should know. What words they are! As so often seems to happen, verses whose whereabouts in Scripture we cannot

quite recall, but whose content is quite unforgettable, turn out to be the work of the Chronicler. A dull writer, they say, yet how many gems await to be unearthed from his unfamiliar pages! 29:11 and 29:14 are a case in point. A conflation of parts of the two verses is used in worship all over the Christian world, among thousands who have no idea where the words come from. Instead of RSV, I quote a version which for this reason is perhaps better known: 'Yours, Lord, is the greatness, the power, the glory, the splendor, and the majesty; for everything in heaven and on earth is yours [Hag 2:8]. All things come from you, and of your own do we give you.'[1] It is a precious thing of undimmed luster and undiminished value. Wilcock, p. 115

"Of all created comforts, God is the lender; you are the borrower, not the owner."
Ernest Rutherford (1871–1937) British Scientist

---

[1] The Holy Communion Service, the *Alternative Service Book 1980* of the Church of England

2 Chronicles

Commentaries:
- *The Message of Chronicles*, by Michael Wilcock. (BST Series) (1987)
- *The Preacher's Commentary*, OT Vol 10, by Leslie C. Allen (1987)

2 Chr 7:14 *if my people, who are called by my name, will humble themselves and pray and seek my face and turn from their wicked ways, then will I hear from heaven and will forgive their sin and will heal their land.*
This is one of the two keys of Chronicles, the other being 1 Chr 17:12, a pair of verses which puts the Chronicler's theology into two nutshells. They are God's words of revelation spoken to David and Solomon as pioneers of a new era and through them to the people of God generation after generation. The Chronicler will construct the rest of his history around this second verse. Its recurring vocabulary will show that its model for spirituality may either be embraced for one's good or rejected at one's peril [cf Deut 30:19]. The low road from sin to disaster could be left by a track which wound back to the high road from obedience to blessing. If every rule in the book had been broken, one more ruling is revealed, vibrant with grace and hope. The prayer had to be accompanied by a resolve to start again with God and leave the bad, old lifestyle behind. It was far from a glib recital of a formula of confession. It reached into the heart and soul, as 6:38 indicated. … Repentance is a matter of heart and mind; it is a mental and spiritual realignment with God's will.
Until we fall on the banana skin of failure, we are apt to walk with a jaunty air of self-confidence, imagining ourselves masters and mistresses of our destiny. If God is to have His way with us, it seems that we have first to fall and humbly realize our need for help from outside ourselves. The wonder is that the grim either-or of verses 17–22 is not God's only word; beyond just deserts lies undeserved grace [Acts 3:19].   Allen, excerpts, pp 214–223

Dave Martin

Taken from The Preacher's Commentary Series Volume 10: 1 & 2 Chronicles by Leslie C. Allen. Copyright © 1991 by Word, Inc. Used by permission of Thomas Nelson. www.thomasnelson.com

Excerpt from Abraham Lincoln's proclamation of a National Fast Day, March 30, 1863:

Whereas, the Senate of the United States, devoutly recognizing the Supreme Authority and just Government of Almighty God, in all the affairs of men and of nations, has by a resolution, requested the President to designate and set apart a day for National prayer and humiliation.
And whereas it is the duty of nations as well as of men, to own their dependence upon the overruling power of God, to confess their sins and transgressions, in humble sorrow, yet with assured hope that genuine repentance will lead to mercy and pardon; and to recognize the sublime truth, announced in the Holy Scriptures and proven by all history, that those nations only are blessed whose God is the Lord.

We have been the recipients of the choicest bounties of Heaven. We have been preserved, these many years, in peace and prosperity. We have grown in numbers, wealth and power, as no other nation has ever grown. But we have forgotten God. We have forgotten the gracious hand which preserved us in peace, and multiplied and enriched and strengthened us; and we have vainly imagined, in the deceitfulness of our hearts, that all these blessings were produced by some superior wisdom and virtue of our own [Deut 8:17–18]. Intoxicated with unbroken success, we have become too self-sufficient to feel the necessity of redeeming and preserving grace, too proud to pray to the God that made us. It behooves us, then, to humble ourselves before the offended Power, to confess our national sins, and to pray for clemency and forgiveness.

2 Chr 21:1: *Then Jehoshaphat rested with his fathers and was buried with them in the City of David. And Jehoram his son succeeded him as king.*
This is the lesson which godly Thomas Fuller (1608–1661) found in the sequence of reigns from Rehoboam to Jehoram. He is commenting on the kings as they appear in the genealogy of Jesus Christ in Matthew 1.

'Lord, I find the genealogy of my savior strangely checkered with four remarkable changes in four generations. Rehoboam begat Abia: a bad father begat a bad son. Abia begat Asa: a bad father begat a good son. Asa begat Jehoshaphat: a good father begat a good son; and Jehoshaphat begat Jehoram: a good father begat a bad son. I see, Lord, from hence that my father's piety cannot be entailed: that is bad news for me. But I see also that actual impiety is not hereditary: that is good news for my son.'

Quoted in Wilcock, p. 207

2 Chr 26:15–16: *His fame spread far and wide, for he was greatly helped until he became powerful. But after Uzziah became powerful, his pride led to his downfall. He was unfaithful to the LORD his God.*
The characteristic which is brought out in several ways in the chapter before us is strength. Three times we are told in so many words that 'he was strong', 'very strong' (26:6, 15, 16). Uzziah's very name announces the theme in the chapter's opening verse, for it may be translated 'The Lord my strength'. …Uzziah was a strong man, and his strength was praiseworthy—until it came to the crunch. Then his strength was his downfall. "I am not an ordinary man", Napoleon once said, "and the laws and morals and customs were never made for me." But among God's people, no leader, however experienced, can risk such a cavalier attitude to the law of God. *'Nobless Oblige'*—nobility has its obligations, and the higher the greater. No one is beyond the kind of temptation that came to Uzziah; it may lie ahead for any of us [Prov 16:18].
Wilcock, p. 221, 229, 230

Ezra

Commentaries:
- *The Preacher's Commentary*, OT Vol. 11, by Mark D. Roberts (1993)
- *The Message of Ezra & Haggai*, by Robert Fyall (2010)

Ezra 1:11: *In all, there were 5,400 articles of gold and of silver. Sheshbazzar brought all these along when the exiles came up from Babylon to Jerusalem.*

'The exiles came up from Babylon to Jerusalem' is a laconic phrase but it expresses nothing less than a reversal of the exile, a new exodus and one of the great moments of history. Unlike the exodus story, no details are given of the journey nor of the feelings of those who undertook it. For that kind of story, we have to wait for chapter 8 when Ezra himself returns. This is a visible demonstration of the unseen providence of God. The event may not have had the overtly miraculous accompaniments of the exodus but it is no less an act of God. The numbers may be small but they represent the return of the nation and, like their forebears leaving Egypt, they carry gifts from their Gentile neighbors. … Ezra often fails to charm at a first reading, largely because it so often seems so low key and factual. Yet, as we look at what is happening and catch the echoes of earlier Scripture and see the book in the overall biblical picture we realize that God is working his purpose out. Ultimately the Bible's theology of history is that God will be God and the world will know it [eg, Isa 40:5]. Fyall, pp. 43–44

Ezra 4:24: *Thus the work on the house of God in Jerusalem came to a standstill until the second year of the reign of Darius king of Persia.*

The work, we are told, came to a standstill. This is a situation the devil loves; if he can trap us into believing we are in a cul-de-sac we will lose heart and stop building. In such circumstances we need to take our stand on God's earlier assurances, not least the praise of 3:11: He is good; his love to Israel endures for ever. This is a God who does exactly what he promised [Num 23:19, Josh 21:45], at the precise moment he promised it and in the face of all the odds. When we come to an apparent graveyard of our hopes, we need to renew our trust in a God who knows his way out of the grave.

Fyall, p. 81

Ezra 10:11: *Now make confession to the Lord, the God of your fathers, and do his will. Separate yourselves from the peoples around you and from your foreign wives.*
Ezra 9–10 is a notoriously difficult Bible passage that upsets our emotional instincts. Admittedly intermarriage between Jews and pagans was wrong, but was it really necessary for families to be broken up? Did fathers have to send away their children forever? Did restoration really need to be this painful? … Was Ezra correct? Honestly, I do not now. Did God hate the continuation of pagan marriages even more than breaking them up? I'm not sure.

Roberts, excerpts, p. 147–149

Nehemiah

Commentary:
- *The Message of Nehemiah*, by Raymond Brown (BST Series) (1998)

Neh 5:9: *So I continued, "What you are doing is not right. Shouldn't you walk in the fear of our God to avoid the reproach of our Gentile enemies?"*
The inconsistent conduct of the offenders not only dishonored God and ignored Scripture; it nullified their witness to the unbelieving world. If their pagan neighbors saw them behaving cruelly towards their own people, how could they possibly be persuaded of the uniqueness and reality of Israel's distinctive faith? Consistent testimony is a central biblical theme and figures prominently in the New Testament teaching about the Christian life. People with consistently attractive Christian lives not only make faith visible and credible but challenge the unbelief of their contemporaries. Edgar Wallace, a prolific writer of thrillers for an earlier generation, was influenced by the Christian living of a Methodist friend, J.B. Hellier. He said, 'I believe that much of the good which is within me came because I knew him. He is an everlasting barrier between me and atheism.' Conversely, these rapacious Israelite slave-owners and money lenders would make their distinctive message a reproach in the eyes of their Gentile enemies. Inconsistent lifestyles seriously damage the effectiveness of Christian witness. W.E. Sangster used to pose the searching question: 'Are some people outside the Church of Jesus Christ because I am inside?'
Brown, p. 94

Neh 9:5-6: *Blessed be your glorious name, and may it be exalted above all blessing and praise. You alone are the LORD. You made the heavens, even the highest heavens, and all their starry host, the earth and all that is on it, the* *seas and all that is in them. You give life to everything, and the multitudes of heaven worship you.*

You alone are the Lord is a significant biblical affirmation for our time, especially in the face of two contemporary challenges: idolatry and pluralism. Modern people have idols other than grotesque statuettes; their idols reign in the heart. They worship prosperity, popularity, pleasure and power, and those who idolize these invisible icons persistently turn their backs on the one and only God. Further, the pluralistic nature of late twentieth century Western society will not tolerate this uncompromising biblical exclusivism. It prefers a 'pick 'n mix religion', a view which regards all religions, ancient and modern, as of equal worth. Many of our contemporaries prefer to select acceptable elements not only from the older world religions but also from the new, such as the bizarre ideas in New Age with its primary focus on the pre-eminent 'self' (self-awareness and self-fulfillment), rather than on the reality of human sin and the crucial need for a Divine Savior. The Christian must be prepared to bear what has been described as the 'scandal of particularity.' Brown, p. 156

"An idol is a good thing, which becomes a great thing, which becomes a god thing, which in the end becomes a nothing." Joshua Knott

Esther

Commentaries:
- *The Message of Esther*, by David G. Firth (2010)
- *The Preacher's Commentary* OT Vol. 11, by Mark D. Roberts (1993)
- *Ezra, Nehemiah, Esther*, by Leslie C. Allen and Timothy S. Laniak (2003)

Est 4:14: *For if you remain silent at this time, relief and deliverance for the Jews will arise from another place, but you and your father's family will perish. And who knows but that you have come to royal position for such a time as this?* Just when it seems most likely that God will be mentioned, we meet a gaping theological silence. As Berlin observes, 'God is most present and most absent in this chapter.' Yet the book assumes God's activity, evident in the God-shaped holes in the narrative, and these become apparent from a close reading of the text. Somehow, in the faithful action of God's people we discover the working of God for his people. ... The question, *And who knows*, leaves it open for Esther to consider. She has become queen at just the right time. His question thus asks Esther to ponder providence. Is it possible that she has been placed in this position just so she can serve God's purposes? It is precisely because we cannot know such things in advance that the question is phrased as it is, but it is a question that many since Esther have also had to consider. Firth, excerpts, pp. 70, 76

Est 4:16: *Go, gather together all the Jews who are in Susa, and fast for me. Do not eat or drink for three days, night or day. I and my maids will fast as you do. When this is done, I will go to the king, even though it is against the law. And if I perish, I perish.*

Prepared by the fast, Esther will go to the king, even though it is against the law [v 11]. It is a supremely dangerous moment for her in that she must risk the king's ire. The famous words *if I perish, I perish*, are an expression of courage uttered by one who has placed her life in the hands of providence but who still knows that martyrdom for her people may be the outcome. At this point Esther has no idea whether her plan will succeed or not, because we cannot compel God to work with us to achieve goals we set. But we do know that God works to achieve his purposes and calls us to join him in this. It is the ambiguity of this world that Esther explores, and is perhaps one of the key reasons why God is not mentioned directly. We only recognize the working of providence by looking back, but we have to commit ourselves to God's providence and live our lives going forward.

Firth, p. 78

"Life can only be understood backwards; but it must be lived forwards."
Soren Kierkegaard (1813–1855)

Est 6:1–3: *That night the king could not sleep; so he ordered the book of the chronicles, the record of his reign, to be brought in and read to him. It was found recorded there that Mordecai had exposed Bigthana and Teresh, two of the king's officers who guarded the doorway, who had conspired to assassinate King Xerxes. "What honor and recognition has Mordecai received for this?" the king asked.*

Like the author of the Hardy Boys mysteries, the author of Esther uses coincidence to develop the plot and to delight the reader. From a Christian perspective, however, we see these happenstances as a sign of God's providence. While from a human perspective life is full of accidents, from a biblical perspective life is full of events that reflect God's sovereign plan. As the Master Author of human history, God weaves together the stories of our lives. To surprise us with joy and to accomplish his inscrutable will, God fills our lives with apparent flukes that, upon deeper inspection, reflect his Sovereign care. Coincidence or Providence? Our answer depends on seeing with the eyes of faith.

Roberts, p. 391, 392

Est 7:5: *King Xerxes asked Queen Esther, "Who is he? Where is the man who has dared to do such a thing?"*
Esther articulates her request with clear resolve. She is asking the king to make a critical choice between his queen and his prime minister. Her

request is crisp, and she delivers an accusation without so much as hinting at the king's complicity. Like Nathan with David, she elicits the king's anger before identifying the culprit (2 Sam 12:1-6). Once Xerxes hears of this unnamed threat to herself and her people (compare 3:8), he is agitated into demanding details. Without hesitation, she answers (with similar staccato in Hebrew), "The adversary and enemy is this vile Haman" (v 6). *Her* enemy is now *his* enemy and thus *the* enemy.

Esther's extreme deference to the gracious Xerxes is matched by her open spite for the "wicked" Haman. The Hebrew adjective is the simple term for evil, the opposite of the Hebrew term for good used of Esther (1:19) and Mordecai (7:9) and the king's choices (3:9).

Esther's accusation triggers the kind of anger that is to be expected from those in power who are threatened. The king was enraged over Vashti's insubordination, as was Haman over Mordecai's indifference. The king's agitated questions in verse 5 reveal his readiness to protect his queen. Esther's appeal was based not only on the king's favor with her but perhaps even more on the king's own honor. Someone close to the king was plotting the destruction of the queen! Had the king been "taken for a ride," bribed unwittingly into giving up his wife? Once Haman was identified as the culprit, the king got up in a rage (v 7).

Larniac, Timothy S., *Ezra, Nehemiahm, Esther*, Grand Rapids, MI: Baker Books, 2003, p. 244

Est 8:2: *The king took off his signet ring, which he had reclaimed from Haman, and presented it to Mordecai. And Esther appointed him over Haman's estate.* As Christian readers we can see in the story of Esther the same principles at work throughout the Bible: the way down is the way up [2 Cor 12:10]; the first shall be last [Mt 19:30]; the way to glory is the way of the cross [Mark 8:34]. All to often, rather than seeking to serve a great God, some want to be great in God's service [Lk 22:24–27]. The difference is crucial. Many excellent young leaders find themselves on the fast track to greatness, but Scripture warns us that the fast track usually leads to a crushing U-turn. That is why we see around us the wreckage of lives destined for glory, but destroyed by the flames of ambition [cf King Amaziah 2 Chr 25:17–26].

Roberts, p. 413

Est 9:28 *These days should be remembered and observed in every generation by every family, and in every province and in every city. And these days of Purim should never cease to be celebrated by the Jews, nor should the memory of them die out among their descendants.*
The book of Esther, with its many peculiarities including the establishment of Purim, leaves Christian readers unsettled and perhaps that is why God included it within our canon—for it continually challenges us to consider our relationship to a world of people that are loved by God in a world system that we are not to love (John 3:16, 1 John 2:15). The book of Esther stands as a warning for those of us who take too much pride in our neatly-formulated doctrines of Scripture. Just when we think we have it all figured out, the reality of Esther challenges our ability to domesticate the Bible. The puzzles of Esther keep us in a position of humbly seeking God's truth rather than pretending to control it with complacency and presumption. Roberts, p. 432

The Books of Wisdom

Personal Note and Introduction

The five books that are generally categorized as the "Wisdom" books contain an enchanting microcosm of the Word of God. One thing that seems to set these books apart from the rest of Scripture is that they tend to contain brief treatments rather than long stories or extensive treatises. I suspect for this reason most of the Wisdom books are rarely taught in Sunday School classes except to be occasionally cross referenced. Unless a reader is committed to reading the Bible in its entirety, these books will tend toward a "dip and skip" approach. But like other Scripture, these books are fascinating and useful for educating us on God's word. We risk missing out on a delightful and edifying experience if we only use them as references to our other studies.

The Wisdom books form an eloquent defense of the Christian faith and thus may be persuasive to the secular skeptic if they are given half a chance. To the skeptic with an open mind I would not recommend reading these books in their canonical order. Instead I would recommend the following:

Proverbs:	The practical book of Reason, Logic, and Knowledge
Psalms:	The book of Emotions
Job:	Why do bad things happen to Good People?
Song of Songs:	The book of Love as it was meant to be
Ecclesiastes:	The Skeptic's Argument and its Answer

While Proverbs occasionally reaches to celestial heights (eg, 8:27–31), it is one of the most "down to earth" books in the canon. In the pages of Proverbs we see the vivid contrast between wisdom and folly. The book is comprised of two main sections: Chapters 1–9 form an extended speech comparing wisdom and folly, which are personified by two women. Both make their proclamations in the public square. Both promise understanding and joy, but only one delivers. The remaining twenty-two chapters contain short, crisp sayings that show different facets of wisdom and folly. Most of the book is thus structured (to quote Spurgeon) like a chest of gold rings rather than a chain of rings.

The keynote of Proverbs is struck with 1:7: Fear of the Lord is the beginning of wisdom. C.S. Lewis has an interesting metaphor that illustrates why we risk a lot by ignoring Proverbs 1:7. In his book *Mere Christianity*, he writes:

> A car is made to run on gasoline, and it would not run properly on anything else. Now God designed the human machine to run on Himself. He Himself is the fuel our spirits were designed to burn or the food our spirits were designed to feed on. But many of us want to feed on something else. Something goes wrong. The machine conks. It seems to start up all right and runs a few yards, and then it breaks down. They are trying to run it on the wrong juice.

Proverbs often stubs our toes as we recognize ourselves in the depictions of folly. We think "we know better" than the demonstrated wisdom of God's Word. The Lord gives us the freedom to be stupid, but longs for us to take hold of the wisdom he grants to those who seek it. Proverbs gives us a glimpse into God's perspective. As we sojourn on his creation, we can profit greatly by reading the divine guidebook.

Once we have mastered the practical truth of Proverbs, we are ready to experience the emotions of the Psalms. The Psalter begins with a simple (the skeptic might say, simplistic) portrayal of two groups: the righteous and the wicked. Like Proverbs with its binary choice of wisdom and folly, we get only two choices in Psalm 1 with no shades of gray. Read out of context, Psalm 1 seems absolutely incorrect since it seems to suggest that the righteous have it made while the wicked will perish. But as commentator Michael Wilcock points out, the Psalm must be read in context. The other 149 psalms (and the rest of Scripture) work through all the "yes, but" protestations we bring up.

The Psalms often use the first person pronoun I, inviting us to take the Psalm as our own. Intense emotions characterize most of the psalms. From frustration, anger, fear, and loathing of enemies to unbridled joy and worship of our creator, the Psalms have it all. Some of the Psalms challenge us. For example, David seems to be self-righteous (eg, Psalm 18:20). In some the Psalmist rails against his enemies in a most unseemly manner (eg 3:7, 35:4–8). Some accuse the Lord of being asleep at the switch (eg most of Psalm 89). Some cry out to the Lord in anguish and pain (eg 38:7). The psalms express nearly all the emotions humans can feel.

But perhaps the most pervasive emotion expressed in the Psalms is praise and adoration of the Lord our God. Many of the psalms begin in agony and woe as the writer focuses on his own circumstances but end in joy and gladness as he turns the focus to God. Psalm 77 is a fine example of this pivot from self to God.

Vigorous praise is found throughout the Psalms, reminding us that the Lord is not only worthy of our worship, but the only thing worthy of our worship. As we lift our eyes to the hills (121:1), we take our eyes off the agony and woe we may see at ground level. The Westminster confession of faith states "Man's chief end is to glorify God, and to enjoy him forever" and the Psalms help us to do just that. They give us the words to describe the indescribable and to express our wonder at His majesty and power.

After mastering the basics of Proverbs and the emotional power of the Psalms, we may be ready to take on the Book of Job. This book eloquently answers the questions most skeptics ask about Christianity: Why do bad things happen to good people? How can a loving God permit such pain to people who are devoted to Him? Many who ask this question are expecting a simple answer and when one is not given, just say "well that proves it. You can't answer me so I just can't believe in God." A complex question will not have a quick answer, but if you read the book of Job you will find the answer (maybe not the one you wanted to hear).

The book of Job also refutes a modern day popular approach sometimes called "the prosperity Gospel." One prominent purveyor of this simplistic approach has built a large following because his audience gets a steady dose of things they want to hear. But a syrupy, sickeningly sweet over-simplification of the gospel is simply wrong. A syllogism that states "I am good, so God prospers me" (or "I am bad so God punishes me") leaves no room for divine sovereignty. This is the argument given by Eliphaz, Bildad, and Zophar in Job. God is reduced to a computer program or a cash register when he in fact is the sovereign God to whom we all must answer.

The book sometimes called 'Song of Solomon' or 'Song of Songs' then takes on the topic of love between a man and a woman as God meant it to be. This book does not shy away from the physical dimension of love. Some outside the faith have a distorted view that Christianity is a prudish cult that frowns on any type of fun, especially sexual pleasure. But Song of Songs emphatically demolishes that stereotype. Sexual love is not only exquisitely pleasurable; it was designed by God. In his wisdom, he knew he needed to build a drive into his species to assure their propagation. But he also designed us to be faithful to a life partner. In that context, sexual love is not only permitted, but applauded by God's word, especially here in the Song of Songs.

The Song also can be read as an illustration of passionate love for God. As humans we are quite familiar with the profound satisfaction we receive from the love act. We do not need to be persuaded or cajoled. We want it. We want it now. We want it often. But the Song reminds us that we need that same passion for our Creator and the Lover of our souls. Ps 63:3 says "Because your love is greater than life, my lips will glorify you." We might say this on Sunday but do we mean it on Monday? The Song reminds us that the same strong emotions that motivate our love for a life partner can motivate our love for God. He after all is our ultimate life partner (Rev 21:3).

Finally we come to the Book of Ecclesiastes, where a "teacher" spews out one cynical and skeptical verse after another. Some scholars think Solomon wrote his Song of Songs when he was fairly young, Proverbs when he was in middle age, and Ecclesiastes when he was an old man. Given the fact that Solomon did not end well, we can see how he could think that all was chasing after the wind and that there is nothing new under the sun. In his personal life he sated himself on wine, women and song and came up empty as many in modern Hollywood do.

Ecclesiastes rails against nearly everything we might consider good, including even wisdom. After Solomon wrote an eloquent encomium of wisdom in Proverbs (eg, "wisdom is more precious than rubies, and nothing you desire can compare with her." [8:11]), he says in Ecclesiastes "Then I applied myself to the understanding of wisdom, and also of madness and folly, but I learned that this, too, is a chasing after the wind." [1:17]. Ecclesiastes can be tedious with its repetition of the same things over and over. It whines and moans much like complainers we see (and abhor) in our modern encounters.

While rays of sunshine occasionally peek through the clouds even in this book (eg 3:22, 5:19,20), it mainly is just one long diatribe. The "teacher" tries dozens of things to bring meaning to his life "under the sun" but in the end, finds there is only one path that works (12:13). Commentator Derek Kidner sums up the book well by quoting Shakespeare. Kidner states:

It is God's work that baffles us: it is not "a tale told by an idiot." Yet what if it is a tale told to an idiot?

Ecclesiastes repeats the phrase "under the sun" over and over again. The book thus emphasizes that we see the world at "ground level" and thus lack the perspective of the Creator. This is why it may appear to be meaningless. God's Word stunningly rejects the cynical position of most of the book of Ecclesiastes. Life on earth does in fact have profound meaning and purpose [Eph 1:3–5]. We catch but a glimpse of the Lord's overarching plan, but He has graciously given us insight that we lacked had we only our senses and logic and scientific instruments to guide us. May we seize what he gives us and know him more intimately [Eph 1:17–18] as we read his word. The five books of wisdom give us a good start in our journey to at least partially comprehending the love that surpasses knowledge [Ps 36:5, 57:10, 108:4, Eph 3:19].

Before closing, I should also mention that our Lord and Savior Jesus Christ makes his appearance in these books as he does the other 61 in the canon. Augustine's statement that "the new testament is in the old concealed, and the old is in the new revealed" is demonstrated in spades in these five books. Christ is seen in Job: "I know that my redeemer liveth" [19:25] and 'Even now my witness is in heaven; my advocate is on high' [16:19]). Our Lord is seen in the Psalms (particularly 22 which he quoted on the cross and 72 which describes his kingdom). He appears in Proverbs in the form of wisdom "I was there when he set the heavens in place, when he marked out the horizon on the face of the deep" [8:27]). The crusty writer of Ecclesiastes seems to leave Christ out, but his very absence teaches us that life is meaningless without Him. Spurgeon comments on 11:7–8: "*Truly the light is sweet, and a pleasant thing it is for the eyes to behold the sun: but if a man live many years, and rejoice in them all; yet let him remember the days of darkness; for they shall be many. All that cometh is vanity.* Take Christ away, and this is a truthful estimate of human life. Put Christ into the question, and Solomon does not hit the mark at all." And finally we see our Lord and Savior in the Song particularly in 2:16: 'My beloved is mine and I am his; he browses among the lilies.'

May we rejoice in the thought that we are loved by God and by his Son and by his Spirit! May our lives reflect that love! And may we honor Father, Son, and Spirit in all we do!

Job

Commentary:
- *The Preacher's Commentary*, OT Vol 12, by David L. McKenna (1982)
- *Job: A Man of Heroic Endurance*, by Charles Swindoll (2004)
- *Cornerstone Biblical Commentary*, Vol. 6, by August H. Konkel (2006)
- *Stars Through the Clouds*: The Collected Poetry of Donald T. Williams (2020)

Job 1:1: *In the land of Uz there lived a man whose name was Job. This man was blameless and upright; he feared God and shunned evil.*
Job's consistency is a commendation that escapes many Christians who claim the grace of Jesus Christ. One well-known financier has said "On the weekend, my priorities are God, family, and business. When I arrive at the office on Monday morning, the order is reversed." Job does not suffer from this contradiction. He has integrity—*being* equals *doing*.

McKenna, p. 30

Taken from The Preacher's Commentary Series Volume 12: Job by David L. McKenna. Copyright © 1991 by Word, Inc. Used by permission of Thomas Nelson. www.thomasnelson.com

Job 8:18: *But when it is torn from its spot, that place disowns it and says, 'I never saw you.'*
According to Bildad, Job has 'prosperity without permanence.' Bildad the simplifier has an answer for everything. Admitting that he cannot refute Job's claim of innocence, he uses three parables to press home the only other conclusion that his doctrine of God's justice will permit: Job is guilty of secret sins! Like the Pharisees of Jesus' time, his life is a whited sepulcher, spotless on the outside, but inside it is full of dead men's

bones [Mt 23:27]. With his faith cemented in place by tradition, Bildad can come to no other conclusion. By pushing his doctrine to its logical extreme, Bildad has hardened the categories and reversed the character of Job from being 'blameless' (1:1) to being 'evil' through and through. Bildad must have closed his speech with the confidence that he has brought the final resolution of the Jobian question. God's justice has been successfully defended, truth has been graphically pictured, tradition is intact, secret sins have been exposed, and Job has no recourse except to repent or be wiped from the face of the earth. Thus speaks Bildad, the grand inquisitor of religious tradition. McKenna, p. 80, 81

Taken from The Preacher's Commentary Series Volume 12: Job by David L. McKenna. Copyright © 1991 by Word, Inc. Used by permission of Thomas Nelson. www.thomasnelson.com

Job 9:33: *If only there were someone to arbitrate between us, to lay his hand upon us both*
Human reason has driven Job to the edge of a chasm over which he cannot see. On the far and unseeable side is the transcendent God—all wise and all-powerful. On the near and seeable side, Job stands with all humankind—ignorant and impotent. Futility is ready to flood his soul once again except for a flash of prophetic insight that sends a shudder through his being. A *mediator*! Job sees the only way across the chasm between God and man [cf discussion on 1 Tim 2:5–6]. Reason is not a dead end after all. In one of the most indelible images and insightful moments of Old Testament Scriptures, Job foresees Christ through the eyes of faith. This is the truth that shakes the earth! Job's hope is not in reason; it is reconciliation [Rom 5:10]! McKenna, p. 89

Taken from The Preacher's Commentary Series Volume 12: Job by David L. McKenna. Copyright © 1991 by Word, Inc. Used by permission of Thomas Nelson. www.thomasnelson.com

Job 15:13: *so that you vent your rage against God and pour out such words from your mouth?*
I can't help but think of that when I see Job, as he sits there enduring this, awash in his grief, trying his best to believe his ears–that this man who was once a friend is saying such graceless words. I'm left with one thought: "Lord, if you are teaching us anything through Job's endurance, teach us

the value of *grace*. Teach us about demonstrating grace. Show us again that grace is always appropriate. Always needed. Not just by a student in Missouri taking a final exam. Not only by a grieving family in Dallas. All of us need it! The person sitting near you in church next Sunday, the lady pushing the cart in the grocery store, the one who's putting gas in his car at the next pump, the man behind you at the movies, waiting to buy his ticket, the student across from you at school. You have no idea what this person is going through. If you did, chances are you'd be prompted to show grace or to say a few encouraging words even quicker. Remember this please: Grace is *always* appropriate, *always* needed.

Job: A Man of Heroic Endurance, Nashville, TN: Thomas Nelson (2004), excerpts, pp. 132-134

Personal Note: Although I generally agree with Swindoll here, there are times when grace is not appropriate. The California Legislature recently enacted a law that basically says a theft of less than $950 will not be prosecuted. This has caused an avalanche of shop-lifting that threatens the livelihoods of many store owners. Grace also is not appropriate when someone does a hateful, heinous crime such as murder or rape. But though Swindoll is exaggerating here, he's basically right more times than not. We need to focus on the general rule, not the exceptions I bring up here.

Job 19:25: *I know that my Redeemer lives, and that in the end he will stand upon the earth.*

What is it that brings the pits and pinnacles of life together? Is it simply an emotional lurch from high to low? Is it an intellectual flash that lets us see clearly when we are stripped of pretense?

When Job hits the bottom of the pit of humiliation, he has no place to go but to stand and look up [2 Cor 12:10]. His stance is represented by his unshaken confidence in his innocence before God. Yet, for the first time, he deals with the shock of recognition that he may not be vindicated while still alive. His only recourse is to turn the clock ahead to eternity. … Deferred gratification of our most urgent desires is a sign of emotional and spiritual maturity. Instant gratification is its opposite and the sign of a secular attitude that cannot see beyond the 'radical now.' In the give and take of exaggerated words and the intricacies of logical debate between Job and his friends, we dare not lose sight of the fact that Job has been

'hobbling toward the holy,' usually two steps forward and one step back. Bursting into the reality of revelation known only to the prophet, Job declares 'I know that my redeemer lives.' His choice of the word *redeemer* is proof of God's inspiration. Earlier, Job had appealed for an independent umpire to plead his case [9:33]. Now he knows that he cannot stand before God in his own righteousness. His blameless behavior (1:1) is not enough to redeem him. A brother who is willing to shed his blood on Job's behalf is his only hope. Job foresees atonement. Although Job is centuries from the birth of the Savior, he lives in that hope by faith!McKenna, pp. 136–137
Taken from The Preacher's Commentary Series Volume 12: Job by David L. McKenna. Copyright © 1991 by Word, Inc. Used by permission of Thomas Nelson. www.thomasnelson.com

Job 23:10: *But he knows the way that I take; when he has tested me, I will come forth as gold.*

The false accusations of Eliphaz are so ridiculous that they collapse under their own weight. Job is wise in not dignifying them with a direct response. Besides, he has other things on his mind. From the summit of his newfound faith, he catches glimpses of the character and purpose of God. More often than not, his view is still clouded by his suffering and hazed by his humanity. Yet, in the fleeting moments when there is a break in the clouds and Job's eyes open, it is like a clear day on which he can see forever. ... Job speaks for all humankind in its search for God (23:3–9). Wherever he looks, he cannot see Him—forward, backward, right hand, left hand, North or South. The eyes of faith open again. Job exclaims, 'But *He* knows the way I take!' (v 10). Even when we cannot see God, He sees us [Ps 139:1–3]! Suddenly, Job's eyes open wide. For the first time, he sees the reason for his suffering. God is not punishing him or acting by whimsy—*He is testing Job* [Zc 13:9]. This realization changes Job's whole perspective. Even though the reason for his suffering is still hidden, in the mind of God it has a purpose [Isa 48:10]. Job's confidence in God tells him that the purpose is good, and, therefore, the suffering is bearable.

McKenna, pp. 165–166

Taken from The Preacher's Commentary Series Volume 12: Job by David L. McKenna. Copyright © 1991 by Word, Inc. Used by permission of Thomas Nelson. www.thomasnelson.com

"The brightest crowns that are worn in heaven have been tried, and smelted, and polished, and glorified through the furnace of tribulation."
                                                Edwin H. Chapin (1814–1880)

Job 28:12: *But where can wisdom be found? Where does understanding dwell?* No one knows the way to wisdom because it is not within the land of the living (28:13, 21); the very best of skill or perception is insufficient to find it. Even outside the world of ordered creation, there is but a rumor of the home of wisdom (28:14, 22); the netherworld, the deep, and the sea declare that she is not there. The place of death can only report rumors about wisdom.

The more difficult an object is to obtain, the greater is its worth; because pure gold, silver, and stones such as blue sapphire, black or white onyx, opaque shiny crystal, bright coral and yellow chrysolite (topaz) are difficult to obtain, they are very expensive. Yet, as to its worth, wisdom is not to be compared with any of these precious jewels. The wisdom of creation is not accessible within creation; therefore nothing within creation can be compared in worth with wisdom.

God alone understands wisdom, knows its source, and has evaluated and approved it. The forces of creation such as wind, rain, and storm were set in place and governed by wisdom. Wisdom was the means by which the orders of the natural world were achieved (Prov 8:22-31). This kind of wisdom is inaccessible to humans. In the final line of the poem, "wisdom" is distinguished from "the wisdom" described in the previous lines by the absence of the article. Absolute wisdom, designated by the use of the article, is denied to humans, but humans have access to a more limited form of wisdom. The wisdom of humans is to fear the Lord and to know about morality, life, and appropriate conduct. Humans should know this kind of wisdom, but the wisdom of God concerning the ultimate order of the universe is a wisdom humans often wish they could know but cannot–their attempts to find it may well leave them self-deceived.

Konkel, August H, *Cornerstone Biblical Commentary*, Vol. 6, Carol Stream, IL: Tyndale, 2006, excerpts, pp. 173, 174, 175

Job 32:20: *I must speak and find relief; I must open my lips and reply.*
Elihu is an angry young man. His youth is revealed by the fact that he waits until all of his elders have exhausted their words. Then, his youthful anger spills onto the pages of Scripture through a phrase that is repeated four times in the brief introduction 'His wrath was aroused' (eg, v. 5). Elihu is mad at the world! Typical of the young, he sees flaws in what is reputed to be the wisdom of age and reacts violently against it. Yet, youthful rage is not without its redeeming value. In every generation, the young serve as check-and-balance for our ideas, values, attitudes, and tastes by their questions and causes, pranks and protests, rage and reaction, music and dress. Although we hate to admit it, youth see clearly through their anger, even though they do not see the whole picture or the long view. Time will take care of that. Young radicals often become old reactionaries. Is it possible that Eliphaz, Bildad, and Zophar see the image of their reactionary age in the mirror of Elihu's radical rage?   McKenna, p. 214
Taken from The Preacher's Commentary Series Volume 12: Job by David L. McKenna. Copyright © 1991 by Word, Inc. Used by permission of Thomas Nelson. www.thomasnelson.com

Job 33:14–15: *For God does speak-now one way, now another- though man may not perceive it.*
In a dream, in a vision of the night, when deep sleep falls on men as they slumber in their beds.
Personal Note: Elihu has hit on something here. Frustrated Christians (and secularists as well) often complain of God's silence. Yet often when we think he is silent, we just aren't listening or are listening only according to our own preconceived notions of how he should speak. Like Job, we too want some dramatic personal revelation from God as we try to cope with our struggles. But God reveals himself in his written word and in words he puts in the mouths of the people we meet. In order to hear God's voice, we need to humble ourselves and recognize that God often communicates through mundane means (Job 34:3). Only the ear of faith is sensitive enough to hear His gracious revelation.

Job 38:4: *Where were you when I laid the earth's foundation? Tell me, if you understand.*

Time collapses on Job. His beginning does not precede the Creator of the universe. Yet, Job has asked the question *why* about his suffering. It is a legitimate question because it arises from his God-given curiosity. To ask *why* is to inquire about the first cause of creation. To know the answer is to be God himself. Behind the question *why* is always the question *how*. Sin is more than the desire to be as wise as God; it is also the urge to be as powerful as God. If the cause of suffering, for instance, can be broken down into explainable pieces, it is assumed that solutions can be found to control the problem. This is the path of scientific process that has made miracles so common among us. God is not condemning science by His questions about the systems of the earth which remain a mystery to the human mind and ultimately out of human control. He is saying that the human mind can take the world apart, but it cannot put it back together again.

Job cannot understand why God controls His creation as He does any more than Job can comprehend creation itself. To believe in God is to live with mystery. Once again, we are suspending in a paradox, best defined as 'truth held absurdly.' With Job, we must believe that God is the Creator of all, the Controller of all, and the Cause of all, but not the one who intervenes in natural law so that every evidence of prosperity or punishment can be interpreted as a cause-and-effect relationship initiated by God. This was the fatal trap into which Eliphaz, Bildad, and Zophar fell. They insisted that human reason could understand everything that happens to human beings by applying the cause-and-effect formula in which God automatically rewards justice and punishes wickedness. No room is left for God's grace or mankind's faith.

McKenna, p. 272–275

Taken from The Preacher's Commentary Series Volume 12: Job by David L. McKenna. Copyright © 1991 by Word, Inc. Used by permission of Thomas Nelson. www.thomasnelson.com

Job 38: 7 *while the morning stars sang together and all the angels shouted for joy?*

>The Novas were the trumpets
>The Black Holes played the bass,
>The comets were the clarinets
>The concert hall was Space.

> The stars were the violins,
> The Angels sang in thirds,
> The Planets danced a minuet
> Jehovah wrote the words.
>
> And still they sang together,
> And with the inner ears,
> The clear-souled man can listen yet
> The music of the spheres.

Commentary, Job 38:7, from *Stars Through the Clouds*, the collected poetry of Donald T. Williams, 2nd edition, Toccoa, GA: Lantern Hollow Press, 2020

Job 38:33: *Do you know the laws of the heavens?*
Personal Note: I suspect that many modern scientists and others of a technical bent would answer *yes* to this question and to many others the Lord asks of Job in this passage. With our modern science and technology, we have seen the very distant and the very small. If we lack an answer, we can just *Google* it. Our wildlife cameras now can answer *yes* to the question of 39:1 and we have domesticated the ox of 39:9. But if we are really honest, we have to admit that we have many gaps in our knowledge. Our telescopes cannot penetrate the dark matter between us and other stars. Although we have now seen the entire sphere of the earth, we will probably never see the whole majesty of the Milky Way's spiral arms. Although we can gather historical evidence of times past, we will never have a video showing what actually happened. And although we can observe the behavior of wildlife, we cannot penetrate the minds of animals. Our knowledge of the physical realms is limited to our senses and instruments. Even we modern humans can learn from Job's humble response to the Lord's intervention (40:4).

Job 42:6: *Therefore I despise myself and repent in dust and ashes.*
Knowing the answer to the question *who*, Job no longer needs to ask the question *why*. Why then does Job conclude his response to God by bowing and repenting once again? The answer is that one who 'sees through' to the great grace of God bows humbly and repents sincerely. By bowing, grace

lifts him up [1 Pet 5:6]; by repenting, grace liberates him [Ps 32:2–5]. So, like the phoenix bird rising out of the dust and ashes with the colors of the sun, God will lift Job to his feet and set him free—reconciled, restored, and ready to serve others with new-found grace [2 Cor 12:10]. Job has 'seen through' to God. McKenna, p. 298–299

Taken from The Preacher's Commentary Series Volume 12: Job by David L. McKenna. Copyright © 1991 by Word, Inc. Used by permission of Thomas Nelson. www.thomasnelson.com

Job 42:17: *And so he died, old and full of years.*
Our hero dies well. Despite the fact that he came through suffering without sin, became a model of God's grace, and prefigured the resurrection of Christ in his restoration, Job died as all humans do. The quality of his days, however, is his own final testimony. We read again, 'So Job died, old and full of days', which tells us that he celebrated the joy of living to the very end. Grace does that for us. Our bodies will age and we will die, but grace is the quality of spirit that is renewed with youthful vigor every day [2 Cor 3:18, 4:16-18]. Job is a modern as well as an ancient model of the silver-haired statesman whose grace and wisdom are indispensable to the life of the society. So ends the journey of Job. It began with a *ring of righteousness*—sounded by self-discipline and tested for perfection. It ends on a *note of grace*—sensitized to suffering and turned to trust. His epitaph might well be rewritten:

*And so Job died, old and **full of grace**.*

McKenna, pp. 311–312
Taken from The Preacher's Commentary Series Volume 12: Job by David L. McKenna. Copyright © 1991 by Word, Inc. Used by permission of Thomas Nelson. www.thomasnelson.com

Psalms

When I feel I cannot make headway in devotion, I open the Psalms and push out my canoe and let myself be carried along on the stream of devotion that flows through the whole book. The current always sets toward God and in most places is strong and deep.
Missionary quoted in Wallace Commentary on Daniel, *p. 154, 155*

Commentaries:

- *Treasury of David* (1885), by Charles Haddon Spurgeon Spurgeon Archives Online
- *The Message of Psalms 1–72*, by Michael Wilcock (2001)
- *The Message of Psalms, 73–150*, by Michael Wilcock (1992)
- *The Preacher's Commentary* OT Vol 13, By Donald M. Williams (1986)
- *The Book of Psalms* (NICOT), by Nancy deClaisse-Walford, Rolf A. Jacobson, and Beth LaNeel Tanner (2014)
- *A Long Obedience in the Same Direction* (Psalms of Ascent 120–134), by Eugene H. Peterson (2000)
- *The Message* (Biblical Paraphrase in modern English), by Eugene H. Peterson (2002)
- *Matthew Henry Commentary* at BlueletterBible.org (1710)

Ps 1:1: *Blessed is the man.* רֶשַׁע שִׁיאָה־יְרְשַׁא

It is striking that the very first word יְרְשַׁא of the entire book of Psalms should be this one. From his original creation of his people [Gn 1:28] right through to the final redeeming of them [Rev 22:14], Scripture is clear that God's long term purpose for them is that they should be blessed. The psalmists celebrate every foretaste of that heavenly promise.

Wilcock, p. 20.

Wilcock, Michael, *The Message of Psalms 1–72* Taken from *The Bible Speaks Today* Series edited by J. Alec Motyer; John Stott. Copyright ©1983 edited by J. Alec Motyer; John Stott. Used by permission of InterVarsity Press, P.O. Box 1400, Downers Grove, IL 60515, USA. www.ivpress.com

Ps 1:1 *who does not walk in the counsel of the wicked or stand in the way of sinners or sit in the seat of mockers.*

Perhaps there is no anthem so genuinely American as "My Way" as sung so epically by Frank Sinatra. The song expresses one of our highest cultural ideals–the ideal of the self-made man, the self-sufficient woman, the rugged individual. "My Way" is a paean to those who strike out on their own to break trail through the wilderness. Psalm 1 is as antithetical to that ideal as it is possible to get. Psalm 1 bears witness to the belief that the road of our own choosing leads only to our own destruction. Psalm 1 sees hope in a different path, the path defined by God's instruction. To some interpreters, the message of Psalm 1 has sounded a bit like "works righteousness." But when it is seen that the way of God's instruction is a gift for those who cannot guide themselves, then we correctly see that Psalm 1 is the opposite of works righteousness. The Psalm offers the free and gracious gift of a better way. But to follow this way that Psalm 1 recommends will require that we unlearn some bad habits. Chief among those bad habits is the habit of relying upon ourselves and seeking to be our own lords and masters. It will require that we relinquish our greedy grasp on what we think of as our own freedom and will. But when we do so, we will discover, as did the psalmist, that there is a better way, a way that is truly free.

Jacobson, Rolf A., *The Book of Psalms* (NICOT), Grand Rapids, MI: Eerdmans, 2014, pp. 63-64

Ps 8:1: *O LORD, our Lord, how majestic is your name in all the earth! You have set your glory above the heavens.*

Verse 1. Unable to express the glory of God, the Psalmist utters a note of exclamation. O Jehovah our Lord! We need not wonder at this, for no heart can measure, no tongue can utter, the half of the greatness of Jehovah. The whole creation is full of his glory and radiant with the excellency of his power; his goodness and his wisdom are manifested on every hand. The countless myriads of terrestrial beings, from man the head, to the creeping worm at the foot, are all supported and nourished by the Divine bounty.

The solid fabric of the universe leans upon his eternal arm. Universally is he present, and everywhere is his name excellent. God worketh ever and everywhere. There is no *place* where God is not. The miracles of his power await us on all sides. Traverse the silent valleys where the rocks enclose you on either side, rising like the battlements of heaven till you can see but a strip of the blue sky far overhead; you may be the only traveler who has passed through that glen; the bird may start up affrighted, and the moss may tremble beneath the first tread of human foot; but God is there in a thousand wonders, upholding yon rocky barriers, filling the flowercups with their perfume, and refreshing the lonely pines with the breath of his mouth. Spurgeon

Ps 13:1: *How long, O LORD? Will you forget me forever?*
We find acknowledged here in Scripture what we all know in experience, that the steady stream of real time never corresponds to the rate at which perceived time moves, dawdling and cantering, disappearing in a flash or seeming to stand still. It is not only with the Lord that a day can be like a thousand years (2 Pet 3:8, cf Ps 90:4). Wilcock, pp 50–51
Wilcock, Michael, *The Message of Psalms 1–72* Taken from *The Bible Speaks Today* Series edited by J. Alec Motyer; John Stott. Copyright ©2001 edited by J. Alec Motyer; John Stott. Used by permission of InterVarsity Press, P.O. Box 1400, Downers Grove, IL 60515, USA. www.ivpress.com

<u>**Personal Note**</u>: As I read this psalm in October 2014, it reaches out and grabs me and insists that I pay attention. This psalm expresses in a most heart-felt way the experience of many a troubled saint, and is particularly poignant for me today. I just went through a six-month frustrating waiting period that then just suddenly concluded beyond my wildest dreams as the Lord's providence dropped an amazing blessing in my lap. Just like the psalmist, I kept asking the Lord "How long" over and over and he kept whispering "just a little while longer. Patience, Dave, patience." The psalms were written so long ago by someone I never met, yet they resonate in my soul thousands of years later. The "I" of the psalmist becomes *me* today in Georgia. How rich is God's word! And how potently relevant!

Ps 16:11: *You have made known to me the path of life; you will fill me with joy in your presence, with eternal pleasures at your right hand*

Trapp's note on the heavenly verse which closes the Psalm is a sweet morsel, which may serve for a contemplation, and yield a foretaste of our inheritance. He writes, "Here is as much said as can be, but words are too weak to utter it. For quality there is in heaven joy and pleasures; for quantity, a fulness, a torrent whereat they drink without let or loathing; for constancy, it is at God's right hand, who is stronger than all, neither can any take us out of his hand; it is a constant happiness without intermission: and for perpetuity it is for evermore. Heaven's joys are without measure, mixture, or end." Spurgeon

Personal Note: As I read this verse in April 2014, I am struck by its profound majesty. The Lord, through his Word, clearly shows me the path of life. I sometimes want to stray off into side roads which look good but which peter out into dark dead ends. The more I stray the harder it is to get back to the path the Lord has shown I should take. But the destination of the Lord's path is never in doubt: eternal pleasures in His presence. Why would anyone want to take a detour from such a destination? Because they think they know the way better than their creator. May I remember that He knows the way [Job 23:10] and He will lead me to his holy hill [Ps 43:3].
Personal Note2: Pastor John Batusic of Chestnut Mountain Presbyterian in Georgia delivered an eloquent message on this Psalm in August 2016. Verses 3 and 4 remind us to spend our time with "excellent" people. God intends for our journey to be in community. The psalmist also prays for discernment about others and not to pursue the other gods (v 4) of the world around us such as personal beauty, wealth, and self-esteem. When folks dip their buckets into the water of the 21st century gods, they come up empty. The appetites of the gods of this world are insatiable and ultimately will not satisfy. In verse 6, the psalmist realizes just how good he has it (may we as well). Do we focus on what is missing from our lives or are we thankful for what we have? Worldly philosophers give us nice messages but there is a Counselor whose advice is always right. The Lord needs to be our focal point. We should always be "aiming for him." Finally the psalm is summed up in verse 11. Are we held captive by the hope of eternal life (Zech 9:12)? Verse 11 says it all. Do we seek eternal pleasures instead of eternally seeking temporary pleasures? That is a question we should ask and answer. May this psalm inspire us!

Psalm 19

"I take this to be the greatest poem in the Psalter and one of the greatest lyrics in the world."
C.S. Lewis (1898–1963)   Quoted in B&B

"I love to think of nature as an unlimited broadcasting station, through which God speaks to us every hour, if we will only tune in."
George Washington Carver (1864–1943)

Ps 19:1–2: *The heavens declare the glory of God; the skies proclaim the work of his hands. Day after day they pour forth speech; night after night they display knowledge.*
God's glory is on tour in the skies, God craft on exhibit across the horizon. Madame Day holds classes every morning, Professor Night lectures each evening.   *The Message*

Psalm 19 is virtually peerless in its poetic power and theological depth. It reveals the God who is continually communicating through His works (vv 1–6) and through His Word (vv 7–14). The psalmist moves in his thought from the general revelation given in heaven and earth, to the special revelation in God's law or *Torah*. Having begun with the vast reaches of the cosmos, he ends with his own heart. God speaks or 'shouts' at us, with all the stops pulled out, in order that we may hear and respond. Behind all the primeval explosion of creation and behind the smoke and fire of Sinai is the loving heart of God seeking our hearts. 'God speaks' is the thesis of this psalm.   Williams, p. 157

From the things that are seen every day by all the world the psalmist, in these verses, leads us to the consideration of the invisible things of God, whose glory shines transcendently bright in the visible heavens, the structure and beauty of them, and the order and influence of the heavenly bodies. This instance of the divine power serves not only to show the folly of atheists, who see there is a heaven and yet say "there is no God" (Ps 14:1), who see the effect and yet say "there is no cause," but to show the folly of idolaters also, and the vanity of their imaginations, who, though the heavens declare the glory of God, yet give that glory to the lights of heaven which those very lights directed them to give to God only, the Father of lights [James 1:17].

All succession and motion must have had a beginning; they could not make themselves, that is a contradiction; they could not be produced by the random collision of atoms, that is an absurdity, fit rather to be bantered than reasoned with; therefore they must have a Creator, who can be no other than an eternal mind, infinitely wise, powerful, and good. From the excellency of the work we may easily infer the infinite perfection of its great author. From the brightness of the heavens we may collect that the Creator is light (1 John 1:5); their vastness and extent bespeaks his immensity, their height his transcendency and sovereignty, their influence on earth his dominion and providence, and universal beneficence; and all declare his almighty power. Matthew Henry Commentary

Hymn: *This Is My Father's World*, Text: Maltbie D. Babcock, Published Posthumously 1901

This is my Father's world,	[Gen 1:1]
And to my listening ears	[Mt 11:15]
All nature sings, and round me rings	[Isa 55:12]
The music of the spheres.	[Job 38:7]
This is my Father's world:	[Ps 95:6]
I rest me in the thought	[Ps 46:10]
Of rocks and trees, of skies and seas;	[Ps 96:11–12]
His hand the wonders wrought.	[Ps 40:5, 66:5]
This is my Father's world,	[Ps 121:2, Ps 50:11]
The birds their carols raise,	[Ps 104:12]
The morning light, the lily white,	[Ps 30:5, Lk 12:27]
Declare their maker's praise.	[Ps 98:4]
This is my Father's world:	[Mt 25:34]
He shines in all that's fair;	[Num 6:25]
In the rustling grass I hear him pass;	[Gn 3:8]
He speaks to me everywhere.	[Ps 19:1–3, Job 33:14–15]

This is my Father's world.	[Mt 6:9]
O let me ne'er forget	[Ps 103:2]
That though the wrong seems oft so strong,	[Ps 73:3–4]
God is the ruler yet.	[Ps 68:16]
This is my Father's world:	[Ps 146:6, Jn 17:24]
Why should my heart be sad?	[Ps 42:5]
The Lord is King; let the heavens ring!	[1 Chr 29:11, Rev 11:15]
God reigns; let the earth be glad!	[Ps 97:1]

Ps 19:7–9: The revelation of God is whole and pulls our lives together. The signposts of God are clear and point out the right road. The life-maps of God are right, showing the way to joy. The directions of God are plain and easy on the eyes. God's reputation is twenty-four-carat gold, with a lifetime guarantee. The decisions of God are accurate down to the nth degree.
The Message

<u>**Personal Note**</u>: Eugene Peterson's paraphrase of these verses bring alive just how amazing and vibrant is God's word. It also brings to mind Philippians 4:8. How are we to think on whatever is true, noble, pure, right, lovely, admirable, excellent and praiseworthy? Soak ourselves in God's word to the point where we are saturated like a sponge so that when we are squeezed, what comes out is good! (to paraphrase Pastor John Batusic).

Ps 22:1: *My God, my God, why have you forsaken me? Why are you so far from saving me, so far from the words of my groaning?*
The first two verses are wrenching. The urgency of the words and the intimacy between the parties jump off the page. The cry is to My God, and there is no formal address or introduction. Instead there are two questions of why. Why has God abandoned? Often God has promised not to forsake (eg Deut 31:6, Pss 9:10; 37:28;33; 94:14). Even if parents do, God will hold fast (27:10). The cries do not stop there, however. The questions continue: Why is God so far away from saving and from these roaring words? "Roaring words" is not an elegant phrase, but it is an exact translation of the Hebrew. This is not groaning or complaining or whining.

These words are expressed in the raspy scream of one in deep distress. The next verse tells us that this is not a temporary issue. Indeed, the pain has lasted too long already.

Verses 3-5 are an abrupt about-face. First, God's lofty position compounds the distance from one crying out. God is sitting or enthroned on Israel's praises. Does that mean there is no room for cries of abandonment? Or is this a title of honor offered as a sincere act of praise? Miller notes, I think rightly, it is both. Crying out in pain and expressing trust are not incompatible. Faith and trust ebb and flow and surge in life, and the appearance of contrasting situations causes a clash in the one suffering. I know what I feel and I know what I believe. The prayer clearly demonstrates the emotional roller coaster of the suffering of a faithful one.

Tanner, Beth LaNeel, *The Book of Psalms* (NICOT), Grand Rapids, MI: Eerdmans, 2014, p. 233

Ps 22:7–8: *All who see me mock me; they hurl insults, shaking their heads: "He trusts in the LORD; let the LORD rescue him. Let him deliver him, since he delights in him."*

Personal Note: This, perhaps the most messianic of all the Psalms, hits the Christian like a sledgehammer. It is hard to believe that a Psalm which so vividly portrays Christ's experience on the cross could have been written a thousand years before it happened. Christ quoted verse 1 on the cross as he felt the weight of the sin of the world on his shoulders and his separation from the Father even more strongly than the nails that pierced his hands and feet (22:16) and the insults of the crowd (Ps 22:6–8, Lk 23:35). This Psalm reminds us that our salvation was extremely costly for the Father and the Son (1 Cor 6:20). We should not take it lightly.

Psalm 23 [cf Ezek 34:31]

It is well to know, as certainly David did, that we belong to the Lord. There is a noble tone of confidence about this sentence. There is no "if" nor "but," nor even "I hope so;" but he says, "The Lord *is* my shepherd." We must cultivate the spirit of assured dependence upon our heavenly Father. The sweetest word of the whole is that monosyllable, "My." He does not say, "The Lord is the shepherd of the world at large, and leadeth forth the multitude as his flock," but "The Lord is *my* shepherd;" if he be a

Shepherd to no one else, he is a Shepherd to me; he cares for me, watches over me, and preserves me. The words are in the present tense. Whatever be the believer's position, he is even now under the pastoral care of Jehovah.

Spurgeon

Ps 23:3: *He restores my soul*
There is an exact parallel to this in caring for sheep. Only those intimately acquainted with sheep and their habits understand the significance of a 'cast' sheep. This is an old English shepherd's term for a sheep that has turned over on its back and cannot get up again by itself. A cast sheep is a pathetic sight. Lying on its back, it's feet in the air, it flays away fanatically struggling to stand up, without success. Sometimes it will bleat a little for help, but generally it lies there lashing about in frightened frustration. … Often the fleece is clogged with filthy manure, mud, burrs, sticks, and ticks. What a relief to be rid of it all. … There will come a day when the Master must take us in hand and apply the keen cutting edge of His word for our lives. It may be an unpleasant business for a time. No doubt we'll struggle and kick about it. We may get a few cuts and wounds. But what a relief it is when it is all over. Oh, the pleasure of being set free from ourselves! … If He is the Good Shepherd we can rest assured that He knows what He is doing. This in and of itself should be sufficient to continually refresh and restore my soul. I know of nothing which so quiets and enlivens my own spiritual life as the knowledge that God knows what He is doing with me.   Phillip Keller, *A Shepherd Looks at Psalm 23*.
Personal Note: This beloved Psalm is even more special in light of Phillip Keller's classic, *A Shepherd Looks at Psalm 23*. I recommend this little book to anyone who wants to experience this Psalm in a rich new way.

Ps 23:6: *Surely goodness and mercy shall follow me all the days of my life: and I will dwell in the house of the LORD for ever.* [KJV] [Ps 27:4, 37:29, 65:4, 84:2, 84:4]
The confidence of Psalm 23 is that of one who is steeped in the theology of the earlier days, when God made his covenant with his people. David knows that God. And since he is the eternal Lord, his people are not surprised to find him as the New Testament Shepherd too: the good Shepherd [Jn 10:11], the great Shepherd [Heb 13:20], the chief Shepherd [1

Pet 5:4] who will one day appear with glory that will never fade away and who will lead them to springs of living water [Ps 28:9, 78:70–72, Isa 40:11, 53:6, Rev 7:17].

Wilcock, p. 87

Wilcock, Michael, *The Message of Psalms 1–72* Taken from *The Bible Speaks Today* Series edited by J. Alec Motyer; John Stott. Copyright ©2001 edited by J. Alec Motyer; John Stott. Used by permission of InterVarsity Press, P.O. Box 1400, Downers Grove, IL 60515, USA. www.ivpress.com

Ps 25:1: *Unto thee, O LORD, do I lift up my soul.* [KJV]
True prayer may be described as the soul rising from earth to have fellowship with heaven; it is taking a journey upon Jacob's ladder, leaving our cares and fears at the foot, and meeting with a covenant God at the top. Very often the soul cannot rise, she has lost her wings, and is heavy and earth bound; more like a burrowing mole than a soaring eagle. At such dull seasons we must not give over prayer, but must, by God's assistance, exert all our powers to lift up our hearts. Let faith be the lever and grace be the arm, and the dead lump will yet be stirred. With all our tugging and straining we have been utterly defeated, until the heavenly loadstone of our Saviour's love has displayed its omnipotent attractions, and then our hearts have gone up to our Beloved like mounting flames of fire.

Spurgeon

Ps 25:4–5: *Show me your ways, O LORD, teach me your paths; guide me in your truth and teach me, for you are God my Savior, and my hope is in you all day long.*
David knew much, but he felt his ignorance and desired to be still in the Lord's school; four times over in these two verses he applies for a scholarship in the college of grace. It were well for many professors if instead of following their own devices, and cutting out new paths of thought for themselves, they would enquire for the good old ways of God's own truth, and beseech the Holy Ghost to give them sanctified understandings and teachable spirits. *For thou art the God of my salvation.* The Three One Jehovah is the Author and Perfector [Heb 12:2] of salvation to his people. Reader, is he the God of your salvation? Do you find in the Father's election, in the Son's atonement, and in the Spirit's quickening all the grounds of your eternal hopes? If so, you may use this as an argument for obtaining further blessings; if the Lord has ordained to save you, surely

he will not refuse to instruct you in his ways. ... We shall not grow weary of waiting upon God if we remember how long and how graciously he once waited for us. Spurgeon

Ps 27:13–14: *I am still confident of this: I will see the goodness of the LORD in the land of the living. Wait for the LORD; be strong and take heart and wait for the LORD.*
'The mills of God grind slowly' and it is no surprise that saints of great vision should sometimes pray prayers whose answers do not arrive until after they have gone to glory, but, they see plenty of the goodness of the Lord before they go. They are the kind of people who know all about the alert, tip-toe expectancy which is what Scripture means by 'wait for the Lord' and which gives his hard pressed people heart and strength [cf Hab 2:3, Isa 25:9]. Wilcock, p. 97
Wilcock, Michael, *The Message of Psalms 1–72* Taken from *The Bible Speaks Today* Series edited by J. Alec Motyer; John Stott. Copyright ©2001 edited by J. Alec Motyer; John Stott. Used by permission of InterVarsity Press, P.O. Box 1400, Downers Grove, IL 60515, USA. www.ivpress.com

"It took me years to discover the premier lesson that God has a timing all His own and that I must not be impatient when His timing doesn't coincide with mine."
David Wilkerson (1930–2011)

Ps 30:5: *For his anger endureth but a moment; in his favour is life; Weeping may endure for a night, but joy cometh in the morning.* (KJV)
Verse 5a may mean not that God's anger is brief and his favor life*long* [lasts a lifetime, NIV], but that his anger is destructive and his favor life*giving*. In New Testament terms it actually lasts more than a lifetime! It is eternal glory, out of all proportion. The church needs to recapture this truth. What Kirkpatrick finely says of the weeping of God's people is true also of that just but merciful anger of God which causes them to weep: it is 'but the passing wayfarer, who only tarries for the night; with dawn, joy comes to take its place' Wilcock, p. 105–106
Wilcock, Michael, *The Message of Psalms 1–72* Taken from *The Bible Speaks Today* Series edited by J. Alec Motyer; John Stott. Copyright ©2001 edited by J. Alec

"Tomorrow is the most important thing in life. Comes into us at midnight very clean. It's perfect when it arrives and it puts itself in our hands. It hopes we've learned something from yesterday." John Wayne (1907–1979)

Ps 31:19 *Oh how great is thy goodness, which thou hast laid up for them that fear thee; which thou hast wrought for them that trust in thee before the sons of men!* [KJV]

Personal Note: As I read this verse in December 2020, I, like many of my neighbors, am suffering from Covid fatigue. Yet even in the midst of this gloomy year 2020, I must pause and reflect not only on the greatness of our God, but on his goodness. If God were great but not good, we would be in a world of hurt. But here and many other places in scripture, we read that God is good [eg, Gen 1:31, 50:20, Ex 18:9, Ps 34:8, 107:9, 116:7, 118:1, 119:68, Mk 1:1, Lk 4:18, Rom 8:28, 12:2] ! In fact, "Gospel" means "Good News." With all the bad news that has been spewing into our lives during this coronavirus crisis, it is "good" that we reflect on the profound truth of this verse.

Ps 36:2 *In their own eyes they flatter themselves too much to detect or hate their sin.*

Personal Note: This verse describes what some call "the up and outers." We all have people in our life who, from our limited perspective, lead good, even noble lives. They are kind to others. They do not indulge in sins of excess such as alcohol, drugs, filthy language, or adultery. They have long, happy and fruitful marriages, unmarred by bitterness and divorce. They go to work, play by the rules, and support worthy charities. Their children behave and are just as good and decent as their parents. Their only issue with God is this verse: they do not detect their sin. They don't think they have any. A reasonable and rational person might say, "So what? What is the big deal?" Overall, they lead good decent lives. But the Lord looks on their hearts (1 Sam 16:7) and knows their motives (1 Cor 4:5) and sees the sin that others do not see. Their problem is that God doesn't grade on a curve. He demands perfection (Mt:5:48) and they fall far short of that

(Rom 6:23). But this is no reason for a believer to be smug. Remember Rom 6:23 says "all". We too are in need of salvation. Our only advantage is that we know it all too well.

Ps 36:5–7: *Your love, O LORD, reaches to the heavens, your faithfulness to the skies. Your righteousness is like the mighty mountains, your justice like the great deep. O LORD, you preserve both man and beast. How priceless is your unfailing love!*
God's love is meteoric, his loyalty astronomic, His purpose titanic, his verdicts oceanic. Yet in his largeness nothing gets lost; Not a man, not a mouse, slips through the cracks. *The Message*
We might despair of reaching the oceanic depths or mountainous (or even celestial) heights of God's qualities, did we not realize it is precisely those things that he brings to bear upon us and our needs. It may be 'too great to grasp' (v5), but it is 'too good to let slip' (v7). Wilcock, p. 126
Wilcock, Michael, *The Message of Psalms 1–72* Taken from *The Bible Speaks Today* Series edited by J. Alec Motyer; John Stott. Copyright ©2001 edited by J. Alec Motyer; John Stott. Used by permission of InterVarsity Press, P.O. Box 1400, Downers Grove, IL 60515, USA. www.ivpress.com

Ps 36:8–9: *They feast on the abundance of your house; you give them drink from your river of delights. For with you is the fountain of life; in your light we see light.* [Ps 65:4]
Their needs supplied [Deut 11:14–15], their craving gratified [Ps 78:29], and their capacities filled [Eph 3:19]. In God all-sufficient they shall have enough, all that which an enlightened enlarged soul can desire or receive [Isa 12:3]. There are pleasures that are truly divine. There is a river of these delights [Ps 46:4], always full, always fresh, always flowing [Ezek 47:12]. The pleasures of sense are putrid puddle-water; those of faith are pure and pleasant, clear as crystal (Rev 22:1). Having God himself for their happiness, they have a fountain of life, from which those rivers of pleasure, knowledge, and joy, all included in this light. Matthew Henry Commentary
Personal Note: Verses 5–9 together are an eloquent testimony to a God who is not just powerful, but to a God who cares and wants to bless humanity. The profusion of blessing issuing from the hand of God is enough to boggle our minds. What a wonderful, loving God we have!

We, with David, should be exhilarated at his goodness and love! Here the psalms give us the words to say to express our wonder. May we take these words on our lips.

Ps 39:3–4: *My heart grew hot within me, and as I meditated, the fire burned; then I spoke with my tongue "Show me, O LORD, my life's end and the number of my days; let me know how fleeting is my life."*

"He who provides for this life but takes no care for eternity, is wise for a moment but a fool forever."
John Tillotson (1630–1694) Quoted in Ward and Wild

Ps 40:1–3: *I waited patiently for the LORD; he turned to me and heard my cry. He lifted me out of the slimy pit, out of the mud and mire; he set my feet on a rock and gave me a firm place to stand. He put a new song in my mouth, a hymn of praise to our God. Many will see and fear and put their trust in the LORD.* [cf Job 5:11, Ps 18:16, 30:11, 69:1–3, Lam 3:55–58]
Psalm 40 has a chiastic structure:

Looking backward	(vv 1–3)
Looking upward	(vv 4–5)
Looking inward	(vv 6–8)
Looking outward	(vv 9–11)
Looking around	(vv 12–15)
Looking forward	(vv 16–17)

This tiptoe expectancy (as distinct from finger-tapping impatience) is the vital thing the Lord looks for in his people, since it shows a positive, active trust [Rom 8:25]. The old Latin title of Psalm 40, *Expectans expectavi*, indicates both its eagerness, and the Hebrew that lies behind the words *waited patiently*, namely the doubling of the verb קַוֹּה קִוִּיתִי: 'Expectantly I expected the Lord to act.' Psalm 40:6–8, understood in Christian terms, sounds the death knell for all attempts to make oneself right with God and fit for heaven. Out of every such slimy pit, out of the mud and mire, he will lift the soul that abandons these hopeless efforts and instead looks eagerly for the blessings that flow from the obedience and sacrifice of Christ. *Expectans expectavi.* Wilcock, p. 142

Wilcock, Michael, *The Message of Psalms 1–72* Taken from *The Bible Speaks Today* Series edited by J. Alec Motyer; John Stott. Copyright ©2001 edited by J. Alec Motyer; John Stott. Used by permission of InterVarsity Press, P.O. Box 1400, Downers Grove, IL 60515, USA. www.ivpress.com

"I was like a stone lying deep in mud but he that is mighty lifted me up and placed me on top of the wall." St. Patrick of Ireland (AD 389–461)
Quoted in Ward and Wild

Ps 40:8: *I desire to do your will, my God; your law is within my heart*
Personal Note: I pause this day to reflect on the delight I've received morning by morning as I have taken in the Word of God. I began reading God's word every morning in May 1994. At this point, I have a string of about 3900 days I began by reading the Word and what an adventure it has been! This morning and yesterday I read the early psalms in Gene Peterson's *The Message*, and verses like (Ps 19:7,9) these resonate in my soul:

> The revelation of God is whole and pulls our lives together.
> The signposts of God are clear and point out the right road.
> God's reputation is twenty-four-carat gold, with a lifetime guarantee.
> The decisions of God are accurate down to the nth degree.

These verses remind me of Philippians 4:8 (NIV): "Finally, brothers and sisters, whatever is true, whatever is noble, whatever is right, whatever is pure, whatever is lovely, whatever is admirable—if anything is excellent or praiseworthy—think about such things." What a wonderful world we would have if everyone did as Paul suggests. And one way we can be sure to "think on these things" is to read God's word.

In a world with so much hate and grief and pain, I am so glad I have this rock of stability, my safe haven to begin my day. The psalmists and prophets often ask the Lord to teach and guide them (eg 25:4–5, 48:14, 71:17, 73:24, 86:11, 119:33, 68, 102, 135, 171, 143:10, Isa 28:29, Isa 30:21, Ps 25:4, Ex 15:13): "Show me your ways, LORD, teach me your paths. Guide me in your truth and teach me, for you are God my Savior, and my hope is in you all day long." Just as David prayed thousands of years ago, I can take his words into my heart and soul and pray the same thing in Maryland in the 21st century.

Our Lord Jesus taught his disciples in the Parable of the Sower that the worries of this life and the deceitfulness of wealth would choke the word like weeds (Mt 13:22), and I can testify to this from personal experience. There is a kind of centrifugal force that draws me away from God every day. But like a homing beacon, I keep coming back to him morning by morning so I don't get too far astray. And Oh, what a blessing his Word is each and every day! If not for this daily dose of the Word, I would fly off!

Unlike any other book, the Scriptures are consistent and complete; they are new every morning (Lam 3:23); I defy anyone to find them boring. Although some sections are tedious (eg Book of Ezekiel) and confusing to me (eg, stories of leaving no survivors), the more I read the more I see that even these fit into the beautiful mosaic that is the Word. The valleys make the mountains all the more glorious. The more we know about God's wrath, the more we appreciate his grace. So I thank my God and Savior for blessing me and millions of others with his rock–solid word. Keep bringing me back, Lord, as I begin to stray into the far country!

Ps 40:17 *But as for me, I am poor and needy; may the Lord think of me. You are my help and my deliverer; you are my God, do not delay.* [NIV]
Ps 40:17 And me? I'm a mess. I'm nothing and have nothing: make something of me.
You can do it; you've got what it takes—but God, don't put it off.
The Message

My Comment: A modern paraphrase from a TV Show: "Can we just fast-forward to eventually?"

Ps 43:3 *Send forth your light and your truth, let them guide me; let them bring me to your holy mountain, to the place where you dwell.*   [cf Neh 9:12]
The psalmist reasons that God's light and God's truth can be his guides out of his present wretched isolation, just as in the previous psalm he has

been reminding himself that God's love and God's song have been his companions in the past. "We are never helpless victims of our emotions," says Clements. "Don't let your feelings dictate to you; you do the dictating." Ask yourself why you are so downcast (42:5, 11) and give yourself a rational answer. Remind yourself that hope means a patient but expectant waiting for God to act. Tell yourself that your day of praise will certainly come, though in God's time, not yours. Wilcock, p. 156–157

Wilcock, Michael, *The Message of Psalms 1–72* Taken from *The Bible Speaks Today* Series edited by J. Alec Motyer; John Stott. Copyright ©2001 edited by J. Alec Motyer; John Stott. Used by permission of InterVarsity Press, P.O. Box 1400, Downers Grove, IL 60515, USA. www.ivpress.com

Personal Note: In Psalm 42, the psalmist has been groping around in the dark. It's almost as if he is in a strange city with darkness all around and no map. But then suddenly he remembers in Psalm 43 that he has a super-deluxe GPS system that guides him out of a rough neighborhood and into the glorious celestial city. When we are lost, we need to turn on the GPS and hear God's voice. He shows us the way if we would but listen for him [2 Tim 4:18].

Ps 51:1: *Have mercy on me, O God, according to your unfailing love; according to your great compassion blot out my transgressions.*
Ps 51:3: *For I know my transgressions, and my sin is always before me.*
Ps 51:1–3: Generous in love—God, give grace! Huge in mercy—wipe out my bad record.
Scrub away my guilt, soak out my sins in your laundry. I know how bad I've been; my sins are staring me down. *The Message*

Among the outpourings of the human heart agonized by the consciousness of sin, this Psalm stands pre-eminent. It surely must be rooted in the events of 2 Samuel 11: David's coveting and then theft of another man's wife, his adultery with her, his murder of her husband, and his conspiracy with his chief of staff to cover up the facts—five of the Ten Commandments broken in one sordid and cynical enterprise, and that by a man who had perhaps already given a hostage to fortune in the words 'I desire to do your will, O my God; your law is within my heart' (Ps 40:8). He begins by saying *I know my transgressions*. He cannot simply mean 'I acknowledge them'; rather, he knows them only too well, for they are always there [v 3], a shameful waking nightmare, now that the word of God has convicted him of them. Then because that word has turned him round, he sees no longer before him the glamour of the woman he stole, nor even beside him the innocence of the man he killed, but behind him the judgment of the God he had turned his back on.... But David in no way regards his innate sinfulness as an excuse. Far from saying 'It wasn't my fault. I couldn't help it,' he feels all the more responsible, all the more ashamed. ... While he has no grounds for presumption, he has good grounds for hope. Wilcock, p. 185, 186, 188

Wilcock, Michael, *The Message of Psalms 1–72* Taken from *The Bible Speaks Today* Series edited by J. Alec Motyer; John Stott. Copyright ©2001 edited by J. Alec Motyer; John Stott. Used by permission of InterVarsity Press, P.O. Box 1400, Downers Grove, IL 60515, USA. www.ivpress.com

Ps 63:1: *O God, you are my God, earnestly I seek you; my soul thirsts for you, my body longs for you, in a dry and weary land where there is no water.*

Observe the eagerness implied in the time mentioned; he will not wait for noon or the cool eventide. Communion with God is so sweet that the chill of the morning is forgotten, and the luxury of the couch is despised. The morning is the time for dew and freshness, and the psalmist consecrates it to prayer and devout fellowship. He who truly longs for God longs for him now. Holy desires are among the most powerful influences that stir our inner nature; hence the next sentence, *My soul thirsteth for thee*. Thirst is an insatiable longing; there is no reasoning with it, no forgetting it, no despising it, no overcoming it by stoical indifference. Thirst will be heard; the whole man must yield to its power; even thus is it with that divine desire which the grace of God creates in regenerate men; only God himself can satisfy the craving of a soul really aroused by the Holy Spirit. ... The absence of outward comforts can be borne with serenity when we walk with God; and the most lavish multiplication of them avails not when he withdraws. Only after God, therefore, let us pant. Let all desires be gathered into one [Mt 13:46]. Seeking first the kingdom of God—all else shall be added unto us [Mt 6:33]. Spurgeon

Ps 65:9–11: *You care for the land and water it; you enrich it abundantly. The streams of God are filled with water to provide the people with grain, for so you have ordained it. You drench its furrows and level its ridges; you soften*

it with showers and bless its crops. You crown the year with your bounty, and your carts overflow with abundance. [cf Job 5:10, Ps 85:12, 104:13–14]
What God has done for us spiritually, as Redeemer, he assures us of concretely, as Creator, by bringing his creative power to bear on the provision of our needs. He is the Provider, not of riches or luxuries, but of necessary and appropriate blessings. For a farming community like Israel, that meant a good harvest. In real-life circumstances, the truth of God becomes equally real. It is he—the repeated *You* of vv 9–11—who brings about the harvest, both in principle and in detail, and it is to him that the rich farmlands are pictured as returning praise. We of the supermarket culture may smile at the rustic image of God the farmer driving a great wagon along the country lanes, so laden with produce that the surplus tumbles off it. But in a world where so many are hungry, those of us who do have enough to eat should be moved to say perhaps more often than we do, '*God* has done this!' [also see Deut 11:14–15, Ezek 34:26–27, Zc 10:1, Joel 2:24, Joel 3:18]   Wilcock, p. 228–229

Wilcock, Michael, *The Message of Psalms 1–72* Taken from *The Bible Speaks Today* Series edited by J. Alec Motyer; John Stott. Copyright ©2001 edited by J. Alec Motyer; John Stott. Used by permission of InterVarsity Press, P.O. Box 1400, Downers Grove, IL 60515, USA. www.ivpress.com

Personal Note: We humans often tend to take our blessings for granted. And they *were granted*: by God. Yet sometimes we claim that no, it isn't God who gives us the crops, it's human grit and ingenuity using fertilizers, pesticides, and modern agricultural science. But recall what Paul states in 1 Cor 3:6: we may plant and we may water, but it is God who gives the growth. The Lord is the first cause of everything, since he created it all. The cycle that produces an inexhaustible supply of water where rain falls, then evaporates and then condenses to rain down again only exists because our creator endowed our planet with a position in the "Goldilocks Zone" where we're not too close to the sun, not to far, just right. He also gave us a magnetic field to protect the atmosphere and earth's surface from excess solar radiation. In addition, he gave us the carbon cycle where animals breathe in oxygen and breathe out carbon dioxide, and the plants, by photosynthesis, breathe in carbon dioxide and breathe out oxygen. On top of all that, he gave us a stable sun that has a perfect balance between the outward pressure of nuclear fusion and the inward pressure of gravity. And on top of all of that, the axial tilt gives us seasons and the large moon maintains the axial tilt for centuries and millennia. Everything is sooooo finely balanced, isn't it? Secular skeptics might still claim that natural processes along with human ingenuity give us the food we eat. And yes, that is partially the case. But if we think about it, the chance that all of these natural processes would combine as they do to our benefit without a creator is very small, even given billions of stars and billions of chances. In the end, we must confess that all natural processes originated from a supernatural designer. This psalm gives us the words to praise and thank him for granting us the bounty we daily enjoy. What joy should stir our hearts as we contemplate the incredible abundance he showers down on undeserving humanity! His carts do overflow! [Ps 23:5]

Ps 71:17: *O God, thou hast taught me from my youth: and hitherto have I declared thy wondrous works*
[KJV].
Personal Note: This verse resonates with my personal experience and I suspect it may have similar relevance for many others. I came to faith in my early 40's, but now that I look back decades later, I see that God had been teaching me even before I began to trust in him. I grew up in a fine church which taught me scripture and hymns. These seeds were planted in my heart at that early age. Though they were dormant for about a couple of decades, they sprouted and bore fruit many years later. I suspect many other "late bloomers" like me have a searing sense of recognition when they survey their youth and realize, "God was there even when I didn't see him."

Ps 73:3: *For I envied the arrogant when I saw the prosperity of the wicked.*
[Ps 37:1–2]
Ps 73:2–5: But I nearly missed it, missed seeing his goodness. I was looking the other way,
looking up to the people at the top, envying the wicked who have it made, who have nothing to worry about, not a care in the whole wide world.
The Message
When he is, so to speak, 'in the sanctuary', the facts come into focus. He realizes that even in his bitterest moments the grace of God unfailingly surrounds him [Ps 139:5]. Distress of mind is not the same thing as loss of faith. Those who look at the world with what seems to them the simple,

innocent perspective of Psalm 1 (and of Ps 73:1) will be disoriented by the hard experience of real life, which seems to contradict it. They need to be reoriented—to be turned so as to see these confusing facts from a different point of view. That new orientation will bring them ultimately to Psalm 150 (and to Ps 73:27–28), and to the recognition that in a deeper sense than they had realized 'God surely is good to Israel.' Psalm 73 is 'the book of Job in a nutshell' [also cf Ps 37 (esp v 7), Jer 12:1–2, Mal 3:14]. Wilcock, p. 8, 9
Wilcock, Michael, *The Message of Psalms 73–150* Taken from *The Bible Speaks Today* Series edited by J. Alec Motyer; John Stott. Copyright ©1992 edited by J. Alec Motyer; John Stott. Used by permission of InterVarsity Press, P.O. Box 1400, Downers Grove, IL 60515, USA. www.ivpress.com

"Too many Christians envy the sinners their pleasures and the saints their joy because they don't have either one." Martin Luther (1485–1546)

Ps 73:13 *Surely in vain I have kept my heart pure and have washed my hands in innocence.*

Ps 73:12-14: The wicked get by with everything; they have it made, piling up riches. I've been stupid to play by the rules; what has it gotten me? A long run of bad luck, that's what—a slap in the face every time I walk out the door. *The Message*

Personal Note: Asaph the psalmist poses a concern many beleaguered Christians may voice at times. Psalm 1 tells us that the righteous prosper and the wicked do not, and yet in real life we see many examples that seem to contradict this seemingly Pollyannaish view. Our foot may almost slip as we say "there's no point to being a good boy. The wicked seem be in a much better position than I am." This Psalm helps us to resolve this conundrum. Our problem is that we are looking at ground level and in short spurts of time (compared to the long view of the Lord, Ps 90:4). The Lord uses his omniscience and omnipotence to assure a reward for the righteous (heaven) and punishment for the wicked (hell). This is not a case of salvation by works. Those who are righteous look forward to heaven, while the wicked think heaven would be a boring place and want to grab all the gusto they can here and now. The pivot verse 16 helps Asaph grasp what he had been missing in earlier verses. Once he enters the sanctuary of the Lord, he is in the frame of mind to understand divine providence without being distracted by short term anecdotes. He doesn't really care about the short term success of the wicked because he is focused on his heavenly destination (vv 23-24). We as believers must, like the apostle Paul, press on to obtain the prize (Phil 3:13-14). Psalm 73 tells us that our focus should not be on the wicked but on our Lord and Savior who will never let us go (Phil 3:12, Rom 8:38-39). Begin with the end in mind!

Ps 73:28 *But it is good for me to draw near to God: I have put my trust in the Lord GOD, that I may declare all thy works.* [KJV]
Verse 28. Had he done so at first he would not have been immersed in such affliction; when he did so he escaped from his dilemma, and if he continued to do so he would not fall into the same evil again. The greater our nearness to God, the less we are affected by the attractions and distractions of earth. Access into the most holy place is a great privilege, and a cure for a multitude of ills. It is good for all saints, it is good for *me* in particular; it is always good, and always will be good for me to approach the greatest good, the source of all good, even God himself. Faith is wisdom; it is the key of enigmas, the clue of mazes, and the pole star of pathless seas. Trust and you will know. *That I may declare all thy works.* He who believes shall understand, and so be able to teach. God's ways are the more admired the more they are known. He who is ready to believe the goodness of God shall always see fresh goodness to believe in, and he who is willing to declare the works of God shall never be silent for lack of wonders to declare.   Spurgeon

Ps 77:8, 10 *Has his unfailing love vanished forever? Has his promise failed for all time? Then I thought, "To this I will appeal: the years of the right hand of the Most High."*

Ps 77:8–10: Is his love worn threadbare? Has his salvation promise burned out? Has God forgotten his manners? Has he angrily stalked off and left us? "Just my luck," I said. "The High God goes out of business just the moment I need him."   *The Message*
Brueggemann highlights the collision between what he calls 'canonical memory', the Biblical story, and 'concrete pain', the present experience that seems to contradict it. But the mood of the psalm's 2nd half contrasts greatly with its first half. The key to the change is the turn from self to

God. *I* am the focus of vv 1–9. They are full of *my* misery, *my* complaints, *my* assumptions—a preoccupation with self as much as our modern culture has revived with great success and feeds assiduously. *You*—*your* power, *your* path, a willingness to meditate on *your* works and consider all *your* mighty deeds is the focus of the 2nd half of the psalm.   Wilcock, pp. 22–23
Wilcock, Michael, *The Message of Psalms 73–150* Taken from *The Bible Speaks Today* Series edited by J. Alec Motyer; John Stott. Copyright ©1983 edited by J. Alec Motyer; John Stott. Used by permission of InterVarsity Press, P.O. Box 1400, Downers Grove, IL 60515, USA. www.ivpress.com

Ps 78:19: *They spoke against God, saying, "Can God spread a table in the desert?"*

Ps 78:19-20: They whined like spoiled children, "Why can't God give us a decent meal in this desert? Sure, he struck the rock and the water flowed, creeks cascaded from the rock. But how about some fresh-baked bread? How about a nice cut of meat?" *The Message*

<u>**Personal Note:**</u> This profound verse speaks of God the Alpha and Omega. Early in redemption history, the Lord answered this question, providing the 'bread of angels' (78:25, Ex 16:31). At the turning point of history, Christ resoundingly answered this verse again as he fed the multitudes in the wilderness (Mk 6:34-44). Throughout scripture, the Lord transforms our desert places into abundant blessings (Ps 30:11, Isa 35:2, 6) and provides nourishment for his people (eg Ps 23:5, Ps 65:9-11, 81:10, 16). And at the final consummation, His people are invited to the wedding feast of the lamb (Rev 19:9, Isa 25:6, 55:1-2, Lk 14:15). No wonder Paul (Eph 3:20) could gush about the Lord doing immeasurably more than all we ask or imagine!

Ps 84:1–2: *How lovely is your dwelling place, O LORD Almighty! My soul yearns, even faints, for the courts of the LORD; my heart and my flesh cry out for the living God.*
Ps 84:12: *O Lord Almighty, blessed is the man who trusts in you.*
The first and last verses make a chiastic inclusio that frames the rest; *how beloved the House* [Ps 23:6, 27:4], *O Lord Almighty, how blessed the man* [Ps 1:1]. God's house is accessible here as well as hereafter. It is anywhere that God's people congregate in his presence. The pilgrimage need mean nothing more exotic than regular churchgoing—a determination not to

'give up meeting together, as some are in the habit of doing' (Heb 10:25), seduced by the modern cult of individualism, leisure, mobility, and lack of commitment. Wilcock, p. 48, 50

Wilcock, Michael, *The Message of Psalms 73–150* Taken from *The Bible Speaks Today* Series edited by J. Alec Motyer; John Stott. Copyright ©1992 edited by J. Alec Motyer; John Stott. Used by permission of InterVarsity Press, P.O. Box 1400, Downers Grove, IL 60515, USA. www.ivpress.com

Personal Note: This psalm has been set to music in one of the most magnificent choral pieces ever written. It is a chorus (named, appropriately, *How Lovely is thy Dwelling Place*) in the *Requiem* of Johannes Brahms. I have both listened to and sung this wonderful song (as a tenor in the Cedar Springs Church choir). For those who like choral music, this is a "must hear" piece.

Ps 86:11: *Teach me your way, O LORD, and I will walk in your truth; give me an undivided heart, that I may fear your name.*

Personal Note: Pastor Jay Harvey of Evangelical Presbyterian Church of Newark Delaware presented a fascinating analysis of this wonderful psalm. God's anointed is confronted with dire circumstances (v 14) he can't face in his own strength (v 1), so he turns to God. He approaches God neither naively nor cynically, but with bold confidence asks God to inject joy into his life (v 4). He asks God for *your strength* and recognizes that this strength can only flow through the servants of God (v 16). David is not complaining with his back turned to the Lord, but praying in full honesty. What is his confidence based on? What decorates his petition? Much like a child who says 'Pretty please, with a cherry on top,' David celebrates God's goodness, faithfulness, and steadfast love (vv 5, 10, 15) in the midst of his distress. This psalm reminds us that joy can be elusive and fleeting if we chase it because true joy can only come from the Spirit's work within us (Gal 5:22). But the true joy which only the Lord grants can persist in spite of circumstances which may threaten us, even death itself (v 13). May we, like David, recognize the true source of all joy (Ps 37:4).

Ps 91:10–11: *then no harm will befall you, no disaster will come near your tent. For he will command his angels concerning you to guard you in all your*

ways; they will lift you up in their hands, so that you will not strike your foot against a stone.

In *all* these things (Rom 8:37): we are not saved *from* them, we are saved *in* them. The negatives are transmuted into positives; by a divine alchemy the lead turns to gold [cf Joel 2:24–25, Job 23:10]. When therefore we stumble at 91:9–10 and protest: 'but harm *does* befall God's people,' however trustingly and obediently they take refuge in him, we do well to ponder Spurgeon's comment, 'It is impossible that any ill should happen to the man who is beloved by the Lord… Ill to him is no ill, but only good in mysterious form. Losses enrich him, sickness is his medicine, reproach is his honor, death is his gain' [Phil 1:21].   Wilcock, p. 82

Wilcock, Michael, *The Message of Psalms 73–150* Taken from *The Bible Speaks Today* Series edited by J. Alec Motyer; John Stott. Copyright ©1992 edited by J. Alec Motyer; John Stott. Used by permission of InterVarsity Press, P.O. Box 1400, Downers Grove, IL 60515, USA. www.ivpress.com

Ps 93:1: *The LORD reigns, he is robed in majesty; the LORD is robed in majesty and is armed with strength. The world is firmly established; it cannot be moved.*

Its many repetitions—*robed in majesty*—*robed in majesty, lifted up*—*lifted up, mightier*—*mightier* – do not impede the flow of Psalm 93, rather they drive it along with a punchy rhythm, though scarcely are we caught up by its momentum before it comes to a sudden end. No complex structure here!   Wilcock, p. 86

Wilcock, Michael, *The Message of Psalms 73–150* Taken from *The Bible Speaks Today* Series edited by J. Alec Motyer; John Stott. Copyright ©1992 edited by J. Alec Motyer; John Stott. Used by permission of InterVarsity Press, P.O. Box 1400, Downers Grove, IL 60515, USA. www.ivpress.com

Ps 95:2 *Let us come before his presence with thanksgiving, and make a joyful noise unto him with psalms.* [KJV]

We must praise God with our voice; we must speak forth, sing forth, his praises out of the abundance of a heart filled with love, and joy, and thankfulness—*Sing to the Lord; make a noise*, a joyful noise to him, with psalms—as those who are ourselves much affected with his greatness and goodness, are forward to own ourselves so, are desirous to be more and more affected therewith, and would willingly be instrumental to kindle and inflame the same pious and devout affection in others also.

Matthew Henry Commentary (1710)

Let all things now living a song of thanksgiving	[Ps 150:6]
To God the Creator triumphantly raise,	[Ps 98:7–9]
Who fashioned and made us, protected and stayed us	[Ps 139:13, 46:1]
Who guides us and leads to the end of our days.	[Ps 86:11, Isa 46:4]
His banners are o'er us, His light goes before us	[Isa 11:10, Ps 119:105]
A pillar of fire shining forth in the night.	[Ex 13:21]
Till shadows have vanished and darkness is banished	[Rev 21:23]
As forward we travel from light into light.	[Ps 43:3]
His law He enforces: the stars in their courses	[Isa 40:26]
The sun in its orbit, obediently shine.	[Jer 31:35]
The hills and the mountains, the rivers and fountains	[Isa 55:12, Ps 36:8]
The deeps of the ocean proclaim Him divine.	[Ps 148:7]
We too should be voicing our love and rejoicing	[Phil 4:4]
With glad adoration a song let us raise	[Ps 98:4]
Till all things now living unite in thanksgiving	[Ps 117:1]
To God in the highest, hosanna and praise!	[Ps 103:22]

Hymn: *Let All Things Now Living*, Words: Katherine K. Davis (1892–1980)
Music: "The Ash Grove", a traditional Welsh melody

Katherine K. Davis, "Let All Things Now Living" © Copyright 1939 by E. C. Schirmer Music Company. Copyright renewed 1966 by E. C. Schirmer Music Company, a division of ECS Publishing. www.ecspublishing.com All rights reserved. Used by permission.

Ps 103:19: *The LORD has established his throne in heaven, and his kingdom rules over all.*

What especially stirs our psalmist is the fact that the Lord rules over all, that is, over everything, the entire creation. He shows at once that by this he means more than the world and the people we see around us, more than the hidden structures of the physical globe or of human society, more even than the entire universe of which our planet is such a tiny part.

His mind flies at once to the angels of God, who though awesome spirit beings, mighty ones who inhabit a heavenly dimension outside the scope of scientific observation, are just as much the Lord's creation as we are. Wilcock, p. 120

Wilcock, Michael, *The Message of Psalms 73–150* Taken from *The Bible Speaks Today* Series edited by J. Alec Motyer; John Stott. Copyright ©1992 edited by J. Alec Motyer; John Stott. Used by permission of InterVarsity Press, P.O. Box 1400, Downers Grove, IL 60515, USA. www.ivpress.com

Ps 104:1–2: *Praise the LORD, O my soul. O LORD my God, you are very great; you are clothed with splendor and majesty. He wraps himself in light as with a garment; he stretches out the heavens like a tent*

It says something about the psalms of Book IV that they should have given rise to so many of our most enduring English hymns. Hard on the heels of *Praise my Soul the King of Heaven* comes *O Worship the King, all Glorious Above*. Fine hymns both, they differ in one respect: Lyte's version of 103 works steadily though the whole psalm, whereas Sir Robert Grant's of 104 is subject to a sudden acceleration halfway through. His first verse represents the psalm's verse 1, his second is verses 2 and 3, his third its verses 5–9, while his fourth sums up the next twenty-one, and his fifth and sixth are his own rounding off of the whole. What Grant did with the psalm is very like what the psalmist himself has done with the biblical story of creation. That was plainly his basis, and it striking how he follows the order of the days of creation in Genesis 1. Not, however, in their proportion! Wilcock, p. 121

Wilcock, Michael, *The Message of Psalms 73–150* Taken from *The Bible Speaks Today* Series edited by J. Alec Motyer; John Stott. Copyright ©1992 edited by J. Alec Motyer; John Stott. Used by permission of InterVarsity Press, P.O. Box 1400, Downers Grove, IL 60515, USA. www.ivpress.com

Hymn: *O Worship the King* (1833), Text: Robert Grant, 1779–1838
Music: Attr. to Johann Michael Haydn

O worship the King, all glorious above,	[Zech 14:16, Mt 2:2]
O gratefully sing God's power and God's love;	[2 Chr 20:21]
Our Shield and Defender, the Ancient of Days,	[Gn 15:1, Dan 7:9]
Pavilioned in splendor, and girded with praise.	[1 Chr 16:27, Ps 72:19]

O tell of God's might, O sing of God's grace,	[Ps 21:13, 71:23, 118:14]
Whose robe is the light, whose canopy space,	[Isa 6:1, Mk 9:3, Isa 40:22]
Whose chariots of wrath the deep thunderclouds form,	[2 Kings 6:17]
And dark is God's path on the wings of the storm.	[Jer 30:23, Nah 1:3]
The earth with its store of wonders untold,	[Gn 2:1]
Almighty, thy power hath founded of old;	[Prov 8:22–23]
Hath stablished it fast by a changeless decree,	[Gn 8:22, Isa 54:10]
And round it hath cast, like a mantle, the sea.	[Prov 8:27–29]
Thy bountiful care, what tongue can recite?	[Ps 65:9, 116:12]
It breathes in the air, it shines in the light;	[Job 33:4, Isa 60:1]
It streams from the hills, it descends to the plain,	[Isa 55:10]
And sweetly distills in the dew and the rain.	[Job 36:27]
Frail children of dust, and feeble as frail,	[Gn 2:7, Ps 103:14]
In thee do we trust, nor find thee to fail;	[Ps 143:8, Josh 21:45]
Thy mercies how tender, how firm to the end,	[Isa 40:11, Ps 105:8]
Our Maker, Defender,	[Isa 54:5, Ps 72:4]
Redeemer, and Friend.	[Job 19:25, Jn 15:13]
O measureless Might, ineffable Love,	[Ps 147:5, Jn 3:16]
While angels delight to hymn thee above,	[Ps 148:2, Rev 7:11, 12]
Thy humbler creation, though feeble their lays,	[Rev 19:5]
With true adoration shall sing to thy praise.	[Ps 104:33]

Ps 107:9: *for he satisfies the thirsty and fills the hungry with good things* Israel's wants were seasonably supplied [Lev 26:4], and many have been wonderfully relieved when they were ready to perish [Ps 116:3,8, Isa 37:33–34]. The same God that has led [Ps 73:24] us has fed us [Ps 81:16] all our life long unto this day, has fed us with food convenient [Ruth 2:17], has provided food for the soul [Ps 63:5], and filled the hungry soul with goodness [Isa 55:2]. Those that hunger and thirst after righteousness [Mt 5:6], after God [Ps 42:1], the living God [Ps 42:2], and communion with

him [Rev 3:20], shall be abundantly replenished with the goodness of his house [Ps 36:8, 84:1–2], both in grace [John 1:16, Rom 5:20b] and glory [1 Cor 15:42–44, John 17:22].   Matthew Henry Commentary. (1710)

Personal Note: I added a lot of scripture references to this Matthew Henry excerpt, because he knows his scripture so well, it simply tumbles off his pen as he writes. He has scripture exuding from his prose as the great hymnists Wesley, Watts, and Lyte have it radiate from their poetry. Henry's familiarity with scripture is quite inspiring to this rank amateur!

Psalm 119

The more you look into this mirror of a gracious heart the more you will see in it. Placid on the surface as the sea of glass before the eternal throne [Rev 4:6, 15:2], it yet contains within its depths an ocean of fire, and those who devoutly gaze into it shall not only see the brightness, but feel the glow of the sacred flame. It is loaded with holy sense, and is as weighty as it is bulky. Again and again have we cried while studying it, "Oh the depths!" Yet these depths are hidden beneath an apparent simplicity, as Augustine has well and wisely said, and this makes the exposition all the more difficult. Its obscurity is hidden beneath a veil of light, and hence only those discover it who are in thorough earnest, not only to look on the word, but, like the angels, to look into it. … May those who shall read the Psalm, accepting, the help of our exposition, feel their hearts burn within them! To this end, at the very outset let our prayer ascend to God, that his Holy Spirit may rest upon us while we devoutly peruse the volume.
Spurgeon, *The Golden Alphabet*

Personal Note about this, the longest Psalm. It is written in the form of an acrostic. Each line of each stanza begins with the same Hebrew letter of the alphabet (reading from right to left). Wilcock finds some key words which tie to the Hebrew letter and give a sense of theme to each stanza (the ones he supplies are shown in the headings below).

Ps 119:19: *I am a stranger on earth; do not hide your commands from me.*
God's people always need to be reminded of this. Everyday we walk familiar roads; this is our hometown, our home country, we say. Yes and no, says God. This is my world and you are here as *garim* (expatriates). We begin to see why the psalmist, a stranger on earth, cries 'Do not hide your

commands from me'. He needs God's handbook for the duration of his residence in God's world. Wilcock, p. 196

Wilcock, Michael, *The Message of Psalms 73–150* Taken from *The Bible Speaks Today* Series edited by J. Alec Motyer; John Stott. Copyright ©1992 edited by J. Alec Motyer; John Stott. Used by permission of InterVarsity Press, P.O. Box 1400, Downers Grove, IL 60515, USA. www.ivpress.com

Teth ט   *tob* –- "Good" טוֹב

Ps 119:65 *Do good to your servant according to your word, LORD.*

This kindness of the Lord is, however, no chance matter: he promised to do so, and he has done it according to his word. It is very precious to see the word of the Lord fulfilled in our happy experience; it endears the Scripture to us, and makes us love the Lord of the Scripture. The book of providence tallies with the book of promise [Josh 21:45, 1Kings 8:24]: what we read in the page of inspiration we meet with again in the leaves of our life-story. ... We have had bread enough and to spare [Phil 3:18], our livery has been duly supplied, and his service has ennobled us and made us happy as kings. Complaints we have none [Phil 2:14]. We lose ourselves in adoring thanksgiving [Ps 95:2], and find ourselves again in careful thanks-living.

Spurgeon

Nun נ   "lamp" נֵר

Ps 119:105: *Your word is a lamp to my feet and a light for my path.*
[Ps 18:28]

We are walkers through the city of this world, and we are often called to go out into its darkness; let us never venture there without the light-giving word, lest we slip with our feet. Each man should use the word of God personally, practically, and habitually, that he may see his way, and see What lies in it. When darkness settles down upon all around me, the word of the Lord, like a flaming torch, reveals my way. Having no fixed lamps in eastern towns, in old time each passenger carried a lantern with him, that he might not fall into the open sewer, or stumble over the heaps of ordure which defiled the road. This is a true picture of our path through this dark world: we should not know the way, or how to walk in it, if Scripture, like a blazing flambeau, did not reveal it. One of the most practical benefits of Holy Writ is guidance in the acts of daily life: it is not sent to astound us with its brilliance, but to guide us by its instruction. It is true the head needs illumination, but even more the feet need direction, else head and feet may both fall into a ditch. Happy is the man who personally appropriates God's word, and practically uses it as his comfort and counselor, — a lamp to his feet. Spurgeon

Ps 119:147 *I rise before dawn and cry for help; I have put my hope in your word.*
Personal Note: This verse sometimes describes my life. I often rise before dawn and the first thing I do is open God's Word. As I go through my day, my attention to spiritual details flags and I feel a centrifugal force pulling me away from God. Were it not for a morning by morning refocusing on His Word, I would be a mess as I was before I was saved in the early nineties. I thank the Lord that he planted a passion deep in my heart for His Word. Though I often disappoint Him, he and His Word never disappoint me.

Sin and Shin שׁ *samara* – "keep or obey" יִתְרַמְיָשׁ

Ps 119:176: *I have strayed like a lost sheep. Seek your servant, for I have not forgotten your commands.*
The value of learning to use all these verses, each with its reference to the word of God, is inestimable. Lord, hear my prayer for understanding according to your word (169): I need to know the right things, in the right spirit, at the right time and for the right purpose. Lord, hear my praise for your willingness to teach me your decrees (v 171); you have made me see what really matters: the truth graven in stone—crudely, the 'bottom line.' Lord, act to restore me because I have retained your commandments (176). Your word is truly in my heart even though I have strayed like a lost sheep. I may know enough about you to write a psalm 176 verses long, but for all this industry and theology, for all this art and skill and grasp of the word, I am as prone to wander, Lord, as the next sheep is. What grace it is that recognizes the frailty of the author of this magnificent psalm, and brings him back repeatedly, by the word of God, to the word of God.

Wilcock, pp. 218–219

Wilcock, Michael, *The Message of Psalms 73–150* Taken from *The Bible Speaks Today* Series edited by J. Alec Motyer; John Stott. Copyright ©1992 edited by J.

Alec Motyer; John Stott. Used by permission of InterVarsity Press, P.O. Box 1400, Downers Grove, IL 60515, USA. www.ivpress.com

Ps 121:8: *the LORD will watch over your coming and going both now and forevermore.*

The only serious mistake we can make when illness comes, when anxiety threatens, when conflict disturbs our relationships with others is to conclude that God [like Baal, 1 K 18:27] has gotten bored looking after us and has shifted his attention to a more exciting Christian, or that God has become disgusted with our meandering obedience and decided to let us fend for ourselves for a while, or that God has gotten too busy fulfilling prophecy in the Middle East to take time now to sort out the complicated mess we have gotten ourselves into. It is the mistake that Psalm 121 prevents: the mistake of supposing that God's interest in us waxes and wanes in response to our spiritual temperature. We know that God created the universe and has accomplished our eternal salvation. But we can't believe that he condescends to watch the soap opera of our daily trials and tribulations; so we purchase our own remedies for that. But Psalm 121 says that the same faith that works in the big things works in the little things. Faith is not a precarious affair of chance escape from satanic assaults. It is the solid, massive, secure experience of God [Ps 46:1], who keeps all evil from getting inside us [Mt 6:13], who guards our life [Ps 18:2], who guards us when we leave and when we return [Ps 139:3], who guards us now [Ps 86:2], who guards us always [Rom 8:38–39]. Peterson, p. 43, 45, 46
Peterson, Eugene H., *A Long Obedience in the Same Direction: Discipleship in an Instant Society*, Downers Grove, IL: InterVarsity Press, Copyright © 2000. Used by Permission.

Ps 122:4: *Where the tribes go up, The tribes of the LORD, To the Testimony of Israel, To give thanks to the name of the LORD.* NKJV

"The soul of one who loves God always swims in joy, always keeps holiday, and is always in a mood for singing." John of the Cross (1542–1591)
Quoted in Ward and Wild

Ps 123:1–2: *I lift up my eyes to you, to you whose throne is in heaven. As the eyes of slaves look to the hand of their master, as the eyes of a maid look to the*

hand of her mistress, so our eyes look to the LORD our God, till he shows us his mercy.

Paul Scherer writes scathingly of people who lobby around in the courts of the Almighty for special favors, plucking at his sleeve, pestering him with requests. God is not a buddy we occasionally ask to join us at our convenience or for our diversion. Too often we think of religion as a far-off, mysteriously run bureaucracy to which we apply for assistance when we feel the need. We go to the local branch office and direct the clerk (sometimes called the pastor) to fill out our order for God. Then we go home and wait for God to be delivered to us according to the specifications that we have set down. But that is not the way it works. We are not presented with a functional god who will help us out of jams or an entertainment god who will lighten tedious hours. We are presented with the God of the Exodus and Easter, the God of Sinai and Calvary. If we want to understand God, we must do it on his terms. Peterson, p 62, 63

Peterson, Eugene H., *A Long Obedience in the Same Direction: Discipleship in an Instant Society*, Downers Grove, IL: InterVarsity Press, Copyright © 2000. Used by Permission.

Ps 124:1–3: *If the LORD had not been on our side—let Israel say— if the LORD had not been on our side when men attacked us, when their anger flared against us, they would have swallowed us alive*

Through the week I get case histories of family tragedy and career disappointments, along with pessimistic recounting of world events. The concluding line is a variation on the theme: "How could you explain that, you who are so sure God is for me?" I am put on the spot of being God's defender. I am expected to explain God to his disappointed clients. I am thrust into the role of a clerk in the complaints department of humanity, asked to trace down bad service, listen sympathetically to aggrieved patrons, try to put right any mistakes I can and apologize for the rudeness of the management. But the proper work for the Christian is witness, not apology, and Psalm 124 is an excellent model. It does not explain God's help; it is a testimony of God's help in the form of a song. The song is so vigorous, so confident, so bursting with what can only be called reality that it fundamentally changes our approach and our questions. ... Don't hesitate to put the psalm (or any other Scripture passage) under the searchlight of your disbelief! Subjected to the most relentless and searching criticism, Psalm 124 will, I think, finally convince us of its honesty. There is no literature in all the world that is more true to life and more honest than the Psalms, for here we have warts-and-all religion. Every skeptical thought, every disappointing venture, every pain, every despair that we can face is lived through and integrated into a personal, saving relationship with God—a relationship that also has in it acts of praise, blessing, peace, security, trust and love. Peterson, p.72, 75

We speak words of praise in a world that is hellish; we sing our songs of victory in a world where things get messy; we live our joy among people who neither understand nor encourage us. But the content of our lives is God, not humanity. We are not scavenging in the dark alleys of the world, poking into garbage cans for bare subsistence. We are traveling in the light [Ps 43:3], toward God who is rich in mercy [Eph 2:4] and strong to save [Isa 63:1]. It is Christ, not culture, that defines our lives [Rom 12:2]. It is the help we experience, not the hazards we risk, that shape our lives [Dan 3:25, Ps 138:7, Isa 43:1–3]. Peterson, p. 79

Peterson, Eugene H., *A Long Obedience in the Same Direction: Discipleship in an Instant Society*, Downers Grove, IL: InterVarsity Press, Copyright © 2000. Used by Permission.

Ps 131:1–2: *My heart is not proud, O LORD, my eyes are not haughty; I do not concern myself with great matters or things too wonderful for me. But I have stilled and quieted my soul*

Psalm 131 is a maintenance psalm. It is functional to the person of faith as pruning is functional to the gardener: it gets rid of that which looks good to those who don't know any better, and reduces the distance between our hearts and their roots in God. It is additionally difficult to recognize unruly ambition as a sin because it has a kind of superficial relationship to the virtue of aspiration. But if we take the energies that make for aspiration and remove God from the picture, replacing him with our own crudely sketched self-portrait, we end up with ugly arrogance. Robert Browning's fine line on aspiration 'A man's reach should not exceed his grasp, or what's a heaven for?' has been distorted to 'reach for the skies and grab everything that isn't nailed down.' Ambition takes the same energies for growth and development and uses them to make something tawdry and cheap, sweatily knocking together a Babel when we could be vacationing in Eden. Peterson, p. 153

Peterson, Eugene H., *A Long Obedience in the Same Direction: Discipleship in an Instant Society*, Downers Grove, IL: InterVarsity Press, Copyright © 2000. Used by Permission.

Ps 133:1 *Behold, how good and how pleasant it is for brothers to dwell together in unity! (NASB)*
Personal Note: Pastor Dee Hammond of Chestnut Mountain Presbyterian in Georgia delivered a message about this beloved psalm on July 3, 2016. The message, titled "A Celebration of Dependence", identified 3 main blessings in the Psalm:

- Blessing of community in unity (vv1–2)
- Blessing of community through presence (v3a)
- Blessing of community throughout eternity (v3b)

Verse 1 stresses community and unity. There are some that think they can be Christian but not go to church. But if one loves Christ, one must also love his bride (the Church). Our presence with one another is essential to Christian community. Our lack of presence is absence and it diminishes the vibrancy of the church (2 John 12, 3 John 13). Unity is also essential. An orchestra can contain many instruments, but if they aren't playing the same sheet of music under some direction, it just sounds like "noise". The motion throughout the psalm is down down down, while other Psalms of ascent stress up, up, up (Ps 121:1, 122:1, 123:1). Blessing flows down as our praise wafts upward.

Ps 139:1–2: *O LORD, you have searched me and you know me. You know when I sit and when I rise; you perceive my thoughts from afar.* [J e r 23:24]
Words like omniscience and omnipresence can be useful shorthand for stating facts about God. With regard to Psalm 139 (one of the summits of OT poetry), they are not perhaps the best words. It is such a personal and deeply felt expression of what the psalmist knows of God that we should want to describe it in simpler, more direct terms. As he himself tells us, it is about how God knows me, how he surrounds me, how he has made me, and how he tests me. A series of verbs reads like an extract from a thesaurus: search/examine, know, perceive/understand, discern/

sift, be familiar with. Rather like the A–Z of the acrostic psalms, pairs of words suggest how comprehensive God's knowledge is: whether I sit or rise, whether I travel or settle down—that is, whatever I do, he knows. He knows my thoughts from afar, my words before I utter then; he knows me *completely* [1 Chr 28:9].　　　　　　　　　　　　　　　　Wilcock, p. 258

Wilcock, Michael, *The Message of Psalms 73–150* Taken from *The Bible Speaks Today* Series edited by J. Alec Motyer; John Stott. Copyright ©1992 edited by J. Alec Motyer; John Stott. Used by permission of InterVarsity Press, P.O. Box 1400, Downers Grove, IL 60515, USA. www.ivpress.com

Ps 139:6: *Such knowledge is too wonderful for me, too lofty for me to attain* [cf Judg 13:17–18].

I cannot grasp it. I can hardly endure to think of it. The theme overwhelms me. I am amazed and astounded at it. Such knowledge not only surpasses my comprehension, but even my imagination. It is high, I cannot attain unto it. Mount as I may, this truth is too lofty for my mind. It seems to be always above me, even when I soar into the loftiest regions of spiritual thought. Is it not so with every attribute of God? Can we attain to any idea of his power, his wisdom, his holiness? Our mind has no line with which to measure the Infinite. We are not surprised that the Most Glorious God should in his knowledge be high above all the knowledge to which we can attain: it must of necessity be so, since we are such poor limited beings; and when we stand a tip toe we cannot reach to the lowest step of the throne of the Eternal.　　　　　　　　　　　　　　　　　　　　　　Spurgeon

Personal Note: This simple verse should give us pause. Modern humanity with all its technological prowess assumes there is no knowledge which is too wonderful. We arrogantly think that given enough time and tenacity, there will ultimately be no secrets we cannot uncover. But what if there is another world that is beyond our human senses and instruments? Pascal sums it up well in this quote (and Job 38:2) which appear to illuminate Ps139:6.

"Our soul is cast into a body, where it finds number, time, dimension. Thereupon it reasons, and calls this nature necessity, and can believe nothing else."

Blaise Pascal (1623–1662)　　　　　　　　　　　　　Quoted in Ward and Wild

Ps 139:23–24: *Search me, O God, and know my heart; test me and know my anxious thoughts. See if there is any offensive way in me, and lead me in the way everlasting.*
[Prov 20:27, Jer 17:10, Ps 19:12, 26:2]
Investigate my life, O God, find out everything about me; Cross-examine and test me, get a clear picture of what I'm about; See for yourself whether I've done anything wrong— then guide me on the road to eternal life.
The Message
Only the one whose heart is open to God's searching eye, who has misgivings (anxious thoughts) about his own discernment, and who is all too aware of the possibilities of something offensive in himself, will be able to follow the Lord in the way everlasting. 'Search all my sense, and know all my heart, who canst make known…Search all my thoughts, the secret springs, the motives that control, The chambers where polluted things Hold empire o'er the soul', the hymn (*Search me O God, My Actions Try*, by Francis Bottome, 1965) based on these verses will repay your meditation. Wilcock, p. 261
Wilcock, Michael, *The Message of Psalms 73–150* Taken from *The Bible Speaks Today* Series edited by J. Alec Motyer; John Stott. Copyright ©1992 edited by J. Alec Motyer; John Stott. Used by permission of InterVarsity Press, P.O. Box 1400, Downers Grove, IL 60515, USA. www.ivpress.com

Ps 141:3: *Set a guard over my mouth, O LORD; keep watch over the door of my lips.*
Verse 3. That mouth had been used in prayer, it would be a pity it should ever be defiled with untruth, or pride, or wrath [Jas 3:9–10]; yet so it will become unless carefully watched, for these intruders are ever lurking about the door [Gen 4:7]. David feels that with all his own watchfulness he may be surprised into sin, and so he begs the Lord himself to keep him. *Keep the door of my lips.* God has made our lips the door of the mouth, but we cannot keep that door of ourselves, therefore do we entreat the Lord to take the rule of it. O that the Lord would both open and shut our lips, for we can do neither the one nor the other aright if left to ourselves.
Spurgeon

<u>Morning Prayer on Words</u> (author unknown) found in my Mother's effects after her death:

O Divine Father, source of my reflection, Strength of my life, origin of my hope; I pause to ponder the words that surround my day, my use and misuse of them, their power to lift or to destroy, to build or to maim. Forgive me, merciful Lord, the folly of things said which would be better left unsaid:

> Heated words that accuse,
> Jealous words that hate,
> Unwarranted words that blame
> Belittling words that taunt,
> Mean words that sour,
> Dishonest words that deny,
> Timid words that disgrace,
> Thoughtless words that sear,
> Hasty words that harm.

Allow instead:

> Kind words that cheer,
> Uplifting words that inspire,
> Tender words that comfort,
> Wise words that guide,
> Affirming words that build,
> Forgiving words that heal,
> Encouraging words that challenge,
> Thoughtful words that redirect,
> Appropriate words that explain,
> Prayerful words that intercede.

May my words flow less from the heat of the moment than from a heart disciplined by Thy will and tempered by Thy Word. Through Him who is the Word of Life. Amen

Ps 150:6: *Let everything that has breath praise the LORD. Praise the LORD.* And so we come to the last psalm of the last Hallel. Its thirteen calls to praise bring Book V and the entire Psalter to a magnificent climax, not only rounding off, but also summing up, all that has gone before. The psalm with which the Psalter ends is as brief and as deceptively simple as the one with which it began. To present either one out of its context is to provoke puzzlement, if not outcry. The good people prosper and everything will work out fine, says 1: and the answer of 150 is, Praise God, so it does. And the perplexed Bible reader says, 'yes, but *does* it?'

So we must see these two psalms in their context. What has happened is that the intervening 148 have worked their way, often painfully, through all the 'yes but's'. They set forth the conflicts, burdens, mysteries, and sufferings that both the individual believer and the assembly have to cope with, and all that God, as their covenant Lord, does for them on their journey of faith. In doing so, they help us to grasp what the first and last psalms are really saying. The progress from 1 to 150 is a movement from obedience to praise. Wilcock, p. 286

Wilcock, Michael, *The Message of Psalms 73–150* Taken from *The Bible Speaks Today* Series edited by J. Alec Motyer; John Stott. Copyright ©1992 edited by J. Alec Motyer; John Stott. Used by permission of InterVarsity Press, P.O. Box 1400, Downers Grove, IL 60515, USA. www.ivpress.com

Personal Note: Postscript on the Psalms

As we look back on the Psalms, what do we make of this seeming grab bag of Hebrew poetry? How is it relevant to our lives more than 2500 years after pen met parchment? Wilcock, Williams, Spurgeon, Henry, and Peterson have already shared many ways these Psalms can impact us. I add a few thoughts here.

One striking feature of the Psalms is their abundant use of first person pronouns. The words I, my, me, and we occur a total of 2,440 times in the Psalms, an average of sixteen times per Psalm. Many times the pronoun refers to God but often it refers to the psalmist. As we read the psalmist's first person accounts, we are invited into the psalmist's own experience, which we find strikingly like our own. The Psalms offer encouragement, strength, and counsel on difficult issues. And they always bring us back to God (mentioned 1,214 times in Psalms).

The Psalms collectively provide punctuation marks in the language of our lives. They often ask questions such as how long? (twenty-two times), why? (thirty-three times), the same questions we repeatedly ask today. The vigorous praise (223 times) and adoration that radiate from so many of the Psalms offer exclamation points for our lives. We should revel in the abundant life the Lord has given us and issue praise and thanks in return. The wise counsel to wait for the Lord and accept his timing (5:3, 27:14, 37:7, 37:34, 38:15, 119:84, 119:166, 130:5–6) puts commas into our sentences, a pause that refreshes. And finally, the absolute truth (25:5, 26:3, 31:5, 40:11, 43:3, 51:6, 86:11) contained in the Psalms and other scripture to which it points provides a decisive period at the end of the sentence ("It is done.", Rev 21:6). Though perplexing and mystifying to us [Eccl 3:11], God's plan is headed to a glorious conclusion. Praise the Lord.

Proverbs

A proverb is a short sentence based on long experience.
Miguel De Cervantes (1547–1616)

Commentaries:
- *Proverbs*, by John A. Kitchen (2006)
- *The Preacher's Commentary*, OT Vol 15, by David A. Hubbard (1989)
- *Proverbs 1–12*, by Bruce Waltke (NICOT Series) (2004)
- Matthew Henry Commentary at BlueLetterBible.org (1710)

<u>Personal Note</u>: We now come to the book of Proverbs, one of the most delightful in the canon. This book speaks simply but eloquently about the contrast between wisdom and folly. It provides practical advice on how to live a joyful life and avoid the snares and pitfalls that so often entangle us. Like the Psalms, the Proverbs sometimes show us people we know. But all too often in the portrait of the fool, we find ourselves looking in the mirror! In his poem "To a Louse", The Scottish poet Robert Burns once said, *"O wad some power the giftie gie us to see ourels as ithers see us."* Burns' "giftie", we find, is the Lord. Through His eyes, we see what we look like to others.

Prov 1:1–2: *The proverbs of Solomon son of David, king of Israel: for attaining wisdom and discipline; for understanding words of insight*
A proverb is a compactly constructed sentence packed with practical insight. It is a stubby sentence pregnant with meaning. It is college in a cup. It is wisdom that you can carry with you as you walk through life. Proverbs presents us with divinely given nuggets of gold that will make rich the one who prizes them enough to understand and apply them at all cost.

Verses 2–6 present ten words that summarize what Proverbs gives the person who heeds its instruction. 'Wisdom' is the first prominent result. The basic meaning of 'wisdom' is skill in living. ... 'Instruction' is also guaranteed. An alternative translation is 'discipline'. This discipline is education through correction. Proverbs will step on your toes, but, in doing so, will discipline you and keep your feet in the right path when you walk in their light. Reading this book is profitable, but not comfortable. ... 'Discernment' is the path to this understanding. Discernment is the ability to look at two things and see what God sees. These proverbs cut through the fog of human reasoning and throw the spotlight of God upon a given situation, revealing God's verdict. Kitchen, p. 38, 39

John A. Kitchen, *Proverbs: A Mentor Commentary*, Copyright © 2006, by Christian Focus Publications, Fearn, Ross-Shire, Scotland. Used by Permission.

Prov 1:2–3: *for gaining wisdom and instruction; for understanding words of insight; for receiving instruction in prudent behavior, doing what is right and just and fair*
Chock full of meaty morsels about wisdom, this paragraph is designed to whet the appetite of even the most casual reader. Its synonyms, piled on one another, are calculated to show wisdom's well-stocked larder. They are an instance of the use of repetition by Hebrew authors to expand, reinforce, and enrich the meaning of a concept. It is their accumulative force that conveys the teacher's intention, more than the precise nuance of each term, though each word wads something to our understanding of wisdom.

Hubbard, p. 45

Prov 1:7: *The fear of the LORD is the beginning of knowledge, but fools despise wisdom and discipline.*
Fear of the Lord—like the four notes that mark the theme of Beethoven's Fifth Symphony, these words are pounded out at the beginning of Proverbs, at the end of the wisdom speeches, and periodically through the rest of the book. Its repetition never lets us forget the theological and spiritual meaning of wisdom. Its recurrence means that we can never slip into secular definitions of insight or prudence; we can never view wisdom as mere cunning or skill. 'Fear of the Lord,' sprinkled as it is throughout the text, salts the whole collection and preserves it from becoming tainted

with flatly humanistic or plainly pragmatic approaches to wisdom.
Hubbard, p. 199

"Man knows mighty little, and may someday learn enough of his own ignorance to fall down and pray."
Henry Brooks Adams (1838–1918) Quoted in Ward and Wild

Prov 1:21: *at the head of the noisy streets she cries out, in the gateways of the city she makes her speech*
Wisdom makes her appeal in 'the noisy streets.' These streets are full of commotion, noise, confusion, and unrest with people shouting and hollering, as they go about transacting their daily business. This is the place that Lady Wisdom speaks her invitation to us. We must tune our ears to hear her voice above the cacophony of life's voices and noises [Mk 4:9, Isa 28:23]. We must discern the call of wisdom from among a myriad of invitations. What wisdom offers is not for the ivory tower, but literally for the push and shove of life. Kitchen, p. 48
John A. Kitchen, *Proverbs: A Mentor Commentary*, Copyright © 2006, by Christian Focus Publications, Fearn, Ross-Shire, Scotland. Used by Permission.

Prov 2:10: *For wisdom will enter your heart, and knowledge will be pleasant to your soul.*

"Knowledge comes, but wisdom lingers."
Alfred Tennyson (1809–1892) Quoted in Ward and Wild

Prov 3:5–6: *Trust in the LORD with all your heart and lean not on your own understanding; in all your ways acknowledge him, and he will make your paths straight.*
Everything we are and all we have must be rested upon the Lord as our security. This does not mean to imply that there is nothing to be trusted in 'common sense', but simply that you don't use it as your sole, or even primary, support in life. Rather, we should bank our all on God and the wisdom of his ways. His ways are above our ways (Isa 55:8–9, Rom 11:33–34), and must be chosen when they seem to contradict our earthly human wisdom. Kitchen, p. 77

John A. Kitchen, *Proverbs: A Mentor Commentary*, Copyright © 2006, by Christian Focus Publications, Fearn, Ross-Shire, Scotland. Used by Permission.

Prov 3:6 *in all your ways acknowledge him and he will make your paths straight.*
Begin, continue, and end every work, purpose, and device with God. Earnestly pray for his direction at the commencement; look for his continual support in progress; and so begin and continue that all may terminate in his glory. And then it will certainly be to thy good, for we never honor God without serving ourselves.   Adam Clarke Commentary (1832)

Prov 3:13–15: *Blessed is the man who finds wisdom, the man who gains understanding, for she is more profitable than silver and yields better returns than gold. She is more precious than rubies; nothing you desire can compare with her.*
Money can put food on the table but not fellowship around it; a house but not a home. By contrast, wisdom gives both physical and spiritual benefits.   A Talmudic proverb says 'Lackest thou wisdom, what has thou acquired? Has thou acquired wisdom, what lackest thou?' [cf Job 28:12–28]   Waltke, p. 257, 258

Prov 4:23: *Above all else, guard your heart, for it is the wellspring of life.*
Solomon calls his son to guard his heart (23), guard his mouth (24), guard his eyes (25), and guard his feet (26–27). This holistic caution will watch over every path of life and keep one in the way of wisdom. Guard your heart! If there were one verse I could give to Christian young people, it would be this one. Nothing is more essential than guarding your heart. The heart is more than simply the sentimental side of us. It is a term that reflects the totality of the inner person (3:5). Your heart is the real *you*. There is nothing of greater value on this earth than the condition of your heart. There is no single action that will more directly affect the outcome and quality of your life than the guarding of your heart. There is not a more portentous predictor of your ultimate end than what you expose your heart to. Above all else, guard your heart!
Kitchen, p. 112–113

John A. Kitchen, *Proverbs: A Mentor Commentary*, Copyright © 2006, by Christian Focus Publications, Fearn, Ross-Shire, Scotland. Used by Permission.

Prov 5:12–13: *You will say, "How I hated discipline! How my heart spurned correction! I would not obey my teachers or listen to my instructors."*
Now the consequences of spurning reproof have come to full fruition. So also the urging to incline the ear to wisdom had not been infrequent (Prov 2:2, 4:20, 5:1, 22:17). Yet, other voices were found that were more pleasant to listen to than that of instruction [eg 1:13, 5:3, 7:17–18]. Beware of listening only to that with which you already agree! Beware of listening only to him who compliments you! Beware of heeding only the advice that brings about your pleasure! Not every dissenting voice is wrong. It might be the voice of wisdom! Kitchen, p. 125

John A. Kitchen, *Proverbs: A Mentor Commentary*, Copyright © 2006, by Christian Focus Publications, Fearn, Ross-Shire, Scotland. Used by Permission.

"Remorse, the fatal egg by pleasure laid."
William Cowper (1731–1800) Quoted in Ward and Wild

Prov 8:1: *Does not wisdom call out? Does not understanding raise her voice?*
Let us not miss the fact stated here: wisdom is ever speaking, calling, inviting, and demanding our attention! God is not silent. He does not sit by quietly, letting the world pass by until someone stops and gives Him attention. He calls to us in creation [Ps 19:1–2], in Christ [Mt 11:28], by the Spirit through the Word of God [1 Cor 2:13, Eph 1:17–18], through our conscience [Isa 30:21], and in His providence [Rom 8:28]. Our failure and foolishness is not for lack of his voice, but for lack of our listening [Job 33:14–15]. …What claims Wisdom has made for herself in this eighth chapter! Breathe deeply and think again of all she has laid credit to for herself. How seriously one must take Wisdom's invitation to draw near her! How carefully one must choose his path! Everything is at stake in our choice! [cf Deut 11:26–28, 30:19, Mt 7:24]. Kitchen, p. 175, 197

John A. Kitchen, *Proverbs: A Mentor Commentary*, Copyright © 2006, by Christian Focus Publications, Fearn, Ross-Shire, Scotland. Used by Permission.

"Sometimes when we say "God is silent," what's really going on is that he hasn't told the story the way we wanted it told. He will be silent when we

want him to fill in the blanks of the story we are creating. But with his own stories, the ones we live in, he is seldom silent."
— Paul E. Miller, *A Praying Life: Connecting with God in a Distracting World*

Prov 8:5–6: *You who are simple, gain prudence; you who are foolish, gain understanding.*
Listen, for I have worthy things to say; I open my lips to speak what is right.
She must emphasize the value of her words, for she has a hard sell; she has some hard things to say, and some uncomfortable truths to tell, and she talks about self-discipline, not self-indulgence. The unfaithful wife's speech is sweet in the beginning and bitter in the end; Wisdom's speech demands discipline in the beginning and promises life in the end.   Waltke, p. 396

Prov 8:22–23: *"The LORD brought me forth as the first of his works, before his deeds of old;*
I was appointed from eternity, from the beginning, before the world began."
Wisdom predates all we know in this world, and was fundamental to the creation of all we know (Prov 3:19–20). How essential, then, to embrace God's wisdom, if we desire to live in God's world? How foolish to attempt to live in God's world without pursuing at all costs His fundamental principle of creating this world? (Ps 104:24) [Jer 33:25].   Kitchen, p. 189
John A. Kitchen, *Proverbs: A Mentor Commentary*, Copyright © 2006, by Christian Focus Publications, Fearn, Ross-Shire, Scotland. Used by Permission.

Prov 10:13: *Wisdom is found on the lips of the discerning, but a rod is for the back of him who lacks judgment.*
This antithetical proverb concerns what it takes to steer a person's life. The first character is 'the discerning.' He has come to the place where he can look at two things and see what God sees in them. He can distinguish wrong from right, good from bad, better from best. He has, through practice in applying God's word, learned to discern God's way in this world (Heb 5:14). What a word for we who live in the age of relativism! We are told today that such discernment is not only useless, but evil. Rather, we must just accept any, and every, voice as equally true. But, that is not the way of wisdom, it is the way of folly.   Kitchen, p. 223–224

Scripture Commentary Sampler

John A. Kitchen, *Proverbs: A Mentor Commentary*, Copyright © 2006, by Christian Focus Publications, Fearn, Ross-Shire, Scotland. Used by Permission.

Prov 10:19: *When words are many, sin is not absent, but he who holds his tongue is wise.*
The person who rattles on and chatters incessantly will not be able to avoid sinning with those words. They will promise something they cannot keep; they will offend someone; they will embarrass themselves; they will reveal their pride by speaking on and on about their own affairs—the possibilities are endless. Kitchen, p.229
John A. Kitchen, *Proverbs: A Mentor Commentary*, Copyright © 2006, by Christian Focus Publications, Fearn, Ross–Shire, Scotland. Used by Permission.

"Discretion in speech is more than eloquence."
Sir Francis Bacon (1561 – 1626)

Prov 12:16: *A fool shows his annoyance at once, but a prudent man overlooks an insult.*
Passion is folly: a wise man may be angry when there is just cause for it, but then he has his anger under check, and is the lord of his anger, whereas a fool's anger lords it over him. It is a kindness to extenuate and excuse insults we receive instead of aggravating them and making the worst of them. Matthew Henry Commentary

"To forbear replying to an unjust reproach, and overlook it with a generous, or if possible, with an entire neglect of it, is one of the most heroic acts of a great mind."
Joseph Addison (1672–1719)   Quoted in Ward and Wild

Prov 13:1 *A wise son heeds his father's instruction, but a mocker does not respond to rebukes.*
There is something that makes us resent most what we most need to hear—what we have done wrong and how we can do better next time. ... A hallmark of the 'wise son' or daughter is the ability to accept even stern or painful advice with open ears. The 'scoffer' of the contrasting line is so attached to foolish behavior, so well defended against changing his ways,

so skeptical of the values of the community that he will 'not listen to any rebuke.' Hubbard, p. 284

Prov 13:3: *He who guards his lips guards his life, but he who speaks rashly will come to ruin.*
A guard at the lips is a guard to the soul [Ps 141:3]. He who is cautious, who thinks twice before he speaks once, guards his life from a great deal of guilt and grief. Matthew Henry Commentary

"He who does not know how to be silent will not know how to speak."
Ausonius (AD 310–394) Latin Poet

Prov 15:23: *A man finds joy in giving an apt reply–and how good is a timely word!*
We speak wisely when we speak opportunely; when it is needed and, as we say, hits the spot. Many a good word comes short of doing the good it might have done, for lack of being well timed.   Matthew Henry Commentary
A wrong answer given when a correct answer is sought is misleading. A right answer given at the wrong time may be well intentioned and technically correct, but damaging. The right answer at the right time is priceless! Kitchen, p. 339
John A. Kitchen, *Proverbs: A Mentor Commentary*, Copyright © 2006, by Christian Focus Publications, Fearn, Ross-Shire, Scotland. Used by Permission.

Prov 15:28: *The heart of the righteous weighs its answers, but the mouth of the wicked gushes evil.*
In sizing up people as potential participants in the life of Fuller Seminary, whether as administrators or trustees, I carefully observed their patterns of speech. Obviously what they said needed to make sense. But I watched for much more than that. Did they wait their turn? Did they step on the lines of others? Did they need to have the last word? Did they try to top everyone else's stories? Did they sound off in their areas of incompetence? Could they say, 'I don't know?' Did they repeat themselves badly or wander aimlessly through their subject matter? Persons with these and other verbal liabilities do not usually make it to my team. They are not sensitive enough, not succinct enough, not modest enough, and not gracious enough to work

well with others. They waste time, hurt feelings, and shatter morale. They, with the rest of us, need to sit longer at the wise teacher's feet and learn that restraint in communication is essential to prudent speech.

Hubbard, p. 221

Prov 16:16: *How much better to get wisdom than gold, to choose understanding rather than silver!*
Heavenly wisdom is better than worldly wealth, and to be preferred above it. Grace is more valuable than gold. Grace is the gift of God's special favor; gold only of common providence. Grace is for the soul and eternity; gold only for the body and time. Grace will stand us in stead in a dying hour, when gold will do us no good.   Matthew Henry Commentary

Prov 16:18: *Pride goes before destruction, a haughty spirit before a fall.*
<u>**Personal Note**</u>: This little proverb has been demonstrated repeatedly down through the ages. When one is proud and at the top of his game, one is blind to the seeds of destruction all around him (2 Chr 26:15–16, Ezek 28:17, Obad 3–4, Acts 12:21–23). The author of this proverb, Solomon himself, personifies the verse. All the arrogant sees is his own self-importance, and that sets up the fall (Isa 14:14–15). A haughty spirit has humbled many a man. May we take this proverb to heart and beware the arrogance that so easily insinuates itself into our being.

Prov 17:9: *He who covers over an offense promotes love, but whoever repeats the matter separates close friends.*

"Meekness takes injuries like pills, not chewing, but swallowing them down." Thomas Browne (1605–1682)   Quoted in Ward and Wild

Prov 17:14: *Starting a quarrel is like breaching a dam; so drop the matter before a dispute breaks out.*
A destructive flood begins with but a tiny leak in the dam. Wise is the man who sees that leak, not for the trickle of water it is at the time, but for the raging torrent it will soon become and then flees from it. So it is with bickering and quarrelling. What begins as a barbed comment soon becomes a biting accusation. That accusation, fueled by pride, quickly breaks out into arguments. The arguments give rise to bitter anger. The anger divides

relationships, breaks up friendships, splits churches, and produces icy homes. O, how much trouble could be avoided if only someone would walk away from that barbed comment! Kitchen, p. 380

John A. Kitchen, *Proverbs: A Mentor Commentary*, Copyright © 2006, by Christian Focus Publications, Fearn, Ross-Shire, Scotland. Used by Permission.

"When angry, count ten before you speak; when very angry, count an hundred." Thomas Jefferson (1743–1826) Quoted in Ward and Wild

Prov 18:2: *A fool finds no pleasure in understanding but delights in airing his own opinions.*

This antithetical proverb lays bare the unteachable, and arrogant, spirit of the fool. The first line makes its point by stating its opposite. A fool has no interest in listening or learning. Rather, as the second line reveals, his only thought is to expose what is on his own mind. The root of the verb 'revealing' (NIV 'airing') can mean to uncover, to reveal, to be away or to go away. The particular form employed here is found only one other time in the Old Testament in Gen 9:21, where Noah got drunk and uncovered himself, sleeping naked in his tent. Thus, it would not be a stretch to understand this as a description of a man with a bit of an exhibitionist tendency. The fool, to his own shame, has only a perverse interest in exposing himself—in this case, his thoughts, feelings, opinions, musings and vaunted insights. He is oblivious to both the divine and public evaluation of him—'a fool'. He lives in a delusional world, where he always has the key insight and always inspires and informs others [cf Eccl 6:11]. Kitchen, p. 392

John A. Kitchen, *Proverbs: A Mentor Commentary*, Copyright © 2006, by Christian Focus Publications, Fearn, Ross-Shire, Scotland. Used by Permission.

Prov 18:22: *He who finds a wife finds what is good and receives favor from the LORD.*

How blessed is the man with a good, and godly, wife! The second line explains how she becomes such a boon to the man—it is the Lord who has given her to him. She is an expression of God's favor resting upon him. A man cannot find a good wife and the favor that goes with her by his direct effort, but only as a divine gift. Surely he has a part in it, but not by directing his efforts at finding a wife, but by directing his energies in pleasing the Lord and walking in His ways. When a man is focused upon honoring God, He will, in His good time, care for the matter of granting a good wife. When God grants her to him, let him never stoop to believe he deserves her. She is a gift [Prov 19:14]. Kitchen, p. 406

John A. Kitchen, *Proverbs: A Mentor Commentary*, Copyright © 2006, by Christian Focus Publications, Fearn, Ross-Shire, Scotland. Used by Permission.

Prov 19:11: *A man's wisdom gives him patience; it is to his glory to overlook an offense.*

Personal Note: In our 21st century world, many people are offended by what is spoken in their presence. In fact, some have developed a kind of science to avoid offending someone. This science speaks of "trigger warnings" and "microaggressions." The very word "micro-aggressions" conveys that these offenses are quite petty; its as if you need either a microscope or special expertise to detect them. The assumption by secular purveyors of this topic is that anything that offends someone else must be avoided at all costs. But this proverb gives another perspective. If everyone is afraid of offending someone else, frank and controversial topics will be avoided and the truth will be shrouded in circumlocution. While we must be sensitive to the feelings of others, we also should not be hypersensitive when we are insulted. We need to "just let it go." Imagine how much more tranquil and harmonious our world would be if everyone took this proverb to heart!

"The remembering of an injury is itself a wrong: it adds to our anger, feeds our sin and hates what is good. It is a rusty arrow and poison for the soul."
Francis of Paola (1416–1507)

Prov 25:16: *If you find honey, eat just enough—too much of it, and you will vomit.*

All things in moderation! Why this restraint? Is it purely for dietetic reasons? Is health his concern? Is it because of weight gain? These may be remotely related as negative side-effects of overindulgence in sweets. But, the point made has more to do with a general theology of pleasure than it does with health issues. This is about more than simply 'honey'. The world believes that pleasure is found through 'more.' If a little is pleasurable, then more will increase that pleasure. Solomon tested this theory and found it to

be false (Eccl 2:1–11). Ultimate pleasure can be found only on the other side of restraint. Kidner well says 'Since Eden, man has wanted the last ounce out of life, as though beyond God's *enough* lay ecstasy, not nausea.' Could it be, then, that God's boundaries are not designed to restrict our freedom and dull our enjoyment, but to expand our boundaries and heighten our pleasure? Kitchen, p. 572
John A. Kitchen, *Proverbs: A Mentor Commentary*, Copyright © 2006, by Christian Focus Publications, Fearn, Ross-Shire, Scotland. Used by Permission.

"Do not bite at the bait of pleasure till you know there is no hook beneath it." Thomas Jefferson (1743–1826)

Prov 26:20–21: *Without wood a fire goes out; without gossip a quarrel dies down.*
As charcoal to embers and as wood to fire, so is a quarrelsome man for kindling strife.
Once the 'whisperer' is removed, the strife 'quiets down.' But oh, how difficult it is to collectively shut down such a talker! You may change the arena in which they do their talking, but will likely never quiet them completely…Whereas in verse 20 the problem was a 'whisperer', here in verse 21 the problem is 'a contentious man.' While they present themselves differently socially, the two are conjoined twins, sharing a corrupt heart. The gossip moves with stealth, while the 'contentious man' is loud and brash. Yet their impulses are not far apart and their results are much the same.   Kitchen, p. 595, 596
John A. Kitchen, *Proverbs: A Mentor Commentary*, Copyright © 2006, by Christian Focus Publications, Fearn, Ross-Shire, Scotland. Used by Permission.

Prov 27:17: *As iron sharpens iron, so one man sharpens another.*
We are better for our social interactions, even the ones we least appreciate. We are a debtor to every person whose path we have crossed, for no social contact need be a waste if we will but learn from it. How much more valuable, then, those friendships in which our companion has our highest good in mind!… No man can be his best or reach the heights God intends for him without those blessed friends who comfort, provoke, challenge, rebuke, chide, affirm, stimulate, and encourage until his thinking is clear, his wisdom mature, his purpose refined, and his faculties sharp. Kitchen, p. 616

SCRIPTURE COMMENTARY SAMPLER

John A. Kitchen, *Proverbs: A Mentor Commentary*, Copyright © 2006, by Christian Focus Publications, Fearn, Ross-Shire, Scotland. Used by Permission.

Prov 31:10–11: *A wife of noble character who can find? She is worth far more than rubies.*
Her husband has full confidence in her and lacks nothing of value.
We now come to the climactic, and concluding, section of the entire book: the well-known treatise on the 'excellent wife.' This section serves not only as an outline of the individual qualities and cumulative worth of a fine wife, but also as a fitting literary conclusion to the whole of Proverbs. In the opening section (Chs 1–9), wisdom was personified as a woman. Here, again, as the book concludes, wisdom appears, this time in the picture of a wise domestic partner. This serves as a fitting inclusio to wrap the whole in the picture of wisdom's beauty and virtues. The ideals of wisdom presented throughout the book of Proverbs are now gathered up and presented in a beautiful, breath-taking, but practical, presentation of wisdom embodied and in motion. Kitchen, p. 710–711

John A. Kitchen, *Proverbs: A Mentor Commentary*, Copyright © 2006, by Christian Focus Publications, Fearn, Ross-Shire, Scotland. Used by Permission.

Prov 31:29: *"Many women do noble things, but you surpass them all."*
My Comment: How precious is my dear wife! I can quote these verses of Proverbs 31 and see her character in every verse. I am truly blessed. She does, indeed, surpass them all!

Prov 31:28: *Her children arise and call her blessed; her husband also, and he praises her*:
As the poem comes to a close, those near her cannot contain their praise. It begins with her children and moves on to the husband, God (v 30), and the broader community (v 31). They see her for what she is: an 'excellent wife' and mother (v 10). Today, it might picture one calling for the attention of assembled guests and clearing his throat to make a toast, or of a crowd leaping to its feet in a thunderous standing ovation. ...Thus ends this remarkable book of wisdom. Wisdom has spoken. Life and death have been set before us. Let us choose life! (Deut 30:19)
Kitchen, p. 721, 723

John A. Kitchen, *Proverbs: A Mentor Commentary*, Copyright © 2006, by Christian Focus Publications, Fearn, Ross–Shire, Scotland. Used by Permission.

Ecclesiastes

Commentaries:
- *The Message of Ecclesiastes*, by Derek Kidner (BST Series) (1976)
- *The Preacher's Commentary*, OT Vol 16, by David A. Hubbard (1991)

Eccl 2:9–10: *I became greater by far than anyone in Jerusalem before me. In all this my wisdom stayed with me. I denied myself nothing my eyes desired; I refused my heart no pleasure.*

Who of us would not like to write a description of our achievements like the Preacher's in verse 9? And who of us would not privately, if not publicly, gloat over the privileges described in verse 10? Pleasure is the blank check whose limits and joys the Preacher sets out to test in 2:1. The task itself was brimful of joy. … Yet despite the high excitement and the quiet satisfaction which the pursuit of pleasure gave Solomon, the wise man, after facing up to the issues and results, branded the whole quest as futile. … He knew the lure of pleasure, and he knew its snare. He had found that pleasure promises more than it can produce. Its advertising agency is better than its manufacturing department. It holds out the possibility of exquisite delight, but the best it can perform is titillation. It seeks to tickle the human spirit but cannot probe its depths. It daubs iodine on human wounds when what it needed is surgery. It may distract us from our problems by diverting our attention, but it cannot free us from those problems.

Hubbard, excerpts, pp 76, 77, 79

Taken from The Preacher's Commentary Series Volume 16: Ecclesiastes, Song of Solomon by David A. Hubbard. Copyright © 1991 by Word, Inc. Used by permission of Thomas Nelson. www.thomasnelson.com

Eccl 8:17: *then I saw all that God has done. No one can comprehend what goes on under the sun. Despite all his efforts to search it out, man cannot discover its meaning. Even if a wise man claims he knows, he cannot really comprehend it.* It is God's work that baffles us: it is not 'a tale told by an idiot.' Yet what if it is a tale told to an idiot? Although as time dwellers we see God's work in tantalizing flashes, the very fact that we can ask about the whole design and long to see it is evidence that we are not entirely prisoners of our world [cf discussion on Jonah 2:1]. In more promising words, it is evidence of not only *how* but *for Whom* we have been made. Kidner, p. 79

He tells how he sought to clutch once more at that will-o'-the-wisp that has flitted just beyond his fingertips each time he has come close—the wisdom beyond the wisdom, the wisdom that will take him further into the mysteries of divine activity than any sage has yet had access. ... The finality of this conclusion informs us that the problem defies solution. More time, greater intelligence, better methods, a new team of researchers—none of these is the answer. The problem lies in the difference between divine and human [Isa 55:8–9], between God and even the brightest of God's creatures. The eager beginning of the quest at 1:13 and its unsatisfied conclusion at 8:17 form a bracket within the book that fences off and billboards its essential message: we are called to live as well as we can within the limits imposed on us [Ps 16:6] by the fundamental differences between us and God. To seek to exceed those limits is both arrogant and dangerous [Isa 14:13–15, Ezek 28:17]. Hubbard, pp 195–197

Taken from The Preacher's Commentary Series Volume 16: Ecclesiastes, Song of Solomon by David A. Hubbard. Copyright © 1991 by Word, Inc. Used by permission of Thomas Nelson. www.thomasnelson.com

Song of Songs

Commentaries:
- *The Message of Song of Songs*, by Tom Gledhill (BST Series) (1994)
- *The Preacher's Commentary*, OT Vol 16, by David A. Hubbard (1991)

Song 1:1: *Solomon's Song of Songs.*
The Bible is about marriage. And at its heart the Spirit of God has placed a collection of wedding songs. They contain no liturgy of worship, no statutes or commandments, no hymns of a psalmist, no oracle of a prophet, no vision of a seer. They are love songs pure and simple, bursting with passion, bright with desire, explosive with longing for physical love. … The Bible is about singing as well as marriage. Biblical faith is personal. It calls for our engagement in it as persons; it grips our lives at their center and evokes a response from the depth of our beings. … Singing opens our eyes and ears to what we have not earlier understood. It draws out of us responses of which we have been previously incapable. It heads us into the heart of wonders and mysteries which only poetry is capable of capturing. … The title is superlative like king of kings (Dan 2:37). It means the best of songs, the outstanding song.… The best of songs is rightly named; its subject is the royal relationship—love strong as death and too fiery for any stream to quench (8:6–7). We sing a song. In the Song treasured in Holy writ, we sing the best song possible.   Hubbard, excerpts, p. 266, 268, 270, 272
Taken from The Preacher's Commentary Series Volume 16: Ecclesiastes, Song of Solomon by David A. Hubbard. Copyright © 1991 by Word, Inc. Used by permission of Thomas Nelson. www.thomasnelson.com

Song 4:7: *You are altogether beautiful, my darling; there is no flaw in you.*
Three important themes are braided together in this section. Each contributes to our understanding of a biblical approach to marriage. The

splendor of matrimony us revealed in the magnificent processional first described at a distance, awesome and mysterious, then viewed close at hand, overpoweringly impressive in the majesty of its military precision and the exquisite details of its accoutrements (3:6–11). ... The *esteem* of each partner for the other is a second essential. In this poem, since the woman has already had ample opportunity to disclose her craving for her lover and the regard in which she holds him, her admiration is noted here only briefly (3:11). He, in contrast, has ample and uninterrupted opportunity to display his feelings toward her. Whatever male reticence may lurk within him he sets aside and boldly describes her beauty and worth. ... The *exclusiveness* of the relationship is the last and, perhaps, most crucial strand in marriage. The woman has eyes only for her Solomon (3:11), despite the possible distraction of sixty hand-picked warriors (3:7–8). The man's heart beats for her alone (4:9). He treasures the uniqueness of their bond: she is accessible to no one else; she is a garden which only his key can unlock (4:12). 'Forsaking all others, will you keep yourself only unto her...only unto him?' That is the central question of the wedding ceremony. It is to be asked and answered at the beginning of the union and every day thereafter. Answering it with a fervent *Yes* will not guarantee untarnished happiness. But it will provide the only context within which true happiness becomes a possibility.   Hubbard, excerpts, pp. 297–299
Taken from The Preacher's Commentary Series Volume 16: Ecclesiastes, Song of Solomon by David A. Hubbard. Copyright © 1991 by Word, Inc. Used by permission of Thomas Nelson. www.thomasnelson.com

Song 8:6–7: *Place me like a seal over your heart, like a seal on your arm; for love is as strong as death, its jealousy unyielding as the grave. It burns like blazing fire, like a mighty flame. Many waters cannot quench love; rivers cannot wash it away. If one were to give all the wealth of his house for love, it would be utterly scorned.*
The love in our song is all-embracing. It embraces pleasure, it embraces pain. It is passionate, yet fearful. It possesses, yet lets go. It liberates, yet binds. It empowers, it weakens. It brings turmoil, it brings peace. It is solemn, yet playful. It is lofty in conception, yet earthy in expression. It is self-centered, it is totally other-centered. It gives, it receives. It longs to give pleasure, it hopes to receive pleasure. Such a union of opposites, such a conflicting array of incompatibilities alone can do justice to the

immensely complex phenomenon of the love between a man and a woman. It transcends logic, rationality, definition, and even sense. Yet this whole thing called love is there to be experienced in all its agony and ecstasy. It is love about which our song sings. Gledhill, p. 230

These magnificent words that pledge deathless love and then describe its power and worth are uttered by the bride. Her formula of mutual possession we have met before (2:16, 6:3, 7:10). Here it is expanded, elaborated, and decorated like a magnificent violin cadenza in the middle of a concerto. The orchestra's instruments are frozen in silence; the conductor joins the audience in rapt attention; the lone musician reaches for sweeter, brighter, stronger tones that even she thought possible. And the result is an outburst of love poetry which is the artistic match of anything William Shakespeare or Elizabeth Barrett Browning ever put to ink. ... Indelible as a seal sharply stamped, unquenchable as a fire with leaping flames, and unbuyable even at an exorbitant price—such is the love she offers. Hubbard, pp. 340–41

Taken from The Preacher's Commentary Series Volume 16: Ecclesiastes, Song of Solomon by David A. Hubbard. Copyright © 1991 by Word, Inc. Used by permission of Thomas Nelson. www.thomasnelson.com

Isaiah

Commentaries:
- *The Book of Isaiah: Chapters 1–39*, by John N. Oswalt (1986)
- *The Book of Isaiah: Chapters 40–66*, by John N. Oswalt (1998)
- *The Prophecy of Isaiah*, by J. Alec Motyer (1993)
- *Studies in Isaiah*, by F.C. Jennings (1935)
- *Matthew Henry Commentary* at www.blueletterbible.org (1710)

Isa 5:20–21: *Woe to those who call evil good and good evil, who put darkness for light and light for darkness, who put bitter for sweet and sweet for bitter. Woe to those who are wise in their own eyes and clever in their own sight.*

Here Isaiah continues his denunciation of those who mock God's ways. In order to justify their own behavior they must, in the most sophisticated reasonings possible, demonstrate that their evil behavior is good, their darkness light, their bitterness sweet. ... Only a prior commitment to the revealed wisdom of God (Prov 1:7, 3:7, 9:10) and a commitment to call good good, despite the reasonings of the wise of this world, can make possible genuine long-lasting righteousness both in individuals and in society. The path of those who chart their own course leads inexorably from self-aggrandizement to the ultimate reversal of moral values [cf Judg 21:25]. This is the vineyard gone completely wrong (5:4). The grapes are all bitter and human sophistry cannot make them sweet.Oswalt, p. 165

Oswalt, John N., *The Book of Isaiah: Chapters 1–39*, Copyright © 1986 by William B. Eerdman Publishing, Grand Rapids, MI USA. Part of *New International Commentary on the Old Testament*, Robert L. Hubbard general editor. Reprinted by permission of the publisher.

"Right is right, even if everyone is against it; and wrong is wrong, even if everyone is for it."
William Penn (1644–1718)   Quoted in Ward and Wild

Personal Note: Contemporary commentator Mark Steyn seems to have been referring to this verse when he spoke on a talk show in March 2019: "What these cultural vandals are doing now is making us live in a permanent year zero, where we have no cultural inheritance and we're just bobbing around in the flotsam and jetsam of a hyper present tense." Steyn's colorful analysis seems to be spot on. The beginning of the twenty-first century has witnessed an alarming moral inversion as secular philosophy has asserted itself and forcefully shoved sacred morality into a closet where it must hide.

The warp speed evolution of morality has been breathtaking as what formerly was thought good just a few years ago is now thought evil and vice versa. When you need a guide book to tell you the correct pronoun to use when addressing a person, you know that you are inhabiting a bizzaro world and cannot keep up with the dizzying pace of change. Secular conventional wisdom seems to have superseded God's eternal word, with disastrous consequences as the family disintegrates and marriage and gender are redefined after thousands of years of tradition with no vote being taken.

The prophet here speaks forcefully across the ages as a tendency that began long ago has culminated today in a wholesale overthrow of what was formerly thought good, replacing it with political correctness. Our modern lifestyle has put bitter for sweet and sweet for bitter and has called evil good and good evil, and we are reaping the woes that the prophet proclaimed here. The irony of this situation is that very few seem to recognize the inversion. As the Apostle Paul puts it, we claim to be wise but become fools when we exchange the Word of God for the word of man, when we exchange God's truth for man's lie (Rom 1:22, 25). We must recover the sacred truth.

Isa 6:3: *And they were calling to one another: "Holy, holy, holy is the LORD Almighty; the whole earth is full of his glory."*

וְקָרָא זֶה אֶל־זֶה וְאָמַר קָדוֹשׁ קָדוֹשׁ קָדוֹשׁ יְהוָה צְבָאוֹת מְלֹא כָל־הָאָרֶץ כְּבוֹדוֹ:

Holy Holy Holy

The seraphim were calling to one another; are we to picture them standing each side of the throne and responding to each other in antiphonal song? At any rate, the song is continuous and its theme is the holiness of the Lord and his presence in all its glory in every place. Hebrew uses repetition to express superlatives or to indicate totality. Only here is a threefold repetition found. Holiness is supremely the truth about God, and his holiness is itself so far beyond human thought that a super-superlative has to be invented to express it. Motyer, pp. 76–77

He is the Lord of hosts, of their hosts, of all hosts; and one of his most glorious attributes, his holiness, without which his being the Lord of hosts could not be so much as it is the matter of our joy and praise; for power, without purity to guide it, would be a terror to mankind. None of all the divine attributes is so celebrated in scripture as this is. This bespeaks, [1.] The zeal and fervency of the angels in praising God; they even want words to express themselves, and therefore repeat the same again. [2.] The particular pleasure they take in contemplating the holiness of God; this is a subject they love to dwell upon, to harp upon, and are loth to leave. [3.] The superlative excellency of God's holiness, above that of the purest creatures. He is holy, thrice holy, infinitely holy, originally, perfectly, and eternally so. Matthew Henry Commentary

Isa 6:5: *"Woe to me!" I cried. "I am ruined! For I am a man of unclean lips, and I live among a people of unclean lips, and my eyes have seen the King, the LORD Almighty."*
He who has been pronouncing woes on others in Chapter 5 must now pronounce woe upon himself. If the experience did come at the outset of his ministry, then its force here is that every member of the nation must come to recognize his or her condition before God. …. Here, then, Isaiah recognizes with sickening force that his character is not, any more than his people's, in keeping with God's character. Their lips do not belong to God, else they would continually pour forth praise like the seraphim. Why,

then, are the lips unclean? Because that of which they are an expression, the heart and the will, do not belong to God [Mt 12:34]. That which God possesses is clean, for it is like him. Thus, it is not merely purification of the lips which is necessary. Nor is it mere ritual purification that is needed. In some way, sin and iniquity must be removed if Isaiah and his people are ever to serve God with clean lips [cf Isa 53:9].   Oswalt, p. 182

Oswalt, John N., *The Book of Isaiah: Chapters 1–39*, Copyright © 1986 by William B. Eerdman Publishing, Grand Rapids, MI USA. Reprinted by permission of the publisher.

Isa 9:6: *For unto us a child is born, unto us a son is given* (KJV)
Ultimately God's truth is not merely in the realm of ideas; ultimately it is meant to be incarnated [Jn 1:14, Heb 1:2]. How will God deliver from arrogance, war, oppression, and coercion? By being more warlike, more oppressive, more coercive? Surely the book of Isaiah indicates frequently that God is powerful enough to destroy his enemies in an instant, yet again and again, when the prophet comes to the heart of the means of deliverance, a childlike face peers out at us. God is strong enough to overcome his enemies by becoming vulnerable, transparent, humble—the only hope, in fact, for turning enmity into friendship [Eph 2:14, Rom 12:21]. Oswalt, p. 245

Oswalt, John N., *The Book of Isaiah: Chapters 1–39*, Copyright © 1986 by William B. Eerdman Publishing, Grand Rapids, MI USA. Reprinted by permission of the publisher.

Isa 14:14–15: *I will ascend above the tops of the clouds; I will make myself like the Most High.*
But you are brought down to the grave, to the depths of the pit.
The human problem is that we will not accept God's gifts within the limits imposed by him. *We* wish to be God, dispensing the gifts. Despite the high pretensions, or precisely because of them, the king is plunged into the underworld. Death mocks every person's claim to be God [Acts 12:21–23]. This truth is entirely congruent with the teaching of Genesis 3. The forbidden fruit was proffered to Adam and Eve as being able to make them like God (Gen 3:5). Instead, it brought them to the ultimate proof of their finitude: death (Gen 3:27, cf Job 20:6–7).
Oswalt, p. 323

Oswalt, John N., *The Book of Isaiah: Chapters 1–39*, Copyright © 1986 by William B. Eerdman Publishing, Grand Rapids, MI USA. Reprinted by permission of the publisher.

Personal Note: In order to absorb its full impact, Isaiah 14:4–20 should be read alongside Phil 2:6–11 for a striking contrast. In the Isaiah passage, the arrogant king is brought down to the depths. The movement in vv 13–14 is up, up, up. But then in v 15 it is abruptly down, down, down, an arresting illustration of Prov 16:18. In the Philippians *kenosis* passage, Christ did not consider equality with God something to cling to. He emptied himself and became low, but then was exalted to the highest place. These two stories powerfully illustrate the biblical message that is expounded again and again, from the building of the tower of Babel (Gen 11) to the hurling of Satan into the lake of fire (Rev 20:15): He who exalts himself will be humbled and he who humbles himself will be exalted (Prov 18:12, Mt 23:12, Lk 14:11, 18:14, 2 Cor 12:10).

Isa 29:16: *Can the pot say of the potter, "He knows nothing"?* [cf Rom 9:19–21]
It is the forgetting of God's right as Maker that leads to ethical relativism. After all, if he is but Bergson's *élan vitale* or Tillich's 'ground of all being', then he has only the most generalized will for any behavior and it becomes impossible of overturning anything. There are no explicit standards to overturn. One must do what one feels. On the other hand, the Maker can say, 'that is good, and that is bad,' because he has a known design which he is seeking to work out. Whether or not 'the Force' even knows that I exist, my existence is of no importance to it. The Maker, says Isaiah, *does* know and cares passionately [30:19, Hos 11:8, Zp 3:17]. Those who say he does not know and care confuse the clay with the Potter, and that is the fundamental error or all strictly human philosophies: they cannot admit of a transcendent God. God is either part of the system or he does not exist.

Oswalt, p. 537

Oswalt, John N., *The Book of Isaiah: Chapters 1–39*, Copyright © 1986 by William B. Eerdman Publishing, Grand Rapids, MI USA. Reprinted by permission of the publisher.

Isa 30:10–11: *They say to the seers, "See no more visions!" and to the prophets, "Give us no more visions of what is right! Tell us pleasant things, prophesy illusions. Leave this way, get off this path, and stop confronting us with the Holy One of Israel!"*
People do not openly request to be told what is wrong and illusory. Isaiah is putting their attitudes into words, verbalizing the implications of their actions and reactions. They did not want a supernatural message (10ab), nor a message of moral demand (10cd), but a ministry that left the surface of life unruffled (*pleasant/smooth*), a ministry of trifles (*illusions*). They did not want holiness, in a life that follows *the way ... the path*; and certainly not the holiness of God himself (11cd). *Leave this way* requests the preachers to pioneer a new morality, is bring us unto the practice of novelties. They did not ask that preaching should cease but only that it be innocuous, void of moral imperatives and without the backing of the ultimate moral absolute of the nature of God.　　　　　Motyer, p. 248

Personal Note: Sadly today, many churches, in order to pump up attendance, mold their message to the world's vision of health, wealth and happiness. One prominent minister of this "prosperity gospel" has built a very large church. He preaches his syrupy message week after week, and his congregation eagerly hangs on his every word. He tells them "pleasant things" and in so doing, dilutes the rich message of the Gospel. My wife and I were watching an interview with this minister on a news show and at one point he had trouble quoting John 3:16, which every minister should know by heart. It appeared that he was trying to bend the word of God to fit his prosperity message instead of just proclaiming it plainly. He reminds me of Pastor Brown in Randy Alcorn's excellent novel *Lord Foulgren's Letters*. Ministers who reduce the gospel to a lowest common denominator in order to enlarge their flock may do more harm to the faith than passionate and vitriolic atheists. The prosperity gospel ignores the reality that bad things happen to good people (eg, book of Job) and that good things happen to bad people (eg Ps 73). It puts *my* pleasure and *my* fulfillment at the center instead of submitting to God as the center. It turns the faith into a simplistic caricature rather than the vibrant, realistic faith portrayed in the pages of the Bible.

Isa 30:21: *Whether you turn to the right or to the left, your ears will hear a voice behind you, saying, "This is the way; walk in it."*
Instead of a stubborn animal which has to be dragged [Ps 32:9] or beaten into going in the proper direction [Num 22:32], here is a person whose teacher is just at his shoulder [Ps 32:8, 73:24, Isa 28:26, 29, 119:102–104] and little more than a word of guidance from time to time is necessary for him to stay on the right path [Ps 119:105]. This is the ideal of the spirit filled life [Rom 8:5], where the contact between us and him is so intimate that only a whisper [Job 4:12, 1 Kings 19:12] is sufficient to move us in his way (Gal 5:16–25). Oswalt, p. 560
Oswalt, John N., *The Book of Isaiah: Chapters 1–39*, Copyright © 1986 by William B. Eerdman Publishing, Grand Rapids, MI USA. Reprinted by permission of the publisher.

Isa 35:8: *And a highway will be there; it will be called the Way of Holiness. The unclean will not journey on it*
How lovely the road to Zion! It is a <u>high</u> way: a path raised above the surrounding land on either side, and keeping the feet of its wayfarers from mud and defilement. Along that road none unclean can walk; it has no attraction for them [Mt 7:13–14]; it is for those who have been themselves sanctified, and for them alone [Rev 21:27]. They may be very ignorant and simple; but the road is so clearly defined [Jer 6:16]: it is such a high way, so far above low self-seeking paths, that even the simple will have no need to stray from it. Nor can any beast of prey invade it and terrify its travelers; absolute security characterizes it. Why is that? Because these passengers Zionward have been bought at great price [1 Cor 6:12], and are well guarded by Him [Jn 10:7–10] who has thus purchased them.   Jennings, p. 417

Isa 35:10: *and the ransomed of the LORD will return. They will enter Zion with singing;*
everlasting joy will crown their heads. Gladness and joy will overtake them, and sorrow and sighing will flee away.
At the end of the Holy Way is Zion, the Holy City [Ps 84:7, 100:4, Heb 11:10]. The result of supernatural protection and provision, but most of all, of redemption, is a gladness that will drive away all sadness forever [Rev 21:1–4, Isa 25:6–8]. This is the apex of the eschatological vision: a day when the people of God can be set free from their own sins and the sins of others

[Isa 6:5–7], when they can come home to their God and be fully restored to his image [1 Cor 15:49], when a lifelong struggle to avoid grief and pain will be ended in their being overwhelmed with gladness and joy [Ps 100:2]. This is the hope of the biblical faith.   Oswalt, p. 626

Oswalt, John N., *The Book of Isaiah: Chapters 1–39*, Copyright © 1986 by William B. Eerdman Publishing, Grand Rapids, MI USA. Reprinted by permission of the publisher.

Personal Note: When I taught this chapter in Sunday School, the phrase which the class latched on to was "gladness and joy will overtake them." All too often, we try to chase after the happiness offered by the world (cf Oswalt on 35:1–2). Commercials and other media entice us to grab hold of the goodies. But even after we have received the objects of our pursuit, we are not satisfied; we still feel empty (Eccl 1:7). Like the dog that finally catches the car, we say "so what do I do with this?" Here in Isaiah, however, instead of *us* pursuing joy, *it* pursues *us*! And when it catches us, "everlasting joy" crowns our heads, not the fleeting pleasure that accompanies earth's tinsel attractions. This verse is repeated in 51:11, doubly emphasizing its importance (see also Ps 23:6). The key to peace, joy, and contentment is not in our attempts to manufacture it for ourselves (Phil 4:12–13). The key is to travel on the holy highway through the narrow doorway (Mt 7:13–14). When we pursue God's way, our way becomes smooth, protected, and sorrow-free [Isa 26:7], and we experience boundless bliss as joy overtakes us on the road.

"Happiness is as a butterfly which, when pursued, is always beyond our grasp, but which if you will sit down quietly, may alight upon you."
                                         Nathaniel Hawthorne (1804–1864)

Hymn: *Joyful, Joyful, We Adore Thee* (1907), Text: Henry Van Dyke, Music: Ludwig van Beethoven

Joyful, joyful, we adore thee,	[Phil 4:4, Hab 3:18]
God of glory, Lord of love;	[2 Chr 7:3]
Hearts unfold like flowers before thee, opening to the sun above.	[Ps 9:1, 139:23]
Melt the clouds of sin and sadness;	[Isa 44:22–23]

Drive the dark of doubt away.	[Mk 9:24]
Giver of immortal gladness, fill us with the light of day!	[Isa 35:10, Lk 11:36]

All thy works with joy surround thee,	[Prov 8:30–31]
Earth and heaven reflect thy rays,	[Hab 3:4, Rev 21:23]
Stars and angels sing around thee, center of unbroken praise.	[Job 38:7, Rev 5:6a, 4:8b]
Field and forest, vale and mountain,	[Isa 55:12]
Flowery meadow, flashing sea,	[Ps 148:9, 7]
Chanting bird and flowing fountain, call us to rejoice in thee.	[Ps 104:12, Ps 36:8–9]

Thou art giving and forgiving,	[1 Chr 29:14, Ps 103:10]
Ever blessing, ever blest,	[Gen 1:22, Ps 84:4]
Well-spring of the joy of living, ocean depth of happy rest!	[Ps 43:4, Mt 11:28]
Thou our Father, Christ our brother,	[John 17:24]
All who live in love are thine;	[John 13:35]
Teach us how to love each other, lift us to the joy divine.	[Ps 119:64, Ps 86:4]

Mortals, join the mighty chorus	[Ps 103:22]
Which the morning stars began;	[Ps 148:3]
Love divine is reigning o'er us, binding all within its span.	[Ps 108:4, 1 Pet 4:8]
Ever singing, march we onward,	[Isa 35:10]
Victors in the midst of strife;	[Ps 60:12]
Joyful music leads us sunward, in the triumph song of life.	[Ps 43:3, 2 Cor 2:14]

Isa 40:9: *O Zion, that bringest good tidings, get thee up into the high mountain; O Jerusalem, that bringest good tidings, lift up thy voice with strength; lift it up, be not afraid; say unto the cities of Judah, Behold your God!* [KJV]

The Lord does not save his people with programs sent from afar. Neither does he save them with theological conceptions coolly administered from on high. He comes! (v 10) This was the glad tidings then and is still the good news today.   Oswalt, p. 54

Oswalt, John N., *The Book of Isaiah: Chapters 40–66*, Copyright © 1998 by William B. Eerdman Publishing, Grand Rapids, MI USA. Part of *New International Commentary on the Old Testament*, Robert L. Hubbard general editor. Reprinted by permission of the publisher.

Isa 40:28 *Do you not know? Have you not heard? The LORD is the everlasting God, the Creator of the ends of the earth. He will not grow tired or weary, and his understanding no one can fathom.*

The solution to their problem is to relearn what they already know and to open their ears to what they have been told. The people of God already possess the truth, and it has come to them from outside. Their God is such (eternal, Creator, untiring) that they need never doubt his capacity; he is also such (possessing unfathomable wisdom) that they must never expect to understand all his ways. As a God of eternity, he does not change; as Creator he has all the glories, attributes, and powers mentioned in vv 12–16; as not growing tired or weary he never has to abandon his purposes as unrealizable or postpone them while he rests. Equally, however, because he works on an everlasting worldwide and ceaseless level, we cannot *fathom his understanding*. His ways belong to eternity, we to time; his vision is for the world, we are local; his ceaselessness keeps him always ahead of the point we have reached.

Motyer, p. 307

Isa 43:1–2: *Fear not, for I have redeemed you; I have summoned you by name; you are mine. When you pass through the waters, I will be with you; and when you pass through the rivers, they will not sweep over you. When you walk through the fire, you will not be burned; the flames will not set you ablaze.* [cf Ps 18:16, 66:12, Dan 3:27, Zc 10:11]

How unspeakably precious are these gracious words! We too have some knowledge of what it means to pass through deep waters, so swift and deep that oftentimes faith finds no footing and has to float on these promises. Precious beyond all thought, again I say, is this trinity of tender words! First "created"—we certainly did not have anything to do with that—then "redeemed"—and that too was his work entirely—and then, old enough to hear Him speak, we hear Him telling us that we belong to Him. He certainly will take care of His own property.

Jennings, p. 504

"We cannot comprehend what an inexhaustible depth this word *gealtika* גְּאַלְתִּיךָ (*I have redeemed thee*) contains within itself...Redemption, redemption, redemption, that should be our creed, our theology, our distinctive character, our daily song of praise, our secret wisdom, our pearl of great price, our invaluable jewel, our one and all." Carl Rudolph Reichel (1718–1794)

Isa 44:9: *All who make idols are nothing, and the things they treasure are worthless.*
The beings on which they lavish their time and attention cannot do anything for them, and as a result their laboriously built-up picture of the universe is a complete fiction. They have created a lie and now they are a part of that lie.   Oswalt, p. 176

Oswalt, John N., *The Book of Isaiah: Chapters 40–66*, Copyright © 1998 by William B. Eerdman Publishing, Grand Rapids, MI USA. Reprinted by permission of the publisher

Personal Note: As I read Oswalt's words, I can't help but think of the man-made pantheon called "science" which assumes it can explain everything. Yes, science is useful and gives us many things. Yes, we should pursue it (as an engineer, I use its principles in my work). But the scientific method can only take us so far. There may be realities which are beyond our ability to observe and measure (cf Jonah 2:1). When science attempts to explain things that it cannot prove (for example, the origins of the universe and evolution) it needs to lose some of its dogmatic insistence and admit that some of the so-called "facts" are really only theories. The circumstantial evidence (which is often fragmentary at best) would be thrown out of court.

Personal Note 2: Isaiah keeps aiming his hammer blows at idolatry in verse after verse. Why this relentless assault? We in our 21st century world may look on all this as a somewhat quaint notion, since we, in our enlightened society would never bow down to figurines. But is that really the case? Pastor John Wood of Cedar Springs Church has repeatedly pointed to the spectacle of sports stadiums. There the people assume all the postures of worship. They sing hymns ("fight songs"). They wave their hands. They shout for joy for touchdowns. What is all this ecstasy for? A little object of rubber that is carried down a field? This is but one example of modern idolatry, which places things other than God in the place which rightfully belongs to him. Others would include rock concerts and celebrity worship, the quest for money and power at all cost, the internet, television, and anything else that dominates our lives (cf Jer 10:14–15).

But lest religious people think they are immune from idolatry, one only need look at the great cathedrals of the world to see that humanity has still not learned the lesson Isaiah preached 27 centuries ago. The Bible's 2nd commandment (Ex 20:4–6) forbids making images of God, but the ceiling of the Sistine Chapel in Rome is a glaring defiance of that commandment. Even evangelical churches can fall prey to idolatry, worshiping their pastors, or music directors, or the ecstatic emotions they experience. The Lord wants his worship to be focused on him, not on our rituals (Isa 1:11–17, Amos 5:23). This message against idolatry needs to be pounded home until we get the message.

Isaiah 52:13–53:12: *The Final Servant Song*

We are now standing on the threshold of the Holy of Holies of our book, and we do well to fear lest a carnal touch should make its defiling mark on this sanctuary, the walls of which are surely whiter than any fuller on earth could whiten them [Mk 9:3, KJV]. Is there not at least one of my readers who will join me in supplication that the Spirit, whose holiness alone accords with that of scripture, will guard us from error, lead us into truth, and so take the things of Christ and show them to us, so as to attract our wandering hearts to Him, and bind them forever? Amen.

Jennings, p. 609

Personal Note: This section of Isaiah has attracted more scholarly attention than perhaps any other passage of scripture. One of the most controversial issues is the identity of the Servant, and much ink has been spilt on just that one topic. I don't pretend to be familiar with even a tiny fraction of the exposition of this topic. Many Jewish scholars assert that the Servant sometimes applies to Israel (e.g. 49:3) and could sometimes even refer to a prophet or king Hezekiah. Oswalt summarizes the controversy as follows: "If so much scholarly effort has produced so little agreement, there must be something about the text itself that resists overneat conclusions" (p. 377). While this may be true by and large, the text does plainly say some things. A strong case can be made (and is in the literature) that the

Servant's identity is the Messiah and that Jesus Christ fulfilled all of these messianic passages in Isaiah.

I attended a bible study led by a messianic Jew named Neil Silverberg (a Jew who later became a Christian minister, *www.ezraproject.org*). He had an amusing story about his orthodox Jewish father. One day he said that he was going to read a passage of Scripture. His father cautioned him "now you know, son, that I only want to hear from the front of the book (ie, the *Tenach*, or Old Testament). Neil read Isaiah 53, and his father exasperatedly said "Neil, *I told you* I only wanted to hear from the front of the book." Neil replied, "But, Dad, this *is* from the front of the book." Isaiah 53 sounds like it could have been written by the Apostle Paul, but it was written 700 years before Paul. Its unique message resonates through the Christian heart more strongly than perhaps any other Old Testament passage (with the *possible* exception of Psalm 22). These verses command our attention and our reverence. For *we* are in them prominently.

Structure:

Kidner sees a symmetrical structure with 5 sets of 3 verses each with God (*I*) and man (*we, us*) sharing in the story:

- Exaltation (52:13–15)   My, I
- Rejection (53:1–3)   We, us
- Atoning significance (53:4–6) We, us, our
- Rejection (53:7–9)   He, My
- Exaltation (53:10–12)   He, I

One of the commentators I read at the time of my study in the year 2000 noted that there were many key words which were repeated at strategic times during these verses. These key words form a golden chain that guides us through the passage. To test this, I made a list of all of the words in these verses and arranged them in order of the *Strong's* number (the unique identifier of each Hebrew Word in the Bible). Being an engineer, I then loaded them into a spreadsheet and sorted them and came up with a list of the recurring words (below). The intricate structure is breathtaking. This poetry was not just thrown together, but has all the marks of a master builder. For example, we read in verse 3 that the Servant was a *man of sorrows*. Then in verse 4 we read the reason for that: he *carried our sorrows*.

52:13: my **servant** will act wisely	53:11: by his knowledge my righteous **servant** will justify many.
52:14: **many** who were appalled at him	53:11 my righteous servant will justify **many**
52:14: he will sprinkle **many** nations	
52:14: his **appearance** was so disfigured	53:12: he bore the sin of **many**.
	53:2: nothing in his **appearance** that we should desire him
52:14: disfigured beyond that of any **man**.	
	53:12: rejected by **men**, a **man** of sorrows.
	53:3: like one from whom **men** hide their faces
	53:7: he did not open his **mouth**…he did not open his **mouth**
52:15: kings will shut their **mouths**	
	53:9: nor was there any deceit in his **mouth**
52:15: they **will see**	53:10: he **will see** his offspring
	53:11: he **will see** the light of life
	53:10: yet it was **the LORD's** will to crush him
53:1: the arm of **the LORD**	
53:6: **the LORD** laid on him the iniquity of us all.	
	53:10 and the will of **the LORD** will prosper in his hand
53:2: he grew up **before** him like a tender shoot	
	53:7: as a sheep **before** her shearers is silent
53:3: he was **despised** and rejected	53:3: he was **despised** and we esteemed him not
	53:4: he took up our infirmities and carried our **sorrows**.
53:3: a man of **sorrows**	
	53:4: he took up our **infirmities** and carried our sorrows.
53:3: familiar with **suffering**	
53:3: we **esteemed** him not	53:4: yet we **considered** him stricken
53:4: **carried** our sorrows	53:12: for he **bore** the sin of many
	53:8: for the transgression of my people he was **stricken**
53:4: **stricken** by God	
53:4: smitten by him and **afflicted**	53:7: he was oppressed and **afflicted**
53:5: he was pierced for our **transgressions**	53:8: for the **transgression** of my people he was stricken
53:12: numbered with the **transgressors**	53:12: made intercession for the **transgressors**
53:5: **crushed** for our iniquities	53:10: yet it was the Lord's will to **crush** him

53:5: crushed for our **iniquities**	53:6: the Lord laid on him the **iniquity** of us all.
53:6: **We all**, like sheep have gone astray	53:6: the Lord laid on him the iniquity of **us all**.
53:6: We all, like **sheep** have gone astray	
53:6: the Lord **laid on** him the iniquity of us all.	53:7: as a **sheep** before her shearers is silent
	53:12: **made intercession** for the transgressors
53:9: with the rich in his **death**	53:12: he poured out his life unto **death**.
53:10: the Lord makes **his life** a guilt offering	53:11: after the suffering of **his soul** he will see

Isa 53:2: *He grew up before him like a tender shoot, and like a root out of dry ground. He had no beauty or majesty to attract us to him, nothing in his appearance that we should desire him.*

Deliverers are dominating, forceful, attractive people, who by their personal magnetism draw people to themselves and convince people what to do. This man does not fit that picture at all. We are not drawn to him and his plans. Rather, we are repulsed by him and them (v 3). Instead of bursting on the scene like a mighty oak or a fruit tree in full bloom, he appears as a sprout (11:1) or "sucker", the normally unwanted shoot that springs up from an exposed root of a tree [Ezek 17:24]. It is a matter of seconds for the gardener to snip it off. ... The Christian thinks inevitably of Jesus Christ, a baby born in the back-stable of a village inn. This would shake the Roman empire? A man quietly coming to the great preacher of the day and asking to be baptized (Mt 3:15). This is the advent of the Savior of the world? No, this is not what we think the arm of the Lord (52:10) should look like. We were expecting a costumed drum-major to lead our triumphal parade. Our eyes are caught and satisfied by superficial splendor [2 Sam 15:6]. This man, says, Isaiah, will have none of that. As a result, our eyes flicker across him in a crowd and we do not even see him. His splendor is not on the surface, and those who have no inclination to look beyond the surface will never see him. Thus the revelation of the arm of the Lord that will deliver the Lord's people is met with shock, astonishment, distaste, dismissal, and avoidance. Such a one as this can hardly be the one who can set us free from the most pervasive of all human bondages: sin, and all its consequences [Jn 8:34–36, Rom 6:14]. To a world blinded by selfishness and power, he does not even merit a second thought.   Oswalt, p. 382,383,384

Oswalt, John N., *The Book of Isaiah: Chapters 40–66*, Copyright © 1998 by William B. Eerdman Publishing, Grand Rapids, MI USA. Reprinted by permission of the publisher

Isa 53:5: *But he was pierced for our transgressions, he was crushed for our iniquities; the punishment that brought us peace was upon him, and by his wounds we are healed.*

How clear, as well as deeply affecting, are the rays of sanctuary light that these words throw on those sufferings that were hidden from every human eye by the three hours of darkness at Calvary. So clear that it is difficult to realize that the words were written more than seven hundred years before the fulfillment. In verse 5, the light of God breaks in on those sufferings and reveals that *ours* was the transgression, *His* the stroke for it; *Ours* was the iniquity, *His* the wound for it; *Ours* was the sin, *His* the death, its wages and due [Rom 6:23]. But here we must let our words be few, and even pause in a silence more expressive than speech, for behind the stroke, the wound, the death, we must apprehend something of the LOVE that was so usward [John 3:16].   Jennings, p. 618

Isa 53:6: *We all, like sheep, have gone astray, each of us has turned to his own way; and the LORD has laid on him the iniquity of us all.*

[Jer 50:6, Ps 119:176]

The picture of straying sheep summarizes all our inadequacy and errancy of nature—our danger too, for the Bible stresses the peril of sheep without a shepherd. The imagery of laying iniquity on summarizes all Isaiah has been teaching about the Servant's substitutionary death. … *We all* and *each* expresses both common culpability and individual responsibility. We cannot blame a 'herd instinct' even though we are all alike implicated. Motyer, p. 431

Isa 53:12: *Therefore I will give him a portion among the great, and he will divide the spoils with the strong, because he poured out his life unto death, and was numbered with the transgressors. For he bore the sin of many, and made intercession for the transgressors.*

In this context, *therefore* brings to mind Phil 2:9. In faithfulness the Servant has descended to the lowest depths. He has fulfilled his Father's will to the last degree [Jn 15:10, Mk 14:36]. Because of that faithful obedience, God will exalt him to the highest heights (52:13). If one had any doubt about how to read the poem, this last verse should dispel it.... The Servant will be exalted to the highest heavens not because he was humiliated (though he was), not because he suffered unjustly (though he did), not because he did it voluntarily (though he did), but because it was all in order to carry the sin of the world away to permit God's children to come home to him [Lk 15:20]. He is exalted because he fulfilled God's purpose for his ministry; and that purpose was redemption [43:1]. Oswalt, p. 405, 407

Oswalt, John N., *The Book of Isaiah: Chapters 40–66*, Copyright © 1998 by William B. Eerdman Publishing, Grand Rapids, MI USA. Reprinted by permission of the publisher

Isa 55:1–2: *Come, all you who are thirsty, come to the waters; and you who have no money,*
come, buy and eat! Come, buy wine and milk without money and without cost. Why spend money on what is not bread, and your labor on what does not satisfy? Listen, listen to me, and eat what is good, and your soul will delight in the richest of fare. [cf Rev 22:17]

Personal Note: We come now to one of my favorite chapters in all of Scripture, and I can't resist adding my thoughts to those of the professional bible scholars. Nearly every verse in Ch 55 is a "fridge quote" (one that is so good, you want to put it on your refrigerator with a magnet).

This chapter has a system of key words that act like a chain to take the reader through the text and weave the words into a rich texture of meaning (similar to Ch 53). A few examples:

55:1: Waters	55:10: watering the earth
55:1: no money	55:2: without money
55:2: Your soul	55:3: your soul
55:2: listen	55:3: give ear
55:7: ways…thoughts	55:8: thoughts…ways
55:2: bread	55:10: bread
55:9: heavens…earth	55:10: heaven…earth

The opening verses are a gracious invitation to get off the treadmill of life where unceasing effort never really gets us to any destination [John 6:27], and to get on to the highway [Isa 35:8] which leads to a celestial city and everlasting joy. The four-fold *come* [cf Rev 22:17] is emphatic as is the doublet *listen, listen*. If we would but listen to the invitation and come at the Lord's call, we would partake of a rich feast (Isa 25:6–8) and would see that life is not a treadmill going nowhere [Hg 1:6], but a fascinating highway taking us to a glorious destination [2 Cor 5:1, Heb 11:10, Rev 21:2].

Isa 55:8–9: *"For my thoughts are not your thoughts, neither are your ways my ways,"*
declares the LORD. *"As the heavens are higher than the earth, so are my ways higher than your ways and my thoughts than your thoughts."*

"We live in the gaslight of our earthly reason instead of the sunlight of our father's glory."
Richard Meaux Benson (1824–1915)   Quoted in Ward and Wild

Personal Note: The contrast between God and everything else (including his people) is a key concept for Isaiah. Many verses describe the transcendence, holiness, and love of God contrasted with man's petty focus on the small picture (Eccl 1:9) and his failure to grasp the significance of God's free gift of salvation. The prophet's central message is well summarized in 55:8–9, and many other rich verses also speak of God's unfathomable ways and thoughts. Some examples: 1 Sam 16:7, Job 11:7, Job 38:4–7, Psalm 139:6, Prov 3:5–7, 19–20, 16:1–4, 21:2, Isa 40:14, 28, Mark 10:27, Rom 11:33–36, 1 Cor 4:5, Eph 3:17–19. These verses provide an answer to man's frustrating question of how a holy and loving God could permit such chaos and violence as we see around us. If man would but tap God's wisdom instead of insisting on his own way (53:6), violence and chaos would cease and be replaced by a glorious new heavens and a new earth. The Lord could, if he wished, be a puppeteer, pulling the strings and making man act in a rational loving way. But his love gives man freedom to do both good and evil. This paradox of God's holiness and love, of his wanting humans to obey him but not compelling them to do so, is at the core of the Christian faith. We cannot understand it at present (our thoughts are not his), and though we see through the glass darkly at the moment (1 Cor 13:12), one day we will comprehend it with astonishing clarity.

Also note the artistic elements of these verses, including the contrast of vs. 8 with previous verse, underlined poetically by an intricate chiastic structure with three levels:

ways…thoughts (vs. 7)	*thoughts…ways* (vs. 8)
my thoughts, *your* thoughts	*your* ways, *my* ways (vs 8)
thoughts…ways (vs. 8)	*ways…thoughts* (vs. 9)

Isa 55:10–11: *As the rain and the snow come down from heaven, and do not return to it without watering the earth and making it bud and flourish, so that it yields seed for the sower and bread for the eater, so is my word that goes out from my mouth: It will not return to me empty, but will accomplish what I desire and achieve the purpose for which I sent it.*   [cf Deut 32:2, Ps 147:15]
Let us consider the rain that is called to witness here. It descends from heaven which is, may we say, its source: so the word that God speaks comes from Him—he is its source. As the rain falls on the thirsty earth, so the word falls on man's dry, thirsty spirit [Deut 32:1–2]. The rain falls indifferently on the mountains and the valleys, but the hard, lofty mountain casts it off, and the valleys receive and profit by it [Heb 6:7]. So the word of God is for all; but lofty pride casts it off, and lowly penitence takes it in. So where the Word is received, the fruit of love, joy, and peace abounds [55:12–13, Deut 32:47].   Jennings, p. 650

Isa 60:9: *bringing your sons from afar, with their silver and gold, to the honor of the LORD your God, the Holy One of Israel, for he has endowed you with splendor.*
When the nations of the earth see the God of the Bible as he really is, no other being that may be called 'god' is left with any divine standing at all. This is what Isaiah teaches, this is what Judaism teaches, and this is what Christianity teaches. Thus it is a double tragedy when believers by their words or their actions make God appear less than all that he is, the *Holy One of Israel*. The phrase serves to express that unique combination of

transcendence with immanence that characterizes the God of the Bible. In his moral perfection [Dt 32:4, Job 34:12], no creature can exist alongside him [Rom 3:23]; in his awesome power [Ps 147:5], no one can contend with him [14:27]; in his sole creatorship, he has no rival [Job 4:17]; in his self-giving to the people of the earth, he is unmatched [30:18]; in the purity of his love, there is nothing else to judge by [Ps 36:5]. In a hundred ways the book has explored the wonder of the Person to whom this phrase applies. Now the *Holy One* who is the final judge is displayed to the nations as the God *of Israel*, who has given himself away to his people in love [John 3:16]. Is it any wonder that they come flying from earth's remotest bounds to throw themselves at his feet? [Rev 21:24]   Oswalt, p. 543

Oswalt, John N., *The Book of Isaiah: Chapters 40–66*, Copyright © 1998 by William B. Eerdman Publishing, Grand Rapids, MI USA. Reprinted by permission of the publisher

Isa 66:22–23: *"As the new heavens and the new earth that I make will endure before me," declares the LORD, "so will your name and descendants endure. From one New Moon to another and from one Sabbath to another, all mankind will come and bow down before me," says the LORD.*

No longer is God behind a great veil, accessible only to a small coterie of the elite [Mk 15:38, Heb 6:19, 10:20]. Now all flesh can revel in the sight of his face with no trace of a frown, but wreathed only in smiles of joy, a face that once even to glance at was certain death, but that now is the source of life itself. This is the goal for which Adam and Even were placed in the garden; this is why God met Abraham in Ur of the Chaldeans; this is why he spoke to Moses from the burning bush; this is why the Servant / Messiah, Jesus Christ, came to live and die and rise again: so that all flesh could hear him speak his good news to the afflicted, the captive, and the broken hearted (61:1), so that all flesh could worship the one true God (40:5)   Oswalt, p. 692

Oswalt, John N., *The Book of Isaiah: Chapters 40–66*, Copyright © 1998 by William B. Eerdman Publishing, Grand Rapids, MI USA. Reprinted by permission of the publisher

Scripture Commentary Sampler

Personal Note: Summary of Isaiah
December 2000

[After our Sunday School class concluded its year long study of Isaiah in the year 2000, I gathered my notes together and wrote my own mini-commentary in the form of an introduction to Isaiah. I reproduce portions of that introduction here. Again, I must emphasize that I am not a seminary-trained biblical scholar, but a layman engineer. Nevertheless, this book has been special to me (I was one of the discussion leaders on this book in 3 different churches over about a 10 year period), so I share my thoughts in the *Sampler*.]

The book of Isaiah is breathtaking in its scope, grandeur, and importance in the Biblical canon. The book abounds in soaring spiritual insight and stirring declarations of the promises of God and his trustworthiness. It is sometimes called the "5th Gospel" since the themes of grace, redemption, and salvation are so prominent. No section of scripture has attracted more scholarly attention (or heated discussion) than Isaiah chapters 40–55. Isaiah is quoted in the New Testament more than all the other prophets put together (mentioned by name 22 times in the NT), and the apostle Paul quotes or alludes to Isaiah eighty times. Many famous NT verses are quotes from Isaiah or strong references to it (examples: Eph 4:30, Eph 6:14, Phil 2:10, Rom 10:15, Rev 21:1, 21:23).

Isaiah also has many rich ties to other books of Scripture. The study notes presented in the Sunday School class referred to nearly every book in the Bible because Isaiah ties to nearly every other book. It has numerous references to the early chapters of Genesis (for example, the frequent use of the Hebrew tohu, formless and void, used in Gen 1:2, in 44:9 and 10 other times, more than any other book). The Exodus also figures prominently in this book (eg: 51:9–11), as do other books of Torah. It appears that Isaiah was intimately familiar with the Psalms. Direct quotes include 12:4 which quotes Psalm 105:1, 57:16 which quotes Psalm 103:9, 42:10 which quotes Psalm 96:1 and other verses have strong references to the Psalms (example: oil of gladness in 61:3 referring to Ps 45:7–8, 66:2 referring to Ps 51:16–17). Isaiah both looks back to Torah and Psalms and forward to the later prophets and the New Testament. The book appears to be a central terminus (along with the Psalms), with all roads in scripture leading to and from it.

Among the prophets, Isaiah is unmatched for the specificity of his predictions and the accuracy of their fulfillments. Some of his predictions were fulfilled in his lifetime (the failure of the siege of Jerusalem by Sennacharib of Assyria, the healing of king Hezekiah), while some were fulfilled long after (the exile to Babylon, King Cyrus permitting the exiles to return to Israel, the suffering Servant / Messiah prophecies). The Cyrus prediction in Chapter 45 is so remarkable that many scholars have theorized a second author (called Deutero-Isaiah) who wrote chapters 40–66 after the Babylonian exile. From the little I've studied this issue, I believe a compelling case has been made for Isianic authorship.

Isaiah stands at the pinnacle of Hebrew poetry, rivaling the Psalms in its mastery of imagery and other poetic devices. The book uses 2,186 different words compared to 2,170 in Psalms, 1,535 in Ezekiel and 1,635 in Jeremiah. Examples of intricate poetic devices abound, including chiasmus (abba structure) that sometimes goes to three levels (e.g., 55:7–9), inclusio (use of either the same word or opposite words to bracket a section (e.g., 26:2: Open the gates with 26:20: shut the doors). The prophet also often uses doublets for emphasis (e.g., 40:1: comfort, comfort), delights in dramatic contrasts (e.g., 50:10–11) and uses key words in different contexts in adjacent verses. The key word technique perhaps reaches its zenith in 52:13–53:12 where the words form a chain that links the whole passage together (e.g., 53:3: a man of sorrows, 53:4: carried our sorrows).

Isaiah is a bit difficult for the modern reader to grasp. The prophet appears to flit from topic to topic without any apparent coherent plan. But most readers look at Isaiah up close and study it in bite size pieces, a few verses or chapters at a time. Like an impressionist painting that looks disorganized up close but splendid when viewed from a distance, the book of Isaiah strikes the reader with its full significance only when seen as a whole. The prophet masterfully weaves strands of salvation, redemption, judgment and hope, and the reliability on the sovereign Lord and in the end presents a magnificent tapestry with profound insight into the nature of God and his plan for mankind. As I step back and view the book from the vantage point of a yearlong study, some patterns emerge and coalesce into a profound and rich message, particularly when viewed against the backdrop of scripture as a whole. Like a precious jewel, the book of Isaiah can be examined from a variety of angles with each sparkling facet revealing another fascinating glimpse of the character of God and his relationship to his people.

Major Themes

The contrast between God and everything else (including his people) is a key concept for Isaiah. Many verses describe the transcendence, holiness, and love of God contrasted with man's petty focus on the small picture and his failure to grasp the significance of God's free gift of salvation. The prophet's central message is well summarized in 55:8–9:

"For my thoughts are not your thoughts, neither are your ways my ways" declares the LORD. "As the heavens are higher than the earth, so are my ways higher than your ways and my thoughts than your thoughts."

The verses that immediately precede 55:8 show the human flip side of this equation. Man is exhorted to forsake his ways and thoughts and replace them with the infinitely superior ways and thoughts of God through obedience to his Word that is absolutely certain (55:10–11). We were made in God's image, but that image has become a caricature since the fall. God graciously offers to teach us his ways and thoughts (50:4, 48:17, 54:13, Ps 32:8–9, Ps 119:102–103), resulting in peace like a river (48:17–18). Our problem is a failure to listen (if only you had paid attention, 48:18).

As stated previously, Isaiah's name means "the Lord is salvation" and the book that bears his name reflects this fervent belief. The word salvation is used twenty-seven times, more than any other book except the Psalms. The description of God as a redeemer is also prominent in Isaiah. Although the word redeem appears more than a hundred times in the OT, redeemer appears only thirteen times, ten of which are in Isaiah (others include Job 19:25 and Psalm 19:14). Carl Rudolph Reichel in his book on Isaiah in the 1750's sums it up beautifully as he comments on 43:1:

We cannot comprehend what an inexhaustible depth this word gealtika (I have redeemed thee) contains within itself…Redemption, redemption, redemption, that should be our creed, our theology, our distinctive character, our daily song of praise, our secret wisdom, our pearl of great price, our invaluable jewel, our one and all. (Quoted in Young, Vol 3, p. 140).

Moreover, Isaiah abounds in references to divine compassion and grace (1:18, 6:7, 12:1, 30:18, 33:24, 43:25,. 44:22, 51:22, 53:5, 53:11, 55:7, 57:16, 65:16). These references are too abundant and emphatic to be mere aberrations from Isaiah's central message. The concepts of redemption, salvation, and grace are perhaps as prominent in Isaiah as they are in Paul's letter to the Romans. The people of 8th Century BC Judah might well have been able to sing Amazing Grace with as much conviction as modern Christians.

An examination of key words in Isaiah shows a striking confluence of words that imply an invitation. The second most abundant (after Lord) key word is see (or eyes, look) which occurs over 140 times. The next most abundant key word is come (nearly a hundred times), and the words for listen occur over eighty times. The prophet says, "Look at this. Listen up. The Lord is inviting you to partake of the compassion and salvation he longs to shower on you." This thought is beautifully encapsulated in 55:1–3 with its five-fold come.

Isaiah often condemns man's use of ritual and cult that are devoid of heart-felt love and worship of God. His book begins with an extended passage on this topic (e.g., 1:12–13). Man thinks that going through forms and rituals can please God. These rituals often are attempts to manipulate God instead of worshiping him, but the Lord sees through these transparent attempts (29:13): The Lord says: "These people come near to me with their mouth and honor me with their lips, but their hearts are far from me. Their worship of me is made up only of rules taught by men." Christ quoted this verse (Mk 7:6) to characterize the legalistic approach of the Pharisees who thought they could curry favor with God by accumulating painstaking observances of the letter of the more than six hundred rules expounded in the Torah. Even today, many think that by going to Church, singing hymns, and parading their adherence to man-made rules and restrictions they can please God. But such form and ritual are smoke in the Lord's nostrils (65:5). The Lord esteems the humble (66:2), not the proud who say "Keep away; don't come near me, for I am too sacred for you!" (65:5). We must realize that "all our righteous acts are as filthy rags" (64:6).

The theme of choices also occurs often in this book. The words choose, chose, and chosen appear twenty-five times. The Lord has chosen Israel (e.g., 45:4) but man also must choose between his own ways and thoughts and those of the Lord. Much hinges on man's choice. Although the Lord repeatedly reaches out to his people (30:18–21, 44:22, 65:1–2) and invites them to a sumptuous banquet (55:1–3, 25:6), man often does not listen (48:18, 66:4) and even spurns the invitation (66:3). The choice is between blessings and curses much like Deut 28. Those who serve God will receive glorious blessings and joy (12:1–3, 35:10, 42:11, 44:23, 52:9, 54:11–15, 55:12–13, 57:18–19, 58:14, 60:4–6, 61:1–3, 62:1–4, 63:7–9, 65:9–10, 66:11–12). But (ominously), those who reject the Lord's grace and salvation will reap what they have sown (2:12, 5:5–7, 9:14, 10:3–4, 14:15, 24:1–3, 30:12–14, 41:11–12, 42:24–25, 45:24, 47:10–11, 48:22, 50:11, 57:20–21, 59:7–8, 61:2, 63:3–4, 65:12–13, 66:6, 66:15, 66:24).

Conclusion

Though long and complex, the Book of Isaiah is a rich and powerful text and is a crucial cornerstone in God's Word. The prophet gives us an enlightening glimpse into the divine character (e.g., Chapter 40) and presents a persuasive case that the Lord will be a refuge in life's storms (33:5–6, 43:2) and can be trusted to keep his promises (40:8, 55:10–11). In the beginning of Isaiah's ministry, we are taken into the very throne room of the Lord (6:1–3) where we see that though God is thrice holy (6:3) he nonetheless extends grace (6:7). Though the Lord is high and lofty, he also lives with the lowly and contrite (57:15, 66:1–2), blending awesome majesty with gracious condescension. Man's problem is his constant lack of trust (49:14) and lack of understanding of God's ways and thoughts (55:8–9). If man would only pay attention (48:18), he would taste the unshakable covenant of peace (54:10) the Lord offers. But man continues to trust his own ways and thoughts (55:7) and lights his own torches (50:11) instead of looking to the Lord's light (50:10). Those who persist in their own ways and seek their own glory will have an unfortunate end (66:24, 14:11).

Fortunately, however, God keeps reaching out to us (30:18–19, 65:2) in spite of persistent rebellion (1:2) and He plans to transform us from a desert land into a fertile one (35:7) by pouring out his Holy Spirit from on high (32:14–20). The Lord redeemed us (43:1) and offered up his Messiah as a guilt offering (53:10) and by his wounds we are healed (53:5). He has swept away our sins like a morning mist (44:22). His plan for mankind is nothing short of a glorious new creation where the curse of Eden is lifted (55:13, 66:7) and He will wipe away all tears (25:8). In this final consummation, he will rejoice and take delight in his people (65:19) even as he does in his Messiah (42:1). The former things will not be remembered (65:18), and the sun and moon will be unnecessary since the Lord himself will be our everlasting light (60:19). He graciously extends his invitation to all (55:1), even to the ends of the earth (49:6, 45:22). Every knee will eventually bow to the Lord (45:23–24). There will be joy and celebration as the ransomed of the Lord enter Zion with singing (35:10), and nature itself will join with singing and clapping of hands (55:12). We will all partake of a rich feast (25:6) and will delight in abundant provision (66:11). Let us anticipate that joyous day and drink deeply from the wells of salvation (12:3)!

Jeremiah

Commentaries
- *The Message of Jeremiah*, by Christopher J.H. Wright (2014)
- *The Preacher's Commentary*, OT Vol 19, by John Guest (1988)

Jer 8:4 *Why then have these people turned away? Why does Jerusalem always turn away? They cling to deceit; they refuse to return.*
After the sermonic prose of chapter 7, we return to Jeremiah's passion and poetry in chapters 8–10, which immediately take us back to the world of chapters 4–6. Once again we reel in a torrent of rhetorical questions, graphic imagery, fierce accusation, dire predictions of invasion, and anticipated lament for a doomed society. It would be a mistake, however, to rush through these chapters imagining we've heard it all before. At one level, we have. The whole sequence is summarized for us in the text itself in 9:12–16. ... On the other hand, there is the pathos of divine grief. So intense is the poetry, and so seamless is the way it switches from one speaker to another, that it is hard to decide at many points whether we are hearing the voice of Jeremiah or of God. Probably we should not try to decide, for the voice on one expresses the heart of the other. There are few places in the whole Bible where we have a more telling glimpse into the inner emotional life of our God than here—only at Calvary do we see and hear more. Wright, pp 121–122

Wright, Christopher J.H., *The Message of Jeremiah* Taken from *The Bible Speaks Today* Series edited by J. Alec Motyer; John Stott. Copyright ©1983 edited by J. Alec Motyer; John Stott. Used by permission of InterVarsity Press, P.O. Box 1400, Downers Grove, IL 60515, USA. www.ivpress.com Taken from The Message of Jeremiah by Christopher J. H. Wright. Copyright (c) 2014 by Christopher J. H. Wright. Used by permission of InterVarsity Press, P.O. Box 1400, Downers Grove, IL 60515, USA. www.ivpress.com

Personal Note: This passage brings to mind a comment made by sportscaster Tim McCarver before a Braves playoff baseball game. He was trying to describe the success of ace pitcher Tom Glavine (who won over 300 games in MLB). McCarver mentioned when you're batting against Glavine "Look away, look away, look away." Glavine's main technique was to pitch the ball low and outside, but close enough that the batter would swing at it. It occurs to me today that we are trying to pitch low and outside to our Lord instead of giving Him our best, right down the center of the plate. Our Lord laments our turning away as this verse states. He is entreating us to return to Him.

Jer 12:1 *You are always righteous, LORD, when I bring a case before you. Yet I would speak with you about your justice: Why does the way of the wicked prosper? Why do all the faithless live at ease?*
We easily feel angry when law-abiding citizens are clobbered with one blow after another—unfair discrimination at work, higher taxes, loss of employment, unrelieved poverty and debt, austerity measures and welfare cuts, or any of life's other adversities—while greedy and influential people in high places or high office can twist the system to their own advantage and enrich themselves with impunity. Especially if the law-abiding citizen is oneself. And how much worse when the extreme wickedness of tyrants and dictators goes unpunished while their riches pile up in foreign bank accounts? Somehow, the calm logic of Deuteronomy's simple moral equations, as summarized in the sermonic discourse of 11:1–17, cannot contain the emotions generated by this inconsistency. We can believe that *ultimately* the wicked will suffer God's judgment and that the moral equilibrium of the universe will be eschatologically restored as God intended it. We can believe all that will happen in the end. But in the meantime ... ? What about now? The delay is hard to bear.
Peter tells us that God delays his judgment in order to allow time for repentance (2 Pet 3:8–9), to give space for grace. But for Jeremiah, it was not a theological explanation that he wanted, but decisive and deserved action right now. ... Once again, we witness Jeremiah's deeply human feelings and we can understand them, for who would not be tempted to react the same way sometimes? And again we have to contrast them with

those of Jesus, and remind ourselves that it is the example of Jesus, not of Jeremiah, that we are commanded to imitate. Wright, p. 150
Wright, Christopher J.H., *The Message of Jeremiah* Downers Grove, Taken from *The Bible Speaks Today* Series edited by J. Alec Motyer; John Stott. Copyright ©2014 edited by J. Alec Motyer; John Stott. Used by permission of InterVarsity Press, P.O. Box 1400, Downers Grove, IL 60515, USA. www.ivpress.com

Jer 13:11 *For as a belt is bound around the waist, so I bound all the people of Israel and all the people of Judah to me,' declares the LORD, 'to be my people for my renown and praise and honor. But they have not listened.'*
Going back to the beginning, Jeremiah turns the human action of choosing, buying, and wearing a piece of clothing into a metaphor for God's relationship with Israel through election and covenant. And the snug fit of a waistband was the picture of how God wanted his people to cling close to him. ... The imagery is striking. *God wanted to put his people on like clothing!* And not just as a man might wear a cloak loosely thrown over the shoulders, but as a close fitting, clinging waistband. And not just for warmth, but for show! Both of these points seem to be included in Jeremiah's message. On the one hand, God had bound Israel to himself in a covenant relationship in which they were to cling to, or hold fast, to him in covenant loyalty, trust, and obedience. This is a strong emphasis in Deuteronomy (4:4, 10:20; 11:22; 13:4; 30:20, cf 1 Kings 11:2, 2 Kings 3:3, 18:6). But that is exactly what they had failed to do, to their own ruin.
On the other hand, God wanted 'to look good' wearing Israel. That is to say, as a whole community they would be a credit to the God they worshipped, living in such a visibly different way among the nations that the name of YHWH would be held in praise and honor. ... Jeremiah's graphic point, therefore, is that not only had the people unbound themselves from their covenant Lord, they had become completely unwearable by him. Israel, far from displaying the splendor of YHWH, were rotting in their own disgrace. ... They were denying their mission, their reason for existence. And so we have to ask, how does our mission as God's people fit this metaphor? Are we living in such a way that the God we claim to worship attracts admiration from those around? Or does God look at us and think, 'I can't be seen wearing people like that!' Wright, pp.158,59,60
Wright, Christopher J.H., *The Message of Jeremiah* Downers Grove, Taken from *The Bible Speaks Today* Series edited by J. Alec Motyer; John Stott. Copyright ©2014

edited by J. Alec Motyer; John Stott. Used by permission of InterVarsity Press, P.O. Box 1400, Downers Grove, IL 60515, USA. www.ivpress.com

Jer 17:12 *A glorious throne, exalted from the beginning, is the place of our sanctuary.*
What good news it is to notice that the fear and trembling do not have the last word. Breaking in upon them is this vision of the throne. Visions such as this one are beginning to flicker across the prophet's mind. They will rise to a crescendo in the next several chapters. Now they are gathering murmurs in a great orchestration toward a fuller awareness of the sovereignty of God. Here the God of judgment is found also to be the God of refuge. His throne, the symbol of His reign and kingdom, is found to be a sanctuary. What might have mounted to panic has now been turned to peace for Jeremiah, who claims his safety in the purposes of God. Like the psalmist, the prophet can proclaim, 'I will say of the Lord, He is my refuge and my fortress, my God in whom I can trust' (Ps 91:2). Guest, p. 130

Jer 18:12: *But they will reply, 'It's no use. We will continue with our own plans; each of us will follow the stubbornness of his evil heart.'*
The sovereign potter desires to fashion Judah into a useful vessel, but she is no longer malleable. Instead she is brittle and set in her resistance to His purposes for hr. Judah does answer His plea, but her answer is *no*. Jeremiah must have felt a distinct agony in receiving the hopeful vision in the potter's house, rushing to deliver its message of repentance, and then seeing only the faces of his hearers set in anger. *'This is hopeless,'* they say. *'So we will walk according to our own plans, and we will every one obey the dictates of his evil heart.'* Self-avowed rebels, shaking their fists in the face of the sovereign God, are in for a lesson. ... Judah's stupidity was obvious to everyone but herself. Judah has violated her own humanity, her own logic, even her own destiny. Guest, p. 138–139

Jer 18:15: *Yet my people have forgotten me; they burn incense to worthless idols, which made them stumble in their ways and in the ancient paths. They made them walk in bypaths and on roads not built up.*
Personal Note: Jeremiah uses the common but powerful biblical metaphor of the journey of life in this verse (cf Jer 6:16). Isaiah 35 asserts

that the Lord has paved a beautiful highway whose destination brings joy and gladness. He lights the path with his word (Ps 119:105) and even guides his people with his voice (John 10:4). But man is stubborn and sees little side roads which entice him into experiences that at first seem exciting and exhilarating but which inevitably result in sorrow and pain (Prov 1:10-19). The way is clear and we are urged to walk in it (Isa 30:21). May we be watching for the Lord's highway signs (Jer 31:21, Hab 2:1) and listening for his guiding voice (Mk 4:23) so that we may arrive at the glorious destination of our life's journey (Jer 31:12, Heb 11:10, Rev 21:1-5).

Jer 23:3: *I myself will gather the remnant of my flock out of all the countries where I have driven them and will bring them back to their pasture, where they will be fruitful and increase in number.*

The clouds begin to lift. The dark era of evil kings will come to an end. And since they had been the ones primarily to blame for the catastrophe engulfing the people, that is good news. …
Here is a sudden shaft of light and hope: if God's hand was sovereign in judgment it could be sovereign also in restoration. And that is precisely the prospect that Jeremiah now holds out.
Sit with the exiles in Babylon and read these verses with them. Scattered and shattered because of the wicked follies of their kings, they are promised a future based on good governance and security. There would be a return to the land, and there would be more conscientious rulers.
The language of verse 3 ripples out to a wider horizon that will be glimpsed only in the following verses. To be fruitful is the blessing of creation. And to increase in number is the blessing of Abraham. These creational and Abrahamic resonances are developed quite explicitly in 31:35–37 and 33:20–26. The exiles were being given hints of a vision beyond their imagining: the ending of exile, when it comes, would be a whole fresh start for God's plan and purpose for the world and for his people. So indeed it would be, but in ways they could not yet dream of.
Wright, pp 243, 244

Wright, Christopher J.H., *The Message of Jeremiah* Downers Grove, Taken from *The Bible Speaks Today* Series edited by J. Alec Motyer; John Stott. Copyright ©2014 edited by J. Alec Motyer; John Stott. Used by permission of InterVarsity Press, P.O. Box 1400, Downers Grove, IL 60515, USA. www.ivpress.com

Jer 26:3 *Perhaps they will listen and each will turn from his evil way. Then I will relent and not bring on them the disaster I was planning because of the evil they have done.*

Personal Note: In the midst of impending disaster, Jeremiah sounds a vibrant note of grace. Even at this late stage of the game, the Lord was willing to relent if the people would but turn to him (cf Acts 3:19, 2 Chr 7:14). The Lord is a God of second chances. Even the evil Ninevites understood this when they repented and said "Who knows? God may yet relent" (Jonah 3:9). Fortunately for us, he doesn't judge the lateness of repentance, only whether it happens or not. The workers who were hired late in the day get the same pay as those who were hired early (see Green's comments on Mt 20:12). As Wright states in his discussion of Ezek 18:21, "After repentance the wicked man is not required to achieve a balancing amount of righteous deeds to cancel the past before being granted the verdict of life. No, the glorious immediacy of the divine declaration [of grace] is breathtaking."

Jer 29:11–14: *"For I know the plans I have for you," declares the LORD, "plans to prosper you and not to harm you, plans to give you hope and a future. Then you will call upon me and come and pray to me, and I will listen to you. You will seek me and find me when you seek me with all your heart."*

Jeremiah 29:11 probably ranks as one of the most quoted and most claimed promises of the Bible. It is found in countless text calendars, pretty pictures, and sacred ornaments. It is rightly trusted as a precious work of assurance from God. But do we take note of its context? This is a surprising word of hope to a people who stood under God's judgment. It is not a glib happy feeling. It is rather the robust affirmation that even in and through the fires of judgment there can be hope in the goodness and grace of God.

What then should be the response to such a surprising word of amazing grace? Not gleeful celebrations. Not mere relief. Rather, the people are called to the restoring grace of God with renewed prayer and seeking him (12–14). The language here is taken straight from Deut 4:29–31, which had anticipated such a return to YHWH in the wake of the judgment of the exile, and had promised that when Israel would thus return with all their heart and soul they would run into the arms of the God of forgiving grace.   Wright, p. 295–296

Wright, Christopher J.H., *The Message of Jeremiah* Downers Grove, Taken from *The Bible Speaks Today* Series edited by J. Alec Motyer; John Stott. Copyright ©2014 edited by J. Alec Motyer; John Stott. Used by permission of InterVarsity Press, P.O. Box 1400, Downers Grove, IL 60515, USA. www.ivpress.com

Jer 31:1 *"At that time," declares the LORD, "I will be the God of all the families of Israel, and they will be my people."*
The last two verses of Chapter 30, if we read them in isolation, sound harsh and jarring after what we have just been reading throughout the chapter. Why is that past oracle of doom repeated here? For the purpose of wrapping it in the smothering embrace of the core covenant promise that Israel had known from their origins. Wright, p. 311

Wright, Christopher J.H., *The Message of Jeremiah* Downers Grove, Taken from *The Bible Speaks Today* Series edited by J. Alec Motyer; John Stott. Copyright ©2014 edited by J. Alec Motyer; John Stott. Used by permission of InterVarsity Press, P.O. Box 1400, Downers Grove, IL 60515, USA. www.ivpress.com

Jer 31:12: *They will come and shout for joy on the heights of Zion; they will rejoice in the bounty of the LORD—the grain, the new wine and the oil, the young of the flocks and herds.*
They will be like a well-watered garden, and they will sorrow no more.
God's promises trip over one another—*he will gather them ... watch over then ... deliver ... and redeem them* (10–11). No wonder these resounding verbs of salvation are echoed by resounding verbs of rejoicing (12–13). This is the joy of the gospel taking hold of a whole community. It *turns mourning into gladness*, the same as Isaiah depicts (35:10; 55:12–13).
Once again we should see the fulfillment of these verses on two horizons. There was, of course, a measure of fulfilment at Horizon 1, when the exiles did return to the land and re-established their farms and families, doubtless with great joy. But there are hints here of an unalloyed abundance and joy that will only be reality at Horizon 3 in the new creation. They will be like a well-watered garden surely echoes the prefill blessing of Eden, while the word translated *bounty of the Lord* (12) and *my bounty* (14) is in fact the simple word *tôb*, 'good', which was the refrain in Genesis 1 that proclaims the goodness of God's creation—in its origin and its destiny. This kind of prophetic vision is the source of the categorical 'no more' and 'no longer' of Revelation 21:4 and 22:3. Wright, pp. 318–319

Wright, Christopher J.H., *The Message of Jeremiah* Downers Grove, Taken from *The Bible Speaks Today* Series edited by J. Alec Motyer; John Stott. Copyright ©2014 edited by J. Alec Motyer; John Stott. Used by permission of InterVarsity Press, P.O. Box 1400, Downers Grove, IL 60515, USA. www.ivpress.com

Personal Note: Let us pause and drink in this picture of our final destination. Although a few rays of sunshine have appeared in the first twenty–eight chapters, the book of Jeremiah has been up to this point a nearly unrelenting picture of gloom, doom, and judgment. Life for some of us may resemble Jeremiah 1–28, but we have to keep our final goal in mind (Phil 3:13). This is where we are headed, and we should bring this verse and others like Jer 29:11–14 to mind when life seems to be caving in around us. In despair there are the seeds of hope. The Lord has revealed his final consummation and has lit the path to it with his Word. Joy will overtake us (Isa 35:10).

Jer 31:33: *"This is the covenant I will make with the house of Israel after that time," declares the LORD. "I will put my law in their minds and write it on their hearts. I will be their God, and they will be my people."*
The heart, in Hebrew, is not so much the seat of the emotions, but rather of the will. The heart is where you do your thinking, choosing, and deciding. It is the inner organ that shapes the outer directions of your life. And that, says God, is where he will put his law. ... What seems to be new in 31:33a is that God not only asks for obedience from the heart, but promises that he himself will implant it there. The two verbs are emphatic. *I will put ... I will write.* And whereas Deuteronomy 6:6 simply asked that the law should be upon your hearts, God's promise here to put his law 'within them' (translated by NIV as *in their minds*). It seems that a genuine internalizing of the law is envisaged. It is no longer merely that Israel should wholeheartedly obey the law when they read or hear it, but that they should live by an inner impulse coming from within, from God's law written on their own hearts. In other words, their whole inclination and habitual action would be to live according to God's standards and ways. Wright, p. 327

Wright, Christopher J.H., *The Message of Jeremiah* Downers Grove, Taken from *The Bible Speaks Today* Series edited by J. Alec Motyer; John Stott. Copyright ©2014 edited by J. Alec Motyer; John Stott. Used by permission of InterVarsity Press, P.O. Box 1400, Downers Grove, IL 60515, USA. www.ivpress.com

Lamentations

Commentaries:
- *The Message of Lamentations*, by Christopher J.H. Wright (2015)
- *The Preacher's Commentary*, OT Vol 19, by John Guest (1988)

Introduction
There is a drive and a rhythm. This is a *journey* through grief, not wallowing in it. Second, there is a sense of intentional completeness. It is as if the poet says, 'Here is all our pain, from A to Z.' It is an encyclopedia of suffering. Nothing more can be said or needs to be said. The book has five chapters, which suggests that Chapter 3 might be the central focus of the message of the book as a whole. That impression is strengthened by the intensification of the acrostic pattern in that chapter. In Chapters 1 and 2, the poet writes 22 stanzas of three lines each, in which the first line of each stanza starts with the letters of the alphabet in sequence. However, in Chapter 3, he triples the acrostic intensity by starting all three lines of each of the 22 stanzas with the same letter (like: AAA, BBB, CCC, etc.). Our Bibles turn each line of chapter 3 into a separate verse, and for that reason, it has 66 one line verses, even though it is actually the same length as Chapters 1 and 2 with their 22 three line verses.

The one voice we never hear in Lamentations is the voice of God. God remains silent throughout. He allows the other voices to speak their A to Z, till they have said all they want or can. He does not interrupt, whether to comfort, explain, or excuse.

Wright, Excerpts from Introduction, pp. 29–45

Wright, Christopher J.H., *The Message of Lamentations*, Taken from *The Bible Speaks Today* Series edited by J. Alec Motyer; John Stott. Copyright © 1983 edited by J. Alec Motyer; John Stott. Used by permission of InterVarsity Press, P.O. Box 1400, Downers Grove, IL 60515, USA. www.ivpress.com

Lam 1:9: *she did not consider her future.*
When she had the chance, *she did not consider her destiny*. If only we could hear those words today and think seriously about our destiny and about the consequences of our roamings. In this culture we insure ourselves against all kinds of losses. We take out policies that cover disability, health, fire, theft, casualty, and so on. We insure ourselves against so many calamities, most of which will never happen, but we don't take care enough about our souls, to insure against the one thing that most certainly will happen. We make so little provision for our eternal destiny. Guest, p. 337

Lam 2:8 *The LORD determined to tear down the wall around Daughter Zion. He stretched out a measuring line and did not withhold his hand from destroying. He made ramparts and walls lament; together they wasted away.*
Again, the language is vivid and forceful. This is a shattered city. God the demolisher is fulfilling the word of Jeremiah 1:10 to the utmost. But is is not just that God is fulfilling his word, he is actually carrying out his plan. *The Lord determined ... and the Lord has done what he has planned* (8, 17). The terrible destruction of Jerusalem was not an act of random violence inflicted on an unsuspecting people. It was not God raging out of control. It was planned. Now that might seem to make it worse. This was not some secret divine machination, an evil cosmic conspiracy, hidden from view until it burst forth in awesome devastation. On the contrary, God had spoken clearly in advance about the judgment he was planning, precisely so that the people could take action to avert it if they chose to. It was not an irreversible plan. It was not pre-determined fate that nothing could change. It was a conditional plan, and if the conditions had changed, so would the plan. That is the clear message of Jeremiah 18.   Wright, pp. 86, 87
Wright, Christopher J.H., The Message of Lamentations, Taken from *The Bible Speaks Today* Series edited by J. Alec Motyer; John Stott. Copyright © 2015 edited by J. Alec Motyer; John Stott. Used by permission of InterVarsity Press, P.O. Box 1400, Downers Grove, IL 60515, USA. www.ivpress.com

Lam 3:7: *He has walled me in so I cannot escape; he has weighed me down with chains.*
Typical of the grief process is the feeling that there is no future, that things will never get better, that God simply cannot be reached. I am ever amazed at the honesty of Scripture. There is no glossing over the realities

of our humanity. It walks right up to them and looks them in the face. Here Jeremiah describes something of a Catch-22 situation. He needs God to comfort him in his grief, but he can't reach God because he is too overwhelmed with grief. Guest, p. 355

Personal Note: I suspect most of us go through dark times like the ones recorded here in scripture. I recall times in my own life when I felt as if I were writing my prayer on a piece of paper and slipping it under the Lord's door, but he never seemed to pick it up (Lam 3:44). It's times like these that we must remember his goodness and cling to the hope which emerges later in this chapter (3:21–33).

Lam 3:22–23: *Because of the LORD's great love we are not consumed, for his compassions never fail. They are new every morning; great is your faithfulness.*
[Ps 90:14, 143:8]

These verses (22–23), resonating as they do with harmonics from all over the scriptures, are deservedly famous. It is grievous that they suffer from being so often extracted from their context in the midst of the surrounding pain of the whole book of Lamentations. But ironically, they are often quoted and sung in the midst of personal suffering and danger by believers who may know nothing of what our Poet describes the horrors of 587 BC—but who do know personal or community suffering. So, in the devotions and songs of multitudes of believers ever since, the sustaining truth at the heart of the Man's memory becomes embedded again in surrounding trauma, bringing a transforming perspective and renewed hope. Wright, p. 112

Wright, Christopher J.H., *The Message of Lamentations*, Taken from *The Bible Speaks Today* Series edited by J. Alec Motyer; John Stott. Copyright © 2015 edited by J. Alec Motyer; John Stott. Used by permission of InterVarsity Press, P.O. Box 1400, Downers Grove, IL 60515, USA. www.ivpress.com

Lam 3:25 *The LORD is good to those whose hope is in him, to the one who seeks him*

Are you ever astonished by the Bible? I hope so. For nothing seems more astonishing to me than that someone who has exploited a whole catalogue of violent metaphors to describe the suffering that God has inflicted on him (1–18) can turn round and say 'The Lord is good …' (25)!

How on earth can he say that? Yet he does. Indeed the poet emphasizes his point by triple repetition of the word *good* (*tôb*) at the start of every line of the stanza (*good...good...good*). Read those scary verses again. And nothing he says now cancels out the suffering described there. It stands still in his memory and in our text. He does not deny it, and neither should we. But he is no longer drowning in it. For his deliberate act of remembrance has brought a moment of calm to his soul, a moment in which he reflects on some of the core truths of Israel's faith.

And the first core truth is the goodness of God—affirmed here, not in the swelling praise of Psalm 136, but in the aftermath of the most horrendous suffering under the hand of God's covenant judgment. For if the God who punishes is the God who is good, then punishment cannot be the last word. ... He is not saying that sufferers like himself should never speak their pain. No, there is a time for yelling out, but there is also a time to calm down under the recital of remembered truth. This poet swings from one to the other without denying the validity of either. God allows (indeed encourages, by including it in Scripture), the strident voice of pain and protest—the classic outpouring of biblical lament, so common in the psalms, so familiar in Jeremiah, and perfected here in Lamentations. But God also calls for the quiet humility of faith, born of penitence and sustained by hope. That is what emerges here in the midst of a storm that has not yet gone away and will return in force by the end of this chapter and remain unabated through the rest of the book.

Wright, pp. 114–115

Wright, Christopher J.H., The Message of Lamentations, Taken from *The Bible Speaks Today* Series edited by J. Alec Motyer; John Stott. Copyright © 2015 edited by J. Alec Motyer; John Stott. Used by permission of InterVarsity Press, P.O. Box 1400, Downers Grove, IL 60515, USA. www.ivpress.com

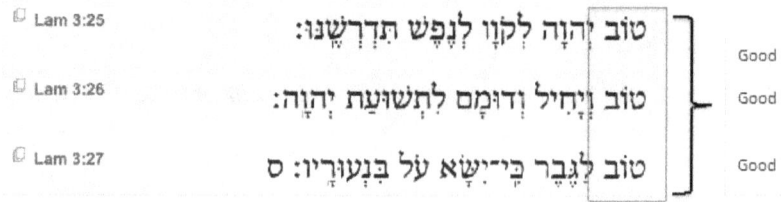

Lam 3:31–32: *For men are not cast off by the Lord forever. Though he brings grief, he will show compassion, so great is his unfailing love.*

The astonishing contrast between the turbulent desperation of verses 1–18 and the calm depths and surprising advice of verses 22–30 demands an explanation. And here we have it. Every line of this stanza begins with *kî –for*. These verses are offered as the reason why the man can speak with such calm assurance about the wisdom of humbly submitting to God even in the midst of suffering. And that reason is part of the bedrock of biblical theology. …The poet has reached what will be the center point of his whole book and the central pillar of his theology, battered though it is by all that surrounds it. God is again the subject of the verbs, as in verses 1–18, but God's actions are modified in a way that changes the world.

Once again, the intensity and skill of the poetry is remarkable. The two outer negatives—'not … forever (31), 'not …from his heart' (33)—frame the climactic central positive: 'he will have compassion according to the magnitude of his lovingkindness' (32). The central and eternal character of God—his compassion and faithful love—outweighs the effects of his reaction against sin and evil. So even though that reaction involves the 'recoil' effect, in which human folly and rebellion generate their own inevitable disastrous results, that punishment will not last forever.

There is an important theological truth here. We should not equate God's love and God's anger, as if they were both eternally equivalent attributes of deity. God's anger against evil is a terrible reality. It is the negative outworking of God's goodness in rejecting and repelling all that is contrary to his nature and will, but it is not eternally definitive of his character. God *is* love. God *is not* anger. On the contrary, God is 'slow to anger', but 'abounding in love.' The imbalance is a thousand to one, according to Deut 7:9–10. We have several verses in scripture that tell us God's anger will not last forever. That indeed is something that makes YHWH incomparable among other claimed deities. Wright, p. 116

Wright, Christopher J.H., The Message of Lamentations, Taken from *The Bible Speaks Today* Series edited by J. Alec Motyer; John Stott. Copyright © 2015 edited by J. Alec Motyer; John Stott. Used by permission of InterVarsity Press, P.O. Box 1400, Downers Grove, IL 60515, USA. www.ivpress.com

Lam 5:21–22: *Restore us to yourself, O LORD, that we may return; renew our days as of old*

unless you have utterly rejected us and are angry with us beyond measure.
Verse 20 is the last question in the book, and like all the other ones, it gets no answer. God does not explain. The prophets had done that already. For the poet and the people whose prayer he is voicing, the question hangs frozen in the air, challenging the frozen present, the unbearable 'now' of bearing the judgment of God in the day of his anger.

There is nothing sentimental or escapist about affirming the massive majesty of the redemptive patience, faithfulness and salvation of the biblical God in confronting and defeating the ravages of evil and sin and delivering us ultimately from all the suffering they wreak on humanity and creation. That is the story that the rest of the Bible tells. Within that story, Lamentations has its place and its voice. … And that story, of course, leads to and centers upon the cross and resurrection of Jesus Christ. Both are indissolubly linked together, and each has its vital necessity. We cannot contemplate the cross without knowing the resurrection to come. But equally, we cannot use our knowledge of the resurrection as a sentimental or escapist way of denying the absolute horror of the cross and the unimaginable depth of suffering that Christ endured at every level of his divine and human being.

But in between Good Friday and Easter day stands Holy Saturday—the literally 'dead time' when the agony of Good Friday has done its worst, but God has not yet stretched out his right hand and mighty arm in glorious resurrection power.

That, as Robin Parry suggests, is where Lamentation positions Israel in 587 BC—along with all those in Christ who share in his sufferings in this world, enduring them with ultimate hope, but without present relief and even with a martyr's death. Like them, Christ on Holy Saturday, Israel at the end of Lamentations remains in the land of exile and death. Waiting. Resurrection has not yet been heralded. Easter day has not yet dawned. But it will.

It will.

Wright, excerpts, pp 162–166

Wright, Christopher J.H., The Message of Lamentations, Taken from *The Bible Speaks Today* Series edited by J. Alec Motyer; John Stott. Copyright © 2015 edited by J. Alec Motyer; John Stott. Used by permission of InterVarsity Press, P.O. Box 1400, Downers Grove, IL 60515, USA. www.ivpress.com

Ezekiel

Commentary:
- *The Message of Ezekiel*, by Christopher J.H. Wright (2001)
- *The Preacher's Commentary*, OT Vol 20, by Douglas Stuart (1989)
- *Cornerstone Biblical Commentary*, Vol 9, By David L. Thompson (2010)

Ezek 2:4: *The people to whom I am sending you are obstinate and stubborn. Say to them, 'This is what the Sovereign LORD says.'*
Who wants a career full of hostility? Is it easy for a missionary to set off for a tribe or territory where he or she is sure to meet not merely hostile disapproval of God's message, but rejection personally? There are many modern-day saints who understand from experience exactly what Ezekiel was calling them to endure, but there are few who enjoy the process. Rare is the person who can set out on a task knowing that people will hate him or her for doing it. But that is exactly what Ezekiel was called to do. His faithfulness stands as a challenge to ours.
Stuart, Douglas, *The Preacher's Commentary*, OT Vol 20, Nashville: Thomas Nelson, 1989, p. 35

Ezek 3:1–2: *And he said to me, "Son of man, eat what is before you, eat this scroll; then go and speak to the house of Israel." So I opened my mouth, and he gave me the scroll to eat.*
The word of God is not a blank check to be filled in to the recipient's benefit, not a draft discussion document awaiting the input of various focus groups. Yes, as affirmed above, the word of God in this particular book of the Bible will be unmistakably Ezekiel's very own, shaped by his character, personality, and passion, but it comes to us through him

ultimately in the same way as it came to him: as the word given by the One on the throne of the universe.

Like Israel, we may listen or fail to listen [3:27], but we are not invited to come up with alternative drafts or argue a case for our own preferred options. Ezekiel's experience indicated that he was about to absorb the word of God totally. He did not just taste it, but it was to fill his stomach so that he had thoroughly digested it. It was to become a part of him, nourishing, energizing, and empowering him [Jer 15:16]. Wright, p. 59, 6
Wright, Christopher J.H. *The Message of Ezekiel,* Taken from *The Bible Speaks Today* Series edited by J. Alec Motyer; John Stott. Copyright ©1983 edited by J. Alec Motyer; John Stott. Used by permission of InterVarsity Press, P.O. Box 1400, Downers Grove, IL 60515, USA. www.ivpress.com

Ezek 9:10: *So I will not look on them with pity or spare them, but I will bring down on their own heads what they have done.*
It would be easy, with all the surrounding scene of armed executioners and carnage to imagine these words being spoken with vicious coldness and implacable malice. But if there was steel in the voice, there were tears in the eyes and unbearable pains in the heart. This is the same God whose mercy longs to triumph over justice (James 2:13), whose love outlasts his punishment on a scale of 1000:1 (Deut 7:9–10), who is slow to anger and rich in love (Ex 34:6). For such a God to be brought to the extremity of having to utter the terrifying words we read here speaks more loudly than anything else could of the horrific, detestable, and intolerable nature of sin, and the moral necessity of its being finally and justly punished. It brings us to the cross. Wright, p. 118–119
Wright, Christopher J.H. *The Message of Ezekiel,* Taken from *The Bible Speaks Today* Series edited by J. Alec Motyer; John Stott. Copyright ©2001 edited by J. Alec Motyer; John Stott. Used by permission of InterVarsity Press, P.O. Box 1400, Downers Grove, IL 60515, USA. www.ivpress.com

Ezek 16:14: *And your fame spread among the nations on account of your beauty, because the splendor I had given you made your beauty perfect, declares the Sovereign LORD.*
The message of the imagery for us is that as the people who claim the name of the Lord, or rather who have been claimed by him as the bearers of the Lord's name, we live in public view. Where God's people live in God's way,

God's name is adorned and beautiful, and something of his splendor is witnessed among them. Do our lives weave the kind of clothing that our Lord would want us to be seen in? Do our actions so shine like jewelry that the watching world is led to give glory to the Father, as Jesus exhorted? (Mt 5:16) Wright, p. 134

Wright, Christopher J.H. *The Message of Ezekiel,* Taken from *The Bible Speaks Today* Series edited by J. Alec Motyer; John Stott. Copyright ©2001 edited by J. Alec Motyer; John Stott. Used by permission of InterVarsity Press, P.O. Box 1400, Downers Grove, IL 60515, USA. www.ivpress.com

Ezek 16:25: *At the head of every street you built your lofty shrines and degraded your beauty, offering your body with increasing promiscuity to anyone who passed by.*

Second only, perhaps, to the genealogies in 1 Chronicles, the lurid allegories of Ezekiel 16 and 23 must qualify as the chapters in the Bible least likely to be read aloud in church—and just as unlikely to be preached from. They are long, they are lewd, and their language in places is, frankly, pornographic.... Most English translations have to tone down the offensive coarseness of some of the original expressions of sexual lust and obscene behavior used in these chapters. These are deliberate shock tactics on a scale probably unsurpassed in the whole arsenal of prophetic assault and battery weapons...In Ezekiel's hands it becomes the dynamite necessary to explode a whole set of religious assumptions, demolishing an unsafe building and clearing the site before any reconstruction can be planned. Wright, p. 128

Wright, Christopher J.H. *The Message of Ezekiel,* Taken from *The Bible Speaks Today Series* edited by J. Alec Motyer; John Stott. Copyright ©2001 edited by J. Alec Motyer; John Stott. Used by permission of InterVarsity Press, P.O. Box 1400, Downers Grove, IL 60515, USA. www.ivpress.com

Ezek 16:53: *However, I will restore the fortunes of Sodom and her daughters and of Samaria and her daughters, and your fortunes along with them,*

The gospel undermines our pride not only by removing any pathetic claim to be less of a sinner than somebody else, but also by insisting that we have no choice who else gets saved alongside us. If God is able and willing to pardon and restore you, then Sodom will be no problem for him. Humbling, shaming, disillusioning words. Yet words that are the very essence of the Gospel. The grace of God is good news for all or it is good news for none. Saved sinners don't get to select their traveling companions.

Wright, p. 153

Wright, Christopher J.H. *The Message of Ezekiel,* Taken from *The Bible Speaks Today* Series edited by J. Alec Motyer; John Stott. Copyright ©2001 edited by J. Alec Motyer; John Stott. Used by permission of InterVarsity Press, P.O. Box 1400, Downers Grove, IL 60515, USA. www.ivpress.com

Ezek 18:2–4: *"What do you people mean by quoting this proverb about the land of Israel:'"The fathers eat sour grapes, and the children's teeth are set on edge'? As surely as I live, declares the Sovereign LORD, you will no longer quote this proverb in Israel. For every living soul belongs to me, the father as well as the son-both alike belong to me. The soul who sins is the one who will die.*

What an enriching and affirming anthropology! The universality and particularity of God's involvement in human life could hardly be more succinctly stated. If someone or something else is really to blame for the mess I have made, then I can dismiss my own personal responsibility. And if God is unfair in the way he punishes people, then to the extent that any of my misfortunes are being inflicted by him, I am not so much a sinner as a victim. Both these tunes are played very loudly in modern and post-modern society. We are not to blame—it is always someone else's fault, directly or indirectly. So we lay the consequences of our personal and collective wickedness at the door of our genes, or psychological stress, or government failures, or market forces, or anything else that is sufficiently vague and removed from uncomfortable proximity to our own choices or actions. Such blame-shifting tactics were unacceptable to Ezekiel then, and unacceptable to God then and now. Wright, p. 189

Wright, Christopher J.H. *The Message of Ezekiel,* Taken from *The Bible Speaks Today* Series edited by J. Alec Motyer; John Stott. Copyright ©2001 edited by J. Alec Motyer; John Stott. Used by permission of InterVarsity Press, P.O. Box 1400, Downers Grove, IL 60515, USA. www.ivpress.com

Ezek 18:21: *"But if a wicked man turns away from all the sins he has committed and keeps all my decrees and does what is just and right, he will surely live; he will not die."*

It becomes increasingly difficult to insist that there are some choices in life that matter in the ultimate sense. Evangelists were once accustomed to calling people to 'choose Christ.' Today such a call, within our consumerist cultures, may be understood to mean little more than 'Give Christ a try for a while and see if he works for you; you can always try something else later if you aren't satisfied.' And in the marketplace of old denominations and new Christian movements, you can have a conveniently customized Christ, tailored to suit your particular religious consumer needs. No such trivial understanding of choice exercised Ezekiel's mind. Neither wickedness nor righteousness is a commodity that can be stored up or counter-balanced. After repentance the wicked man is not required to achieve a balancing amount of righteous deeds to cancel the past before being granted the verdict of life. No, the glorious immediacy of the divine declaration is breathtaking. He has turned to do righteousness and so *he will live*. No wonder Micah [7:18] exclaimed, 'Who is a God like you, who pardon's sins and forgives the transgression of the remnant of his inheritance?' Who indeed? Praise his name! Wright, pp 197–209

Wright, Christopher J.H. *The Message of Ezekiel*, Taken from *The Bible Speaks Today* Series edited by J. Alec Motyer; John Stott. Copyright ©2001 edited by J. Alec Motyer; John Stott. Used by permission of InterVarsity Press, P.O. Box 1400, Downers Grove, IL 60515, USA. www.ivpress.com

Ezek 18:32: *For I take no pleasure in the death of anyone, declares the Sovereign LORD. Repent and live!*

The conclusion Yahweh draws uses few words but carries huge theological freight along several lines. First, he directly and plainly applies the rule of dynamic personal responsibility to the people of Israel, making explicit the point implicit all along: Yahweh will judge each Israelite for his or her own actions (18:30). No confusion on Yahweh's part of hiding in tradition on their part will save sinners among them…. Then follows an open invitation for Israel to turn away from their wicked deeds, and, by inference from the case studies considered [vv 4-27], to turn to live by the law of the Lord (18:30-31). No impediment can be raised, either in their own lives or in some alleged determination by prior generations that need prevent this redirection of human behavior. Yahweh here addresses their rebellious hearts, from which flow their sinful deeds. Without specifying how it would happen, Yahweh directs Israel to put away her rebellion—all of it—and find a new heart and new spirit (18:31).

Finally, Yahweh urges their repentance by revealing his own passionate desire in this matter. Yahweh's desire was implicit in the warnings and invitations already recorded in the book, but had yet to be put into words. ... The chapter ends with a two-word (in Hebrew) climactic plea: "Turn back and live!" Yahweh put the crucial repentance and consequent life in hortatory terms. Here is what Yahweh really wants!   Thompson, David L., *Cornerstone Biblical Commentary*, Vol 9, Carol Stream, IL: Tyndale, 2010, excerpts, pp. 123-124

Ezek 33:11: *As surely as I live, declares the Sovereign LORD, I take no pleasure in the death of the wicked, but rather that they turn from their ways and live. Turn! Turn from your evil ways!*
What, in fact, does God want from the Israelites? Repentance! What will it produce? Forgiveness! This is the message Ezekiel must preach and the people must hear, according to verses 10-11. It is a great message. The pessimism of verse 10 (how can we live?) was understandable from a human point of view. From the divine point of view, however, there was great hope. What Israel needed to do was to turn from its sin toward God—making Him Lord and thus accepting Him as Savior. For the rest of the book this invitation to turn to the Lord, obeying His word and receiving His deliverance is a central theme.   Stuart, p. 302

Ezek 36:25–27: *I will sprinkle clean water on you, and you will be clean; I will cleanse you from all your impurities and from all your idols. I will give you a new heart and put a new spirit in you; I will remove from you your heart of stone and give you a heart of flesh. And I will put my Spirit in you and move you to follow my decrees and be careful to keep my laws.*
No longer was it enough to expect God to circumcise their hearts in the graphic metaphor of Deut 30:6. Much more radical surgery is needed now. So, in repetition of 11:19, God proposes a heart transplant. He will remove the heart of stone, which made Israel cold, unresponsive, and dead to the Lord's words of command or appeal; and he will implant in its place a heart of flesh—which is living, warm, and soft, and which speaks of close kinship and intimate relationship. God will transform Israel's whole mindset and fundamental orientation of will, desire, and purpose. God's grace will give what God's law requires. ... There is, of course, a tension here between the role of human will and choice and the role of divine causation. One pole of that tension affirms human freedom.

The other affirms divine sovereignty. No amount of theology will ever be able to provide a complete correlation of both truths which does not leave us still conscious of mysteries somewhere beyond our grasp. Wright, p. 296, 297

Wright, Christopher J.H. *The Message of Ezekiel,* Taken from *The Bible Speaks Today* Series edited by J. Alec Motyer; John Stott. Copyright ©2001 edited by J. Alec Motyer; John Stott. Used by permission of InterVarsity Press, P.O. Box 1400, Downers Grove, IL 60515, USA. www.ivpress.com

Ezek 37:9–10: *Then he said to me, "Prophesy to the breath; prophesy, son of man, and say to it, 'This is what the Sovereign LORD says: Come from the four winds, O breath, and breathe into these slain, that they may live.'" So I prophesied as he commanded me, and breath entered them; they came to life and stood up on their feet-a vast army.*

The whole scene is permeated by the various activities of *rûah* חוּרָה (mentioned 10 times in 36:1–14) —human, natural, and divine: breath, wind, and Spirit. And the single total effect of all this activity of *rûah* is life: life out of utter darkness [Gen 2:7, John 20:22]. Here again the links between Israel and humanity are apparent. Israel has been called to be a blessing to all the nations. Their election and redemption were for the sake of the rest of humanity. Likewise, therefore, just as their sin and punishment mirrored the fallen-ness of the whole race, so too their restoration would prefigure God's gracious purpose of redemption for humanity. Resurrection for Israel anticipated resurrection for all [Isa 26:19, Eph 2:6, 1 Cor 15:52, 1 Th 4:16]. Wright, p. 310

Wright, Christopher J.H. *The Message of Ezekiel,* Taken from *The Bible Speaks Today* Series edited by J. Alec Motyer; John Stott. Copyright ©2001 edited by J. Alec Motyer; John Stott. Used by permission of InterVarsity Press, P.O. Box 1400, Downers Grove, IL 60515, USA. www.ivpress.com

Ezek 43:7: *He said: "Son of man, this is the place of my throne and the place for the soles of my feet. This is where I will live among the Israelites forever. The house of Israel will never again defile my holy name"*

Chapters 40–42 are a celebration. They harness the wagon of contemporary reality to the star of hope. The account is an architectural symphony, an intricate composition that counter points the predicament of exile and the promise of restoration in a grand celebration of God's sure purposes. ... In the coming of the Messiah, Jesus initiated another level in the fulfillment of Ezekiel's vision. For in Jesus, the perfection of God's holiness and beauty did indeed take physical form and tabernacled among us, in divine glory, full of grace and truth (John 1:14). Wright, p. 336, 340

Wright, Christopher J.H. *The Message of Ezekiel,* Taken from *The Bible Speaks Today* Series edited by J. Alec Motyer; John Stott. Copyright ©2001 edited by J. Alec Motyer; John Stott. Used by permission of InterVarsity Press, P.O. Box 1400, Downers Grove, IL 60515, USA. www.ivpress.com

Ezek 47:12: *Fruit trees of all kinds will grow on both banks of the river. Their leaves will not wither, nor will their fruit fail. Every month they will bear, because the water from the sanctuary flows to them. Their fruit will serve for food and their leaves for healing.*

As is so often the case with biblical prophetic symbolism, then, Ezekiel's river of living water has several layers of significance. For the exiles, this river spoke of the reversal of the curse, death, and barrenness of exile through their return to the land as a people restored to God's blessing and favor. Beyond that, it spoke of the true source of all life and healing—the presence of the living God in his sanctuary. For those who believe in the Messiah, Jesus, the river of living water [John 4:10–14, cf Jer 2:13, 17:13, Zech 14:8, John 7:38, Rev 7:17, 22:1–3] speaks of the continuing welling up of the Spirit of God which brings life and blessing to the believer here and now and flows out to others. We need to remember that all renewal in the church or in the world flows by God's grace from God's presence and is not something we generate or control. And ultimately the river of Life, in Ezekiel and Revelation [22:1–3], anticipates the new creation [Rev 21:5] in which God will have lifted the curse [Rev 22:3] from the earth for ever and will dwell in life-giving abundance among his redeemed people [Rev 21:3] gathered from all the nations [Rev 5:9]. Wright, p. 359

Wright, Christopher J.H. *The Message of Ezekiel,* Taken from *The Bible Speaks Today* Series edited by J. Alec Motyer; John Stott. Copyright ©2001 edited by J. Alec Motyer; John Stott. Used by permission of InterVarsity Press, P.O. Box 1400, Downers Grove, IL 60515, USA. www.ivpress.com

Ezek 48:35: *And the name of the city from that time on will be: THE LORD IS THERE.*

The name of the city speaks the great truth about God's people. John heard the same truth amplified as a loud voice from the very throne of God himself in the holy city: 'Now the dwelling of God is with men, and God himself will be with them and be their God.' (Rev 21:3). And in the meantime we, who live in the certain hope of that great day, have the equally certain promise of the Lord's presence in whatever earthly city we are called to live and witness. 'For wherever two or three come together in my name, there I am with them' (Mt 18:20).

Wright, p. 368

Wright, Christopher J.H. *The Message of Ezekiel,* Taken from *The Bible Speaks Today* Series edited by J. Alec Motyer; John Stott. Copyright ©2001 edited by J. Alec Motyer; John Stott. Used by permission of InterVarsity Press, P.O. Box 1400, Downers Grove, IL 60515, USA. www.ivpress.com

Daniel

Commentaries:
- *Hearing the Message of Daniel*, by Christopher J.H. Wright (2017)
- *The Message of Daniel*, by Ronald Wallace (1984)
- *The Preacher's Commentary*, OT vol 21, By Sinclair B. Ferguson (1988)
- *The Story of God Bible Commentary, Daniel*, by Wendy L. Widder (2016)
- Sermons by Jay Harvey (2012)
- Sermons by John Batusic (2016, 2017)

Dan 1:17 *To these four young men God gave knowledge and understanding of all kinds of literature and learning. And Daniel could understand visions and dreams of all kinds.*

The chapter draws to a close with the third occurrence of the phrase "God gave" (1:2, 1:9, 1:17). This time, God gave Daniel and his friends the unique ability to excel in the king's service. The young men were exceptional to begin with or they would not have been among the exiles selected for royal training. However, God enabled them to succeed above and beyond their normal capacities. The placement of this statement immediately after the Hebrew stand against the defiling food of Babylon suggests that God was blessing them in particular for their faithfulness. We can expect them to succeed in the chapters to follow because they are skilled and because God has gifted them.

God's hand steers the events of this chapter, from the defeat of King Jehoiakim to the treatment of Daniel in exile to the success of the Hebrew youth in the king's court. Although the historical circumstances may have suggested otherwise, the God of Israel had not been defeated. Instead, he is the one in control.

As he did in Genesis 11, the true God has come to Shinar, but this time he has come subversively: his temple vessels are tucked away in a foreign god's treasury and some of his choicest human vessels are in the palace of a foreign king. In the chapters that follow, God will once again confront proud humans confused about their place before the divine. Some will repent. Others will not. But before the city of Babylon falls, God will make clear who his God and who is not.

God's involvement in the affairs of human history is largely subtle. His unseen providential hand guides the circumstances of mighty kings and lowly exiles, and his sovereignty provides a stability that enables his people to live in faithful confidence. … When the mountains give way, we need a gentle reminder that there is still one thing left to stand on. God's sovereignty.

Widder, Wendy L., *The Story of God Bible Commentary, Daniel*, Grand Rapids, MI: Zondervan, 2016 excerpts, pp. 30-33

Dan 2:1 *In the second year of his reign, Nebuchadnezzar had dreams; his mind was troubled and he could not sleep.*

Nebuchadnezzar had everything a person could dream of possessing: power, fame, influence. Not only so, but he was in the process of creating an empire that would memorialize him for posterity and a city whose gardens would be known as one of the wonders of the ancient world. Why, then, should a mere dream fill him with such anxiety? The answer is that Nebuchadnezzar was a man whose heart was set on goals that would in the long run prove to be mirages in the desert. He lived exclusively for this world; thus the horizons of his ambitions always moved with the change and decay of this world. … As long as Nebuchadnezzar sought security and rest in possessions or power or future reputation, he could never be content. Nebuchadnezzar, like so many people, had everything except the one thing he most needed: peace.

Ferguson, Sinclair B., *The Preacher's Commentary*, OT vol 21 Nashville: Thomas Nelson, 1988, pp. 45-46

Dan 3:25: *He said, "Look! I see four men walking around in the fire, unbound and unharmed, and the fourth looks like a son of the gods."*

As we go through various trials, we may feel that our hair has been singed and our robes have been scorched. But the Lord here fulfills Isaiah's

prophecy in Isa 43:1–2, where He promises to sustain his people through their trials with his protective presence. When others peer into the furnace of our lives, do they see our Savior protecting and sustaining us?
Jay Harvey, Oct 21, 2012

Dan 4:4: *I, Nebuchadnezzar, was at home in my palace, contented and prosperous.*
Nebuchadnezzar was a builder in many different ways:

- He built an empire
- He built a culture
- He built an educated, multi-racial government administration
- He built a city—Babylon. He glorified it and beautified it, so that it was not for nothing that the famous 'Hanging Gardens of Babylon' are among the seven wonders of the ancient world.

Altogether, it was a remarkable and creditable achievement. Humanly speaking, Nebuchadnezzar had plenty to be pleased about and proud of; his boasting has its basis in fact. Even theologically speaking, we recall that it was God who had raised him up and given him authority, power, and wide dominion with all the wealth and opportunities that go along with such a position. … By the standards of his own age, Nebuchadnezzar was a competent, efficient, and constructive ruler. However, as so often, the Bible sees beyond and behind the external splendor to the reality as God knows it. The Bible, speaking for God, looks inside Nebuchadnezzar's heart [1 Sam 16:7] and sees the pride that filled it. And it looks underneath the glory of Babylon and sees the social evil that it was built on.
Nebuchadnezzar's pride, you see, was not just your ordinary, everyday kind of pride. He still had the delusions of divinity that we saw earlier in Chapter 3. He was still refusing to acknowledge what God had been trying to teach him for years. … It is tragic that the world of Christian ministry is littered with bloated egos and wonderful gifts being prostituted to the idols of pride. Wright, pp. 89–90

Dan 5:6: *Then the king's countenance was changed, and his thoughts troubled him, so that the joints of his loins were loosed, and his knees smote one against another.* KJV

Personal Note: Pastor John Batusic of Chestnut Mountain church vividly sets the scene in his message on January 30, 2016: An invading army is approaching the city and what does the king do? He throws a party! The dance band on the titanic plays on in the large banquet hall, the wine flows, there is dancing and a general hubbub of conversation and laughter. But then all of a sudden, the music and dancing stops, the wine stops flowing, and table talk is hushed as fear comes over the drunken party-goers. All that can be heard is the king's knees knocking together. A hand writes something on the wall, so the king calls for the usual wise guys, who have repeatedly been called before in the book of Daniel, always with the same result: they have no answer for the king. So they call in Daniel who is offered honors if he can read the handwriting on the wall. Daniel reads the succinct message: "It's over; You don't measure up; Your kingdom is gone." Rev18:22–23 completes the picture: "The music of harpists and musicians, pipers and trumpeters, will never be heard in you again. No worker of any trade will ever be found in you again. The sound of a millstone will never be heard in you again. The light of a lamp will never shine in you again. The voice of bridegroom and bride will never be heard in you again." Batusic asks, "So what about us? King Belshazzar never learned the message that God rules the world, but have we? The writing is on the wall for us today. Can we read it?"

Dan 7:27: *Then the sovereignty, power and greatness of the kingdoms under the whole heaven will be handed over to the saints, the people of the Most High. His kingdom will be an everlasting kingdom, and all rulers will worship and obey him.*

So history proceeds. Human empires come and go. Kings, presidents, and prime ministers do what they do. But ultimately God remains the supreme governor and final judge. And nothing will be overlooked or swept under the carpet. This is the Auditor-in-Chief, the one to whom all hearts are open, all desires known, and from whom no secrets are hidden. This is the God who sees and knows, who looks considers, and senses all that is done on by every human being on earth (Ps 33:13–15) and not only their actions, but their thoughts and motives. All earthly authority then—even that which is used boastfully and destructively—is delegated and derivative, subject to being revoked and terminated. And even when human powers are doing their worst, the kingdom of God is at work.

Wright, pp 166–167

Dan 8:8: *The goat became very great, but at the height of his power his large horn was broken off*
To be the conqueror is usually so costly that it is hardly worth the effort. This is why Paul insisted that in Christ we are more than conquerors (Rom 8:37). How often it happens in human history that men and women put everything into some life achievement; the end is good; the effort is full of nobility; the best of their skill and resources are freely given and freely expended; it is magnificent, and they attain exactly the goal they set themselves and even more—but at the moment of attainment, everything collapses simply because they have tried too well, given themselves too whole-heartedly. The power to enjoy the achievement when it came has been sacrificed by the colossal expenditure to get there.   Wallace, p. 141

Dan 11:35: *Some of the wise will stumble, so that they may be refined, purified and made spotless until the time of the end, for it will still come at the appointed time.*
Personal Note: Pastor John Batusic of Chestnut Mountain Church in Georgia sees the overarching theme of Daniel 11 as the reliability of God's Word. Many events are predicted with amazing accuracy in this chapter. Some scholars have asserted that the predictions were "too accurate" and that they were penned after the fact. But Pastor John says these critics won't submit to the Word, but want the Word to submit to them. You can bend it, fold it, spindle it, and mutilate it, but you can't break the Word of God because the Lord is Lord of His book.

Hosea

Commentary:
- *The Preacher's Commentary*, OT Vol 22, by Lloyd Ogilvie (1990)
- *Cornerstone Biblical Commentary*, Vol 10, (Minor Prophets) by Richard D. Patterson (2008)

Hos 1:2: *When the LORD began to speak through Hosea, the LORD said to him, "Go, marry a promiscuous woman and have children with her, for like an adulterous wife this land is guilty of unfaithfulness to the LORD."*
Hosea was called to make the same choice that was before God. The prophet was commanded to select and marry a woman who was involved in physical adultery just as God was confronted with the choice to be faithful to the people of Israel who were committing spiritual adultery by departing from the Lord. Here we have the first clear rendition of the central theme that will reoccur constantly throughout the symphony of unqualified grace in the Book of Hosea. It is the haunting, pulsating theme of unbroken love from a broken heart. God cannot give up His bride of Sinai regardless of what unfaithfulness she has committed. … We must linger to listen to this theme and allow it to capture our minds. It must become like a familiar song that we hear and then cannot get out of our minds for days. The theme of the unqualified love of God grips our repetitive thought patterns for a lifetime—for eternity. God chooses to choose us even when we have rejected His faithfulness. There are no depths to which we can sink where He will not find us and seek to woo us back into a right relationship with Himself.   Ogilvie, p. 27

Taken from The Preacher's Commentary Series Volume 22: Hosea, Joel, Amos, Obadiah, Jonah by Lloyd J. Ogilvie Copyright © 1990 by Word, Inc. Used by permission of Thomas Nelson. www.thomasnelson.com

Hos 3:1: *The LORD said to me, "Go, show your love to your wife again, though she is loved by another man and is an adulteress. Love her as the LORD loves the Israelites, though they turn to other gods and love the sacred raisin cakes."*

Get inside Hosea's skin. Feel the hurt and anguish. Sense the pain over the rejection of his love for Gomer. Empathize with his desire to block his ears to the gossip about his wife's adultery. Allow your heart to be broken with his as he learns that she not only has other lovers, but that she has gone from flagrant promiscuity to cult prostitution to being sold into slavery. Give vent to the judgment, indignation, and the rage Hosea justifiably feels. And the shame. Don't leave that out. ... Now try to imagine the consternation and utter astonishment Hosea must have felt when Yahweh commanded, 'Go again to this woman.' The very idea sent shock waves through the prophet's heart. ... The word 'again' leaps off the page. It is the *againness* of God's pursuing, persistent love that Hosea is to emulate. ... Yahweh's love is not conditional on Israel's repentance. He loves His people even while they are looking to other gods, defying His command. Ogilvie, excerpts, pp 66, 68, 69

Taken from The Preacher's Commentary Series Volume 22: Hosea, Joel, Amos, Obadiah, Jonah by Lloyd J. Ogilvie Copyright © 1990 by Word, Inc. Used by permission of Thomas Nelson. www.thomasnelson.com

Hos 4:6: *my people are destroyed from lack of knowledge.*

There is nothing more important. With it life is sublime; without it there is constant stress. It is the secret of true success, the source of wisdom beyond our understanding, the strength to endure in hard times. It is our ultimate goal, life's greatest privilege, and our most urgent need. ... What is it? Knowledge of God. Our purpose and passion is to know God [Eph 1:17]. ... Knowledge of God is more than ideas about Him. Knowledge of God involves the total inner person: intellect, emotion, and will. ... We were created to know, to love, to glorify, and to serve God. Knowledge of God is our purpose. We were meant to experience intimacy with God, an intrinsic encounter, one that reveals and brings into union the essential nature and inner being of God and us [Eph 3:16]. In that relationship His nature is recreated in us. From recreation flows integrity, obedience to discover and do His will, to live His commandments, and to do the truth. We are destroyed without that knowledge. Our lives are wrong side up [7:8] !

Ogilvie, excerpts, pp. 75, 82
Taken from The Preacher's Commentary Series Volume 22: Hosea, Joel, Amos, Obadiah, Jonah by Lloyd J. Ogilvie Copyright © 1990 by Word, Inc. Used by permission of Thomas Nelson. www.thomasnelson.com

Hos 6:6: *For I desire mercy, not sacrifice, and acknowledgment of God rather than burnt offerings.*
What we should do because of God's *hesed* [lovingkindness] to us sometimes becomes our effort to earn it. Subtly, it soon becomes a substitute to the knowledge of God, within a responsive relationship with Him. Essentially though, often we cannot be bothered with God. We want to do His basic requirements, then get on with our own agendas. Our sacrifices can include dutiful prayer, attendance at worship, church work, service, and good works. What is to be done in intimate communion *with* God we do *for* God, and eventually we do it *without* God. All these responsibilities are crucial for authentic discipleship. But the danger is that we can become so preoccupied with working for the Lord in our self-justifying effort that our own personal relationship with Him becomes perfunctory rather than primary.   Ogilvie, pp. 114–115
Taken from The Preacher's Commentary Series Volume 22: Hosea, Joel, Amos, Obadiah, Jonah by Lloyd J. Ogilvie Copyright © 1990 by Word, Inc. Used by permission of Thomas Nelson. www.thomasnelson.com

Hos 7:13-14: *I long to redeem them but they speak lies against me. They do not cry out to me from their hearts but wail upon their beds. They gather together for grain and new wine but turn away from me.*
This section details many of the dangers inherent in turning away from a wise and holy God. Covenant-breaking Israel cast off its proper allegiance to the Lord in favor of what was at best a dead orthodoxy mingled with pagan ritual. The results proved to be disastrous. From top to bottom, Israelite society became plagued with all manner of crimes. Corporately and individually, the abandonment of God's standards of righteousness for the pursuit of pagan beliefs brought morality to a new low. Deceit, intrigues, adultery, prostitution, and drunken revelry were rampant. By bringing Yahweh down to the level of Baal, God's people were deceiving themselves in the pursuit of sensual pleasures.

Such is the fate of any nation or society that abandons the true revelation of God so as to recreate him in its own selfish image and exchange pleasure for God's guidance (Prov 11:14; 14:34; 29:18; Isa 2:1-6). Paul predicted that such an egoistic hedonism would be a distinguishing mark of earth's final era before the return of Christ (2 Tim 3:1-5).

Patterson, Richard D., *Cornerstone Biblical Commentary, Vol 10*, Carol Stream IL: Tyndale, 2008 p. 46

Hos 14:1: *Return, O Israel, to the LORD your God. Your sins have been your downfall!*

Hosea is eminently the prophet of God's grace and the need for human repentance. Both themes reach a triumphant crescendo in the final chapter of the prophecy. We cannot read Hosea Chapter 14 without feeling a tug in our souls. … The first step in returning to God is to accept responsibility for departing from Him. When we have stumbled and are flat on our faces, we tend to blame others and circumstances for tripping us. … We all know what it is like to sense a growing distance between us and the Lord. Prayer becomes strained, life becomes increasingly stressful, and our heart becomes restless. The danger is that we settle for this kind of spiritual mediocrity. We feel the emptiness but seek to forget it by filling our lives with distractions. Then when life crumbles or a crisis strikes, we are brought face to face with the person we have become. We stumble because we wandered away from a trusting relationship with God.

Ogilvie, pp 211, 213

Taken from The Preacher's Commentary Series Volume 22: Hosea, Joel, Amos, Obadiah, Jonah by Lloyd J. Ogilvie Copyright © 1990 by Word, Inc. Used by permission of Thomas Nelson. www.thomasnelson.com

Joel

Commentaries:
- *The Books of Joel, Obadiah, Jonah, and Micah*, by Leslie C. Allen (1976)
- *The Message of Joel, Micah, and Habakkuk*, by David Prior (1998)

Joel 1:10-11: *The fields are ruined, the ground is dried up; the grain is destroyed, the new wine is dried up, the oil fails. Despair, you farmers, wail, you vine growers; grieve for the wheat and the barley, because the harvest of the field is destroyed.*

Personal Note: This passage will resonate with American consumers in the Coronavirus pandemic of 2020. All of a sudden, the store shelves were picked clean of items like toilet paper, paper towels, and anti-bacterial wipes. For a few weeks, other items such as meats were scarce (I recall being in a large grocery store where a worker had a little cart loaded with Ground Beef and customers were congregating around the cart to get them while they were available). In America the Land of Plenty, this was a very disconcerting situation.

Joel 2:24–25: *The threshing floors will be filled with grain; the vats will overflow with new wine and oil. I will repay you for the years the locusts have eaten.*

The oracle looks forward to a bountiful harvest that would make any farmer's eyes glisten. It was the practice to spread wheat over the threshing floor ready for the oxen to go round and round loosening the grain and chopping the stalks. Grapes and olives were taken to troughs where they were trodden to extract the juice which flowed into the vats below. These were happy scenes, which made all the previous toil worthwhile [cf Deut 11:14–15, Ps 65:9–11]. Welcome indeed would be the event when the

Lord crowned the year with his generous bounty. Where sin abounds, grace superabounds [Rom 5:20]: God would make up for the produce lost in the years when locusts had ravaged the crops. He would give full compensation. Instead of the locusts eating, the theme is now the people eating the abundance of the Lord's provision. For an obedient people, there is only the prospect of well being, as long as they abide near the fount of every blessing [Prov 3:10–11, Ps 36:8–9]. Allen, p. 95, 96

Allen, Leslie C., *The Books of Joel, Obadiah, Jonah, and Micah*, Copyright © 1976 by William B. Eerdman Publishing, Grand Rapids, MI USA. Part of *New International Commentary on the Old Testament*, Robert L. Hubbard general editor. Reprinted by permission of the publisher.

Personal Note: Verse 25 reverberates eloquently in my soul. My life during much of the 1990's was one of unmitigated sorrow and despair as I reaped the consequences of bad choices I had made. But even though it was all my own silly fault, the Lord graciously pulled me out of the muck and mire I had made of my life, set my feet on firm ground, and put a new song in my heart (Ps 40:1–3). And since that time, my life has completely turned around. The Lord has indeed restored the years the locusts had eaten! May he be forever praised (Ps 13:6)!

Joel 3:16 *The LORD will roar from Zion and thunder from Jerusalem; the earth and the heavens will tremble. But the LORD will be a refuge for his people, a stronghold for the people of Israel*

It is only when our comfortable surroundings are being shaken to the core that we truly experience the relevance of old familiar truths. This statement about the Lord (16) is a classic example. If our world seems safe and sure, who needs a refuge? If we have our lives well organized with plenty of material, social, religious, and human resources to surround us, we hardly need a stronghold somewhere to run into. Many self-sufficient, competent and adjusted people genuinely see no point in having faith in God; he is superfluous—only for wimps and losers.

The sad and serious aspect of such complacency, of course, is even this kind of respectable atheism (practical, usually not intellectual) tends to be shaken at one time or another. That produces an internal conflict which can be worse than the adversity that causes it. Having effectively dismissed faith in God as a crutch for emotional cripples, they find that the same quiet pride in which they sailed on in their serenity now paralyzes them in their agony.

It is of prime importance for the messengers of God in every generation to communicate not a God of the gaps or of the gullible, but a sovereign Lord of heaven and earth, who, in Christ, has called for every knee to bow before him. Although the hurt, the damaged, and the broken hearted will be more likely to bow the knee before him, the missing link is humility, not hopelessness. Prior, p. 96

Taken from *The Message of Joel, Micah & Habakkuk* by David Prior. Copyright (c) 1999 by David Prior. Used by permission of InterVarsity Press, P.O. Box 1400, Downers Grove, IL 60515, USA. www.ivpress.com

Joel 3:18: *In that day the mountains will drip new wine, and the hills will flow with milk;*

all the ravines of Judah will run with water. A fountain will flow out of the LORD's house.

This picture of superabundance surpasses the years of blessing following the restorative work of God after the locust plagues (2:22–24). Nothing anyone has experienced, even in the most halcyon days of God's blessing, can begin to compare with what will be available to the people of God on that day. The promised land had originally been 'a land flowing with milk and honey' (Jos 5:6). Now, after all the vicissitudes of famine, war, locusts, and other plagues, its fertility was to be assured. This superabundance would also indicate that the curse, pronounced on the land by God after the disobedience of Adam and Eve (Gen 3:18) had at long last been lifted. The true source of all this superabundance is made very plain: *A fountain shall come forth from the house of the Lord and water the valley of Shittim* (18). This spring of water is seen to be a supernatural provision, coming from the worshiping life of the people of God. As their holiness is renewed and deepened by the presence of God in their midst, so this profound satisfaction will become a reality as a fruit of their life with God.

Prior, pp. 98, 99

Prior, David, *The Message of Joel, Micah, & Habakkuk*, Taken from *The Bible Speaks Today* Series edited by J. Alec Motyer; John Stott. Copyright ©1998 edited by J. Alec Motyer; John Stott. Used by permission of InterVarsity Press

Personal Note on the Book of Joel

Like most of scripture, the book of Joel can be read on many different levels. The apocalyptic language of chapter 1 has ties to many other books of the Bible (locusts are mentioned fourty-five times in over a dozen other biblical books). In particular, the locusts are described in Joel 1:6 as having teeth like lions and are described the same way in Rev 9:8. Chapter 1 describes sorrow and destruction in vivid and horrifying detail. The locusts eat everything (1:3–4); new wine is snatched from the people's lips (1:5); vines and trees are stripped bare (1:7); fields are ruined and harvests destroyed (1:10–11); the vine and apple tree are dried up and the fig tree has withered (1:12); seeds are shriveled up and storehouses are in ruins (1:17); cattle have no pasture (1:19). The scene from chapter 1 is one of unmitigated disaster.

But then, rays of sunshine begin to gleam. The Lord returns to his people when they return to him (1:13, Jer 29:11–13, James 4:8) and the result is boundless bliss and unmitigated joy. The mountains drip new wine, hills flow with milk, and the ravines run with water (3:18). The fountain flows out of the Lord's house (3:18, James 1:17, Ezek 47:12, Ps 103:1–5). The Lord even restores what the locusts have eaten (2:25).

Life sometimes looks like Joel Chapter 1 when it bursts in on us with one sorrow after another. In times like that we, like the ancient Israelites, should redouble our efforts to seek the Lord in prayer. We need to ask the question of 2:14 ("who knows?") before we can experience the blessings of 2:23–25. Some of the blessings described in this little book will only be realized in when we reach the glory of the end times (eg Isa 25:6–8), but I believe the Lord also aims to bless us here and now (John 10:10). The key is to stay on his divinely lit path (Ps 16:11, 119:105, Prov 3:5–8, Isa 2:5, Isa 30:21). For that path is the only one which in the end leads to true joy and contentment [Isa 35:8–10].

Amos

Commentaries:
- *The Message of Amos*, by J. Alec Motyer (1974)
- *The Preacher's Commentary*, OT Vol 22, by Lloyd Ogilvie (1990)

Amos 4:7–8: *"I also withheld rain from you when the harvest was still three months away.*
I sent rain on one town, but withheld it from another. One field had rain; another had none and dried up. People staggered from town to town for water but did not get enough to drink, yet you have not returned to me," declares the LORD.

Troubles apparently fall by chance—rain here, drought there, seemingly haphazard, luck for one, ill luck for the other. But over against them all is the first person singular of divine decision and action. Everything on earth comes from a God who rules and reigns in heaven. The biblical view is that God is sovereign both over history and experiences of man. Words could not be plainer, and unless we wish to trim Him down to the poor limits of a God nice enough to suit our emotions, small enough to fit within our logic and effete enough to leave room for our wills, we shall bow before the Sovereign revealed in this passage and throughout the rest of the Bible.
Motyer, p. 97

Taken from *The Bible Speaks Today* Series edited by J. Alec Motyer; John Stott. Copyright ©1983 edited by J. Alec Motyer; John Stott. Used by permission of InterVarsity Press, P.O. Box 1400, Downers Grove, IL 60515, USA. www.ivpress.com Taken from *The Message of Amos* by J. Alec Motyer. Copyright (c) 1984 by J. Alec Motyer. Used by permission of InterVarsity Press, P.O. Box 1400, Downers Grove, IL 60515, USA. www.ivpress.com

Amos 5:23–24: *Away with the noise of your songs! I will not listen to the music of your harps.*

But let justice roll on like a river, righteousness like a never-failing stream!
There is no doubt that they went in for religion in a big way at Gilgal. Somehow the vivacity of it all and the thrill of it all communicates itself. One can almost hear the singing. But God could not! All he heard was noise. There cannot be a passage in the Bible more deliberately expressing divine distaste than this: *I hate...I despise...take no delight...will not accept...will not look upon...take away from me the noise...I will not listen.* Their religion was dutiful, exceedingly costly, apparently whole-hearted, emotionally satisfying. But if religion does not get through to God, it has failed centrally [cf Isa 1:11, Hos 6:6, 9:4]. ...The Lord is looking for lives whose energies, abundantly and perpetually, are flowing out in righteousness and justice [1 Kings 10:9, Ps 33:5, 56:1]: the cultivation and holding of sound moral principles of life, and the practice of these principles in personal and social behavior. And religion is pointless unless this is its outflow. The trouble with Gilgal was that they kept their religion in a box, a sealed compartment with no communicating exits. It made no difference to life before or after, and therefore it had no significance before God.

Motyer, p. 131, 133

Motyer, J. Alec, *The Message of Amos,* Taken from *The Bible Speaks Today* Series edited by J. Alec Motyer; John Stott. Copyright ©1974 edited by J. Alec Motyer; John Stott. Used by permission of InterVarsity Press, P.O. Box 1400, Downers Grove, IL 60515, USA. www.ivpress.com

"He who seeks God in some external routine will find the routine and lose God."
Meister Eckhart (1260–1327)   Quoted in Ward and Wild

Amos 8:2 *"What do you see, Amos?" he asked. "A basket of ripe fruit," I answered.*
Then the LORD said to me, "The time is ripe for my people Israel; I will spare them no longer."
The Israelite society suffered the loss of stability and regularity, where absolutes are no longer recognized and rules are there to break. The further man gets from his moorings in God, the further he gets from all moorings [cf Prov 4:19].

Motyer, p. 179

Motyer, J. Alec, *The Message of Amos,* Taken from *The Bible Speaks Today* Series edited by J. Alec Motyer; John Stott. Copyright ©1974 edited by J. Alec Motyer; John Stott.

Used by permission of InterVarsity Press, P.O. Box 1400, Downers Grove, IL 60515, USA. www.ivpress.com

Amos 8:11: *"The days are coming," declares the Sovereign LORD, "when I will send a famine through the land- not a famine of food or a thirst for water, but a famine of hearing the words of the LORD."* [cf 1 Sam 3:1]
By far the greatest manifestation of the judgment of God on Israel's unrepentant hypocrisy will be a famine of hearing the words of the Lord. Note that it will not be a famine of the words of the Lord, but a famine of hearing. Hypocrisy has ripened to the place that the people no longer seek God's words, nor do they listen when He speaks. A virus of unresponsiveness has debilitated the audio nerve in the souls of the people. For years the people did not want to hear God; now He will grant their desire.... The phrase 'words of the Lord' is synonymous both with communion with Him and communications from Him. We cannot do without either. But we try. We seek to fill our spiritual hunger with substitutes. ... Beneath all our surface needs is the one great need for God Himself. Only communion with him and communication from Him will give us security, stability, and strength. Ogilvie, pp 361
Taken from The Preacher's Commentary Series Volume 22: Hosea, Joel, Amos, Obadiah, Jonah by Lloyd J. Ogilvie Copyright © 1990 by Word, Inc. Used by permission of Thomas Nelson. www.thomasnelson.com

Obadiah

Commentaries:
- *The Books of Joel, Obadiah, Jonah, and Micah*, by Leslie C. Allen (1976)
- *The Preacher's Commentary*, OT Vol 22, By Lloyd J. Ogilvie (1990)

Obad 3: *The pride of your heart has deceived you, you who live in the clefts of the rocks and make your home on the heights, you who say to yourself, 'Who can bring me down to the ground?'*

The Edomites became a people to match the rocky, ragged crags and serrated ridges of the Seir territory. They were a hard, earthy people, proud, cruel, and fierce. Their problem was not syncretism with other gods; they had no gods at all. ... We think of the contemporary Edomites where arrogance rules their lives. They are the materialists whose security is in human power and possessions. Accountable to no one but themselves, they perpetuate the cult of humanism. Bloated egoism results. Their motto is, 'What's good is what makes me feel great.' These are the truly dangerous people—the real enemies of God. And our enemies too, because their lack of accountability to anyone greater than themselves makes them willing tools of the archenemy, Satan. ... But God is not mocked. He brings down the arrogant, if not in their lifetime, in their death and in history's evaluation of them. ... Greatness is not measured in our achievement for our own glory but in the measure that we glorify God. Without that, life is an empty quest for human greatness.   Ogilvie, excerpts, p. 391, 395
Taken from The Preacher's Commentary Series Volume 22: Hosea, Joel, Amos, Obadiah, Jonah by Lloyd J. Ogilvie Copyright © 1990 by Word, Inc. Used by permission of Thomas Nelson. www.thomasnelson.com

Obad 21: *Deliverers will go up on Mount Zion to govern the mountains of Esau. And the kingdom will be the LORD's.*

The territorial and imperialistic emphasis of the passage is embarrassing to the Christian reader, but it is of a piece with general OT theology, whereby the blessing of God was intimately bound up with material possession of the land of promise. Accordingly the land had a sacramental significance: spiritual restoration to divine favor is inextricably linked with material restoration to Palestine. The Christian is handed the book of Obadiah as part of the OT heritage he has received with Christ. He will interpret the hope of territorial expansion [1 Chr 4:10, Isa 54:2] in terms of his inspired teachers in the NT, finding in it encouragement to possess the land whose horizons he can now understand to be far wider and higher [Eph 3:18–19] than Obadiah was privileged to grasp. But his interpretation will be no more spiritual than the literal one of Obadiah, for whom matter was ideally the incarnation of spirit. Allen, p. 172

Allen, Leslie C., *The Books of Joel, Obadiah, Jonah, and Micah*, Copyright © 1976 by William B. Eerdman Publishing, Grand Rapids, MI USA. Part of *New International Commentary on the Old Testament*, Robert L. Hubbard general editor. Reprinted by permission of the publisher

Jonah

Commentaries:
- *The Message of Jonah*, by Rosemary Nixon (2003)
- *The Books of Joel, Obadiah, Jonah, and Micah*, by Leslie C. Allen (1976)

Jonah 1:5 *All the sailors were afraid and each cried out to his own god. And they threw the cargo into the sea to lighten the ship.*
Benighted heathens as they are, they resort to S.O.S. prayers. They are doomed to obtain no help from that expedient, because the cosmopolitan crew worships various gods of their own and not Yahweh. It is a case of 'All is lost! To prayer! To prayer!', but the situation is too serious for false religion to solve…. Thrown back on their own resources, the seamen jettison the cargo. They try to deal with the storm God had thrown upon the sea with a counter-throw. But if religion was no solution, neither is the way of works. The problem lies elsewhere, beyond the sailors' knowledge. One feels sorry for them, caught up unawares in the consequences of the sin of that wretch Jonah, and so the narrator intends.   Allen, p. 207
Allen, Leslie C., *The Books of Joel, Obadiah, Jonah, and Micah*, Copyright © 1976 by William B. Eerdman Publishing, Grand Rapids, MI USA. Part of *New International Commentary on the Old Testament*, Robert L. Hubbard general editor. Reprinted by permission of the publisher

Jonah 1:8–9: *So they asked him, "Tell us, who is responsible for making all this trouble for us? What do you do? Where do you come from? What is your country? From what people are you?"*
He answered, "I am a Hebrew and I worship the LORD, the God of heaven, who made the sea and the land."
Ironically, it is his claim to fear the Lord, a claim blatantly at odds with his response to God's call which the narrator considers most significant.

In putting Jonah on the spot, the pagan sailors were putting his God on the spot. It is they who force the issue. The pagans were more committed to their faith than Jonah was to his; at least they prayed and sought divine assistance. By contrast, Jonah, who enjoyed all the blessings of knowing the Lord, epitomized the privatization of faith. But the Lord would have none of this. It is often easier to stand by creedal statements than to walk by them. The role of the world is to challenge believers to identify themselves as witnesses to the Lord God and to walk or live by the beliefs by which they stand. Nixon, p 105, 106

Nixon, Rosemary, *The Message of Jonah* Leicester Taken from *The Bible Speaks Today* Series edited by J. Alec Motyer; John Stott. Copyright ©1983 edited by J. Alec Motyer; John Stott. Used by permission of InterVarsity Press, P.O. Box 1400, Downers Grove, IL 60515, USA. www.ivpress.com

Jonah 2:1: *From inside the fish Jonah prayed to the LORD his God*
We would be justified in believing the belly of Sheol to be Jonah's tomb, but the prayer now on the prophet's lips transforms the belly of the fish into a place of potential new life, a womb.

By hiding or protecting ourselves from God's reality we become deluded. Like Jonah, we might dig our hiding places so deep that we become entombed. We may become blind to the unsavory reality within us, and deaf to the cries of those around us. We can even build our defenses so high that it takes some kind of disaster before we can be exposed to God's reality. To pray is to admit that Another Reality, One which is distinct from our own, exists. It is a Reality which is different from ours and possibly therefore threatening. It is a Reality which constantly seeks to be in relationship with us. The Lord God is this Reality. Yahweh is the only safe hiding place, the only secure refuge [Ps 46:1]. Only here may we acknowledge and expose our total defenselessness, powerlessness, and vulnerability. To unmask ourselves in prayer is to begin to discover who we really are in the presence of this faithful One. In prayer, the heart, the eyes, and ears of the human soul are opened to the possibility of being touched and healed by this Other Reality, the brooding Holy Spirit of God. Prayer is the breath of life. Nixon, p. 136, 137

Nixon, Rosemary, *The Message of Jonah* Leicester Taken from *The Bible Speaks Today* Series edited by J. Alec Motyer; John Stott. Copyright ©2003 edited by J.

Alec Motyer; John Stott. Used by permission of InterVarsity Press, P.O. Box 1400, Downers Grove, IL 60515, USA. www.ivpress.com

Personal Note: Human beings sometimes assume that the only reality is one that can be examined and measured by our senses and scientific instruments. But what if we are wrong? [Eccl 8:17]. Scientists recently discovered that we only "see" five percent of the universe and the rest may constitute "dark matter" and "dark energy". The notion of a reality outside our senses is vividly described by Philip Yancey in his book *Rumors of Another World: What on Earth are we Missing?* He speaks of "thin places" where only a thin vale separates the natural world from the supernatural. Yancey writes: "If I see myself as one more species of animal, with no life beyond this one and no accountability to a Higher Power, then why not follow the pleasure instinct to the end? On the other hand, if I see this planet as God's world, and my longings as rumors of another world, then I want to connect those clues to God's overall plan. I want to bring the two worlds together, and I do so by accepting that we human beings must look beyond ourselves—above ourselves—for direction in ordering our desires." (Yancey, p. 60–61)

Jonah 3:2–3: *Go to the great city of Nineveh and proclaim to it the message I give you."*
Jonah obeyed the word of the LORD and went to Nineveh.
So often, God's call is just unreasonable. Notice however, that God does not negotiate with the prophet to arrive at a mutually agreeable calling. Certainly the call remained as unreasonable in Chapter 3 as it had been in chapter 1. In terms of our limited human understanding, God's ways sometimes appear not only unreasonable, but eccentric and anarchic.... Mission involves taking risks, traversing boundaries, crossing over into dangerous places only to discover that God is already there.

Nixon, p. 157, 162

Nixon, Rosemary, *The Message of Jonah* Leicester Taken from *The Bible Speaks Today* Series edited by J. Alec Motyer; John Stott. Copyright ©2003 edited by J. Alec Motyer; John Stott. Used by permission of InterVarsity Press, P.O. Box 1400, Downers Grove, IL 60515, USA. www.ivpress.com

Jonah 4:9: *But God said to Jonah, "Do you have a right to be angry about the vine?"*

Jonah and his self-pity fade away, and the Jonahs among the listening circle feel that Yahweh is putting the question to them personally. The story is deliberately left open-ended and the listeners are brought face to face with the existential challenge of the story, just as in the parable of the Prodigal Son, the appeal to the elder brother was really addressed to the religious snobs of Jesus' day (Lk 15:2, 31, 32). Did those scribes and Pharisees slink away into the spiritual night, or did some at least greet the prodigal tax-collectors as their long-lost brothers? And whose side did the listening circle take? Jonah's whose petty attitude they had constantly been invited to condemn? Or did they identify themselves with the divine Hero, whose love is broader than the measures of man's mind? [Eph 3:19] A Jonah lurks in every Christian heart, whimpering his insidious message of smug prejudice, empty traditionalism, and exclusive solidarity. He that has ears to hear, let him hear and allow the saving love of God which has been outpoured in his own heart to remold his thinking and social orientation [Rom 12:2]. Allen, p. 234, 235

Allen, Leslie C., *The Books of Joel, Obadiah, Jonah, and Micah*, Copyright © 1976 by William B. Eerdman Publishing, Grand Rapids, MI USA. Part of *New International Commentary on the Old Testament*, Robert L. Hubbard general editor. Reprinted by permission of the publisher

Jonah 4:10–11: *But the LORD said, "You have been concerned about this vine, though you did not tend it or make it grow. It sprang up overnight and died overnight. But Nineveh has more than a hundred and twenty thousand people who cannot tell their right hand from their left, and many cattle as well. Should I not be concerned about that great city?"*

In the text he (Jonah) remains silent as the Lord God offers him the way to life. I have forgiven, he whispers, and waits patiently for his and our reply.

Nixon, Introduction, p 41

Nixon, Rosemary, *The Message of Jonah* Leicester Taken from *The Bible Speaks Today* Series edited by J. Alec Motyer; John Stott. Copyright ©2003 edited by J. Alec Motyer; John Stott. Used by permission of InterVarsity Press, P.O. Box 1400, Downers Grove, IL 60515, USA. www.ivpress.com

Micah

Commentaries:
- *The Books of Joel, Obadiah, Jonah, and Micah*, by Leslie C. Allen (1976)
- *The Message of Joel, Micah, and Habakkuk*, by David Prior (1998)

Mic 6:8: *He has told you, O man, what is good; And what does the LORD require of you But to do justice, to love kindness, And to walk humbly with your God?* [NASB]

God wants our very selves, our lives and our love. This is the costliest sacrifice we can bring, a living sacrifice of our souls and bodies (Rom 12:1). This is the only reasonable response we can make to his redeeming love. … Micah's three-fold requirement cannot be conveniently dissected, packaged, and labeled. The three quantities hold together. It is only by applying ourselves to the third (to walk humbly with your God), that we can begin to practice the first two (to do justice and to love kindness). That is, also, what it means to love the Lord your God with all your heart, soul, mind, and strength and to love your neighbor as yourself (Mk 12:28–34). They do not come down from heaven wrapped in parcels. They are expressed in and through people who walk humbly with their God.
Prior, p. 177

Prior, David, *The Message of Joel, Micah, & Habakkuk*, Taken from *The Bible Speaks Today* Series edited by J. Alec Motyer; John Stott. Copyright ©1998 edited by J. Alec Motyer; John Stott. Used by permission of InterVarsity Press, P.O. Box 1400, Downers Grove, IL 60515, USA. www.ivpress.com

Personal Note: Micah 6:6–8 has been set to music beautifully in an excellent choral work called *Offertory*, by John Ness Beck.

Mic 7:18: *Who is a God like you, who pardons sin and forgives the transgression of the remnant of his inheritance? You do not stay angry forever but delight to show mercy.*

The fourth and final movement of this liturgical symphony is a choral piece of devotion and doxology. It begins in the style of a hymn, extolling the compassionate nature of God. A theme from the opening movement is taken up and developed, the burden of God's wrath resting upon the sin-conscious hearts of the community. They have come in repentance, but that is not enough to win back the blessing of God. He is no petulant princeling to be wooed away from a fit of capricious temper. Nothing they can do will avail of itself to secure God's acceptance. The sole ground of their hope lies in the noble character of God as one who forgives [Ps 103:8-12], forgets [Isa 65:17], and offers a fresh beginning [2 Cor 5:17]. ... The heartfelt appreciation of divine grace that impassions this finale is an emotion that can be experienced only by those who have come to see sin through God's eyes. Believers know that the purpose of God's dealings with them is to train them in the ways of righteousness and harmony with him. To this end, chastisement may play a part, but over and beyond it lies the mystery of grace. Allen, p. 401, 402

Allen, Leslie C., *The Books of Joel, Obadiah, Jonah, and Micah*, Copyright © 1976 by William B. Eerdman Publishing, Grand Rapids, MI USA. Part of *New International Commentary on the Old Testament*, Robert L. Hubbard general editor. Reprinted by permission of the publisher

Nahum

Commentary:
- *The Books of Nahum, Habakkuk, and Zephaniah*, by O. Palmer Robertson (NICOT) (1990)
- *Cornerstone Biblical Commentary*, Vol 10, (Minor Prophets) by Richard D. Patterson (2008)

Nah 1:6: *Who can withstand his indignation? Who can endure his fierce anger? His wrath is poured out like fire; the rocks are shattered before him.*
Nahum initially declares (1:2-3) that God is a God of justice who will not allow his person or power to be impugned. He will deal justly with the ungodly. The theme of judgment is balanced by the knowledge that God is "slow to get angry." His judicial wrath is not always immediate. At times, he holds back his wrath against his foes until the proper occasion. God's government, including his judicial processes, is on schedule, even though to a waiting humanity his timing may seem to lag. ...Nahum gives a graphic picture of the limitless and invincible power of God. Accordingly, he can ask whether any could stand in the face of such an almighty one when he executes his wrath. The answer is "No one, no one at all!" By implication, this response anticipates the subject of his prophecy: Not even mighty Nineveh, home to the Assyrian world empire, would be able to withstand the sovereign God of all nature. The creator, controller, and consummator of this world and its history is the same one who will not leave the guilty unpunished. Patterson, excerpts, pp. 365, 366

Nah 3:1: *Woe to the city of blood, full of lies, full of plunder, never without victims!*
The bloodthirsty city aptly describes the life-style of a metropolitan community devoted to the glory of man rather than the glory of God.

E.B. Pusey appropriately recalls the contrast found in Augustine's *City of God*: 'Two sorts of love had made two sorts of cities: the earthly love of self to the contempt of God; the heavenly love of God even to the contempt of self. The one glorieth in itself, the other in the Lord.' ... Bloodthirsty indeed was the ancient city of Nineveh. On one of the sculptured reliefs found in Ashburnipal's palace is a scene featuring the king and queen celebrating victory over the Elamites. Depicted near the banqueting table is a fruit tree with the severed head of the king of Elam dangling from one of the branches. Bloodthirsty indeed. Let all generations remember the atmosphere for banqueting created by this specter situated about the table of the Assyrians. Carved in stone by their own hands and so representing how they themselves chose to be remembered—so be it.

Robertson, pp 100, 101

Nah 3:19: *Nothing can heal your wound; your injury is fatal. Everyone who hears the news about you claps his hands at your fall, for who has not felt your endless cruelty?*

Why can there be no *lessening* of his punishment? Because although the wheels of God's justice grind slowly, they grind exceedingly fine. The time comes when the longsuffering of God will endure no more. Then he shall bring swift vengeance on his enemies. Such a message applies to every oppressor. At a certain point, the time comes when the Lord will endure no more. For a while he may suffer the tyrant to live in luxury bought with the blood of his martyrs [Rev 6:9–10]. But a complete reckoning shall be required.

Perhaps the most tragic dimension of the demise of the king of Assyria is Nahum's note that all people everywhere will rejoice in his end. *All who hear your story will clap their hands over you.* Universally the response shall be the same. Without newspapers, television, radio, or satellite, the word will spread overnight. When an oppressive monarch like Ashurbanipal falls, the reverberations are heard to the ends of the earth. A vigorous, jubilant, uninhibited applause shall break out spontaneously at the death of Nineveh's king.

The reason for this response among the nations is plain to see. The prophet poses his final question in unavoidable terms: *upon whom has not your cruelty been inflicted?* To the mighty monarch he says, What can you

expect? Shall those whose eyes you have gouged out shed tears at your death? Shall the tongues you have chopped off recite your praises? The ultimate tragedy of persistent sin is vividly displayed in the final word about the king of Assyria. God will destroy him along with his nation, and people will universally break out in shouts of jubilation, clapping their hands at the destruction of their tormentor.
Robertson, excerpts, pp. 129–130

Habakkuk

Commentaries:
- *The Message of Joel, Micah, and Habakkuk*, by David Prior (1998)
- *The Preacher's Commentary*, OT Vol 23 by Walter Kaiser. (1992)

Hab 1:5: *"Look at the nations and watch- and be utterly amazed. For I am going to do something in your days that you would not believe, even if you were told."*
In answer to his honest prayer, God tells him to look again, and to look further afield. Habakkuk is instructed to turn his eyes away from his own little world and watch God at work on a wider canvas. Like us, the prophet had become preoccupied, if not obsessed, with his own situation. His horizons had narrowed to the limits of his own vision and experience [Eccl 1:14]. He could not lift himself above the daily events of his particular circumstances [Col 3:2]. Because God seemed to be inactive, indeed absent, he was becoming sucked into a downward spiral of doubt and despair. … God listened to Habakkuk and addressed the prophet's burning concern in specific detail. He still does so today. But we need to be open to God's lateral thinking. His perception and perspective are much wider than ours. He sees the end from the beginning and he sees the whole picture. … Our judgments are radically affected by time, space, and mortality. God stands outside all three. Yet, in his compassion and concern, he takes our prayers very seriously [Ps 56:8, 66:19].   Prior, p. 212, 213

Prior, David, *The Message of Joel, Micah, & Habakkuk*, Taken from *The Bible Speaks Today* Series edited by J. Alec Motyer; John Stott. Copyright ©1998 edited by J. Alec Motyer; John Stott. Used by permission of InterVarsity Press, P.O. Box 1400, Downers Grove, IL 60515, USA. www.ivpress.com

Hab 2:3: *For the revelation awaits an appointed time; it speaks of the end and will not prove false. Though it linger, wait for it; it will certainly come and will not delay.*

This verse appears to be self-contradictory—wait for it, it will not delay. The apparent conflict can be explained, as John Calvin suggested, in that the vision may appear to tarry from the human perspective while from the divine side its certainty is never in doubt and its fulfillment is never delayed [cf Ps 27:13–14, 130:5–6, Isa 25:9, Rom 8:25]. Kaiser, p. 167

<u>Personal Note</u>: One of the men in my prayer group said "God is sometimes kinda slow, but he's never late."

Hab 3:17–18: *Though the fig tree does not bud and there are no grapes on the vines, though the olive crop fails and the fields produce no food, though there are no sheep in the pen and no cattle in the stalls, yet I will rejoice in the LORD, I will be joyful in God my Savior.* [cf Job 1:21]

It is one thing to thank and praise God for all the good things in our lives, to rejoice in our blessings. It is quite another to rejoice in the midst of nothing, when all these blessings have been summarily and completely removed. The prophet has learned to rejoice, not in any particular quantity or quality of blessings, but in God himself [1 Th 5:18]. God never changes. If we learn—if we are liberated—to find our joy in the Lord, regardless of any good things we may or may not receive from his hand, then he remains a continuous source and cause of rejoicing. ... This is because God is the Lord, the Creator of the universe and the covenant-keeping God, who can be known and appreciated for his unchanging characteristics of compassion [Ps 103:3–4] and holiness [Isa 6:3]. He never changes in these qualities. He remains a cause for great joy because he is who he is [Neh 8:10].

Prior, pp 275–276

Prior, David, *The Message of Joel, Micah, & Habakkuk,* Taken from *The Bible Speaks Today* Series edited by J. Alec Motyer; John Stott. Copyright ©1998 edited by J. Alec Motyer; John Stott. Used by permission of InterVarsity Press, P.O. Box 1400, Downers Grove, IL 60515, USA. www.ivpress.com

<u>Personal Note</u>: These verses were keynotes in our church during the depths of the Coronavirus pandemic in March and April of 2020. The store shelves were indeed empty. But even during tough times like this, we need to remember our gracious Lord and Savior who has given us more than we can ask or even imagine! [Eph 3:20].

Zephaniah

Commentaries:
- *The Message of Obadiah, Nahum, and Zephaniah*, by Gordon Bridger (2010)\
- *The Books of Nahum, Habakkuk, and Zephaniah*, by O. Palmer Robertson (1990)

Zp 1:4: *"I will stretch out my hand against Judah and against all who live in Jerusalem. I will cut off from this place every remnant of Baal, the names of the pagan and the idolatrous priests"*
A few weeks after the striking of the Twin Towers in New York on that fateful day in September 2001, Anne Graham Lotz was asked 'How could God let something like September 11th happen?' Part of her reply was as follows, 'I believe that God is deeply saddened by this just as we are; but for years we've been telling God to get out of our schools, to get out of our government, and to get out of our lives. And being the gentleman that he is I believe that he has calmly backed out. How can we expect God to give us his protection if we demand that he leaves us alone?' Bridger, p. 197

Zp 1:5: *those who bow down on the roofs to worship the starry host, those who bow down and swear by the LORD and who also swear by Molech*
Syncretism involves the mixing of different religious systems, practices, and loyalties. It's a feature of western society in the 21st century. We live in a pluralistic society; and for many people pluralism means not only that we have many different religions in post-modern Britain, but that each religion is equally valid. This is perfectly illustrated in New Age religion, which combines ideas and practices from different religions in a 'pick and mix' way. No doubt those who encouraged such syncretistic practices believed they were acting in a more culturally relevant way. But

God's Word has always been clear: 'You shall have no other gods before me.' (Deut 5:7). ... The Bible speaks about God as a jealous God. He has a right to our exclusive loyalty. To compromise, to hedge our bets, to 'pick and mix' our religion or to engage in multi-faith worship is to invite the judgment of God.
Bridger, pp 206, 207

Zp 3:17: *The LORD your God is with you, he is mighty to save. He will take great delight in you, he will quiet you with his love, he will rejoice over you with singing.*

Now the prophet moves into the 'holy of holies' by a rapturous description of the love of God for his people. This verse is the John 3:16 of the OT. That Almighty God should derive delight from his own creation is significant in itself [cf Gn 1:31, Ps 149:4, Isa 65:19]. But that the Holy One should experience ecstasy over the sinner is incomprehensible. The mutuality of the loving response of Redeemer and redeemed is seen in the that fact that some of the same terms used in the admonition to his people now describe the response of God himself to his people [Deut 30:9]. The whole scene depicts a grand oratorio as God and his people mutually rejoice in their love for one another. ... Almighty God, quiet in his love. God the mighty savior [Isa 60:16], quietly contemplating, contented in his love for you. If the prophet's mode of expression appears excessive, it must be remembered that God in his very essence is love (1 John 4:8). As the direct source of all true love, he not only is capable of achieving every depth of salutary love experienced by his creation. He by his very nature may excel every human emotion of true love [Ps 36:5]. If a human being with all the limitations of his nature may revel in the purity of essential love in short, snatched moments, then certainly the Almighty himself may reach even greater depths of love and sustain these depths without restriction of time [Jer 31:3].
Robertson, excerpts, p. 334–341

Haggai

Commentary:
- *The Preacher's Commentary*, OT Vol 23, by Walter Kaiser (1992)

Hag 1:5: *Now this is what the LORD Almighty says: "Give careful thought to your ways."*
The prophet urges this 4 times in 38 verses (1:5, 1:7, 2:15, 2:18). Haggai was pointing to the people's desperate need to examine their hearts and search out the direction of their lives [Lam 3:40]. If God's work was not at the top of their priorities, how could they be sure they had not fallen into serious idolatry? Was not the genius of idolatry putting any idea, person, goal, or commitment on par or above the living God? Kaiser, p. 258

<u>**Personal Note**</u>: Pastor Joshua Knott (EPC Delaware) delivered a message on 6/23/2013 on this and surrounding verses. In verse 2, the people offer a "pleasant" way to put off the building. Knott pointedly asks what needs to be built in your life and are you putting it off? The prophet asks us to consider our ways, and Knott asks, "How is your me first and God second way working for you?" The prophet then connects the dots between the people's covenant breaking sin and the consequences (eg, v 6). The Lord loves us too much to leave us content with the blessings of this world so we miss those of the eternal life to come. God's grace makes sin hurt, and we need to stop fighting the spirit and be led by the spirit. That is where the freedom and joy are to be found!

Hag 2:7 *'I will shake all nations, and the desired of all nations will come, and I will fill this house with glory,' says the LORD Almighty.*
So the word for discouraged people who feel they may be off to the hinterlands of God's service is this: God's work done in God's ways will never lack in splendor, eternal significance or the personal presence of our

Lord. The kingdom, the glory, and the person of our Lord will remain when everything else has given way. They are unshakable. Let us, therefore, forsake all negative attitudes about the work of God: his Name, his Cause, and His Kingdom will most certainly triumph over everything!

Kaiser, p. 273

Zechariah

Commentaries:
- *Zechariah*, by Richard D. Phillips (REC Series) (2007)
- *The Message of Zechariah*, by Barry Webb (BST series) (2003)
- *The Preacher's Commentary*, OT Vol 23, by Walter C. Kaiser (1992)

Zech 1:3 *Therefore tell the people: This is what the LORD Almighty says: 'Return to me,' declares the LORD Almighty, 'and I will return to you,' says the LORD Almighty.*

The simple but profound solution to Israel's current state of sin was to 'return' to the Lord. No other single word epitomized the prophets more accurately than this single word to 'turn' or 'return'. In all of Scripture, that is the one prerequisite to receiving any of God's blessings. The summons to return is God's call to us to reverse our directions; when we are following our own goals and aims God asks us to do a 180 degree turn and make Him the goal and aim of our lives.

We return to the Lord, for we live only by God's grace. He asks only that we be willing to turn our backs on our sins and turn to face Him, the only source of every blessing. It is so important we do so that Zechariah three times notes that it is the Lord who says we should return to Him. Thus he drums into our consciousness an idea we would usually resist.

Kaiser, pp 303–304

Zech 3:3–4: *Now Joshua was dressed in filthy clothes as he stood before the angel. The angel said to those who were standing before him, "Take off his filthy clothes." Then he said to Joshua, "See, I have taken away your sin, and I will put rich garments on you."*

Joshua is manifestly unfit to be in the presence of God [Isa 6:5, Isa 64:6, Lk 5:8], let alone serve him as high priest. And that means that the

whole community is in trouble, because Joshua is their mediator and representative.... It is not merely the problem of having done unclean things, but of being an unclean man. Joshua stands before the angel of the Lord turned inside out, with what he really is on full display, covered with shame and condemned in the court of heaven. Satan, the accuser, does not even need to present the case against him: the filthy clothes Joshua wears do it for him. There is surely no hope for this man, or for those he represents. But now something totally unexpected happens. The Lord declares that Joshua is a saved man, a burning stick snatched from the fire (2b), and that he simply will not allow any charge Satan brings against him to stand.... The essence of the matter is captured in the pronouncement of verse 4: 'See, I have taken away your sin.' This is good news indeed for Joshua. What better news could any man hear?   Webb, p. 86, 87
God's command is: 'Take away the filthy garments from him' (v 4), for the Angel said he would clothe him instead with 'rich robes'. What a graphic picture of the free, gracious forgiveness and removal of sin from all who confess their sin to our Lord! Joshua could no more cleanse himself than we can! Someone had to take the filthy clothes away from him. These 'rich robes' are the garments of salvation [Isa 61:10]. They are the perfect righteousness of our Lord in which all who believe are attired. Joshua was reinstated and reconsecrated by this act of replacing his garment, and, since he was a 'sign', so were all who believed thereby assured of complete cleansing from God.   Kaiser, pp 332–333

Zech 9:9: *Rejoice greatly, O Daughter of Zion! Shout, Daughter of Jerusalem! See, your king comes to you, righteous and having salvation, gentle and riding on a donkey, on a colt, the foal of a donkey.*
These spontaneous outbursts of exuberant joy are an expression of enormous jubilation and celebration over the fact that the earth will finally receive her King. Isaac Watts paraphrased Psalm 98, which celebrates the same event; with the words 'Joy to the world, the Lord has come. Let earth receive her King.' Few events in the history of our planet are more worthy of shouting over. ... Like his celebrated entrance into Jerusalem on Palm Sunday, Jesus will come once again as King of kings and Lord of lords in order to rule and reign forever and forever. What a triumphant return that will be! If

ever there was a reason to shout, this is it. The Messiah King is Lord of the whole earth! Kaiser, p. 386, 388

Zech 12:10: *"And I will pour out on the house of David and the inhabitants of Jerusalem a spirit of grace and supplication. They will look on me, the one they have pierced, and they will mourn for him as one mourns for an only child, and grieve bitterly for him as one grieves for a firstborn son."*
Godly sorrow is the garden in which all sorts of good fruits are grown, especially the repentance that leads to salvation. Zechariah makes clear the source of such mourning, stating that godly sorrow is the gift of the Holy Spirit. Charles Spurgeon wrote 'There never was any real godly sorrow, such as worketh repentance acceptable unto God, except that which was the result of the Holy Spirit's work within the soul.' It is not, Spurgeon adds, the product of mere conscience, which though pricked is not able to rise to these spiritual heights. It is not produced by mere terror of judgment, without the quickening of God's Spirit. True mourning, which rises up to be received by God, always grieves for the sin and not just for the situation into which it has brought us. … What is it about Jesus that causes such sorrow when we see him pierced? First, it is his loveliness, the excellency of him who bore our sins. Here is one utterly pure in heart, one so holy that before him angels veil their faces. In him there never was any sin, and to this his whole life bears testimony. … Why, we ask, looking to him now pierced, is it he that bears our punishment? We perhaps grow callous to suffering, but here is One who truly does not deserve any of what he is receiving. We are the ones who deserve it.   Phillips, pp. 272–273
Personal Note: This majestic verse, with it's mention of "only son" and "first born son" reminds us of John 3:16.

Zech 13:1 *"On that day a fountain will be opened to the house of David and the inhabitants of Jerusalem, to cleanse them from sin and impurity."*
Ezekiel 36:25 employs this theme: 'I will sprinkle clean water on you and you shall be clean.' Zechariah foresees a whole fountain of such cleaning fluid opening up not just a sprinkling but an abounding, flooding provision of grace, as the remedy for the great sorrow of those who look on the One whom they have pierced. The idea is that of a pent-up spring now let loose, so that the waters long confined may now gush forth in abundance. … It

is a particularly apt depiction of Jesus Christ's cleansing blood, shed on the cross. This cleansing, the prophet says, will be made available to the house of David and the inhabitants of Jerusalem. Given the earlier statement that God's spirit will make us mourn for the pierced one (12:10), it is clearly the blood of the Messiah that comes forth to cleanse. ... The hymnist William Cowper put it this way in his famous hymn

> *There is a fountain filled with blood drawn from Immanuel's veins*
> *And sinners plunged beneath the flood lose all their guilty stains.*

Phillips, p. 280–281, p. 289

Malachi

Commentaries:
- *Haggai, Zechariah, and Malachi: God's Restored People,* by John L. Mackay (2003)
- *The Preacher's Commentary,* OT Vol 23, by Walter Kaiser (1992)
- *The Message of Malachi,* by Peter Adam (2013)

Mal 1:2: *"I have loved you," says the LORD." But you ask, 'How have you loved us?'*
Like a banner over a Bible conference this theme of God's love hangs over every message the prophet delivers. His banner over us is Love [Song 2:4]. Love proceeds from His own character and being; thus no definition of God's love can be separated from what he is and does.
Kaiser, p 458
The community was disillusioned, discouraged, doubting, and cynical. It is a measure of the extent of polarization between them and God that this is the first of 27 questions that the NIV identifies in Malachi's 55 verses. That is an average of just over one question every two verses. The relationship between God and the people was confrontational, as he probed their loyalty and they questioned the value of serving him. If God loves us, where is the evidence to prove it? Perhaps all the promises and visions of the prophets were no more than religious talk, without substance. Where are the hard facts to back up the claim that God loves us? Mackay, p. 279

Mal 2:16: *"I hate divorce," says the LORD God of Israel*
How contemporary Malachi's situation sounds! There are two ways of approaching marriage—that of the world, which views it as little more than a mutually convenient arrangement that may be terminated when it becomes inconvenient, and that of God. Increasingly, the church has

caved in to pressure to accept as valid grounds for divorce what the civil authorities deem permissible. It is too embarrassing to ask if a divorce was granted on Scriptural grounds. But marriage is a creation ordinance of God, and he still wishes it to be honored both within and without the church. The teaching of Paul still stands that divorce is not right (1 Cor 7:10,11). There are exceptional circumstances mentioned, but they are just that—exceptional. They are not the basis for easy and unthinking breaches of the marriage bond. When that becomes prevalent in a country, the whole social and religious fabric of the land is corrupted. The marriage bond and the family are divine institutions which cannot be set aside without horrendous consequences. Mackay, p. 315

Personal Note: The ESV translation of this verse is significantly different than NIV and NASB.

Mal 2:17: *You have wearied the LORD with your words. "How have we wearied him?" you ask. By saying, "All who do evil are good in the eyes of the LORD, and he is pleased with them" or "Where is the God of justice?"*

They saw the wicked prosper, so they assumed that God delighted in the wicked. Notice that their focus was on others, not on God, and that they envied success. ... Life would be simpler if God judged all sins immediately. We would know immediately that we had done something wrong or failed to do something right. We would never have to ask 'Where is the God of justice'. Waiting on God to act is demanding in many ways. And why does God make us wait? It is worth commenting that this is an odd question, because it assumes God should serve us, that God should meet our expectations and our timetable. It assumes that our desire should prevail, and that God is answerable to us. This is not the case, and it is good to recognize this stance is ridiculous, and repent of it. ... We may wonder at God's patience with evil people. But of course, we praise him for his patience with ourselves! Adam, excerpts, p. 97, 101

Mal 3:2–3 *But who can endure the day of his coming? Who can stand when he appears? For he will be like a refiner's fire or a launderer's soap. He will sit as a refiner and purifier of silver; he will purify the Levites and refine them like gold and silver.*

God, the Refiner of silver [Ps 66:10, Zc 13:9], will know by His testing process exactly when we have been purified [1 Th 5:23, 1 Jn 1:9]. There is a dramatic moment when the refiner knows that all the dross has gone from the silver [Prov 25:4]. Peering over it, the silver suddenly becomes a liquid mirror in which the image of the refiner is reflected [Gn 1:27, Mt 5:48, 1 Pet 1:15]. Then he knows his task is done. So it is with us; when our Lord can observe His image reflected in us, then the trial-by-fire suffering has accomplished its perfect work. Kaiser, p. 497

Mal 3:14: *You have said, 'It is futile to serve God. What did we gain by carrying out his requirements and going about like mourners before the LORD Almighty?'*
'What do we profit?' is such a revealing question. It shows that they are fundamentally self-centered, not God-centered. This is the embarrassing question that comes to us mid-way through our lives as Christians, and the painful question that can come near the end of years of ministry. What have I got out of all this? What reward do I have for my goodness and service to God? ... If the words 'what do we profit?' reveal much about our deep and destructive motivation, the following words reveal much about their deep and destructive tendency to envy those who have not even bothered to keep God's commands or to sorrow for their sins. ... Yes, sinners do get away with blue murder. But God is patient with you when you sin, even the sin of envy. You are here to serve God; God it not here to serve you! You will never be content if you compare yourself with others, and you are the only person who can stop yourself doing it. Don't blame others for your attitude to them. Envy is the enemy of contentment.
Adam, p. 110, 112

Matthew

Commentaries:
- *The Message of Matthew,* by Michael Green (1988)
- *The Gospel of Matthew,* by Charles Haddon Spurgeon (1834–1892)
- *The Preacher's Commentary,* NT Vol 24, *by Myron S. Augsberger* (1982)
- *Living Insights,* Vol 1a, by Charles Swindoll (2020)
- Matthew Henry Commentary www.BlueletterBible.org (1710)

Mt 1:23b: *"and they will call him Immanuel"-which means, "God with us."* That child of prophecy [Isa 7:14], that child who was to be a 'sign', has come at last. And he is no less than God with us. The Hebrews had such an exalted conception of God that they did not even make any image of him—something which so amazed their Roman conquerors that they dubbed them 'atheists', people without gods. Against that background, Matthew claims, not that God has given us a representation of himself, but that he has come in person to share our situation. What a claim, right at the outset of the Gospel! It is so ultimate, so exclusive. It does not fit with the pluralist idea that each of us is getting through to God in his or her own way. No, says Matthew. God has got through to us in *his* way [Jn 14:6]. And Jesus is no mere teacher, no guru, no Muhammad or Gandhi. He is 'God with us'. That is the essential claim on which Christianity is built. It is a claim that cannot be abandoned without abandoning the faith in its entirety.   Green, pp 59–60

Taken from *The Bible Speaks Today* Series edited by J. Alec Motyer; John Stott. Copyright © 1983 edited by J. Alec Motyer; John Stott. Used by permission of InterVarsity Press, P.O. Box 1400, Downers Grove, IL 60515, USA. www.ivpress.com. Taken from *The Message of Matthew* by E. Michael Green. Copyright (c) 2001 by E. Michael Green. Used by permission of InterVarsity Press, P.O. Box 1400, Downers Grove, IL 60515, USA. www.ivpress.com

"Great little one! Whose all-embracing birth lifts earth to heaven, stoops heaven to earth."
Richard Crashaw (1613–1649)   Quoted in Ward and Wild

Mt 5:9: *Blessed are the peacemakers, for they will be called sons of God.*

> *Lord, make me an instrument of Thy peace;*
> *Where there is hatred, let me sow love;*
> *Where there is injury, let me sow pardon;*
> *Where there is doubt, let me sow faith;*
> *Where there is despair, let me sow hope;*
> *Where there is darkness, let me sow light;*
> *And where there is sadness, let me sow joy.*
> *O Divine Master,*
> *grant that I may not so much seek to be consoled as to console;*
> *To be understood, as to understand;*
> *To be loved, as to love;*
> *For it is in giving that we receive,*
> *It is in pardoning that we are pardoned,*
> *And it is in dying that we are born to Eternal Life.*
> *Amen*
>
> Prayer of Francis of Assisi (1182–1226)

Mt 5:16: *In the same way, let your light shine before men, that they may see your good deeds and praise your Father in heaven.* [cf John 15:8]
Until he has illuminated us we can never shine with his reflected light. The imperative of shining is based on the indicative of being lit up by him. Then people will see our good deeds and praise not us but our heavenly Father, who is the source of the light they see reflected [Gal 1:24 NIV].

Green, p. 92

Green, Michael *The Message of Matthew*, Taken from *The Bible Speaks Today* Series edited by J Alec Motyer; John Stott. Copyright © 1988 edited by J. Alec Motyer; John Stott. Used by permission of InterVarsity Press, P.O. Box 1400, Downers Grove, IL 60515, USA. www.ivpress.com

Mt 5:43–45: *You have heard that it was said, 'Love your neighbor and hate your enemy.' But I tell you: Love your enemies and pray for those who persecute you, that you may be sons of your Father in heaven.*

Nowhere is the challenge of the Sermon greater. Nowhere is the distinctness of the Christian counter-culture made more obvious. Nowhere is our need of the power of the Holy Spirit (whose first fruit is love) more compelling. We are to go beyond forbearance to service, beyond refusal to repay evil to resolve to overcome evil with good [Rom 12:21]. Alfred Plummer summed up the alternatives with admirable simplicity: 'To return evil for good is devilish; to return good for good is human; to return good for evil is divine.'
John Stott, *The Message of the Sermon on the Mount*, p. 103, 122

Mt 5:48: *Be perfect, therefore, as your heavenly Father is perfect.* [cf Heb 12:23b]
Jesus espouses not limited love, but unlimited love, love to the just and the unjust, to evil and good alike, that is the mark of the Great Lover. And it must not be sporadic, but a settled mark of our characters, just as the regular following of day by night is a mark of the settled character of God himself. That is the meaning of perfect, τέλειοι *teleioi*. Be like God in undiscriminating and undifferentiating love towards all and sundry. That is the mark of the Master. That is the mark of the disciple.

Green p. 98

Green, Michael *The Message of Matthew*, Taken from *The Bible Speaks Today* Series edited by J. Alec Motyer; John Stott. Copyright © 1988 edited by J. Alec Motyer; John Stott. Used by permission of InterVarsity Press, P.O. Box 1400, Downers Grove, IL 60515, USA. www.ivpress.com

Mt 6:10: *your kingdom come, your will be done on earth as it is in heaven.*
God, our dear heavenly father! His name hallowed, his kingdom extended, his will done. Our needs supplied, our sins forgiven, our temptations overcome. What a prayer! And all in fifty-seven [Greek] words—no vain repetitions [6:7, KJV] here! Green, p. 101

Green, Michael *The Message of Matthew*, Taken from *The Bible Speaks Today* Series edited by J. Alec Motyer; John Stott. Copyright © 1988 edited by J. Alec Motyer; John Stott. Used by permission of InterVarsity Press, P.O. Box 1400, Downers Grove, IL 60515, USA. www.ivpress.com

Mt 6:19–21: *Do not store up for yourselves treasures on earth, where moth and rust destroy, and where thieves break in and steal. But store up for yourselves*

treasures in heaven, where moth and rust do not destroy, and where thieves do not break in and steal.
[cf Prov 23:5, Eccl 2:8–11, Isa 5:9, Isa 55:2, James 5:1, 1 Pet 1:4.]
Worldly riches have in themselves a principal of corruption and decay; they wither of themselves, and make themselves wings. ... There are treasures in heaven, as sure as there are on this earth; and those in heaven are the only true treasures, the riches and glories and pleasures that are at God's right hand, which those that are sanctified truly arrive at, when they come to be sanctified perfectly. ... The heart follows the treasure, as the needle follows the loadstone, or the sunflower the sun. Where the treasure is there the value and esteem are, there the love and affection are (Col. 3:2), that way the desires and pursuits go, thitherward the aims and intents are leveled, and all is done with that in view. Matthew Henry Commentary

Mt 6:34: *Therefore do not worry about tomorrow, for tomorrow will worry about itself. Each day has enough trouble of its own.*
Our business is with today: we are only to ask bread day by day, and that only in sufficient abundance for the day's consumption. To import the possible sorrows of tomorrow into the thoughts of today is a superfluity of unbelief. When the morrow brings sorrow, it will bring strength for that sorrow. Today will require all the vigor we have to deal with its immediate evils; there can be no need to import cares from the future. Oh my heart, what rest there is for thee if thou wilt give thyself up to thy Lord, and leave all thine own concerns with him! Mind thou thy Lord's business, and he will see to thy business. Spurgeon, p. 76

"Worry is interest paid on trouble before it falls due"
William Ralph Inge (1860–1954) Quoted in Ward and Wild

Mt 7:5: *You hypocrite, first take the plank out of your own eye, and then you will see clearly to remove the speck from your brother's eye.*
The judging faculty is best employed at home. Our tendency is to spy out splinters in other men's eyes and not to see the beam in our own. Fancy a man with a beam in his eye pretending to deal with so tender a part as the eye of another, and attempting to remove so tiny a thing as a mote or a splinter! Jesus is gentle, but he calls that man a hypocrite, who fusses about

small things in others and pays no attention to great matters at home in his own person. ... May none of us provoke the Lord to say to us, 'thou hypocrite!'
Spurgeon, p. 78

Mt 7:12: *So in everything, do to others what you would have them do to you, for this sums up the Law and the Prophets.*
Put yourself in another's place, and then act to him as you would wish him to act towards you under the same circumstances. This is a right royal rule, a precept always at hand, always applicable, always right. Oh, that all men acted on it, and there would be no slavery, no war, no swearing, no striking, no lying, no robbing, but all would be justice and love! What a kingdom is this which has such a law! Lord teach it to me! Write it on the fleshly tablets of my renewed heart! Write it out in full in my life!
Spurgeon, pp. 80–81

Mt 7:13: *Enter through the narrow gate.*
Notice how here, as so often in Jesus' teaching, we are challenged to decide. There is no middle ground, embracing most of us, and leaving on either side the very good and the very bad. How comfortable if that were the case! But Christianity is not about being very good, or very bad, or very comfortable. It is about being in God's kingdom or not. It is about allegiance to God or rebellion [cf Allen on 1 Chr 10:13–14]. It is about being on the road that starts narrow but opens out into the life of heaven, or staying on the broad road of our self-centeredness until it contracts to a dead halt in final destruction [Prov 14:12]. An awesome choice. And we find that at the end of the Sermon, we are not permitted merely to admire the teaching, we are challenged to bow to the preacher. Have you entered in? Are you on the road? [cf Isa 35, Jer 6:16]
Green, p. 108

Green, Michael *The Message of Matthew*,Taken from *The Bible Speaks Today* Series edited by J. Alec Motyer; John Stott. Copyright © 1988 edited by J. Alec Motyer; John Stott. Used by permission of InterVarsity Press, P.O. Box 1400, Downers Grove, IL 60515, USA. www.ivpress.com

"Better, though difficult, the right way to go than wrong, though easy, where the end is woe."
John Bunyan (1628–1688)
Quoted in Ward and Wild

Mt 7:24: *Therefore everyone who hears these words of mine and puts them into practice is like a wise man who built his house on the rock.*
In this age of permissiveness and pluralism, his claims stand out sheer and stark. He does not agree that it does not matter what you believe in so long as you are sincere. He does not allow that we are all climbing up to God by the route of our choice. He does not fit in with our shallow pluralism. Instead he says there are only two ways we can build. Not many ways, just two [Deut 30:19, Jer 17:5–8]. We can either build on him and his teaching, which we will find is as solid as rock; or else we can build on any other religion or philosophy in the world, and we will find that it is sand, and in the last day it will spell ruin. … The theological and religious world is full of hearing; it is overloaded with God-talk. What will thrill the heart of God, and make the pagans realize that the gospel is true, is practical, generous obedience—obedience that transforms our characters (5:11–12), affects our influence (5:13–16), shows itself in practical righteousness (5:17–48), touches our devotional life (6:1–18), radically alters our ambitions (6:19–34), transforms our relationships (7:1–12), and marks us out as totally wholehearted servants of the King (7:13–27). That is what Jesus is looking for. That is the mark of the disciples he calls. That is the kingdom manifesto detailed with immense authority at the outset of his public ministry.

Green, p. 109, 110

Green, Michael *The Message of Matthew*,Taken from *The Bible Speaks Today* Series edited by J. Alec Motyer; John Stott. Copyright © 1988 edited by J. Alec Motyer; John Stott. Used by permission of InterVarsity Press, P.O. Box 1400, Downers Grove, IL 60515, USA. www.ivpress.com

"We have grasped the mystery of the atom and rejected the sermon on the mount." Omar N. Bradley (1893–1981) American WW II General

Personal Note about the Sermon on the Mount
One theme running through the last part of the Sermon on the Mount is the concept of binary choices [cf Deut 11:26–28, 30:19, Lev 26:3, Ps 1:1, Isa 34:9, Mt 7:13, Lk 6:43, wisdom and folly in the book of Proverbs]:

- Treasures on earth vs. Treasures in heaven (6:19–20)
- Cannot serve both God and Money (6:24)
- The wide and narrow gate (7:13–14)

- Good fruit and bad fruit (7:17–18)
- House on sand and house on rock (7:24–27)

In our modern world, we don't like the concept of black and white, but want nuanced shades of gray. Yet when we think about life, we often are faced with choices of one way or the other. Life is a series of thousands of forks in the road. At each fork we must choose. The more often we choose the wrong fork, the more we deviate from the path to happiness and eternal joy. Any one choice is probably not absolutely critical, but the cumulative impact of many wrong turns is to change our destination. The Word of God and the Holy Spirit give us signposts leading to fulfillment. We do well to heed these signposts [Jer 31:21] to assure we arrive at the destination we seek. The "scenic route" (the wide gate) often ends in our running out of gas and having a flat tire. But the route lit by God's word [Ps 43:3, 119:105] delivers us to a glorious destination.

Mt 10:32: *Whoever acknowledges me before men, I will also acknowledge him before my Father in heaven. But whoever disowns me before men, I will disown him before my Father in heaven.*
When we are confronted by Christ, life's basic issues are at stake. We are 'playing for keeps.' People shove God out of their lives because they have other gods, because He interferes with what they want, yet ultimately it is because the way of Christ is too demanding. We are called to live for two worlds, for the eternal overlaps of the world of time. If we should gain this world alone, we would have only this world! ... When the Titanic sank in 1912, in the office of the Cunard Line in New York City there was a board listing names of passengers in only two columns, and they were headed 'saved' and 'lost'. The open confession of Christ will be honored by His act of vouching for us to the heavenly Father; while an open denial will receive a consequent denial before the heavenly Father.   Augsberger, p. 133

Mt 11:28–30: *Come unto me, all ye that labour and are heavy laden, and I will give you rest.*
Take my yoke upon you, and learn of me; for I am meek and lowly in heart: and ye shall find rest unto your souls. For my yoke is easy, and my burden is light.   [KJV]

Jesus came to end the search by taking us into his loving arms [Isa 40:11]. He came to lift burdens off our aching backs [Ps 68:19, 81:6], not to tie them on [Mt 23:4]. He offers 'rest', not cessation from toil, but peace and fulfillment and a sense of being put right [Ps 62:5]. We have only to come, to entrust ourselves to him, and we shall find that rest [Phil 4:7]. Millions have done so, and have enjoyed that given rest. His yoke is gentle, but not in the sense that it is less demanding than Judaism. In some ways it is more demanding. But it is the yoke of love, not of duty. It is the response of the liberated, not the duty of the obligated. And that makes all the difference.
Green, p. 143

Green, Michael *The Message of Matthew*,Taken from *The Bible Speaks Today* Series edited by J. Alec Motyer; John Stott. Copyright © 1988 edited by J. Alec Motyer; John Stott. Used by permission of InterVarsity Press, P.O. Box 1400, Downers Grove, IL 60515, USA. www.ivpress.com

"You have made us for yourself, and our heart is restless until it finds its rest in you." Augustine of Hippo (AD 354–430)

Mt 13:45–46: *Again, the kingdom of heaven is like unto a merchant man, seeking goodly pearls: Who, when he had found one pearl of great price, went and sold all that he had, and bought it.* KJV

There are other pearls in the market. There are other things of great value. But none is to compare with the pearl of great value. That is how some people find the kingdom of God. They try many faiths, many ideologies, and they gain much from them. But one day, they find the loveliest thing in the world and they give all to gain it. So the message of these twin parables is clear. People find the kingdom in many ways. Some come upon it by accident, some after a long and patient search. But it is immensely worthwhile, however we come to it. It is treasure [6:21]. It is a beautiful pearl. It is worth any sacrifice. Do the disciples of Matthew's day realize this? Do they teach it?
Green, p. 160

Green, Michael *The Message of Matthew*,Taken from *The Bible Speaks Today* Series edited by J. Alec Motyer; John Stott. Copyright © 1988 edited by J. Alec Motyer; John Stott. Used by permission of InterVarsity Press, P.O. Box 1400, Downers Grove, IL 60515, USA. www.ivpress.com

"Cheap grace is grace without discipleship, grace without the cross, grace without Jesus Christ, living and incarnate. Costly grace is the treasure hidden in the field; for the sake of it a man will gladly go and sell all that he has. It is costly because it costs a man his life, and it is grace because it gives a man the only true life." Dietrich Bonhoeffer (1905–1945)
German theologian executed in a Nazi camp

Mt 15:31: *The people were amazed when they saw the mute speaking, the crippled made well, the lame walking and the blind seeing. And they praised the God of Israel.*
How easy it would have been for Jesus to send His disciples halfway down the hill to stop their ascent and say "The Master is resting now. He's not taking any visitors. Go home." But Jesus did not have the disciples take on the role of bouncers or bodyguards–and neither did He start behaving like an unreachable superstar who could only be contacted through an agent. Instead, Jesus showed that His compassion is not bound to a particular schedule. As the crowds made their way to where He was seated, they laid down the needy people at His feet, and He healed them. What a deliriously happy scene! Those who had been lame were made able to walk. Those who were blind now saw clearly. Those who had been disabled now danced with joy. And those who had been speechless were now singing praises. In unanimity, the crowd "glorified the God of Israel" (15:31). The glory of God is the fruit of compassion.
Charles Swindoll, *Living Insights*, Vol 1a (Matt 1-15), Carol Stream, IL: Tyndale, 2020, p. 334

Mt 18:21 *"Peter asked 'Lord, how many times shall I forgive my brother? 7 times?'*
Peter suggested seven times, and he must have felt he was offering the moon: the rabbis reckoned that three times was enough. But Jesus' reply will have shattered him. *'Not seven times, but seventy-seven times'*, better, seventy times seven. It means, 'Go on and on forgiving.' Not of course, 490 times, but constantly. God's pardon is like that. Ours must mirror it if we are in his family [Mt 6:14–15, Lk 6:36]. And because we are forgiven people, we will be able to summon the motivation and the power to forgive. To say, 'I forgive you' is not enough. It needs to be repeated whenever we feel the

sense of grievance rising up in us afresh. As we determine not to hold the grievance against our brother or sister, but to accept his or her penitence wholeheartedly as God does, gradually the heart catches up with the head, and forgiveness, repeatedly reiterated, becomes part of us and enters deep into the wounded feelings. We are at last able to say 'It is finished.'

Green, p. 198

Green, Michael *The Message of Matthew*,Taken from *The Bible Speaks Today* Series edited by J. Alec Motyer; John Stott. Copyright © 1988 edited by J. Alec Motyer; John Stott. Used by permission of InterVarsity Press, P.O. Box 1400, Downers Grove, IL 60515, USA. www.ivpress.com

Mt 18:26–27: *"The servant fell on his knees before him. 'Be patient with me,' he begged, 'and I will pay back everything.' The servant's master took pity on him, canceled the debt and let him go.*

This story of the unforgiving servant drives home the message of the last two pericopae like a pile driver. But it is one thing to be told a truth, and quite another to hear a brilliant short story in which you side with the underdog and then find yourself accusing not the man in the story but yourself [cf 2 Sam 12:7]! The sins of every disciple have been piling up for years like debts; every day, every hour adds to them. They can never be paid. And God says 'I release you from your debt.' Once again we see how opposed Matthew rightly is to cheap grace. It will not do to claim to be forgiven and then to prove by our actions that our lives have not changed. The pardon of God is dynamic, life-changing. We cannot go through heaven's narrow door if our lives are bulging with resentment. God puts his precious gift in our hands—but only if we open them up to him, not clench them in anger against our brethren. We have already seen this principle taught after the Lord's Prayer (6:14–15). Now it comes again, in brilliant color in this wonderful story. There is no escaping it by pious platitudes about God's willingness to forgive us whatever we do. Green, p. 199

Green, Michael *The Message of Matthew*,Taken from *The Bible Speaks Today* Series edited by J. Alec Motyer; John Stott. Copyright © 1988 edited by J. Alec Motyer; John Stott. Used by permission of InterVarsity Press, P.O. Box 1400, Downers Grove, IL 60515, USA. www.ivpress.com

Mt 20:12: *'These men who were hired last worked only one hour,' they said, 'and you have made them equal to us who have borne the burden of the work and the heat of the day.'*

Despite its familiarity, the parable is a total reversal of normal values, and is certainly no recipe for industrial peace! The unions would be up in arms if an employer acted like this today.

The point of the story is plain. Length of service and long hours of toil in the heat of the day constitute no claim on God and provide no reasons why he should not be generous who have done less. All human merit shrivels before his burning, self-giving love [Eph 2:8–10]. Grace, amazing grace, is the burden of this story. ... Many poor Christians who came to faith only at the end of their life will be high in the kingdom because they knew they had done nothing to boast of, and never gave rewards a thought. They just responded to the unexpected love that sought them and accepted them. That is the attitude that brings joy to the heart of God, the great lover. Green, p. 212, 213

Green, Michael *The Message of Matthew*,Taken from *The Bible Speaks Today* Series edited by J. Alec Motyer; John Stott. Copyright © 1988 edited by J. Alec Motyer; John Stott. Used by permission of InterVarsity Press, P.O. Box 1400, Downers Grove, IL 60515, USA. www.ivpress.com

"Men have no right to complain of the bounty of God when he honors unworthy persons by large rewards beyond what they deserve."

John Calvin (1509–1564)

Mt 22:12 *'Friend,' he asked, 'how did you get in here without wedding clothes?' The man was speechless.*

It seems clear that the generous king not only provided the feast free for the wedding of his son; not only invited everyone to it; but also provided beautiful festal robes for all to wear. In this way, the poor need not be ashamed of their rags, and the rich no right to be proud of their dinner jackets and gowns. All came in on the same footing, just as in the parable of the workers in the vineyard. There is room neither for embarrassment nor for pride in the feast of the kingdom. Both attitudes ruin the enjoyment. Green, p. 231

Green, Michael *The Message of Matthew*,Taken from *The Bible Speaks Today* Series edited by J. Alec Motyer; John Stott. Copyright © 1988 edited by J. Alec Motyer;

John Stott. Used by permission of InterVarsity Press, P.O. Box 1400, Downers Grove, IL 60515, USA. www.ivpress.com

Mt 22:21: *Then he said to them, "Give to Caesar what is Caesar's, and to God what is God's."*
The coin bears Caesar's image: give it back to him. You bear God's image [Gn 1:27], so give yourself back to him [Rom 12:1]. When we do give ourselves without reserve to the God who gave us everything and formed us in his own image, and when we set out to give Caesar what is Caesar's and to give God what is God's, then we have within ourselves a spring of action which is always questing, always seeking integrity in a world of compromise. We must wrestle to discern the areas where Caesar has no right to dictate. These areas must be handed back to God. Green, p. 234
Green, Michael *The Message of Matthew*,Taken from *The Bible Speaks Today* Series edited by J. Alec Motyer; John Stott. Copyright © 1988 edited by J. Alec Motyer; John Stott. Used by permission of InterVarsity Press, P.O. Box 1400, Downers Grove, IL 60515, USA. www.ivpress.com

"We are God's money. But we are like coins that have wandered away from the treasury. What was once stamped on us has been worn down by our wandering. The One who restamps his image upon us is the One who first formed us. He himself seeks his own coin, as Caesar sought his own coin." Augustine of Hippo, *Tracates on John* 40.9.

Mt 26:10: *Jesus said to them, "Why are you bothering this woman? She has done a beautiful thing to me"*
In striking contrast both to the sustained hatred of Caiaphas and the Jewish hierarchy, and to the terrible treachery of Judas, we have, sandwiched between them, the story of the unnamed woman who made the offering of her costliest treasure to the Master she loved. We are undoubtedly meant to contrast the extravagance of the woman's grateful love with the plans of Caiaphas and Judas to put Jesus to death. It seemed improbable that one woman's present to Jesus should be recounted in the preaching of the gospel all over the world, and down through the centuries, but so it has turned out [26:13]. Those twin facts, that nothing done for Jesus is wasted, and nothing forgotten, should nerve disciples to take the cap off

their alabaster jars of precious possessions and pour them out for Jesus.
Green, p. 268, 269, 270

Green, Michael *The Message of Matthew*,Taken from *The Bible Speaks Today* Series edited by J. Alec Motyer; John Stott. Copyright © 1988 edited by J. Alec Motyer; John Stott. Used by permission of InterVarsity Press, P.O. Box 1400, Downers Grove, IL 60515, USA. www.ivpress.com

Mt 27:3: *When Judas, who had betrayed him, saw that Jesus was condemned, he was seized with remorse and returned the thirty silver coins to the chief priests and the elders.*

He repented himself; that is, he was filled with grief, anguish, and indignation, at himself, when reflecting upon what he had done. When he was tempted to betray his Master, the thirty pieces of silver looked very fine and glittering, like the wine, when it is red, and gives its colour in the cup [Prov 23:31]. But when the thing was done, and the money paid, the silver was become dross, it bit like a serpent, and stung like an adder [Prov 23:32]. Now he curses the bag he carried [Gn 42:35], the money he coveted, the priests he dealt with, and the day that he was born. The remembrance of his Master's goodness to him, which he had so basely requited, the bowels of mercy he had spurned at, and the fair warnings he had slighted, steeled his convictions, and made them the more piercing. Matthew Henry Commentary

Mt 28:7: *Then go quickly and tell his disciples: 'He has risen from the dead and is going ahead of you into Galilee. There you will see him.'*

Mt 28:12–13: *When the chief priests had met with the elders and devised a plan, they gave the soldiers a large sum of money, telling them, "You are to say, 'His disciples came during the night and stole him away while we were asleep.'"*

From the grave two messages have gone back: one to the disciples, carried by the women, to the effect that Jesus is alive; the other to the chief priests, carried by the soldiers, to the effect that the body has been stolen. Nobody on that Easter day could deny that the body was gone and the tomb was unattended. Nobody attempted to deny it. The only possible reason for the story of the guard is that it was true. There had been a guard. It had not prevented the resurrection. Probably, when the earthquake dislodged the stone, the guard entered to ensure that all was well, found that the tomb was empty, saw the angelic presence, and fled to tell the chief priests, once they had sufficiently recovered to get to their feet. This disaster called for an explanation. So the chief priests bribed the soldiers, and circulated the story that the disciples had stolen the body while the guard was asleep on duty. Highly embarrassing, but not so embarrassing as admitting the truth of the resurrection. The authorities were simply making the best of a bad situation. Green, pp. 317, 318

Green, Michael *The Message of Matthew*,Taken from *The Bible Speaks Today* Series edited by J. Alec Motyer; John Stott. Copyright © 1988 edited by J. Alec Motyer; John Stott. Used by permission of InterVarsity Press, P.O. Box 1400, Downers Grove, IL 60515, USA. www.ivpress.com

Mt 28:19–20: *Therefore go and make disciples of all nations, baptizing them in the name of the Father and of the Son and of the Holy Spirit, and teaching them to obey everything I have commanded you. And surely I am with you always, to the very end of the age.*

So ends this Gospel, which has clearly depicted who Jesus is, what his message contains, how his kingdom comes, and the cost and challenge of discipleship. Jesus, reveling in his Father's company and authority, had come to bring outsiders into the kingdom. And now, at the climax of the Gospel, his disciples are called to follow his lead, to go and make disciples of all nations. That task will be complete only when he comes again at the end of all history. Such was the glorious hope that nerved Matthew to give his all for his Master. May it inspire us! Green, p. 323

Green, Michael *The Message of Matthew*,Taken from *The Bible Speaks Today* Series edited by J. Alec Motyer; John Stott. Copyright © 1988 edited by J. Alec Motyer; John Stott. Used by permission of InterVarsity Press, P.O. Box 1400, Downers Grove, IL 60515, USA. www.ivpress.com

Laud and honor to the Father,	[Rev 1:6]
Laud and honor to the Son,	[2 Pt 1:17]
Laud and honor to the Spirit,	[2 Cor 3:18]
Ever Three and ever One;	[Mt 28:19]
One in might and One in glory,	[Eph 4:4 6]
While unending ages run.	[Mt 28:20]

Hymn: *Christ is Made the Sure Foundation,* Text: Latin, 7th Century, *trans. by John Mason Neale* (1861), *1818–1866,* Melody by Henry Smart, 1876 (Final verse)

Mark

Commentaries:
- *The Gospel According to Mark*, by James R. Edwards (2002)
- *The Preacher's Commentary*, NT Vol 25, by David McKenna (1982)
- *Mark: Good News from Jerusalem*, by Geoffrey Grogan (1995)
- Charles Haddon Spurgeon Sermon (1856)

Mk 1:41: *Filled with compassion, Jesus reached out his hand and touched the man. "I am willing," he said. "Be clean!"* [contrast Lev 13:45–46]
To match the most difficult of human needs, Jesus responds with the deepest of human feelings. As with us, Jesus knows the full range of human emotion. He knows cheer, anger, laughter, disappointment, sighing, displeasure, surprise, impatience, exhilaration, and depression. When we read that Jesus is moved with compassion, it means that He feels Himself so deeply into the sufferings of the leper that it is just as if He Himself is suffering as a leper [cf Rom 12:15, Lev 13:45]. Jesus is not moved with pity—that is too condescending; not with sympathy—that is too superficial; not with empathy—that is too distant. Not just mind for mind, hand for hand, or even heart for heart, but stomach for stomach, blood for blood, gut for gut, Jesus feels His way into the leper's needs.   McKenna, p. 55

Mk 1:20: *Without delay he called them, and they left their father Zebedee in the boat with the hired men and followed him.*
Mark 1 is one of the busiest chapters in the New Testament, and it gives us quite a selection of the kind of things Jesus was doing early in his ministry and which he continued to do. Here he is marked out as unique at his baptism, after which we find him preaching, gathering followers, teaching, casting out evil spirits, healing, praying, and cleansing a man with leprosy. Anybody reading it for the first time is likely to be struck

with awe at the activities and the power of this Man, and would see at once that there is something special about him. This comes out in Mark's use of one of his favorite words. It is used eleven times in this one chapter. What is the word? It is the Greek word ευθυς (*euthus*), translated a number of different ways in the NIV. In vv 12, 18, and 43, it is 'at once', in v 20 'without delay', in v 23 'just then', in v 28 'quickly', in v 29 'as soon as' and in v 42 'immediately'. Mark is underlining for his readers that the life of Jesus at this time was one of constant activity.   Grogan, pp. 51, 52

Mk 2:16: *When the teachers of the law who were Pharisees saw him eating with the "sinners" and tax collectors, they asked his disciples: "Why does he eat with tax collectors and 'sinners'?"*
Jesus' fellowship with tax collectors and sinners—and its condemnation by the scribes—illustrates the radical nature of grace. ... The righteousness of God escapes those who seek to establish their own righteousness [Phil 3:9], whereas those who are too far off to hope for the righteousness of God are graciously granted it. ... The fact that Jesus can be found in the company of people such as Levi reminds us of the difference between his mission and that of the scribes. They come to enlighten; he comes to redeem. Given that mission, it is as senseless for Jesus to shun tax collectors and sinners as for a doctor to shun the sick. The grace of God extends to and overcomes the worst forms of human depravity. Ironically, in one sense great sinners stand closer to God than those who think themselves righteous, for sinners are more aware of their need of the transforming grace of God.

Edwards, excerpts, pp. 85, 86
Edwards, James R. *The Gospel According to Mark*, Copyright © 2002 by William B. Eerdman Publishing, Grand Rapids, MI USA. Part of *The Pillar New Testament Commentary* Series, D.A. Carson general editor. Reprinted by permission of the publisher

Mk 4:26–28: *He also said, "This is what the kingdom of God is like. A man scatters seed on the ground. Night and day, whether he sleeps or gets up, the seed sprouts and grows, though he does not know how. All by itself the soil produces grain-first the stalk, then the head, then the full kernel in the head."*
The kingdom of God should be likened to something grand and glorious, to shimmering mountain peaks, crimson sunsets, the opulence of the potentates, the lusty glory of a gladiator. But Jesus likens it to *seeds*. The

paradox of the gospel—indeed the scandal of the incarnation—is disguised in such commonplaces. The God whom Jesus introduces will not be kept at celestial arm's length. Jesus does not tell us how high and lofty God is but how very near and present he is, and how the routines of planting and harvesting are mundane clues to the nature and plan of God. ... A seed is not spectacular nor does its laborious growth attract attention. Night and day a farmer waits for seeds. Life goes on as it always has. But simultaneously and independent of the farmer another process is at work. Slowly, imperceptibly, the seed sprouts and grows. ... Despite the farmer's absence and ignorance, the soil brings forth 'all by itself' (αὐτόματος *automatos*). The seed contains within itself a power of generation and an orderly process of growth. ... Despite inauspicious beginnings and the absence of human involvement, the seed contains within itself fruit-bearing potential. Edwards, excerpts, pp. 142, 143

Edwards, James R. *The Gospel According to Mark*, Copyright © 2002 by William B. Eerdman Publishing, Grand Rapids, MI USA. Part of *The Pillar New Testament Commentary* Series, D.A. Carson general editor. Reprinted by permission of the publisher

Mk 7:26 *The woman was a Greek, born in Syrian Phoenicia. She begged Jesus to drive the demon out of her daughter.*
An encounter between this woman and a scribe or Pharisee would be hard to imagine in the tradition of the elders. Of all the people who approach Jesus in the Gospel of Mark, this individual has the most against her from a Jewish perspective. Verse 26 reads like a crescendo of demerit: she is a woman, a Greek Gentile, from infamous pagans of Syrian Phoenicia. Even Levi the tax collector must have raised his eyebrows at this woman who has the pluck to beg Jesus to 'drive a demon out of her daughter.' Despite her notorious credentials, she does not apologize or cower in obsequiousness. Her only cover letter is her desperate need. ... Despite such obstacles, the woman's 'heart' is true even if her credentials are wrong. ... This believing woman submits her cause entirely to Jesus and she is not disappointed. 'For such a reply, you may go,' says Jesus, 'the demon has left your daughter [v 29].' What an irony! Jesus seeks desperately his chosen disciples—yet they are dull and uncomprehending; Jesus is reluctant even to speak to a walk-on pagan woman—and after one sentence she understands his mission and receives his unambiguous commendation. How is this possible? The answer

is that the woman is the first person in Mark to hear and understand a parable of Jesus. The brief parable of the children and the dogs at the table has disclosed to her the mystery of the kingdom of God. She is not distant and aloof, attempting to maintain her position and control. She does what Jesus commands of those who would receive the kingdom and experience the word of God: she enters the parable and allows herself to be claimed by it. Edwards, excerpts, pp. 218–222
Edwards, James R. *The Gospel According to Mark*, Copyright © 2002 by William B. Eerdman Publishing, Grand Rapids, MI USA. Part of *The Pillar New Testament Commentary* Series, D.A. Carson general editor. Reprinted by permission of the publisher

Mk 7:37: *People were overwhelmed with amazement. "He has done everything well," they said. "He even makes the deaf hear and the mute speak."*
Both in substance and in spirit, the words 'He has done everything well' (v 37) connote the creative act of God when He said [Gn 1:31] 'It is good.' In a burst of spiritual maturity given by revelation, the people see God at work in Jesus Christ. Verse 37 has the ring of a doxology. Mark has taken us through a cycle which began with the Feeding of the Five Thousand in chapter 6 and finished with the People's Confession of Christ in 7:37. He now opens another cycle, paralleling the first one. Feeding the multitudes, confronting the Pharisees, healing the sick, and hearing the confession of Peter are just ahead for us. Like a great drama of rising and falling action, Mark is building the plot, developing the characters, and recording the events that will lead us to the grand denouement when we, with all his readers, will confess that Jesus Christ is the Son of God and His gospel is the Good News [1:1]. McKenna, p. 156

Mk 8:36 *For what shall it profit a man, if he shall gain the whole world, and lose his own soul?* [KJV]
Spiritually man is a great trader—he is trading for his own welfare; he is trading for time and for eternity; he keeps two shops: one shop is kept by an apprentice of his, a rough unseemly hand, of clayey mould, called the body; the other business, which is an infinitely more vast concern, is kept by one that is called "the soul" a spiritual being, who does not traffic upon little things, but who deals with hell or heaven, and trades with the mighty realities of eternity. Now, a merchant would be very unwise who should

pay all attention to some small off-hand shop of his, and take no account whatever of a large establishment. And he would, indeed, be negligent, who should very carefully jot down every trifle of the expenditure of his own household, but should never think of reckoning the expenses of some vast concern that may be hanging on his hands. But the most of men are just as foolish—they estimate the profits (as they conceive them to be) which are gained in that small corner shop called the body, but they too seldom reckon up the awful loss which is brought about by a negligence of the soul's concerns in the great matters of eternity. Let me beseech you, my brethren, while you are not careless of the body, as, indeed, you ought not to be, seeing that it is, in the case of believers, the temple of the Holy Ghost, to take more especial care of your souls. Decorate the tenement, but suffer not the inhabitant to die of starvation; paint not the ship while you are letting the crew perish for want of stores on board. Look to your soul, as well as to your body; to the life, as well as to that by which you live. Oh that men would take account of the soul's vast concerns, and know their own standing before God. Oh that ye would examine yourselves. It men would do so, if all of you would now search within, how many of you would be bankrupts?
Charles Haddon Spurgeon Sermon Profit and Loss, July 6, 1856

Mk 10:43–44 *Not so with you. Instead, whoever wants to become great among you must be your servant, and whoever wants to be first must be slave of all.*
At no place do the ethics of the kingdom of God clash more vigorously with the ethics of the world than in the matters of power and service. The ideas that Jesus presents regarding rule and service are combined in a way that finds no obvious precedent in either the OT or Jewish tradition. In a decisive reversal of values, Jesus speaks of greatness in service rather than greatness of power, prestige, and authority. The preeminent virtue of God's kingdom is not power, nor even freedom, but service. Ironically, greatness belongs to the one who is not great, the διάκονος *diakonos*, the ordinary Greek word for waiting on tables. The preeminence of service in the kingdom of God grows out of Jesus' teaching on love for one's neighbor, for service is love made tangible. Edwards, p. 325

Edwards, James R. *The Gospel According to Mark*, Copyright © 2002 by William B. Eerdman Publishing, Grand Rapids, MI USA. Part of *The Pillar New Testament Commentary* Series, D.A. Carson general editor. Reprinted by permission of the publisher

Mk 10:45: *For even the Son of Man did not come to be served, but to serve, and to give his life as a ransom for many.*
Jesus is in the business of upsetting all the accepted standards of the world. Categorically rejecting rank and power, He establishes servanthood as His standard of greatness. By rank, a servant is last of all. In power, a servant has none. In a single sentence that rises like a mountain peak above all previous statements about His purpose, Jesus personalizes servanthood as the standard of greatness. Greatness is not to be sought; if it comes, it comes through giving. Ultimate good rules the servanthood of Jesus. Without rank and without power, He gives up His life as a ransom for many. McKenna, pp. 210–211

"A Christian is a perfectly free lord of all, subject to none. A Christian is a perfectly dutiful servant of all, subject to all." Martin Luther (1485 – 1546)
Quoted in Ward and Wild

Mk 12:29–31: *"The most important one," answered Jesus, "is this: 'Hear, O Israel, the Lord our God, the Lord is one. Love the Lord your God with all your heart and with all your soul and with all your mind and with all your strength.' The second is this: 'Love your neighbor as yourself.' There is no commandment greater than these."*
This passage from Deut 6:4–6, known as the *Shema*, was recited morning and evening by every pious Jew. As a creedal summary it was and is as important to Judaism as the Lord's Prayer or the Apostle's Creed to Christianity. Four times in v 30 the word 'all' is repeated, emphasizing the necessity of a total response of love to the lordship of God. God is the one and only Lord, not only of Israel but of every individual as well. God lays rightful claim to every facet of human personality: heart (= emotions), soul (=spirit), mind (=intelligence), and strength (=will). ... The fact that Jesus adds the commandment from Lev 19:18 to the *Shema* indicates that it takes both commandments to realize the one will of God. ... For Jesus, the requirements of the *Shema* cannot be fulfilled in ritual or sacrifice but

in unfeigned love of God, wholly and genuinely. The *Shema* must also be complimented by the love of neighbor. Love of neighbor, moreover, is the chief means of loving God, and is received as love of God. ... The two commandments are not blended into a compromising hybrid. The order in which Jesus declares the commandments implies that love of God is prerequisite to loving one's neighbor. Whoever does not find the source of love in God will fail to exhibit God's unique love to one's neighbor. Love of God is prior to love of neighbor and establishes its possibility. For Jesus, love fulfills the law; love *for* God releases the love *of* God.

Edwards, pp. 372–373

Edwards, James R. *The Gospel According to Mark*, Copyright © 2002 by William B. Eerdman Publishing, Grand Rapids, MI USA. Part of *The Pillar New Testament Commentary* Series, D.A. Carson general editor. Reprinted by permission of the publisher

Mk 14:11 *They were delighted to hear this and promised to give him money. So he watched for an opportunity to hand him over.*

Despite its economy, Mark's account implies that Judas was fully responsible for his betrayal of Jesus. It is he who goes to the chief priests, not they to him; and in one of the bitterest lines in the Gospel, his treachery causes them joy. The account closes with no Hamlet-like soliloquy lamenting a tragic decision, but with Judas' icy resolve to complete his insidious plan. Judas is thus not a victim of circumstances or a pawn dominated by greater forces. He is a sovereign moral agent who freely chooses evil in 'handing Jesus over' (παραδίδωμι *paradidōmi*). That word, the final part of the sandwich in vv 1–11, combines the two essential truths of Jesus' passion: the freely chosen evil of humanity, and the overarching providence of God. Divine grace uses even human evil for its saving purpose.

Edwards, p. 418

Edwards, James R. *The Gospel According to Mark*, Copyright © 2002 by William B. Eerdman Publishing, Grand Rapids, MI USA. Part of *The Pillar New Testament Commentary* Series, D.A. Carson general editor. Reprinted by permission of the publisher

Mk 14:3: *While he was in Bethany, reclining at the table in the home of a man known as Simon the Leper, a woman came with an alabaster jar of*

very expensive perfume, made of pure nard. She broke the jar and poured the perfume on his head.

Most expensive perfume had been poured over his head and probably most of those present will never have smelled such perfume before. The expensive nature of the nard was due, at least in part, to the fact that it had to be brought from India, a very long and arduous journey in those days. It was probably the most valuable thing she had. What matters most in our giving to Jesus is that we give him ourselves [cf Mark 12:17, Rom 12:1], but this self-giving can sometimes find an expression in a physical offering that is sacrificial. Mary's nard and the widow's two small copper coins (12:42) were very different in their monetary value, but they were united in this—they were sacrificially given. Grogan, p. 240

Personal Note: When I led our Sunday School discussion of this story in Mark's gospel, I thought a little "show and tell" would be helpful. So I went on a quest to find some of this *nard* perfume. Some of the commentaries mentioned that it was also called *spikenard*. So I went to various stores in search of it. After I went to about a dozen different stores, I finally found some in a health food store. It is distributed by Starwest Essential Oils and is also known as *Nardostachys jatamansai* and comes in a little ten ml vial. It has a very strong smoky odor almost like sandalwood incense. If a large quantity of this was poured on Jesus' head, the smell must have filled the home. He may well have smelled it as he hung on the cross a couple of days later. This brings to mind Gen 8:21 and Lev 1:13 and other verses which speak of an aroma pleasing to the Lord.

Mk 14:68 *But he denied it. "I don't know or understand what you're talking about," he said, and went out into the entryway*

While Jesus was undergoing a formal trial above, a trial of different sorts was taking place below. A servant girl spies Peter and accuses him of being with 'the Nazarene'. Peter stumbles over himself and retorts with surliness, 'I neither know him nor have any idea what you mean.' Marks's two Greek verbs for 'know' are only an apparent redundancy. The first (οἶδα *oida*) tends to denote theoretical knowledge, and the second (ἐπίσταμαι *epistamai*) practical knowledge. Peter's denial is thus a total denial—in theory and in practice! Peter then quits the fire for the forecourt or 'entryway' (v 68). The change of locations puts Peter even further from Jesus. But a change of place is no substitute for a change of heart. Like a guilty conscience, the servant girl accuses Peter a second time, and this time she enlists the bystanders in her accusation. Peter must now deny his association with Jesus before more people. The imperfect tense of the Greek verb for 'deny' in v 70 means that Peter 'went off' as we say, on an extended denial. The contagion spreads and the bystanders recognize his Galilean dialect. Although Peter hopes to escape notice, he ends up betraying Jesus by what he says, where he stands, and how he says it! ... Mark may have concluded this section with Peter's story to remind his persecuted congregation in Rome that not even the best Christian or lead apostle is immune to apostasy. Nor is he beyond the promise of grace! The church can be honest about sin—even the sins of an apostate apostle—because it is so convinced of grace. 'Where sin increased, grace increased all the more.' (Rom 5:20). Edwards, pp 450–452

Edwards, James R. *The Gospel According to Mark*, Copyright © 2002 by William B. Eerdman Publishing, Grand Rapids, MI USA. Part of *The Pillar New Testament Commentary* Series, D.A. Carson general editor. Reprinted by permission of the publisher

Mk 15:30: *come down from the cross and save yourself!*
Could he come down from the cross? From the standpoint of his power, yes, of course! From the standpoint of his sacrificial commitment to the Father's loving purpose of salvation for sinners—no he could not! Remember that insistent 'must' that he used in instructing his disciples on the road to Jerusalem (8:31, 9:12). What is physically possible is sometimes morally or spiritually impossible. So it was with Jesus. Grogan, p 266

Hymn: *How Deep the Father's Love for Us*, by Stuart Townend ©1995 Thankyou Music

How deep the Father's love for us,	[Eph 3:18]
How vast beyond all measure	[Eph 3:19]
That He should give His only Son,	[John 3:16, 1 Jn 4:9]
To make a wretch his treasure.	[1 Tim 1:16, Deut 7:6]
How great the pain of searing loss,	[Lk 22:44]
The Father turns his face away	[Mt 27:46, Ps 22:1]
As wounds which mar the Chosen One,	[Isa 52:14]
Bring many sons to glory.	[John 17:22]

Luke

Commentaries:
- *The Gospel According to Luke*, by James R. Edwards (2015)
- *Insights on Luke*, by Charles Swindoll (2012)
- *The Preacher's Commentary*, NT Vol. 26, by Bruce Larson (1983)
- *Cornerstone Biblical Commentary*, Vol. 12, by Allison A. Trites (2006)
- *The Return of the Prodigal Son*, by Henri J.M. Nouwen (1992)
- *The Prodigal God*, by Timothy Keller (2008)

Lk 1:46–49: *And Mary said, My soul doth magnify the Lord, And my spirit hath rejoiced in God my Saviour. For he hath regarded the low estate of his handmaiden: for, behold, from henceforth all generations shall call me blessed. For he that is mighty hath done to me great things; and holy is his name.* KJV
The essence of the *Magnificat* does not consist in its particular language or figures of speech, but in its revolutionary blueprint of divine favor. It is a hymn not of the proud but of the powerless; not of just deserts, but of unexpected grace; not of a world fully controlled and determined by human powers, but overturned by divine comedy. God is the subject of nearly every verb, and the verbs are all transitive: they do not declare who God is, but what God *does* as the powerful deliverer of the needy and oppressed. God does not turn away from want and oppression, but toward both in compassion and rescuing intervention. In most religions a meeting with God requires the low to ascend high, sinners to become saints. The *Magnificat* reverses all protocol and expectations: God who is high becomes low. He sees human need and initiates a revolution that reorders reality: the transcendent God intercedes on behalf of a lowly young woman and calls her blessed; the Almighty gives mercy to those who fear him and scatters the strong, proud, and rich, while filling the

hungry and needy with all good things. ... The God of the *Magnificat* advocates the small, insignificant, and needy: God's salvific intrusion in the incarnation does not erase, but includes the lowly state of Mary and 'the fruit of her womb.' Edwards, p 56

Edwards, James R. *The Gospel According to Luke* Copyright © 2015 by William B. Eerdman Publishing, Grand Rapids, MI USA. Part of *The Pillar New Testament Commentary* Series, D.A. Carson general editor. Reprinted by permission of the publisher

Luke 2:11 *Today in the town of David a Savior has been born to you; he is the Messiah, the Lord.*

'Today' belongs to the lexicon of Luke's load-bearing theological vocabulary. Its occurrence here announces Jesus' advent; in 4:21, it is the first word of Jesus' inaugural sermon in Nazareth; at 23:43, it is the final promise of Jesus from the cross: 'Today you will be with me in paradise.' The angel identifies the newborn Jesus as Messiah, Lord, and Savior. The first two titles appear in tandem, 'Messiah-Lord' Χριστὸς κύριος in Greek, a construction found nowhere else in the NT. The identification of the Messiah-Lord as 'savior' counteracts the claims and cult of Caesar Augustus in v 1, who repeatedly promoted himself as 'savior of the common folk' and 'savior of the world'. ... The titles ascribed to Caesar Augustus—Son of God, savior, bringer of peace, hope and good news—are all attributed by Luke to the newborn Jesus, as a divine alternative to the Roman imperial political-theology. Contrary to imperial propaganda, the true Son of God and Savior of the world—and thus the ultimate good news for the world—are not contained in a decree of Caesar but in the divine proclamation from heaven. The savior is not the mighty Augustus in Rome, but an infant lying in a feed trough in the city of David. Edwards, p. 76

Edwards, James R. *The Gospel According to Luke* Copyright © 2015 by William B. Eerdman Publishing, Grand Rapids, MI USA. Part of *The Pillar New Testament Commentary* Series, D.A. Carson general editor. Reprinted by permission of the publisher

Lk 2:13–14: *Suddenly a great company of the heavenly host appeared with the angel, praising God and saying, "Glory to God in the highest, and on earth peace to men on whom his favor rests."*

Scripture Commentary Sampler

Hymn: *Angels, from the Realms of Glory*, Text: James Montgomery, 1816, Melody: Henry Smart, 1867

Angels from the realms of glory,	[Mk 13:27]
Wing your flight o'er all the earth.	[Mt 24:31]
Ye who sang creation's story,	[Job 38:7]
now proclaim Messiah's birth.	[Lk 1:35]
Come and worship, come and worship,	[Ps 95:6, 100:2]
worship Christ the newborn King.	[Mt 2:11]
Shepherds in the fields abiding,	[Lk 2:8]
watching o'er your flocks by night,	[Lk 2:8]
God with man is now residing,	[Jn 1:14]
yonder shines the infant light.	[Isa 9:2]
Come and worship, come and worship,	[1 Chr 16:9, Ps 86:9]
worship Christ the newborn King.	[Lk 2:15]
Sages leave your contemplations,	[Mt 2:1]
brighter visions beam afar	[Isa 33:17]
Seek the great desire of nations,	[Isa 11:10, Ps 33:18]
ye have seen his natal star	[Mt 2:9]
Come and worship, come and worship,	[Rev 14:7]
worship Christ the newborn King.	[Mt 2:2]
Saints before the altar bending,	[Rev 8:3]
watching long in hope and fear	[Mic 7:7]
Suddenly the Lord descending	[Mal 3:1]
in his temple shall appear	[Mt 12:6]
Come and worship, come and worship,	[Rev 15:4]
worship Christ the newborn King.	[Lk 2:20]
All creation, join in praising,	[Ps 103:22]
God the Father, Spirit, Son	[Mt 28:19]
evermore your voices raising	[Rev 4:8]
to the eternal Three in One	[2 Cor 13:14]
Come and worship, come and worship,	[Heb 12:28, Ps 132:7]
worship Christ the newborn King.	[Lk 2:28–32]

Lk 5:5: *Simon answered, "Master, we've worked hard all night and haven't caught anything. But because you say so, I will let down the nets."*
Jesus begins Peter's journey of discipleship not by calling him away from his profession, but by challenging him to bolder practice of it. Jesus does not assert his lordship at Peter's weakest point but at its strongest point—his professional expertise as a fisherman! Nor does Jesus wait for an appropriate moment. Few fishermen endure failure in the art admirably and people who fish for a living rather than for sport may endure it even less admirably. We need not ask what goes through the mind of a professional fisherman in a foul mood when a nonfisherman orders him to do again in bad conditions what he has already tried and failed to do in good conditions. 'Master, we've worked hard all night and haven't caught anything. But because you say so, I will let down the nets' (v 5). Two voices are audible in Peter's reply—the professional fisherman and the fledgling disciple, the man of this world and the man of faith. Peter knew from experience the futility of fishing after sun-up, when fish can see the nets, and he reminds Jesus, who is considerably less experienced in such matters, of this fact. ... When Peter calls Jesus *Master* ἐπιστάτης *epistatēs* there is already a hint of his ultimate allegiance. It is less a theological title than acknowledgment of a practical relationship, 'You're the boss.' Edwards, p. 154
Edwards, James R. *The Gospel According to Luke* Copyright © 2015 by William B. Eerdman Publishing, Grand Rapids, MI USA. Part of *The Pillar New Testament Commentary* Series, D.A. Carson general editor. Reprinted by permission of the publisher

Lk 6:35: *But love your enemies, do good to them, and lend to them without expecting to get anything back. Then your reward will be great, and you will be children of the Most High, because he is kind to the ungrateful and wicked.*
The give-to-gain mentality is only logical. Loving others in the hope of receiving love in return isn't a sacrifice; it's an investment with a reasonable expectation of reward. Jesus, by contrast, called for self-giving without the expectation of anything in return. His brand of discipleship requires faith, confidence that all good things come from God [Jas 1:17]. The Lord doesn't reward His people for extending grace; that's nothing more than works-based righteousness. Instead, He calls His own to imitate Him, which gives them access to all that is His. ... You might call this the grace

principle. Those who exist in a grace relationship with God can count on it no less than the law of gravity. Imitate Christ, and we partake in all that is His. As we extend grace, the grace of God comes to is in greater quantities, not only to benefit us but to shower those around us with the goodness of God.

Swindoll, p. 159

Lk 7:43: *Simon replied, "I suppose the one who had the bigger debt canceled." "You have judged correctly," Jesus said.*
Simon's problem was that he thought he was better than he was and he misunderstood the nature of God who is the giver of unconditional love. The essence of the gospel is ἀγαπάω agapaō, which is the Greek word for the love of God, a love unlike any other love [Ps 36:5, Jer 31:3]. Every other kind of love is to some degree conditioned. It's a trade-off: 'I will if you will.' God's love is very different. Through Jesus, God is saying that He loves you just the way you are now. There's nothing you can do that can make Him love you more than He does right now. If you will respond to His love and give Him your life, He is not going to leave you as you are. You are a mess, obviously. He will reprogram you, make you transparent, set you free. All these strange quirks in you are going to go—in one year or in five thousand years. But when you are what He intended when He thought of you, He will not love you one bit more than He does right now. That kind of love is the most powerful force in the world.

Larson, pp. 141–142

Lk 9:20 *"But what about you?" he asked. "Who do you say I am?" Peter answered, "God's Messiah."*
A genuine confession of Jesus requires of believers more than a proxy endorsement of the judgment of others. 'But what about you? Who do you say I am?' presses Jesus. Peter's answer to that question requires a personal risk in which he stands alone with and before Jesus. His answer becomes the first voice in the chorus of the apostolic tradition that every follower of Jesus must acknowledge and confess for himself or herself. ... Jesus' question cannot be answered by simply amassing more data. Like all ultimate commitments in life, his question cannot be answered by

knowledge alone. It requires risk and trust that either commit one to, or separate one from, his identity and mission.   Edwards, pp. 269–270
Edwards, James R. *The Gospel According to Luke* Copyright © 2015 by William B. Eerdman Publishing, Grand Rapids, MI USA. Part of *The Pillar New Testament Commentary* Series, D.A. Carson general editor. Reprinted by permission of the publisher

Lk 11:52: *Woe to you experts in the law, because you have taken away the key to knowledge. You yourselves have not entered, and you have hindered those who were entering.*

The conclusion of Luke 11 may appear offensive to those who hold to a stereotype of 'gentle Jesus, meek and mild.' Jesus appears to be a rude guest who offends against good manners of ritual purity, who rebukes Pharisees for being internally filthy, and who concludes with an expose of the worst offenses of both Pharisees and lawyers. Such a profile poses a challenge for an age, like ours, that equates Christianity with 'niceness' and 'tolerance.' … The denunciations of the Pharisees and lawyers demonstrate that 'love of enemies' does not mean saying what people want to hear, but telling the truth that they may not want to hear. 'Doing good to those who hate you' does not mean being nice in the face of hatred and injustice, but speaking and acting in ways that have the potential to reduce or eliminate hatred and injustice. The great violation of *agape* love-ethic is not confrontation, but indifference. Jesus is not indifferent. Edwards, p. 360

Edwards, James R. *The Gospel According to Luke* Copyright © 2015 by William B. Eerdman Publishing, Grand Rapids, MI USA. Part of *The Pillar New Testament Commentary* Series, D.A. Carson general editor. Reprinted by permission of the publisher

Lk 13:24 *Make every effort to enter through the narrow door, because many, I tell you, will try to enter and will not be able to.*

God's grace carried with it a bracing challenge; it was not the offer of what Dietrich Bonhoeffer called "cheap grace." Rather it entailed proper human response, which involves intense effort (the Greek ἀγωνίζομαι *agōnizomai* means "struggle" or "fight"). The daunting potential of failure was real, and they were so warned. Like the Corinthians, the disciples were warned not to receive the grace of God in vain (2 Cor 6:1). A long, steady obedience in the same direction that Jesus was taking was called for on the part of his true disciples.

It was not enough to use the right words, calling Jesus "Lord." People could do that and yet not have a real relationship with the Savior. Personal contact, symbolized by such friendly activities as eating and drinking, did not guarantee that they were bona fide believers. Neither did sharing Christian teaching with others substitute for their own direct knowledge of God, experienced in their personal relationship with Jesus. Such activities, devoid of spiritual connection with the Son of God himself, would not do. These persons who just superficially went through the motions did not pass muster. This sham piety was a subterfuge for refusal to meet the high demands of true discipleship and genuine knowledge of the Lord Jesus himself.

Trites, Allison A., *Cornerstone Biblical Commentary*, Vol. 12, Carol Stream, IL: Tyndale, 2006. pp. 205-206

Lk 14:11: *For all those who exalt themselves will be humbled, and those who humble themselves will be exalted.*

The passive voice is another 'divine passive,' a reference to God without using God's name, meaning 'God will humble the exalted and exalt the humbled.' The Pharisees seek to exalt themselves, and in so doing they cease being models and rulers of God's people. ... The Pharisees regard Jesus' intimacy with the social riff-raff a source of defilement, but Jesus is not worried about associating with the 'poor, the crippled, the lame, and the blind' (vv 13, 21). If anything defiles Jesus, it is his association with the *Pharisees*, for they are obsessed with self promotion rather than surrendering trust to 'the one who calls.' Christian discipleship is not self-promotion, but freedom from it, freedom from self-obsession itself.

Edwards, p. 418

Edwards, James R. *The Gospel According to Luke* Copyright © 2015 by William B. Eerdman Publishing, Grand Rapids, MI USA. Part of *The Pillar New Testament Commentary* Series, D.A. Carson general editor. Reprinted by permission of the publisher

Lk 15:12: *The younger one said to his father, 'Father, give me my share of the estate.' So he divided his property between them.*

The uniqueness of the parable does not consist in the sons. We all know people like the rebellious younger son or the resentful older one. At one time or another, in fact, most of us have been like one or the other. But we have never known anyone like the father, nor would we claim to be such ourselves. The father is the first party named and the last to speak, the unique and causal figure in both halves of the parable. ... None of the problems posed in the parable can be solved without the father, who is the last remaining link of each son to the family. ... The parable is about the indomitable love of the Father.   Edwards, pp 437–438

Edwards, James R. *The Gospel According to Luke* Copyright © 2015 by William B. Eerdman Publishing, Grand Rapids, MI USA. Part of *The Pillar New Testament Commentary* Series, D.A. Carson general editor. Reprinted by permission of the publisher

Personal Note: We come now to what I consider to be one of the summits of the Gospel, the moving and compelling story the Prodigal Son, which has been brilliantly explained in Henri Nouwen's treatment, *The Return of the Prodigal Son*. I led a discussion on this parable in our Doulous Sunday School class and it was a personal joy to me. It is a moving portrayal of God's grace. I believe many of us have, like the younger son, tried to find fulfillment in some "distant country" only to discover that our dreams were illusions and that the only contentment and rest we could find is in our heavenly father's home.

More recently, Timothy Keller has provided a new angle on this beloved parable in *The Prodigal God*. Keller's main take is that this parable is not about one lost son, but about two.

Pastor Joe Focht of Calvary Chapel, Philadelphia, summed up the younger son's request in vs 12 well. The younger son basically said, "Father, I want yours but I don't want you. I want your blessing but I don't want your presence" [cf Ps 16:11, contrast with 2 Cor 12:14b]. All too often we behave the same way towards our heavenly father. May we, like the prodigal, "come to our senses" (Lk 15:17) and return to our father's outstretched arms to partake of the grace he offers in such abundance.

The parable's elaborate chiastic structure helps us to understand its rich message:

Scripture Commentary Sampler

The Prodigal Son
Luke 15:1–2, 11–32

1 A son is lost – "Give me my share"
| 2 Goods wasted in extravagant living
| | 3 Everything lost – "He spent everything-he began to want"
| | | 4 The great sin – "feeding pigs for gentiles"
| | | | 5 Total rejection – "no one gave him anything"
| | | | | 6 A change of mind – "he came to himself-I perish here"
| | | | | 6 An initial repentance – "make me a servant"
| | | | 5 Total acceptance – "his father ran and kissed him."
| | | 4 The great repentance – "I am no more worthy to be called your son."
| | 3 Everything gained - a robe, ring, and shoes
| 2 Goods used in joyful celebration
1 A son is found – "My son was dead and is alive, was lost and is found."

Source: Matt Slick, http://www.carm.org/parables/parableprodigal.htm

Lk 15:13: *Not long after that, the younger son got together all he had, set off for a distant country and there squandered his wealth in wild living.*

[Prov 29:3]

The 'distant country' is the world in which everything considered holy at home is disregarded. Leaving home is much more than an historical event bound to time and place. It is a denial of the spiritual reality that I belong to God with every part of my being, that God holds me safe in an eternal embrace, that I am indeed carved in the palms of God's hands [Isa 49:16] and hidden in their shadows [Isa 51:16]. Leaving home means ignoring the truth that God has 'fashioned me in secret, molded me in the depths of the earth and knitted me together in my mother's womb [Ps 139:13–15].' Leaving home is living as though I do not yet have a home and must look far and wide to find one. Nouwen, p. 37

There are endless 'ifs' hidden in the world's love. These 'ifs' enslave me since it is impossible to respond adequately to all of them. The world's love is and always will be conditional. As long as we live within the world's delusions, our addictions condemn us to futile quests in the 'distant country', leaving us to face an endless series of disillusionments while our sense of self remains unfulfilled. … Here the mystery of my life is unveiled. I am loved so much that I am left free to leave home. The blessing is there from the beginning. I have left it and keep on leaving it. But the Father is always looking for me with outstretched arms to receive me back and whisper again in my ear: 'You are my Beloved, on you my favor rests.' Nouwen, p. 43, 44

Lk 15:17–18: *"When he came to his senses, he said, 'How many of my father's hired men have food to spare, and here I am starving to death!.'*
Loneliness and wretchedness have a salutary effect. The young man 'came to his senses.' "Want," writes Plummer, "rekindles what his revelry had extinguished." The Greek expression behind 'came to his senses' εἰς ἑαυτὸν *eis heauton*, is a translation of the Hebrew *bilebo*, meaning 'in the heart.' Luke uses this phrase eleven times—all in Special Luke—to signify inner ruminations that result in resolutions to act (1:29, 7:39, 11:38,12:17,32, 16:3, 18:4, [small variations] 18:11, 7:30, 15:17, 18:9). The first consequence of 'coming to one's senses' is clarity of thought and honest self-appraisal that in this present state, he is utterly 'perishing' (v 17). It is an essential admission, for only the lost can be found. Scholars worry that his repentance was not entirely altruistic, that hunger rather than remorse drove him home. That seems to me like worrying whether people are in the church for the 'right' reasons. Is it necessary that his motives be perfect for the father to receive him? Fortunately for all of us, the God of Jesus—and the father in the parable—is willing to accept a sinner on almost *any* terms!
Edwards, pp. 440-441 Edwards, James R. *The Gospel According to Luke* Copyright © 2015 by William B. Eerdman Publishing, Grand Rapids, MI USA. Part of *The Pillar New Testament Commentary* Series, D.A. Carson general editor. Reprinted by permission of the publisher

Lk 15:29: *But he answered his father, 'Look! All these years I've been slaving for you and never disobeyed your orders. Yet you never gave me even a young goat so I could celebrate with my friends.'*
Outwardly the elder son was faultless. But when confronted by his father's joy at the return of his younger brother, a dark power erupts in him and boils to the surface. The elder brother's complaint is one that comes from a heart that feels it never received what it due. Trust and gratitude are the disciplines for the conversion of the elder son. Resentment and gratitude cannot coexist, since resentment blocks the perception and experience of life as a gift. My resentment tells me I didn't receive what I deserve. The

choice for gratitude rarely comes without some real effort. But each time I make it, the next choice is a little easier, a little freer, a little less self-conscious. Because every gift I acknowledge reveals another and another until, finally, even the most normal, obvious, and seemingly mundane event or encounter proves to be filled with grace. Acts of gratitude make one grateful because, step by step, they reveal that all is grace [1 Chr 29:14, James 1:17].   Nouwen, excerpts, pp 72-73, 85, 86

How will the father respond to his older son's open rebellion? A man of his time and place might have disowned the son on the spot. Instead he responds again with amazing tenderness. "My son," he begins, "despite how you've insulted me publicly, I still want you in the feast. I am not going to disown your brother, but I don't want to disown you either. I challenge you to swallow your pride and come into the feast. The choice is yours." … The listeners are on the edge of their seats. Will the elder brother be softened by this remarkable offer and be reconciled to the father? Just as these thoughts pass through our minds, the story ends! Why doesn't Jesus finish the story? It is because the real audience for this story is the Pharisees, the elder brothers. Jesus is pleading with his enemies to respond to the message. What is that message? He is redefining sin, what it means to be lost, and what it means to be saved.
Timothy Keller, *The Prodigal God*, excerpts, pp 27–28

Personal Note: The elder son's reaction is an arresting portrait of the ugly sin of envy. When we think about this human emotion, we should recoil in revulsion not only at its failure to give thanks for blessings already received, but on the illogical assumption upon which it rests: I am hurt when something good happens to someone else (Gen 26:14, Mt 20:12, Eccl 4:4). Simple envy has caused untold bitterness and strife over the centuries and still does today. Envy is not just wicked, ungrateful, and illogical, it is corrosive—but not to the object of our envy, only to the envier (cf discussion on 1 Sam 18:7–8). Proverbs 14:30 puts it well: "A heart at peace gives life to the body, but envy rots the bones." May we all be quick to recognize and quell envy in our own lives so that it does not rot our bones.

Lk 18:10: *Two men went up to the temple to pray, one a Pharisee and the other a tax collector.*

The Pharisee mentions God, but does not pray to God, for he rests his case on his catalog of virtues. He rehearses his service as above and beyond the call of duty and put God in his debt. He is thankful not to God, but simply that he is not like other people whom he considers inferior. In his mind, his virtues are real and his sins illusory. The tax collector knows his situation to be much different. Without merits to stand on, he must stand humbly before God; without merits to speak for him, he must plead to God; without merits to be rewarded, his only option is to plead for God's mercy. The Pharisee stands before God in self-congratulation; the tax collector stands before God in prayer. Edwards, p. 506
Edwards, James R. *The Gospel According to Luke* Copyright © 2015 by William B. Eerdman Publishing, Grand Rapids, MI USA. Part of *The Pillar New Testament Commentary* Series, D.A. Carson general editor. Reprinted by permission of the publisher

Lk 19:9–10: *Jesus said to him, "Today salvation has come to this house, because this man, too, is a son of Abraham. For the Son of Man came to seek and to save what was lost."'*

Grace is forever scandalous because it is forever undeserved. It is doubly scandalous for Zacchaeus, a rich oppressor, who seems so much less deserving of grace than Lazarus, the wretched outcast (16:19–31). Grace is a scandal because it insists on including those whom we seek to exclude. The story of Zacchaeus illustrates such grace. It ends not with Zacchaeus seeking Jesus but with Jesus seeking him, not in Zacchaeus's moral perfection, but with his recovery and restoration as 'a son of Abraham.' The ironic interaction between Zacchaeus and Jesus is not unlike a former student of mine, a Hindu at the time, who began to read the NT—and discovered that the NT was 'reading him'! The decisive seeker is not Zacchaeus, but Jesus, who accomplishes God's mission, as foretold by the prophets (Ezek 34:11–16), 'to seek and save what is lost.' Edwards, p. 533
Edwards, James R. *The Gospel According to Luke* Copyright © 2015 by William B. Eerdman Publishing, Grand Rapids, MI USA. Part of *The Pillar New Testament Commentary* Series, D.A. Carson general editor. Reprinted by permission of the publisher

"It is not Santa Claus coming to town looking for who has been bad or good, but Jesus coming to town to seek and save that which was lost. And oh, how we fit that bill." Larry DeHeer (Church elder and Christian mentor to me)

Lk 24:5–6: *But the men said to them, "Why do you look for the living among the dead? He is not here; he has risen!"*
With all due respect to the venerable *Merriam-Webster's Collegiate Dictionary*, death need not be 'a permanent cessation of all vital functions.' At least not any more. The resurrection of Jesus Christ is a historical fact that carries far-reaching implications. He did not merely emerge from the tomb, resuscitated to exist a few more years. He was resurrected to a new kind of life, one that transcends the frail, fleeting existence we now endure. While these bodies get sick and suffer injury, Jesus will never feel pain again. While our present relationships are doomed to end through betrayal, distance, or death, He will never feel abandonment or rejection again. While seasons of joy must eventually yield to sorrow, He will always know joy. Because Jesus was raised, we now have hope of that kind of life through Him. The dominion of evil has been vanquished, its power to harm us limited to the realm of space and time. If we trust in Him, we will be like Him. While evil may kill the body, we will be raised to receive eternal life in His kingdom. Swindoll, p. 517

Hymn: *See, What a Morning*, Words and Music by Keith Getty and Stuart Townend
Copyright © 2003 Kingsway Thankyou Music

One with the Father, Ancient of Days	[John 10:30, Dan 7:13]
Through the Spirit who clothes faith with certainty	[Rom 5:5]
Honor and blessing, glory and praise	[Rev 7:12]
To the King crowned with pow'r and authority	[Mt 28:18, Eph 1:21, Rev 11:15]
And we are raised with Him	[Eph 2:6]
Death is dead, love has won, Christ has conquered	[1 Cor 15:54, Rev 17:14, Col 2:15]
And we shall reign with Him	[2 Tim 2:12, Rev 22:5]
For He lives: Christ is risen from the dead	[1 Cor 15:4, Rom 1:4]

John

"St. John's Gospel is God's love letter to the world."
Henry Ward Beecher (1813–1887)

Commentaries:
- *The Message of John*, by Bruce Milne (1993)
- *The Preacher's Commentary*, NT vol 27, by Roger L. Fredrikson (1985)
- *Living Insights*, vol 4, by Charles Swindoll (2014)

John 1:1: *In the beginning was the Word, and the Word was with God, and the Word was God.*
Ἐν ἀρχῇ ἦν ὁ λόγος καὶ ὁ λόγος ἦν πρὸς τὸν θεόν καὶ θεὸς ἦν ὁ λόγος
Is there any way one can plumb the depths of John's prologue to his Gospel? Such intense power in so few words! Living with this prologue is like standing in the foothills of an awesome mountain range catching a breathtaking glimpse of massive, snowcapped peaks reaching up through the haze. Or it is like being overwhelmed by haunting melodies that introduce the themes of a mighty symphony. The prologue is far more than an introduction to the Gospel. It is really a dramatic summary, a revelation, of all that will take place throughout the earthly ministry of our Lord. ... In using 'the Word', the λόγος (*Logos*), John was speaking to both the Jewish and Greek worlds—those two widely divergent cultures. The Greeks were sophisticated, inquisitive, and philosophic [Acts 17:21]; the Jews righteous, traditional, and struggling to be faithful to the Law. How amazing that John could share the Gospel narratives with these two cultures at the same time, using a single, simple concept that carried such profound meaning for both.   Fredrikson, pp. 25, 26, 28

John 1:3: *Through him all things were made; without him nothing was made that has been made.*

John's point is that it is through Jesus alone that all things exist, whether physical planets or spiritual hierarchies. He towers above all and cannot be reduced to one of a series, whether as a stage in the process of human evolution or in the history of human ideas. Since he is fully divine, he cannot be reduced to an intermediate state; since he is a person, he cannot be dissolved into an ideal [Col 1:16]. Milne, p. 39

Milne, Bruce, *The Message of John*, Taken from *The Bible Speaks Today* Series edited by J. Alec Motyer; John Stott. Copyright ©1983 edited by J. Alec Motyer; John Stott. Used by permission of InterVarsity Press, P.O. Box 1400, Downers Grove, IL 60515, USA. www.ivpress.com Taken from *The Message of John* by Bruce Milne. Copyright (c) 1993 by Bruce Milne. Used by permission of InterVarsity Press, P.O. Box 1400, Downers Grove, IL 60515, USA. www.ivpress.com

John 1:14: *The Word became flesh and made his dwelling among us. We have seen his glory, the glory of the One and Only, who came from the Father, full of grace and truth.*
Καὶ ὁ λόγος σὰρξ ἐγένετο καὶ ἐσκήνωσεν ἐν ἡμῖν καὶ ἐθεασάμεθα τὴν δόξαν αὐτοῦ δόξαν ὡς μονογενοῦς παρὰ πατρός πλήρης χάριτος καὶ ἀληθείας

"Founders of other religions say 'I send prophets to help you find God.' Christianity says, 'I'm God, and I came to find you.'"
Pastor Tim Keller, Veritas Forum, Berkeley California, March 7, 2008

This statement is one of the most significant and memorable ever penned. Its implications are limitless. It has provided the church over the centuries with a key to understanding the mystery of Jesus Christ. It represents the heart and climax of the gospel. The remaining twenty and a half chapters will be spent unfolding its significance. ... The tense is aorist, implying a definite and completed action; there is no going back on the Incarnation. The act of self-humbling on the part of God is irreversible [Phil 2:8]; he is eternally Emmanuel, God with us. Milne, pp. 46–47

Milne, Bruce, *The Message of John*, Taken from *The Bible Speaks Today* Series edited by J. Alec Motyer; John Stott. Copyright ©1993 edited by J. Alec Motyer; John Stott. Used by permission of InterVarsity Press, P.O. Box 1400, Downers Grove, IL 60515, USA. www.ivpress.com

John 3:3: *In reply Jesus declared, "I tell you the truth, no one can see the kingdom of God unless he is born again."*
The dialogue with Nicodemus is a crucial section of the whole Bible since it expresses most clearly the truth of regeneration by the Holy Spirit, the fact that it is by the secret, powerful operation of God the Spirit alone that one can experience salvation. To experience God's salvation is not simply a matter of illumination; it is a matter of regeneration. It is not just a new *seeing*, but a new *being*. You must be born again. Regeneration also makes clear the radical difference between Christians and non-Christians. We are either one or the other, born again (1 Pet 1:23, Eph 2:4–5), or dead in sins (Eph 2:1); we have come to the light [1 Pet 2:9], or are still in darkness [Mt 8:12]; we are saved from condemnation [Rom 8:1], or under condemnation [Rom 5:16]. There is no middle ground [cf Dan 12:2, Mt 25:46].

Milne, p. 79

Milne, Bruce, *The Message of John*, Taken from *The Bible Speaks Today* Series edited by J. Alec Motyer; John Stott. Copyright ©1993 edited by J. Alec Motyer; John Stott. Used by permission of InterVarsity Press, P.O. Box 1400, Downers Grove, IL 60515, USA. www.ivpress.com

John 3:4: *"How can a man be born when he is old?" Nicodemus asked. "Surely he cannot enter a second time into his mother's womb to be born!"*
Personal Note: Pastor Ben Phillips had a vivid description of this passage. Being 'born again' should be right in Nicodemus' wheelhouse. He had studied the Scriptures and was intimately familiar with Ezek 36 and 37. Yet in all his intellectual study he missed the main point. I pray that I might not be like Nicodemus—getting a lot of head knowledge but failing to grasp the significance of God's word as a guide to my redemption and eternal life.

John 3:16: *For God so loved the world that he gave his one and only Son, that whoever believes in him shall not perish but have eternal life.*
If the depth of love is measured by the value of its gift, then God's love could not be greater, for his love-gift his most precious possession—his only, eternally beloved Son. He could not love more.   Milne, p. 79

Milne, Bruce, *The Message of John*, Taken from *The Bible Speaks Today* Series edited by J. Alec Motyer; John Stott. Copyright ©1993 edited by J. Alec Motyer; John

Stott. Used by permission of InterVarsity Press, P.O. Box 1400, Downers Grove, IL 60515, USA. www.ivpress.com

John 3:30: *He must increase, but I must decrease.* [KJV]
Jesus must advance into the center of the stage and John must retire to the wings, as the Messiah assumes his rightful rule in his kingdom and the bridegroom takes increasing claim over his bride. Few greater motto texts for ministry have ever been uttered. Only a great man can accept his own demise with joy. Milne, p 81.
Milne, Bruce, *The Message of John,* Taken from *The Bible Speaks Today* Series edited by J. Alec Motyer; John Stott. Copyright ©1993 edited by J. Alec Motyer; John Stott. Used by permission of InterVarsity Press, P.O. Box 1400, Downers Grove, IL 60515, USA. www.ivpress.com

John 5:10 *and so the Jewish leaders said to the man who had been healed, "It is the Sabbath; the law forbids you to carry your mat."*
Legalism is the establishment of standards carefully selected by people for the purpose of celebrating human achievement under the guise of pleasing God. Legalism is a righteousness defined by humans, who frequently cite God as the source of their standard. In reality, the standards come from culture, tradition, and most frequently the personal preferences of those who maintain positions of power or influence.
Legalism denies God's grace and presumes to earn His favor through deeds. It is a man-made righteousness that exalts humanity rather than the Lord. Legalism produces either pride or depression in the people under its spell—pride for those who keep the list to their own satisfaction, depression for those who recognize their utter inability to keep the list perfectly. Criticism is the primary motivation. The goal of legalism is to give as much criticism as possible and to avoid receiving it at all costs.
Legalism is wrong because it produces in people what the Lord desires least: pride, self-loathing, hypocrisy, and self-righteousness.
Charles Swindoll, *Living Insights*, Vol 4, Carol Stream, IL: Tyndale, 2014, excerpts, pp. 109-110

John 8:58: *"I tell you the truth," Jesus answered, "before Abraham was born, I am!"*

He is the eternal Christ sharing the everlasting life of the Father [1:1–2], the changeless Lord [Ps 102:27, Mal 3:6a] who towers over history [Ps 93:1–2, Col 1:16], Master of time [Ps 90:4], Ruler of the ages [Ps 90:2], undiminished by the passing of the centuries, the same yesterday, today, and forever (Heb 13:8). To a generation conscious of the brevity of life we feel constantly threatened by time's flow [Isa 40:6–8, Ps 90:12]. It runs through our fingers and escapes us no matter how frantically we try to fill it and hold it back. But Christ has all time in his hands; as we rest our lives in him our fragile, ephemeral consciousness finds meaning and permanence.
Milne, p. 136

Milne, Bruce, *The Message of John*, Taken from *The Bible Speaks Today* Series edited by J. Alec Motyer; John Stott. Copyright ©1993 edited by J. Alec Motyer; John Stott. Used by permission of InterVarsity Press, P.O. Box 1400, Downers Grove, IL 60515, USA. www.ivpress.com

John 10:28: *I give them eternal life, and they shall never perish; no one can snatch them out of my hand.*
Jesus refers to some of the supreme privileges of those who believe in Jesus. They are:

- a summoned group (*my sheep listen to my voice*, v 27)
- a gifted group (gift of *eternal life*, v 27)
- a secured group (*no one can snatch them out of the Father's hand*, v. 29)

Christ's people are his possession. He has committed himself to them even as they for their part have, however falteringly, committed themselves to him. In this too the Father and the Son are one (30). The flock has been given to the Son by the Father and he stands behind the Son in his guardianship of the flock. Hence the forces of opposition and destruction have to confront the awesome and limitless power of the Father, who is 'greater than all.' No profounder security is conceivable for the follower of Jesus [John 6:39–40, Phil 1:6, Rom 8:38–39]. Milne, p. 153

Milne, Bruce, *The Message of John*, Taken from *The Bible Speaks Today* Series edited by J. Alec Motyer; John Stott. Copyright ©1993 edited by J. Alec Motyer; John Stott. Used by permission of InterVarsity Press, P.O. Box 1400, Downers Grove, IL 60515, USA. www.ivpress.com

John 11:37: *But some of them said, "Could not he who opened the eyes of the blind man have kept this man from dying?"*
He seemed able to cope with all other eventualities; could he not somehow have prevented this? Is this, then, the limit of Jesus' power? Some trials he can deal with, some sicknesses he can cure, some human tragedies do indeed yield to his word of power, but there are others concerning which we sadly conclude that 'he could not' [Mk 9:23–24]. Were that to be the case then all our hopes are finally vacuous. A 'so far' Savior is in the end no Savior at all. On the first reaction the Jews are right, though their understanding is superficial. On the second, they could not be more wrong! Jesus proceeds immediately to demonstrate how wrong they are, and how wrong every other has been over the centuries who has set limits to the possibilities and power of Jesus Christ.   Milne, p. 166

Milne, Bruce, *The Message of John*, Taken from *The Bible Speaks Today* Series edited by J. Alec Motyer; John Stott. Copyright ©1993 edited by J. Alec Motyer; John Stott. Used by permission of InterVarsity Press, P.O. Box 1400, Downers Grove, IL 60515, USA. www.ivpress.com

John 13:34–35: *"A new command I give you: Love one another. As I have loved you, so you must love one another. By this all men will know that you are my disciples, if you love one another."*
To love like Jesus is to love inclusively, indiscriminately, and universally [Mt 5:46–48]. When that kind of love flows within a congregation the world will take note that 'they have been with Jesus.' Nor need this standard daunt us. Tertullian reported in the late second century the comment of the pagans in his day 'Behold, how these Christians love each other!' Their mutual love is the magnet which drew the pagan multitudes to Christ. It has the potential to do so still. … Mother Theresa's prayer has direct application within every Christian community: "Dearest Lord, may I see you today and everyday in the person of your sick and, whilst nursing them, minister unto you. Though you hide yourself behind the unattractive disguise of the irritable, the exacting, the unreasonable, may I still recognize you and say 'Jesus, my patient, how sweet it is to serve you.'"   Milne, p. 207

Milne, Bruce, *The Message of John*, Taken from *The Bible Speaks Today* Series edited by J. Alec Motyer; John Stott. Copyright ©1993 edited by J. Alec Motyer; John Stott. Used by permission of InterVarsity Press, P.O. Box 1400, Downers Grove, IL 60515, USA. www.ivpress.com

John 14:6: *Jesus answered, "I am the way and the truth and the life. No one comes to the Father except through me."*

<u>**Personal Note**</u>: Among those outside the Christian faith, this verse is among the most offensive in the entire Bible. Such people say, "How can you be so sure that of all the religions of the world, yours alone is the correct one? Millions fervently believe in Islam, Hindu, Buddhism, and other religions. How can you say that you are right and all of them are wrong?" The conver-sation then often progresses to debates which attempt to use reason and logic to defend the faith. Some excellent arguments in this genre, called *apologetics* (eg, Thomas Aquinas' 5 proofs for the existence of God, C.S. Lewis's *Mere Christianity*, Josh MacDowell's *Evidence that Demands a Verdict*) have been written over the centuries.

In the end, however, no logic or reason will ever prove the truth of John 14:6. The Christian believes that human reason and logic are insufficient to communicate a wisdom which comes from above (1 Cor 2:14, Isa 55:8–9). We believe that God has testified about himself and his Son through two main vehicles: his Word and the Holy Spirit. We finite beings cannot fully comprehend the story from our omniscient and omnipotent God. It's like humans trying to explain nature to grasshoppers; as though we walked into a college class on quantum mechanics and had never had a single science class in our lives. But we believe his Spirit reveals profound truths to those he has chosen to save. And those who have been touched by that Spirit have absolutely no trouble with this verse.

John 15:13 *Greater love has no one than this: to lay down one's life for one's friends.*

There is no love, too, so gentle, so patient, so enduring, as Christ's love. Again and again you have questioned it, wounded it, forsaken it; again and again you have returned to it with tears, confession, and humiliation, and have found it as unchilled and unchanged as his nature [Heb 13:8]. It has borne with your doubts, has been silent beneath your murmurings, has veiled your infirmities, and has planted itself a thousand times between you and your unseen implacable foe. It has never declined your fickleness, nor frozen with your coldness, nor upbraided you for your backslidings [Ps 103:9], but all day long, tracking your wandering, winding way, it has hovered around you with a presence that has encircled you within its

divine, all-enshrouding, and invisible shield [Ps 28:7, 139:5]. Truly there is no love like Christ's! [1 John 3:16].
Octavius Winslow from "None Like Christ"

John 16:8 *When he comes, he will convict the world of guilt in regard to sin and righteousness and judgment*
Sin, at root is a refusal of grace, the proud titanic assertion that we can atone for ourselves. These three ideas, sin, righteousness and judgment, belong to the common stock of ethical concepts which jostle in today's pluralistic society. In the prevailing relativistic atmosphere, ethical absolutes are dismissed. People claim the right to determine for themselves what will count as sin, what will be their standard of righteousness, and where judgment has or has not been properly expressed. Jesus, through the Holy Spirit's witness, challenges this ethical autonomy, uncovers the rebellion against God which underlies it, and confronts the world with the true character of sin, the true meaning of righteousness and the true place of judgment. Through the Spirit of God the human heart is summoned to repentance and then offered the salvation which is life indeed.   Milne,p. 230, 231
Milne, Bruce, *The Message of John,* Taken from *The Bible Speaks Today* Series edited by J. Alec Motyer; John Stott. Copyright ©1993 edited by J. Alec Motyer; John Stott. Used by permission of InterVarsity Press, P.O. Box 1400, Downers Grove, IL 60515, USA. www.ivpress.com

John 17:3: *Now this is eternal life: that they may know you, the only true God, and Jesus Christ, whom you have sent.*
The world in and of itself cannot satisfy us; that was never the intention. Beyond the world we seek the world's Lord, the ever-living God of glory, grace, and majesty, Father, Son, and Spirit. Eternity will bring the deepening of our knowledge through ever richer appreciation of him who is without end. To receive eternal life is not the end of our journey; in the deepest sense it is only the beginning. Eternal life is in essence quality of life rather than quantity of life. True, it participates in the victory over the grave which the Son has won through his death and rising, and is therefore 'endless', but that is certainly not its most important feature. Eternal life is not so much everlasting life as knowledge of the everlasting One [Eph 1:17–19]. Milne, p. 241, 240

Milne, Bruce, *The Message of John*, Taken from *The Bible Speaks Today* Series edited by J. Alec Motyer; John Stott. Copyright ©1993 edited by J. Alec Motyer; John Stott. Used by permission of InterVarsity Press, P.O. Box 1400, Downers Grove, IL 60515, USA. www.ivpress.com

John 18:9 *This was to fulfill the word that he had spoken: "Of those whom you gave me I have lost not one." * [ESV]

John 18:11: *So Jesus said to Peter, "Put your sword into its sheath; shall I not drink the cup that the Father has given me?"* [ESV]

<u>**Personal Note**</u>: Pastor Ben Phillips of Chestnut Mountain Presbyterian Church expounded the first section of John 18 on Good Friday 2019 with a message titled "Two Gifts that No One Else Wants." The first gift is, well, *us*! We all have sinned and fallen far short of the glory of God [Rom 3:23]. In the ancient world, the best gift a father could give a young man was an unsullied bride. This gift would be enthusiastically and gratefully received. But God the Father gave his Son disgusting people like you and me (and if you don't think you're disgusting to the Father, you need to do a more honest self-appraisal). Yet the Son received this gift eagerly and gratefully and clutched his bride to his bosom. He did not want one of us to be taken from him [Jn 10:28]. The second gift was even harder. The Lord tells Jeremiah "take from my hand this cup of the wine of wrath, and make all the nations to whom I send you drink it." Though Christ certainly did not deserve the cup of God's wrath, he also took it without reservation [John 12:27]. He was so passionately committed to the Father's plan of redemption that he received the Lord's cup of wrath to save the people the Lord had given him. Good Friday, says Pastor Ben, was a really *Good* Friday. The Son laid down his life [Jn 15:13] for low-lifes like you and me because in the end, our lives are precious [Isa 43:4] to Father, Son, and Holy Spirit as mystifying as that sounds.

John 18:39–40: *"But it is your custom for me to release to you one prisoner at the time of the Passover. Do you want me to release 'the king of the Jews'?" They shouted back, "No, not him! Give us Barabbas!"*

The choice that faced the mob in Jerusalem is still before our world. Whom will we follow? Whom will we make our king? Barabbas continues to represent an alluring alternative, the fulfilling of this-worldly ambitions and dreams, the gratification of human lusts and hungers, the nationalist dream, the political kingdom. Jesus still stands before us also offering his way of truth, a knowledge of the Father which, beginning in the valley of confession and repentance, leads forward along the pathway of daily surrender to him as Lord. Though on the surface less attractive, however, that choice frees those who make it to serve him in the world. It carries them at last beyond the passing shadows of the earthly into the enduring order of the kingdom which will have no end. Who is our king? Jesus or Barrabas? The world still chooses. So must we all.   Milne, p. 269

Milne, Bruce, *The Message of John,* Taken from *The Bible Speaks Today* Series edited by J. Alec Motyer; John Stott. Copyright ©1993 edited by J. Alec Motyer; John Stott. Used by permission of InterVarsity Press, P.O. Box 1400, Downers Grove, IL 60515, USA. www.ivpress.com

John 19:30: *When he had received the drink, Jesus said, "It is finished." With that, he bowed his head and gave up his spirit.*

That he should actually experience death was simply unthinkable. Accordingly they argued that Jesus did not truly die on the cross, but was still alive when he was taken down from it. The same error was to resurface in Islam centuries later and remains a part of Islamic criticism of Christianity to this day. There is not a single shred of evidence in its support. The theory is undermined by all the relevant historical data and it is high time it was exposed for the nonsense that it is. In truth, Jesus died and was laid in a tomb, He enters into the full reality of death, not merely walking with us right up to the door only to pull back at the final second, leaving us to walk the dark valley on our own [Ps 23:4]. He comes all the way with us right into the grey, after-death world of funeral parlors and the making of arrangements for the disposing of the body, the world of strained faces, hushed voices and tear-stained eyes. He takes his place within the world of the receding past where death's destructive power is so real and irreversible; dead ...buried ...gone. But in the midst of it all, the claim asserts itself: he is the king, even here.

Milne, p. 283, 286

Milne, Bruce, *The Message of John,* Taken from *The Bible Speaks Today* Series edited by J. Alec Motyer; John Stott. Copyright ©1993 edited by J. Alec Motyer; John Stott. Used by permission of InterVarsity Press, P.O. Box 1400, Downers Grove, IL 60515, USA. www.ivpress.com

John 20:22: *And with that he breathed on them and said, "Receive the Holy Spirit"*

As God breathed His life into that first man and He became a living soul [Gn 2:7], so now His Son shares the intimacy of his own life with His disciples that they may be a new humanity, recreated and empowered for their mission. As Jesus breathes on these men He says, 'Receive the Holy Spirit.' This is a gift to be accepted now, a foretaste of the Person of the Holy Spirit who is yet to come and remain in them permanently after Jesus has returned to the Father. ... Too often the institutional church has not been 'breathed on' and consequently has lacked the spiritual authority to deal with sin. Then it becomes a 'do-good club' enmeshed in a maze of legalisms or simply a friendly collection of people. But there is no loosing of sin. Fredrikson, pp 276–77

Acts

Commentaries:
- *The Message of Acts*, by John R.W. Stott (1990)
- *The Preacher's Commentary*, NT Vol 28, by Lloyd J. Ogilvie (1983)
- *Cornerstone Biblical Commentary*, Vol 12, by William J. Larkin (2006)
- *Living Insights*, Vol 5, by Charles Swindoll (2016)
- *The Book of Acts*, by Chuck Smith (2013)

Acts 1:8: *But you will receive power when the Holy Spirit comes on you; and you will be my witnesses in Jerusalem, and in all Judea and Samaria, and to the ends of the earth*

He granted them power. He didn't outline a program. He didn't give them a detailed strategy. Such a thing wouldn't stand the test of time, as we observe in the business world. Rather than set down a specific business model, God gave each member of the organization the mind of the CEO, in a manner of speaking. Instead of laying out a concrete battle plan, the Lord gave each soldier a brain that thinks in synchronization with the mission and values of the General.

The Greek term for "power" (δύναμις *dynamis*) refers to one's ability or capacity; it suggests "being able". ... If the task is to lift a great weight, the "ability" is physical strength. If the task is to defeat an army, the "capacity" is that of a seasoned general. The Lord's promise leaves the *dynamis* indefinite. In other words, whatever is required, we will receive the power to do what God asks.

To impact a rapidly changing world, the power of the Holy Spirit must be released. I am amazed at how few Christians really know the dynamics of the Holy Spirit. All the power it took to raise Christ from the dead [Eph 1:19-20]–not loud power but silent, effective, dynamic power–has been given to us. But we know so little about the potential energy of having the presence of God within, how to let Him fill and control us [Col 1:9], and how to transform that power into positive change in the world. ... If we pay attention, the book of Acts will fill in some deep gaps in our understanding of the Holy Spirit. I urge you to make the Holy Spirit a subject of intense study, not only to gain theological knowledge, but to discover how to release the incredible power of God residing within you. Charles Swindoll, *Living Insights*, Vol 5, (Acts) Carol Stream, IL: Tyndale, 2016, excerpts, pp. 22, 25, 26

Acts 2:2: *Suddenly a sound like the blowing of a violent wind came from heaven and filled the whole house where they were sitting.*
Suddenly a wind began to stir in the room [Jn 3:8], gently at first [1 K 19:12], then it grew stronger. The followers of Jesus looked up from their prayers. Now the wind was rushing with a rumble like thunder. The wind was blowing, rushing with irresistible force. And what it does when it rushes, so too the Holy Spirit was doing in their souls: blowing out the cobwebs of fear and the layered dust of uncertainty. The presence of the wind outwardly was soon an inward rushing of new thought, emotion, and will. The Lord's people were being stirred up, quickened, brought back to life because he had come. ... When the Spirit comes into us, He is Companion and Friend in life's challenges, but loves us so much that He burns away what will debilitate us or prevent us from fully becoming the persons we were meant to be. He refines and galvanizes. The dross is burned off and the pure metal is left [Prov 25:4]. What a great promise! We don't have to stay the way we are. This is a character transplant. The indwelling Lord makes us like himself. He kindles enthusiasm, warmth, spontaneity. Just as the wind of the Spirit engendered new thought, so too, the fire of the spirit set the followers of Jesus aflame with emotional intensity [2 Tim 1:6–7]. The Spirit never bypasses our humanity; He transforms it and then flows through it [John 3:34]. Ogilvie, pp. 58–59
Taken from The Preacher's Commentary Series Volume 28: Acts by Lloyd J. Ogilvie Copyright © 1991 by Word, Inc. Used by permission of Thomas Nelson. www.thomasnelson.com

"Adorable Spirit, may the rushing wind of your mercy blow away all trace of sin within us, and may your unquenchable fire purify our souls."
Desiderius Erasmus (1469–1536)

Acts 2:37–38: *When the people heard this, they were cut to the heart and said to Peter and the other apostles, "Brothers, what shall we do?" Peter replied, "Repent and be baptized, every one of you, in the name of Jesus Christ for the forgiveness of your sins. And you will receive the gift of the Holy Spirit"*
The great need in the church today is for preaching that pierces the heart. But you won't hear of that at a church growth seminar. Instead, they say you ought to make the church services more palatable for the world and more comfortable for sinners. Entertain them but don't convict them. Lace your sermons with big doses of humor and pop psychology, but never make the people squirm. The church does not need a softer gospel. The church needs to be cut to the heart. Smith, p. 31

Acts 9:17: *Placing his hands on Saul, he said, "Brother Saul"*
There are many Saul's of Tarsus in the world today. Like him they are richly endowed with natural gifts of intellect and character; men and women of personality, energy, initiative, and drive; having the courage of their non-Christian convictions; utterly sincere, but severely mistaken; traveling, as it were, from Jerusalem to Damascus instead of from Damascus to Jerusalem; hard, stubborn, even fanatical in their rejection of Jesus Christ. But they are not beyond his sovereign grace. Stott, p. 180

Acts 10:5: *Now send men to Joppa to bring back a man named Simon who is called Peter.*
What strikes me as I read this is that if the angel could instruct Cornelius to send men to Joppa for Peter, the angel could certainly have shared the gospel with him. Likewise, God could have divinely intervened for the Ethiopian eunuch [Ch 8], but He sent Philip. What does that tell us? God uses human instruments to share the gospel and to do His work. What a privilege to be used by God to bring His glorious truths to those whose hearts are open and seeking! We would have no effect at all apart from the power and direction of the Holy Spirit. All the heart-work is done by Him, but what a joy to know that He allows us to be the instruments of

His work. And on top of that, He rewards us as though we had done the work ourselves! Smith, p.163

Acts 10:19 *While Peter was still thinking about the vision, the Spirit said to him, "Simon, three men are looking for you.*
God was taking the initiative, giving guidance in the outward movement of his mission across ethnic boundaries. He told Peter that three men were seeking him, and he instructed him to go with them without making prejudicial distinctions ("without hesitation"). He was preparing Peter for what he would learn soon enough: These men were Gentiles! Divine fiat is again the rationale: "I have sent them." The command and rationale from the Spirit and from the vision mutually illumine each other. If he was not to keep on calling common what God had declared clean, he was to treat Gentiles without prejudicial distinction even to the extent of enjoying their hospitality.

God's initiative in the matter of the gospel coming to Cornelius, then, is total. He commands the intended audience to summon the gospel messenger. He commands the gospel messenger to obey the summons. So strong was the prejudice, that if God had not acted to remove the boundary and overcome the distance between Jew and Gentile, it would never have happened. But God was determined that his mission would be fulfilled continuously, moving from its inaugural center among the Jewish people of promise across every ethnic and geographic boundary. So determined was he that he took the extraordinary steps of providing visions for Jew and Gentile and issuing the Spirit's command as part of providential "coincidences" to make sure the boundaries came down. Larkin, William J., *Cornerstone Biblical Commentary*, Vol 12, Carol Stream, IL: Tyndale, 2006, excerpts, pp. 474-475

Acts 10:34–35: *Then Peter began to speak: "I now realize how true it is that God does not show favoritism but accepts men from every nation who fear him and do what is right."*
The Lord was way out in front of His people, beckoning them on in the movement of His Spirit. They constantly were trying to catch up to know what He wanted in the light of careful observation of what He did. Our molds were shattered, walls of separation between people were razed [Eph

2:14], and the church was led beyond the exclusivity of its religion to an inclusive exclusivity—an inclusion of all races and national backgrounds and an exclusion of prejudice and judgmentalism. It didn't happen all at once, or without resistance and division, as we shall see. But the Lord had not come in the Incarnation nor returned in power of the Spirit to establish a new religion, or even just to renew Israel, but to save the world. Christianity was and is a movement made up of Christ-centered, filled, transformed, and transforming people. Ogilvie, p. 174

Taken from The Preacher's Commentary Series Volume 28: Acts by Lloyd J. Ogilvie Copyright © 1991 by Word, Inc. Used by permission of Thomas Nelson. www.thomasnelson.com

Acts 12:23–24: *Immediately, because Herod did not give praise to God, an angel of the Lord struck him down, and he was eaten by worms and died. But the word of God continued to increase and spread.*
One cannot fail to admire the artistry with which Luke depicts the complete reversal of the church's situation. At the beginning of the chapter, Herod is on the rampage—arresting and persecuting church leaders; at the end he is himself struck down and dies. The chapter opens with James dead, Peter in prison, and Herod triumphing; it closes with Herod dead, Peter free, and the word of God triumphing. Such is the power of God to overthrow hostile human plans and to establish his own in their place. Tyrants may be permitted for a time to boast and bluster, oppressing the church and hindering the spread of the gospel, but they will not last. In the end, their empire will be broken and their pride abased [Dan 4:30]. Stott, p. 213

Acts 15:11: *No! We believe it is through the grace of our Lord Jesus that we are saved, just as they are.*
The struggle is to live by faith alone as the basis of our righteousness with Him. It is difficult for us to be convinced that something more is not also necessary for our justification, and not only for our own but for others. Our temptation is to establish standards, practices, and regulations in addition to faith. Self-justification and judgmentalism result. We are not alone. The early church struggled for faith. That's the central issue of Acts 15. The epicenter we talked about earlier was still being straddled by many in the church with one foot in Judaism and the other at the foot of the cross. The gap was widening. … The struggle for faith alone for justification is as real today as

it was for Luther and Calvin during the watershed days of the Reformation. It is a struggle in our time, not only for the organized church, but for each of us, every day. We ask, 'Isn't there something else I can do or be to be sure of God's approval?' The struggle for faith alone never ends. It's a part of our own inability to accept a gift. And deeper than that: we want to be loved because of what we do for God. Unconditional love is both difficult to receive, and at times, almost impossible for us to extend to others. Acts 15 is as real as this morning's headlines. Ogilvie, pp. 223, 224

Taken from The Preacher's Commentary Series Volume 28: Acts by Lloyd J. Ogilvie Copyright © 1991 by Word, Inc. Used by permission of Thomas Nelson. www.thomasnelson.com

Acts 17:6: *And when they could not find them, they dragged Jason and some of the brothers before the city authorities, shouting, "These men who have turned the world upside down have come here also"* [ESV]

I love that accusation. What a tremendous charge to have leveled at you! Wouldn't it be exciting to be brought into court with the accusation that you've turned the world upside down? Only the charge is not exactly correct. They weren't turning the world upside down; they were turning the world right-side up. The world—then and now—is messed up. People place a greater value on material things, and love unrighteousness rather than righteousness. So the more appropriate accusation would have been, 'These men have turned the world right-side up.' Smith, p. 273

Acts 17:11: *Now the Bereans were of more noble character than the Thessalonians, for they received the message with great eagerness and examined the Scriptures every day to see if what Paul said was true.*

What is impressive is that neither speaker nor hearers used Scripture in a superficial, unintelligent or proof-texting way. On the contrary, Paul 'argued' out of the scriptures (NIV: 'reasoned with them', 17:2) and the Bereans 'examined' them to see if his arguments were cogent. And we may be sure that Paul welcomed and encouraged this thoughtful response. He believed in doctrine, but not in indoctrination. As Johann Albrecht Bengel wrote about verse 11, 'a characteristic of the true religion is that it suffers itself to be examined into, and its claims to be decided upon.' Thus Paul's arguments and his hearers' studies went hand in hand. I do not doubt that he also bathed both in prayer, asking the Holy Spirit of truth to open his mouth [Eph 6:19] to explain and his hearers' mind to grasp [Eph 1:17, 3:17–19], the good news of salvation in Christ. Stott, pp 274, 275

"Read not to contradict and confute, nor to believe and take for granted, nor to find talk and discourse, but to weigh and consider."
Francis Bacon (1561 – 1626)

Acts 17:27: *God did this so that they would seek him and perhaps reach out for him and find him, though he is not far from any one of us.*
There is within every man that clamant cry for a meaningful relationship with God. Henry Drummond put it this way: There is within the very protoplasm of man little tentacles that are reaching out for God. Man is not complete without God. Man today is conscious of that void, which is why he tries to fill the emptiness with excitement, danger, entertainment, and every other diversion he can think of. The philosophers Paul addressed knew it too, which is why they had filled their lives with so much idolatry. But nothing will fill a void that has been designed for God Himself. Nothing else will satisfy our souls. Smith, p. 283

Acts 20:6 *But we sailed from Philippi after the Festival of Unleavened Bread, and five days later joined the others at Troas, where we stayed seven days.*
One wonders how church history would have unfolded differently if Paul had followed his original itinerary and sailed directly for Syria from Corinth. Paul would not have bumped into Luke in Philippi; Luke would not have traveled with Paul to Jerusalem and had the opportunity to interview Peter, John, Mary, John Mark, and other eyewitnesses; perhaps he would not even have written the Gospel bearing his name or this account of the church. It's pointless to speculate how God would have arranged to give us these treasures by some other means; as always, His plan unfolded like He wanted! The evil intended by Paul's enemies merely advanced the Lord's agenda. Paul adapted, God prevailed. Swindoll, pp. 398-399

Acts 24:25: *As Paul discoursed on righteousness, self-control and the judgment to come, Felix was afraid and said, "That's enough for now! You may leave. When I find it convenient, I will send for you."*

Felix and Drusilla had thought hearing Paul would be an entertaining encounter. What they had not anticipated was that moral implications and the cutting edge of judgment would follow the glorious explanation of righteousness in Christ. The governor and his wife were alarmed by the penetrating power of the gospel Paul preached. Like so many who trifle with Christianity as one more set of ideas or philosophic musings [Acts 17:21], they suddenly saw the personal cost of commitment to Christ. Felix did not want his morals meddled with or his motives questioned. But the real issue was that his lust for money was more urgent than the pull within him to respond to Paul's message. He wanted an under-the-table exchange of money from Paul for his release [v 26]. The tragedy was that the Roman and his wife missed the opportunity [Jer 46:17] to come alive and live forever [Mk 10:22, Mt 25:10]. The irony was that two years later Felix was deposed and transferred. He left Caesarea devoid of political power, and, because he rejected Christ, devoid of any meaning or hope in his life. ... A character study of what prompted Felix to say 'that's enough for now' leads into an honest inventory of the ways we put off the Lord. F.W. Boreham, the great Australian preacher, said 'We make our decisions, and then our decisions turn around and make us.' Felix is a classic study in procrastination. The result of his indecision was that he missed his opportunity to allow the Lord to fill the emptiness of his things-oriented, power-hungry, money-grasping heart.   Ogilvie, excerpts, pp. 322–323
Taken from The Preacher's Commentary Series Volume 28: Acts by Lloyd J. Ogilvie Copyright © 1991 by Word, Inc. Used by permission of Thomas Nelson. www.thomasnelson.com

Acts 28:30–31: *For two whole years Paul stayed there in his own rented house and welcomed all who came to see him. Boldly and without hindrance he preached the kingdom of God and taught about the Lord Jesus Christ.*

The propitious, powerful age of the kingdom is now. Christ in the power of the Holy Spirit is doing what He did as Jesus of Nazareth. The Acts of the Holy Spirit continue in our churches, pulpits, and classrooms. Nothing or no one can ultimately hinder Him. He is the divine Logos[1], the Creator[2] and Recreator[3], the Healer[4], the Liberator[5], the indwelling fullness of the Godhead[6]. He is the Lord. We can confidently expect miracles, changed lives, and churches on fire with joy and power. And why not?   Ogilvie, p. 361

Taken from The Preacher's Commentary Series Volume 28: Acts by Lloyd J. Ogilvie Copyright © 1991 by Word, Inc. Used by permission of Thomas Nelson. www.thomasnelson.com

Just as Luke's gospel ended with the prospect of a mission to the nations, so Acts ends with the prospect of a mission radiating from Rome to the world. Luke's description of Paul preaching 'with boldness and without hindrance' symbolizes a wide open door, through which we in our day have to pass. The Acts of the Apostles have long ago finished. But the acts of the followers of Jesus will continue until the end of the world, and their words will spread to the ends of the earth.   Stott, p. 405

[1] Jn 1:1   [2] Jn 1:3   [3] 1Pet 1:23   [4] Lk 7:7   [5] Jn 8:36   [6] Col 1:19

Romans

Commentaries:
- *The Message of Romans*, by John R.W. Stott (1994)
- *Romans*, by James R. Edwards (1992)
- *The Preacher's Commentary*, NT Vol 29, by D. Stuart Briscoe (1982)
- *The Message* (Biblical Paraphrase in modern English), by Eugene H. Peterson (2002)

Rom 1:18: *The wrath of God is being revealed from heaven against all the godlessness and wickedness of men who suppress the truth by their wickedness*
The moment we embark on a study of the Roman epistle we are confronted with the statement that the wrath of God is part of the righteousness of God—a concept so unnerving to many and distasteful to others that innumerable attempts have been made to avoid the subject. Even a cursory glance at Paul's argument, however, will show that any attempt to avoid what he had to say about the wrath of God at the beginning of his presentation of the gospel would be disastrous. ... Divine wrath should never be confused with human anger, for it contains none of the uncontrolled passion, the unreasonable outbursts, the self-vindication that are unfortunate ingredients in human wrath. God's wrath is 'right': it is a holy response to the unholy, a just reaction to the unjust, a pure reaction of the impure. In fact, for God not to express wrath at much of what goes on in our world would be wrong. Briscoe, pp. 38–39

Rom 2:1: *You, therefore, have no excuse, you who pass judgment on someone else, for at whatever point you judge the other, you are condemning yourself, because you who pass judgment do the same things.*
Those people are on a dark spiral downward. But if you think that leaves you on the high ground where you can point your finger at others, think again.

Every time you criticize someone, you condemn yourself. It takes one to know one. Judgmental criticism of others is a well-known way of escaping detection in your own crimes and misdemeanors. *The Message*
Paul uncovers in these verses a strange human foible, namely our tendency to be critical of everybody but ourselves. We are often as harsh in our judgment of others as we are lenient towards ourselves. We work ourselves up into a state of righteous indignation over the disgraceful behavior of other people, while the very same behavior seems not nearly so serious when it is ours rather than theirs. We even gain a vicarious satisfaction from condemning in others the very faults we excuse in ourselves. Freud called this moral gymnastic 'projection' but Paul described it centuries before Freud. Stott, p. 82

Taken from *The Bible Speaks Today* Series edited by J. Alec Motyer; John Stott. Copyright ©1983 edited by J. Alec Motyer; John Stott. Used by permission of InterVarsity Press, P.O. Box 1400, Downers Grove, IL 60515, USA. www.ivpress.com Taken from *The Message of Romans*. Copyright (c) 2001 by John Stott. Used by permission of InterVarsity Press, P.O. Box 1400, Downers Grove, IL 60515, USA. www.ivpress.com

"The business of finding fault is very easy and that of doing better very difficult."
François de Sales (1567–1622)   Quoted in Ward and Wild

Rom 3:23: *for all have sinned and fall short of the glory of God*   [Ps 143:2]
There are degrees of sinning and therefore differences, yet nobody even approaches God's standard [Eccl 7:20]. Bishop Handley Moule put it dramatically: 'the harlot, the liar, and the murderer are short of it (God's glory) but so are you. Perhaps they stand at the bottom of a mine and you on the crest of an Alp, but you are as little able to touch the stars as they.'
Stott, p. 109

Stott, John R.W., The Message of Romans Taken from *The Bible Speaks Today* Series edited by J. Alec Motyer; John Stott. Copyright ©1994 edited by J. Alec Motyer; John Stott. Used by permission of InterVarsity Press, P.O. Box 1400, Downers Grove, IL 60515, USA. www.ivpress.com

Rom 3:24: *and are justified freely by his grace through the redemption that came by Christ Jesus*

The cross should be enough to break the hardest heart, and melt the iciest. Justification (its source God and his grace, its ground Christ and his cross, and its means faith alone, altogether apart from works) is the heart of the gospel and unique to Christianity. No other system, ideology or religion proclaims a free forgiveness and a new life to those who have done nothing to deserve it but a lot to deserve judgment instead. On the contrary, all other systems teach some form of self-salvation through good works of religion, righteousness, or philanthropy. Christianity, by contrast, is not in its essence a religion at all; it is a gospel, the gospel, good news that God's grace has turned away from his wrath [5:9], that God's Son has died our death [5:8] and borne our judgment [Isa 53:6], that God has mercy on the undeserving [Ps 103:10], and that there is nothing left for us to do, or even contribute. Faith's only function is to receive what grace offers.
Stott, p. 117, 118
Stott, John R.W., The Message of Romans Taken from *The Bible Speaks Today* Series edited by J. Alec Motyer; John Stott. Copyright ©1994 edited by J. Alec Motyer; John Stott. Used by permission of InterVarsity Press, P.O. Box 1400, Downers Grove, IL 60515, USA. www.ivpress.com

"The only thing of our very own which we contribute to our salvation is the sin which makes it necessary."   William Temple (1881–1944)

Rom 3:27: *Where, then, is boasting? It is excluded. On what principle? On that of observing the law? No, but on that of faith.*
Try to imagine a heaven full of people who had earned their right to be there rather like a political dinner where supporters pay $1000 a plate. What arrogance and boasting—what cliques and class distinctions—what arguments and suspicions! Heaven would be no heaven at all! Through God's grace this cannot happen. There will not be a trace of boasting for the simple reason that entrance is limited strictly to those who have been justified by faith. ... Only those who will, by faith, accept justification from the hand of a just God who made it all possible will enjoy its benefits. Receiving something you could never earn and do not deserve is grounds for humility, not arrogance. Gratitude, not boasting, is the language of the redeemed.
Briscoe, p. 94

Rom 5:1–2: *Therefore, since we have been justified through faith, we have peace with God through our Lord Jesus Christ, through whom we have gained access by faith into this grace in which we now stand. And we rejoice in the hope of the glory of God.* [Ezek 37:26]

Justified believers enjoy a blessing far greater than a periodic approach to God or an occasional audience with the king. We are privileged to live in the temple and in the palace. We do not fall in and out of grace like courtiers who may find themselves in and out of favor with their sovereign, or politicians with the public. No, we stand in it, for that is the nature of grace.

Christian hope is not uncertain like our ordinary everyday hopes about the weather or health; it is a joyful and confident expectation that rests on the promises of God, as we saw in the case of Abraham. And the object of our hope is the glory of God, namely his radiant splendor which will in the end be fully displayed. Already his glory is being continuously revealed in the heavens and the earth (Ps 19:1, Isa 6:3). Already it has been uniquely made manifest in Jesus Christ the incarnate word (John 1:14, 2:11), most notably in his death and resurrection. One day, however, the curtain will be raised and the glory of God will be fully disclosed [1 Cor 13:12].
Stott, p. 140

Stott, John R.W., *The Message of Romans* Taken from The Bible Speaks Today Series edited by J. Alec Motyer; John Stott. Copyright ©1994 edited by J. Alec Motyer; John Stott. Used by permission of InterVarsity Press, P.O. Box 1400, Downers Grove, IL 60515, USA. www.ivpress.com

Rom 5:9: *Since we have now been justified by his blood, how much more shall we be saved from God's wrath through him!*

<u>**Personal Note**</u>: This verse brings to mind a message delivered by Pastor John Wood of Cedar Springs Presbyterian Church in the 1990's. The sermon was titled *How Much More*, and its moving message sticks with me today. Pastor Wood told an arresting account about a young pastor he met at a conference. Mr. Wood asked him to tell his story. The man as a child lived in an abusive and poverty stricken home. He had to sleep on sheets that were soaked with urine because he repeatedly wet his bed and his punishment for that offense was to have to sleep on those sheets night after night. One night, the abusive father killed the mother and the son was whisked away to an orphanage, where the conditions were not much better.

After several years, news came of a family who was considering adopting this boy. The venue for their introduction was to be a bowling alley. At the bowling alley, the young man kept praying to the Lord, "Please let me bowl just one strike, so I can impress these people." But he kept bowling gutter ball after gutter ball. He had given up hope of adoption. But the couple accepted him[1], gave him new clothes[2], adopted him[3], and gave him their name[4]. Pastor Wood used this powerful metaphor to describe our vain efforts to please the Lord by our efforts and to realize that his grace is his free gift. Even when we bowl gutter balls in our attempts to impress the Lord, he is reaching out to us in love, just as the father did to the Prodigal in Luke 15.

[1]Ezek 43:27   [2]Isa 61:10   [3]Rom 8:16   [4]Acts 11:26, 1 Pet 4:16

Rom 6:23: *For the wages of sin is death, but the gift of God is eternal life in Christ Jesus our Lord.*

The contrast between sin and grace is now sharpened to a razor's edge. Sin and God are depicted as warlords, the one paying the wages of death, the other offering release and freedom for life. Sin promises to pay subsistence wages, to provide for our needs, but that is an illusion, for in reality it pays death. … Because of sin humanity gets what it has coming to it; death is our due or 'right'. But God does not pay the wages of 'rights' nor compensate according to deserts. He freely forgives those who renounce their 'rights' of sin. God, who is rich in mercy [Eph 2:4], remits our debts and freely grants what we do *not* deserve—eternal life in Christ Jesus. That is the meaning of grace.   Edwards, pp. 175–176

Excerpt from Romans by James R. Edwards, copyright © 1992. Used by permission of Baker Books, a division of Baker Publishing Group.

Personal Note: The paradox of apparent bondage and freedom is a hallmark of Christianity, and the Apostle develops this theme masterfully in chapters 7 and 8 as he describes the battle between flesh and spirit. What appears to the outside world as freedom (I can do anything I want) and bondage (a list of do's and don'ts I must perform) are the reverse of the reality of the Christian walk. The freedom to do what I want nearly always leads to bondage. The seductress of Prov 7:21–22 entices us into her lair with smooth talk, but the end is not what we expected (v 23). The freedom we exercise at first leads to bondage later. Excessive buying on credit and drug addiction are two modern examples of this tendency. With searing hindsight, we later ask the Apostle Paul's question: "What benefit did you reap at that time from the things you are now ashamed of?" (Rom 6:21). On the other hand, the apparent restrictions placed on my activities by my faith and by the Holy Spirit at first appear to be bondage. But freedom within form is actually the only path to true freedom, contentment, and joy. The question all must ask is "do I want to be free or do I want to be a slave"? The Christian discovers that to be free to sin is to be a slave to sin; but to be a slave to the triune God is the only path to true freedom.

Rom 7:25–26a *What a wretched man I am! Who will rescue me from this body that is subject to death? Thanks be to God, who delivers me through Jesus Christ our Lord!*

vv 24–25 I've tried everything and nothing helps. I'm at the end of my rope. Is there no one who can do anything for me? Isn't that the real question? The answer, thank God, is that Jesus Christ can and does. He acted to set things right in this life of contradictions where I want to serve God with all my heart and mind, but am pulled by the influence of sin to do something totally different.   *The Message*
He concludes rather in crushing finality: What good are these things if I still do evil? When one discovers not only a power at work within oneself against one's best desires, but also a powerlessness to combat it, then one must look for help beyond oneself. Paul is not in the market for a self-help program. He is not hoping for a lucky break or a turning over a new leaf. He is the drowning man crying out for rescue! The word for wretched ταλαίπωρος *talaipōros*, means that the situation is critical and beyond his power to change it. If salvation is to come it must come from a *who,* not a *what.* It must come from outside, and apart from his own resources—or it will not come. … This cry of dereliction is not the last sound of an empty universe. It is a prelude to grace. The Greek word χάρις *charis* for *thanks* is the word *grace.* This encomium exposes the nerve of Paul's gospel that reverberates in triumphant refrain throughout chapter 8. While we were in the pit of despair, God demonstrated his grace in Jesus Christ. When human hope is exhausted, salvation is at hand. Where nothing can be expected from humanity, everything may be expected from God. Creation out of nothing will happen again.   Edwards, pp. 193–194

Excerpt from Romans by James R. Edwards, copyright © 1992. Used by permission of Baker Books, a division of Baker Publishing Group

Rom 8:1–2: *Therefore, there is now no condemnation for those who are in Christ Jesus, because through Christ Jesus the law of the Spirit of life set me free from the law of sin and death.*

In sublime contrast to the questions which have beset the argument since chapter 6, chapter 8 begins with a thunderous proclamation. Especially in 7:7–25, Paul's blow by blow account of indwelling sin reminded one of a ringside announcer reporting a losing struggle. But the long and doleful report is now interrupted with ecstatic news. The contest has been decisively reversed. Sin and law may have been the overwhelming favorites, but victory belongs to 'those who are in Christ Jesus.' The fires of hope had dwindled to a cold flame when reinforcements finally arrived.

Credit for the victory, as irrevocable as it was unexpected, belongs to the Spirit. Unforeseen, and from the outside, like a ray of hope extending backward from the future to the present, the Holy Spirit has broken into the dreary domain of sin, law, and death with freedom from oppression, strength for the struggle, and hope for the future. ... Before this chapter, the Spirit is mentioned only five times, and afterward only nine times. But in Chapter 8 the Spirit occurs twenty-one times—a record for any chapter in the NT. ... Chapter 8 begins with the triumphant crash of Beethoven's Emperor Concerto. The Greek behind *therefore now* (ἄρα *ara* νῦν *nyn*) signals an emphatic break from the preceding train of thought. To be in Christ Jesus is to experience something not offered by the law of Moses. Paul's tireless efforts have shown that the law reveals sin (3:20), aggravates sin (7:8–9), and condemns both sin and sinner (7:11); and the burden of this awareness causes him to cry out 'What a wretched man I am!' (7:24). His only recourse is to cry for help outside himself, and help he finds in Jesus Christ. Edwards, pp. 195–199

Excerpt from Romans by James R. Edwards, copyright © 1992. Used by permission of Baker Books, a division of Baker Publishing Group

Rom 8:5–6: *For those who live according to the flesh set their minds on the things of the flesh, but those who live according to the Spirit, the things of the Spirit.* NKJV

Paul has asserted that the only people in whom the law's righteous requirement can be fulfilled are those who live not κατὰ σάρκα *kata sarka* (according to the flesh) but κατὰ πνεῦμα *kata pneuma* (according to spirit or better the Spirit), that is who follow the promptings and surrender to the control of the Spirit rather than the flesh [John 3:6, 6:63 Gal 5:25]. It is this antithesis between the flesh and the spirit which Paul now develops in vv 5–8. To 'set the mind' (φρόνημα *phroneo*) on the desires of *sarx* or *pneuma* is to make them the 'absorbing objects of thought, interest, affection, and purpose'. It is a question of what preoccupies us, of the ambitions which drive us and the concerns which engross us, of how we spend our time and our energies, of what we concentrate on and give ourselves up to [Phil 4:8]. All this is determined by who we are, whether we are still 'in the flesh' or are now by new birth 'in the spirit'. Stott, p. 223

Stott, John R.W., *The Message of Romans* Taken from *The Bible Speaks Today* Series edited by J. Alec Motyer; John Stott. Copyright ©1994 edited by J. Alec Motyer; John Stott. Used by permission of InterVarsity Press, P.O. Box 1400, Downers Grove, IL 60515, USA. www.ivpress.com

Personal Note: One very wise member of my Men's prayer group had a pithy saying related to this verse: "The Holy Spirit must not just be *resident in* your life, he must be *president of* your life."

Hymn: *Spirit of God, Descend upon My Heart* (1854), Text: George Croly, 1780–1860,

Spirit of God, descend upon my heart;	[Ezek 36:26]
Wean it from earth; through all its pulses move;	[Col 3:2]
Stoop to my weakness, mighty as thou art,	[2 Cor 12:9]
And make me love thee as I ought to love.	[Eph 6:24]
I ask no dream, no prophet ecstasies,	[Ezek 11:24]
No sudden rending of the veil of clay,	[Isa 64:1]
No angel visitant, no opening skies;	[Luke 2:9]
But take the dimness of my soul away.	[Eph 1:18]
Teach me to feel that thou art always nigh;	[Jas 4:8]
Teach me the struggles of the soul to bear.	[Rom 5:3–4]

To check the rising doubt, the rebel sigh,	[Mt 14:31, Ezek 2:8]
Teach me the patience of unanswered prayer.	[Job 30:20]

Teach me to love thee as thine angels love,	[Rev 7:11]
One holy passion filling all my frame;	[Col 1:29]
The kindling of the heaven-descended Dove,	[Ps 68:13]
My heart an altar, and thy love the flame.	[Rom 12:1, 2 Tim 1:6]

Rom 8:18: *I consider that our present sufferings are not worth comparing with the glory that will be revealed in us.*
Paul concedes that suffering is numbingly, painfully real, but *in comparison with glory* it looks different than when viewed alone, for it is dwarfed by the grandeur of glory awaiting believers. Moreover, it is only 'for a season.' The Greek word for present, *kairos*, means momentary, limited duration of time. Suffering is limited to this life and pales in comparison to God's coming glory. The apostle is not minimizing suffering, but maximizing glory. Edwards, p. 212
Excerpt from Romans by James R. Edwards, copyright © 1992. Used by permission of Baker Books, a division of Baker Publishing Group

Rom 8:30: *And those he predestined, he also called; those he called, he also justified; those he justified, he also glorified.*
Verses 29–30 are cast in the past tense, as though Paul were looking back on God's will, though some of it still remains to be realized. The affirmations of these things are therefore grounded more in experience than in reason and logic. They are a revelation from God's perspective which sees the embroidery of human life not as we see it, from the backside of knots and tattered ends, but from the finished side of the pattern. The challenge of the present is to believe that by God's grace the knots and rough ends are actually weaving a pattern which is already known to God, even if unclear to us. The glory of the future will be to see the completed pattern, but even now something of it is visible in hindsight. On the threshold of such ineffable mysteries, however, it is the hymn writers, not theologians, who are the best commentators.
Edwards, p. 219
Excerpt from Romans by James R. Edwards, copyright © 1992. Used by permission of Baker Books, a division of Baker Publishing Group

Personal Note: This verse is sometimes referred to as the "golden chain of redemption."

Rom 8:38–39: *For I am persuaded that neither death nor life, nor angels nor principalities nor powers, nor things present nor things to come, nor height nor depth, nor any other created thing, shall be able to separate us from the love of God which is in Christ Jesus our Lord.* NKJV

Here then are five convictions about God's providence (28), five affirmations about his purpose (29,30), five questions about his love (31–39), which together bring us fifteen assurances about him. We urgently need them today, since nothing seems stable in our world any longer. Insecurity is written across all human experience. Christian people are not guaranteed immunity to temptation, tribulation or tragedy, but we are promised victory over them. God's pledge is not that suffering will never afflict us, but that it will never separate us from his love. Our confidence is not in our love for him, which is frail, fickle, and faltering, but in his love for us, which is steadfast, faithful, and persevering.   Stott, pp 259–260

Stott, John R.W., *The Message of Romans* Taken from *The Bible Speaks Today* Series edited by J. Alec Motyer; John Stott. Copyright ©1994 edited by J. Alec Motyer; John Stott. Used by permission of InterVarsity Press, P.O. Box 1400, Downers Grove, IL 60515, USA. www.ivpress.com

Rom 10:2: *For I can testify about them that they are zealous for God, but their zeal is not based on knowledge.*

Scripture says that 'it is not good to have zeal without knowledge' (Pr 19:2) [cf Hos 4:6]. Sincerity is not enough, for we may be sincerely mistaken. The proper word for zeal without knowledge, commitment without reflection, or enthusiasm without understanding, is fanaticism. And fanaticism is a horrid and dangerous state to be in.   Stott, p. 280

Stott, John R.W., *The Message of Romans* Taken from *The Bible Speaks Today* Series edited by J. Alec Motyer; John Stott. Copyright ©1994 edited by J. Alec Motyer; John Stott. Used by permission of InterVarsity Press, P.O. Box 1400, Downers Grove, IL 60515, USA. www.ivpress.com

"Zeal without knowledge is like fire without light."
Thomas Fuller (1608–1661)   Quoted in Ward and Wild

Personal Note: Zeal without knowledge has led to some of the greatest discord and tragedy in the history of the church. One example of this was the persecution of the great Italian scientist Galileo in the 17th Century. Galileo looked through his "spyglass" and saw moons revolving around Jupiter and crescent phases of the planet Venus. This was irrefutable evidence of the Copernican theory that the earth revolved around the sun. The leaders of the church at the time saw this as a threat to Christianity. But there is absolutely no scriptural basis for refuting Galileo's theories. The Bible has only a few verses which even mention the Sun and its relationship to the earth, and most of these are very poetic in nature (eg, Ps 19:4–6, Gen 1:14 ff). Even today many of our newspapers mention "sunrise" even though we know that it merely reflects the earth's rotation. There is no verse which explicitly states that the sun revolves around the earth. So why were these Church leaders so intent on quashing the brilliant scientist? They had zeal that was not based on knowledge, pure and simple. But lest we moderns smugly state that this un-enlightened view has firmly been placed in the rear-view mirror, one only need look at some called "fundamentalists" who vociferously proclaim their own position on debatable areas of scripture such as Creation, Eschatology, the role of women in the church and other peripheral issues. We need to avoid the tendency of "fire without light" as Thomas Fuller puts it. We need to remember Acts 17:11.

Rom 11:33–36: *Oh, the depth of the riches of the wisdom and knowledge of God! How unsearchable his judgments, and his paths beyond tracing out! "Who has known the mind of the Lord? Or who has been his counselor?" "Who has ever given to God, that God should repay him?" For from him and through him and to him are all things. To him be the glory forever! Amen.* [Ps 145:3, 147:5]

"God cannot be grasped by the mind. If God could, he would not be God." Evagrius of Pontus (305–400)   Quoted in Ward and Wild

Paul's horizons are vast. He takes in time and eternity, history and eschatology, justification, sanctification, and glorification. Now he stops, out of breath. Analysis and arguments must give way to adoration. 'Like a traveler who has reached the summit of an Alpine ascent', wrote F.L. Godet of Neuchatel, Switzerland, 'the apostle turns and contemplates. Depths are at his feet, but waves of light illumine them, and there spreads all around an immense horizon which his eye commands.' Before Paul goes on to outline the practical implications of the gospel, he falls down before God and worships [cf Job 36:25–26]. ... His decisions are unsearchable and his ways inscrutable. This is the New Testament equivalent of Isaiah 55:8–9, where God declares his thoughts to be higher than our thoughts, and his ways than our ways. But of course! How could finite and fallen creatures like us ever imagine that we could penetrate into the infinite mind of God [Ps 92:5. 106:2]? His mind (what he thinks) and his ways (what he does) are altogether beyond us (Job 5:9, 11:7; Ps 139:6; Isa 40:28). It is frankly ludicrous, as Paul's two Old Testament quotations make clear, to imagine that we could ever teach or give God anything. No, No. We are not God's counselor; he is ours [Ps 16:7]. We are not God's creditor; he is ours [Ps 116:12]. We depend entirely on him to teach [Ps 119:33] and to save us [Hos 13:4, Jude 25]. The initiative in both revelation and redemption lies in his grace. The attempt to reverse roles would be to dethrone God and to deify ourselves. So the answer to both questions in verses 34–35 is, 'Nobody!' Stott, pp 309–311

Stott, John R.W., The Message of Romans Taken from *The Bible Speaks Today* Series edited by J. Alec Motyer; John Stott. Copyright ©1994 edited by J. Alec Motyer; John Stott. Used by permission of InterVarsity Press, P.O. Box 1400, Downers Grove, IL 60515, USA. www.ivpress.com

Rom 12:1: *Therefore, I urge you, brothers, in view of God's mercy, to offer your bodies as living sacrifices, holy and pleasing to God-this is your spiritual act of worship.*

So begins the most aesthetic formulation of Christian ethics in Scripture. Earlier buds of ethics (6:12–23, 8:12–13) now come to full flower. The issue concerns not religious renewal or increased spiritual consciousness, but the transformation of bodily existence into an expression of spiritual worship. ... If Christian morality were simply a deterrence of divine wrath, then it would not be morality at all, for it would not be free. It would simply be some sort of moral ransom rooted in fear. True Christian ethics are ethics of gratitude. The obedience pleasing to God is characterized by free and willing submission because of God's prior sacrifice of his Son on our behalf. ... It is one thing to give *things* to God (money, time, talents, services, sacrifices, etc.) but quite another to give *oneself*. God sent his Son not to enlighten our minds, raise our emotional level, cultivate our talents, or improve our morals, but to redeem the whole person, and beyond that the world itself. As creator of the universe, sustainer of all things, and eternal judge, God is Lord of all things. If God loves the whole person, then the only fitting response is to return the whole person to that love. Edwards, pp. 282–283

Excerpt from Romans by James R. Edwards, copyright © 1992. Used by permission of Baker Books, a division of Baker Publishing Group

"God does not desire 'something' from us—he desires us, ourselves; not our works, but our personality, our will, our heart."   Emil Brunner (1889–1966)   Quoted in Ward and Wild

Personal Note: Pastor Mike Garrett of Westminster Presbyterian Church in Snellville GA preached on this text in Oct 2014. He noted that the Old Testament preached sacrifices of animals, but now under the new covenant, the Apostle Paul says, in effect "I don't want your dead sacrifices; I want your living sacrifice." God doesn't just want a "thank you for saving me," he wants the rest of you as well. There is so much more to all of us than the drop we put in the collection plate. You can't fit all of you on the memo line of your check. We are called to take what we were created to do and offer it back to the creator. Pastor Garret sums up: "May the Holy Spirit pester you with the with the question, 'am I doing what I was created to do?' This is the secret to discovering a life that adds up."

Rom 12:2: *Do not conform any longer to the pattern of this world, but be transformed by the renewing of your mind. Then you will be able to test and approve what God's will is-his good, pleasing and perfect will.*
J.B. Phillip's paraphrase catches the alternative: 'Don't let the world around you squeeze you into its own mold, but let God remold your minds from within'. We human beings are imitative by nature. We need a model to copy, and ultimately there are only two. There is this world, literally 'this age', which is passing away, and there is God's will which is good, pleasing and perfect [Mt 5:48]. Here then are the stages of Christian moral transformation: first our mind is renewed by the Word and the Spirit of

God; then we are able to discern and desire the will of God; and then we are increasingly transformed by it. Stott, pp 323, 324

Stott, John R.W., The Message of Romans Taken from *The Bible Speaks Today* Series edited by J. Alec Motyer; John Stott. Copyright ©1994 edited by J. Alec Motyer; John Stott. Used by permission of InterVarsity Press, P.O. Box 1400, Downers Grove, IL 60515, USA. www.ivpress.com

Personal Note: When he expounded on this text, Pastor John Wood of Cedar Springs Presbyterian Church picked up on the Greek word μεταμορφοῦσθε *metamorphoo* (transform), from which we get the English word "metamorphosis". He used the perhaps best known example of metamorphosis in the insect world: the caterpillar emerging from the chrysalis as a butterfly. Christians have two tendencies. One is to behave as if we are a caterpillar with "pasted on wings" rather than a real butterfly. Our transformation is only a sham—we have not emerged from the chrysalis; we have only tried to bypass and simulate it. The other extreme is to continue to grub around in the mud as a caterpillar even though we have been transformed. We should instead be soaring to new heights as we continue to take in God's word and are sanctified by the Holy Spirit.

1 Corinthians

Commentaries:
- *The Message of 1 Corinthians*, by David Prior (1985)
- *1 Corinthians*, by John MacArthur (1984)
- *Cornerstone Biblical Commentary*, Vol 15, by William Baker (2009)

1 Cor 1:18: *For the message of the cross is foolishness to those who are perishing, but to us who are being saved it is the power of God.*
For Paul, the cross was no mere message; it was the cataclysmic event in human history by which God has now divided people into two groups, the only two groups that ultimately mean anything and that are utterly and purposely divisive: the destroyed and the saved. Thus, when proclaimed faithfully, the message of the cross creates this division, similar to the way Jesus' parables and activities were calculated to divide people into disciples and enemies (Mk 4:10-12). Thus, the "foolish" or spiritually dense who think the gospel message dumb when they hear it, place themselves in the "destroyed" category. By contrast, the "saved" recognize and experience God's work through the cross ... For Paul, this is no simple general truth about God and human wisdom. The cross itself is the divine moment in history when God shatters all human efforts to explain the world and its purposes, however noble and brilliant, that came before it and will come after it.
Baker, William, *Cornerstone Biblical Commentary*, Vol 15, Carol Stream, IL: Tyndale, 2009, pp. 37-38

1 Cor 2:14: *The man without the Spirit does not accept the things that come from the Spirit of God, for they are foolishness to him, and he cannot understand them, because they are spiritually discerned.*

Without a ministry from the Spirit there can be no communication and no growth into maturity: the truth is incomprehensible and the things of the Spirit are even regarded as foolishness [Isa 29:11]. Vast tracts of human experience, endeavor, and adventure lay beyond the grasp of these Christians at Corinth, so long as they remain unspiritual. When a person has been born again by the Spirit of God, he becomes potentially a 'spiritual man' but he is not automatically going to continue walking in the spirit [Gal 5:25]. We must beware any tendency to sit back on our haunches and to feel that we have 'arrived'. We must determine to love God with every fiber of our being [Deut 6:5, Ps 103:1]. Prior, p. 53, 54

Taken from *The Bible Speaks Today* Series edited by J. Alec Motyer; John Stott. Copyright ©1983 edited by J. Alec Motyer; John Stott. Taken from *The Message of 1 Corinthians* by David Prior. Copyright (c) 1985 by David Prior. Used by permission of InterVarsity Press, P.O. Box 1400, Downers Grove, IL 60515, USA, www.ivpress.com

Personal Note: Throughout the first two chapters of this letter, the Apostle paints a vivid contrast between human (natural) and divine (spiritual) wisdom. Many secular philosophers and scientists claim that there is no spiritual wisdom. They believe that human thought is so advanced as to have moved beyond its need for spiritual enlightenment which, after all, is just a crutch used by those who lack the intelligence of the thought leaders of the day with their Ivy-League degrees. But as the 18th Century philosopher Immanuel Kant pointed out, when we take a good hard look at human intelligence, it is fenced in by the 5 senses (even when enhanced by powerful instruments) and experience. Paul here boldly asserts that there is an intelligence that cannot be detected by our senses and our instruments. The so-called enlightened scientists of our time think they have everything figured out and anyone who asserts a truth that cannot be proven is just a pathetic charlatan who won't listen to reason. But who, here is being close-minded? Who is dismissing, a priori, a truth that only the Holy Spirit can reveal? Since secular science dismisses the need for a God, it implicitly also dismisses any need for spiritual revelation. That is a tragic predicament that modern man has created and which he cannot escape until he humbles himself and admits that he cannot "discover" all relevant facts but must await revelation from beyond.

1 Cor 3:19: *For the wisdom of this world is foolishness in God's sight.*

The final paragraph of chapter 3 reverts to the theme of worldly wisdom and the futility of any kind of boasting about powerful personalities and leaders. This is certainly how the world thinks, but the wisdom of this world is folly with God (19). Those who are truly wise in God's sight are those who deliberately reject such worldly wisdom and adopt an attitude to people and to things which everyone else will call foolish (18). This attitude sees nothing as grounds for boasting, because everything and everybody is a gift from God to undeserving sinners. So it is totally out of place to boast about people and things which, quite undeservedly, have been placed in our laps by a lavishly generous God [4:7].   Prior, p. 61

Prior, David, *The Message of 1 Corinthians,* Taken from *The Bible Speaks Today* Series edited by J. Alec Motyer; John Stott. Copyright ©1985 edited by J. Alec Motyer; John Stott. Used by permission of InterVarsity Press, P.O. Box 1400, Downers Grove, IL 60515, USA. www.ivpress.com

Personal Note: In these first few chapters of 1 Corinthians, the apostle pounds home the contrast between human and divine wisdom. In today's information age, we may be tempted to imagine that we have transcended the world of the Corinthians. *They* may have been limited in their wisdom, but if there's anything *we* don't know, we can just *Google* it. But if we are so wise, why is our world so messed up? The answer, says Paul, is that we are relying on our senses and understanding instead of tapping the rich treasure of God's wisdom. Many other scriptures relate to this topic (eg Isa 55:8–9, Prov 3:5–6, Rom 11:33–36, Job 38:4, James 3:17). Humanity so often imagines that it has everything "figured out" only to discover later that God was right after all.

1 Cor 4:5: *Therefore judge nothing before the appointed time; wait till the Lord comes. He will bring to light what is hidden in darkness and will expose the motives of men's hearts. At that time each will receive his praise from God.*
[cf Prov 16:2, 1 Chr 28:9, Ps 44:21]

Because Paul sees himself and the others as stewards, he exhorts the Corinthians not to slip into any judging attitude: do not condemn us, and also do not eulogize us. Leave that to the Lord: he will do all the judging. If a man deserves to be commended for his stewardship, then the Lord will indeed commend him. Do not pronounce judgment before the time, i.e., before all the evidence is out in the open, and that will be only when the

Lord comes. The final phrase of verse 5 is interesting because the emphasis in the original falls on the first and last words: *Then...from God*, i.e., then, and not before, certainly not now, when all judgment cannot be anything but 'pre-judice'; commendation from God, and not from anybody else, in Corinth or anywhere else. Prior, pp. 62, 63

Prior, David, *The Message of 1 Corinthians*, Taken from *The Bible Speaks Today* Series edited by J. Alec Motyer; John Stott. Copyright ©1985 edited by J. Alec Motyer; John Stott. Used by permission of InterVarsity Press, P.O. Box 1400, Downers Grove, IL 60515, USA. www.ivpress.com

Personal Note: This verse, sometimes overlooked, is one of the most eloquent in the entire Pauline corpus. It builds on Paul's previous discussion of the contrast between human and divine wisdom, and makes a startlingly practical application. Much of human strife and conflict arises from assuming we know a person's motives when we really don't. We are only guessing. Only God truly knows (1K 8:39, 2 Chr 6:30b). While there may be some cases where external evidence points convincingly to an internal motive, in many cases, the motive cannot be known. So we make judgments based on part of the evidence. We condemn our brothers and sisters because we *think* we know why they did something. Paul is calling us to a higher standard when we judge others. We must remember that only *he*, not we, "will bring to light what is hidden in darkness and will expose the motives of men's hearts." This verse urges us to suspend judgment the next time we think we have an "open and shut" case against someone. Our world would be a much more harmonious place if we paused before condemning our fellows and contemplated the profound truth of this verse.

1 Cor 5:12: *What business is it of mine to judge those outside the church? Are you not to judge those inside?*
The words of Jesus are categorical in their warning to us: Judge not, that you be not judged (Mt 7:1). Indeed the drift of that passage in the Sermon on the Mount indicates that we notice faults in others precisely because they are true of ourselves, and normally in greater measure. In other words, we are given the facility to notice the failings of others, not to sit in judgment of them, but to examine and correct ourselves over these selfsame matters. They act as mirrors for ourselves. Prior, p. 84

Prior, David, *The Message of 1 Corinthians,* Taken from *The Bible Speaks Today* Series edited by J. Alec Motyer; John Stott. Copyright ©1985 edited by J. Alec Motyer; John Stott. Used by permission of InterVarsity Press, P.O. Box 1400, Downers Grove, IL 60515, USA. www.ivpress.com

1 Cor 6:12: *"Everything is permissible for me"-but not everything is beneficial. "Everything is permissible for me"-but I will not be mastered by anything*
Personal Note: This verse summarizes a challenge for all humanity. In modern America, we take our liberty very seriously. It is enshrined in our founding documents and is considered almost sacred by many. The Coronavirus lockdowns of 2020 have focused our attention on liberty in a profound way. But Paul here provides insight into all the implications of our liberty. For close to two centuries in America, our liberty was constrained by conscience and social norms. Yes, we could steal, but that is clearly not what our Lord wants, and widespread larceny would make a huge negative impact on our economy which thrives on the lubricating oil of instant credit. I can buy goods on line and just give them a number. The creditor doesn't know me but trusts me because the overwhelming majority of Americans are good and decent people who play by the rules and do not cheat their fellows. Adam Smith's "invisible hand" is guided by the Lord's guiding hand. His Holy Spirit convicts us long before a case could be brought to court. So while we could decide to do something nasty, most of the time we don't. Liberty without any boundaries would lead to chaos and the breakdown of civilization. It is only within bounds that liberty gives us a flourishing society. The Lord nudges us in the right direction (Isa 30:21) and the more we submit to his guidance, the better it is for all of us.

1 Cor 8:1–2: *We know that we all possess knowledge. Knowledge puffs up, but love builds up. The man who thinks he knows something does not yet know as he ought to know.*
Knowledge on its own, particularly of the kind paraded by these Corinthian experts, only *puffs up*, leaving its possessor like an inflated balloon. This is not the first time he has had to fire this warning shot across their bows. Knowledge is important; we all possess some; but on its own it is inflated and empty. A Christian needs to be filled with love because *love builds up.* Prick a balloon and it bursts; lean on a wall and it holds your weight. Any

true knowledge does not lead to pride in what we know, but to humility about what we don't know. That truth flew in the face of the Gnostic approach to religion, which was essentially acquisitive and self-centered, asking such questions as "how far can I go" and "what's in it for me?" That grasping approach is the exact opposite of *agape*-love which wants to give, to help, to build up others. All our knowledge is now partial (1 Cor 13:8) [cf 1 Cor 4:5] and it is therefore extremely arrogant to put the greatest store by knowledge, especially the very esoteric and exclusive kind of knowledge paraded by the Gnostics. Prior, p.143

Prior, David, *The Message of 1 Corinthians,* Taken from *The Bible Speaks Today* Series edited by J. Alec Motyer; John Stott. Copyright ©1985 edited by J. Alec Motyer; John Stott. Used by permission of InterVarsity Press, P.O. Box 1400, Downers Grove, IL 60515, USA. www.ivpress.com

"Knowledge is proud that he has learned so much; Wisdom is humble that he knows no more."
William Cowper (1731–1800)   Quoted in Ward and Wild

Personal Note: *Knowledge puffs up* is a biting assessment we see alive and kicking in our 21st century world. The news media and internet are saturated with analysts and pundits who claim they have knowledge that "the unenlightened" lack. The Apostle here (and elsewhere in this letter) reminds us that our knowledge is only partial and fragmentary. When scientists make bald statements that make theory sound like facts, we need to remember that no one, not even the scientists, and not even *Google*, has all the answers. We can interpret the evidence we see to make tentative conclusions, but those conclusions are only tentative. In our fallen world, all of us, including Christians, may think they know a lot and may take pride in that knowledge, but we need to heed Paul's pungent caution here. None of us know yet what we ought to know. How many times have we read a spy thriller or watched an exciting movie where the ending totally surprised us? And yet we think that life can't surprise us? Revelation of truth comes gradually as the Holy Spirit doses out that truth at just the rate we need. Paul reminds us that the Lord is the only one with special knowledge (Rom 11:33–34). We need his special revelation if we are to thrive under his protective hand.

1 Cor 12:31: *And now I will show you the most excellent way.*
It is well known that the Greek word for love in the New Testament, (ἀγάπη) *agape*, was not previously in common use. It was taken into the Greek of the New Testament because the love of God, seen in Jesus of Nazareth, required a new word. God's love completely transcends all human ideas or expressions of love. 'It is a love for the utterly unworthy, a love which proceeds from a God who is love. It is a love lavished on others without a thought of whether they are worthy to receive it or not. It proceeds rather from the nature of the lover, than from any merit of the beloved' (L. Morris, quoted in Prior, p. 226)

Prior, David, *The Message of 1 Corinthians,* Taken from *The Bible Speaks Today* Series edited by J. Alec Motyer; John Stott. Copyright ©1985 edited by J. Alec Motyer; John Stott. Used by permission of InterVarsity Press, P.O. Box 1400, Downers Grove, IL 60515, USA. www.ivpress.com

1 Cor 13:4–5: *Love is patient, love is kind. It does not envy, it does not boast, it is not proud. It is not rude, it is not self-seeking, it is not easily angered, it keeps no record of wrongs.*
Ἡ ἀγάπη μακροθυμεῖ χρηστεύεται ἡ ἀγάπη οὐ ζηλοῖ ἡ ἀγάπη οὐ περπερεύεται οὐ φυσιοῦται
οὐκ ἀσχημονεῖ οὐ ζητεῖ τὰ ἑαυτῆς οὐ παροξύνεται οὐ λογίζεται τὸ κακόν

The verbs Paul uses here are in the present continuous tense, denoting actions and attitudes which have become habitual, ingrained gradually by constant repetition. They sound ordinary, obvious, almost banal, but they are probably the most difficult habits to cultivate. It is not coincidental that these four verses perfectly describe the character of Jesus himself, and of nobody else. This becomes clear when we substitute 'Jesus' for 'love' in this passage, and then by contrast substitute our own name instead [what a challenge!]. Prior, p. 229

Prior, David, *The Message of 1 Corinthians,* Taken from *The Bible Speaks Today* Series edited by J. Alec Motyer; John Stott. Copyright ©1985 edited by J. Alec Motyer; John Stott. Used by permission of InterVarsity Press, P.O. Box 1400, Downers Grove, IL 60515, USA. www.ivpress.com

In verses 4–5 we find the most comprehensive biblical description of the fullness of love. Each ray gives a facet, a property, of ἀγάπη *agape* love.

Unlike most English translations, which include several adjectives, the Greek forms of all those properties are verbs. They do not focus on what love *is* so much as on what love *does* and does not do. *Agape* love is active, not abstract or passive. It does not simply feel patient, it practices patience. It does not simply have kind feelings, it does kind things. It does not simply recognize the truth, it rejoices in the truth. Love is fully love only when it acts (1 Jn 3:18) [Jas 4:17]. MacArthur, p. 337

It keeps no record of wrongs οὐ λογίζεται τὸ κακόν
Love lets the past die. It moves people to a new beginning without settling the past. Love does not have to clear up all misunderstandings. In its power, the details of the past become irrelevant; only its new beginning matters. Accounts may go unsettled; differences remain unsolved; ledgers stay unbalanced. Conflicts between people's memories of how things happened are not cleared up; the past stays muddled. Only the future matters. Love's power does not make fussy historians. Love prefers to tuck all the loose ends of the past rights and wrongs in the bosom of forgiveness.
Lewis Smedes, *Love Within Limits: Realizing Selfless Love in a Selfish World*

1 Cor 13:6–7 *Love does not delight in evil but rejoices with the truth. It always protects, always trusts, always hopes, always perseveres.*

"I have found the paradox that if I love until it hurts, then there is no hurt but only more love."
Mother Teresa of Calcutta   Quoted in Ward and Wild

1 Cor 13:7 (Love) *bears all things, believes all things, hopes all things, endures all things.* NKJV
πάντα στέγει πάντα πιστεύει πάντα ἐλπίζει πάντα ὑπομένει
Love bears what is otherwise unbearable; it believes what is otherwise unbelievable; it hopes in what is otherwise hopeless; and it endures when anything less than love would give up. After love bears, it believes. After it believes, it hopes; after it hopes, it endures. There is no 'after' for endurance, for endurance is the unending climax of love. MacArthur, p. 355

1 Cor 15:42–44: *So will it be with the resurrection of the dead. The body that is sown is perishable, it is raised imperishable; it is sown in dishonor, it is* *raised in glory; it is sown in weakness, it is raised in power; it is sown a natural body, it is raised a spiritual body.*

In the whole of this section, we are particularly hamstrung by the limitations of English in rendering key Greek words…Perhaps the most helpful single clue is to note Paul's contrast between the bodies we have now for our natural human existence and the bodies we will be given when we enter into our full inheritance in heaven. The first body has all the limitations of our earthiness; the second body has all the capacity of God's Spirit [Eph 1:23, 3:19]. From this perspective it is obvious that the first body (flesh and blood) cannot inherit the kingdom of God, because decay and corruption cannot be part of what is eternally corruptible (vs 50) [cf Isa 35:8–9]. In summary, we must acknowledge that in this whole discussion Paul is struggling to describe the indescribable.   Prior, p. 274

Prior, David, *The Message of 1 Corinthians,* Taken from *The Bible Speaks Today* Series edited by J. Alec Motyer; John Stott. Copyright ©1985 edited by J. Alec Motyer; John Stott. Used by permission of InterVarsity Press, P.O. Box 1400, Downers Grove, IL 60515, USA. www.ivpress.com

Personal Note: Pause and reflect on the Apostle's profound transformational statement. In 2 Cor 4, Paul reminds us that while our outer bodies are wasting away, our inner bodies are being renewed day by day (2 Cor 4:16). And here at the close of this letter, he proclaims the wonderful end of this divine process of renewal. The change is stunning; it is staggering. Our bodies in this life are mere clogs we carry around compared to the bodies we will have at our resurrection thanks to the grace and sacrifice of our Lord Jesus Christ. Given our current bodies with all their frailties, it is hard for us to imagine what these new bodies will be like. No more pain. No more sickness. No more decay. No more flaws and blemishes. No more getting tired. No more tears. This is the glorious destiny that awaits us. May we not forget where we are headed as we endure our light and momentary troubles (2 Cor 4:17). May we eagerly seek to prepare ourselves for this magnificent calling as our sovereign Lord sanctifies us through and through (1 Thes 5:23).

2 Corinthians

Commentaries:
- *The Second Epistle to the Corinthians* (NICNT), by Paul Barnett (1997)
- *The Story of God Bible Commentary: 2 Corinthians*, by Judith A. Dichl (2020)
- *2 Corinthians* (USB Series), by James M. Scott (1998)
- Charles Haddon Spurgeon Sermons on Line

2 Cor 3:18: *But we all, with unveiled face, beholding as in a mirror the glory of the Lord, are being transformed into the same image from glory to glory, just as by the Spirit of the Lord.* NKJV

Whether intentionally or not, in this summary comment about the new covenant, Paul has given his readers what will prove to be one of his most potent theological declarations. It spans the covenants, implying the blindness under the old covenant while affirming the brightness of sight of those within the new. Moreover, it spans from the creation of humanity as *imago dei* (image of God) and the fall with its rebellion and death, to conversion-illumination and from there through metamorphosis to glorification [Gn 1:27, 3:23, 1 Cor 15:42-44]. It teaches that we all in whom the image of God is defaced are able through the gospel to see the image in its perfection, in the face of Jesus Christ. And we are enabled not only to see that image, but to be progressively transformed into it by the sovereign Spirit.   Barnett, p. 208, 209

2 Cor 4:7: *But we have this treasure in jars of clay to show that this all-surpassing power is from God and not from us*

God has the sovereign freedom to choose to fill human beings with his love and power and glory, based on their actions, behavior, and acceptance of

Jesus Christ. He has the right and the desire to mold, form, and transform men and women in the way that he sees best. ... Believers are transformed from ignoble "clay pots" to become "clean vessels," useful for spreading the gospel message around the world. Paul refers to humanity as "earthenware vessels," made by the sovereign Potter, who has chosen to fill the menial vessels in Corinth with his glorious, saving gospel.

Still, why would a powerful, sovereign God do this for frail, dishonorable humanity? Paul goes on to say that God wants to demonstrate *his* power in contrast to the power of human beings (4:7). Paul recognizes the total sufficiency to achieve his purposes through his servants. ... In the Potter's hand, and under his transforming, "kiln" power, even mud can be fashioned into a vessel worthy of being filled with God's glory.

Diehl, Judith A., *The Story of God Bible Commentary:2 Corinthians*, Grand Rapids, MI: Zondervan, 2020, p. 174

2 Cor 4:16–18 *Therefore we do not lose heart. Though outwardly we are wasting away, yet inwardly we are being renewed day by day. For our light and momentary troubles are achieving for us an eternal glory that far outweighs them all. So we fix our eyes not on what is seen, but on what is unseen. For what is seen is temporary, but what is unseen is eternal.*

Few verses from the pen of the apostle Paul come with such spiritual impact as this antithesis in which he contrasts the present age to the coming age. Comparison of three successive verses reveals the following:

vs. 17		vs. 18		5:1
Momentary slight suffering	=	what is seen	=	earthly tent / house
Eternal weight of glory	=	what is not seen	=	a building from God

What is not seen is the yet to be revealed building from God that will belong to the coming age, the incomparable weighty and eternal glory of God. Thus, we do not focus on the present time including its suffering and disappointment. Rather we fix our gaze on the glorious hope that will be realized in the age to come [Col 3:2, Heb 11:10, Rev 21:2]. As we do so, God will re-create our inner person even though our outer person is decaying.

Barnett, p 251, 254, 255

"Age is not decay; it is the ripening, the swelling, of the fresh life within, that withers and bursts the husk."
George MacDonald (1824–1905)   Quoted in Ward and Wild

Benjamin Franklin's epitaph
The body of B. Franklin, Printer (Like the Cover of an Old Book, Its Contents torn Out And Stript of its Lettering and Gilding) Lies Here, Food for Worms. But the Work shall not be Lost; For it will Appear once More In a New and More Elegant Edition, Revised and Corrected By the Author.

2 Cor 5:1: *Now we know that if the earthly tent we live in is destroyed, we have a building from God, an eternal house in heaven, not built by human hands.* As we try to absorb these thoughts about this life and the life to come, it is easy to miss the purpose of God's big plans and promises: God created people for eternal life, and while that is guaranteed (5:5), he never promised that our current life would be easy. God gave us his Spirit to help us in the life that we live now. Speaker and author Josh McDowell once said that this life is "boot camp"; we are now being trained for whatever God has planned for us in the eternal future. ... Paul affirms that life in this body is a gift from God and that the human body is the place where we are being taught, trained, and tested, and we will be judged accordingly (5:10). He reminds his readers that their hope and confidence (5:6) rests in eternal things, not in the worldly wisdom of his opponents. Paul's message of hope did not demand that believers abuse or discard their physical bodies, but their hope rested in the resurrected Christ and in their future, eternal, resurrected bodies to come.

With this in mind, Paul tells his Corinthian readers that they have fixed their focal point on the wrong thing: temporal afflictions, mortality, and physical death. They should refocus on what they know about God's power, his gracious intervention, his Spirit, his gift of life, and the eternal hope of glory. The very same power of God that raised Jesus from the dead is placed within the believer to energize him or her to do what he or she is called to do. ... The gift of God's glory will last forever, while earthly trials of today are that so visible and and so heavy will not.
Diehl, excerpts, pp. 188-189

Oh think! To step ashore and that shore Heaven;
To breathe new air, and that celestial air;
To feel refreshed and know 'tis immortality.
Oh think! To pass from storm and stress
To one unbroken calm; to wake and find it Glory.

Dr Peter S Ruckman [Ps 17:15]

http://www.kjv1611.org.uk/Heaven.htm

2 Cor 5:17: *Therefore, if anyone is in Christ, he is a new creation; the old has gone, the new has come!*
THIS TEXT IS exceedingly full of matter, and might require many treatises, and even multitudes of folios, to bring forth all its meaning. Holy Scripture is notably sententious. Human teachers are given to verbiage; we multiply words to express our meaning, but the Lord is wondrously laconic; he writeth as it were in shorthand, and gives us much in little. One single grain of the precious gold of Scripture may be beaten out into acres of human gold leaf, and spread far and wide. A few books are precious as silver, fewer still are golden; but God's Book hath a bank note in every syllable, and the worth of its sentences it were not possible for mortal intellect to calculate. ... There are three stages of the human soul in connection with Christ: the first is without Christ, this is the state of nature; the next is in Christ, this is the state of grace; the third is with Christ, that is the state of glory. Without Christ, this is where we all are born and nurtured, and even though we hear the gospel, and the Bible be in all our houses, and even though we use a form of prayer, yet until we are born again, we are without God, without Christ, and strangers from the commonwealth of Israel. .... The riper the Christian becomes, the nearer to the glory, the closer to the perfection which is promised, the more completely will he think and act, and live and move, in Christ his Master, being one with Jesus in all things.
Charles Haddon Spurgeon, 'The Believer a New Creature', July 18, 1869

2 Cor 5:21: *God made him who had no sin to be sin for us, so that in him we might become the righteousness of God.*

This justly famous verse is one of the most critical in this letter and, indeed, within the writings of the Apostle Paul. This verse makes powerful assertions about Christ, his life and death. It points first to the sinlessness of his incarnate life [Isa 53:9, Mk 7:37, 1 Pet 1:19] and then to his sin-laden death [Isa 53:12]. It is to be inferred that the efficacy of his death arises from the sinlessness of his life. Because in his death God made this sinless man sin for us, those who are in him by faith commitment become the righteousness of God [Rom 5:17]. Barnett, p. 314

"He became what we are that he might make us what he is."
[cf Phil 2:7, 3:21, 1 Cor 15:42–43]
Athanasius (AD 296–373) Bishop of Alexandria Quoted in Ward and Wild

2 Cor 12:7–9: *To keep me from becoming conceited because of these surpassingly great revelations, there was given me a thorn in my flesh, a messenger of Satan, to torment me. Three times I pleaded with the Lord to take it away from me. But he said to me, "My grace is sufficient for you, for my power is made perfect in weakness."*
Power in weakness runs as a thread throughout this letter, reaching its most powerful expression here. Accordingly we agree with Hughes that Christ's reply to Paul here is the summit of the epistle. The words spoken at the cross 'he saved others, but he can't save himself' (Mk 15:31) point to power made perfect in weakness. The powerful salvation of God has been wrought in the powerless crucified one. The stake / thorn remains, and Paul continues to be buffeted. But the Lord's reply stands: his grace <u>is</u> sufficient; his power <u>is</u> being made perfect in the unremoved weakness of the thorn. Barnett, pp 572–573

Personal Note: These verses, which succinctly describe the paradox of strength in weakness, are among the most famous from the Apostle's pen. Both the Old and New Testaments abound in verses that reinforce this concept. The stronger we try to be apart from God, the weaker we become [Jn 15:5], while the more we submit to his grace, the more able we are to tap the inexhaustible dynamo of strength he lavishes upon us. The paradox is counter-intuitive, but human intuition falls flat before the wisdom of God.

May we never forget that God is the source of all we have (James 1:17), including our wealth, our talents, and our intellect [Dt 8:17–18].

2 Cor 13:14: *May the grace of the Lord Jesus Christ, and the love of God, and the fellowship of the Holy Spirit be with you all.*
The letter ends with a grace benediction. Usually Paul closes his letters with a simple formula. Here, however, he employs a much more elaborate benediction that, in parallel structure, lists both the three persons of what we now call the Trinity and their main gifts to the church. Paul is expressing not a pious wish, but rather a confident matter of fact. This statement concludes the letter on a very positive note, for Paul's confidence in the renegade Corinthians (7:4, 16) is based ultimately on God and his presence in their midst. After all, the Corinthians reveal that they are a letter of Christ, written by the Spirit of the living God (3:3). Paul apparently expects them to pass the test after all (13:5). ... Paul affirms that these gifts are *with you all*. This is an amazing statement in view of the dissension and strife in the church at Corinth. Paul does not normally include the word *all* in this part of the closing grace benediction; therefore, its inclusion here is probably highly significant. Paul is saying that, despite the current factions and rebellion, his affirmation of Trinitarian blessing applies to the whole Corinthian congregation. Paul's confidence is rooted in his Trinitarian conviction expressed earlier in the letter: The *God* who is faithful and who vouches for Paul's word in the face of accusations has given the apostle a message of the *Son of God, Jesus Christ*; he has established Paul with the Corinthians in Christ; and he has given his *Spirit* in their hearts as a guarantee (1:18-22; 1:15a; 3:3-4).
Scott, James M., *2 Corinthians*, Grand Rapids, MI: Baker Books (1998), pp. 265-266

Galatians

Commentaries:
- *The Message of Galatians*, by John R.W. Stott (1968)
- *The Preacher's Commentary*, NT Vol 31, by Maxie D. Dunnam (1982)

Gal 1:6 *I am astonished that you are so quickly deserting the one who called you to live in the grace of Christ and are turning to a different gospel*
Paul's was the explosive gospel of free grace. He had experienced it and it had turned his life around, and this was what he shared. Because of his own pilgrimage away from the dead-end of an arduous self-effort at salvation by keeping the law and seeking to be righteous, Paul was absolutely convinced that a person can do nothing to gain favor with God. He had been on that road for a long time and he knew its frustration and futility. … Fervent self-righteousness had sent Paul to Damascus to root out and persecute the Christians. God turned him around and now he knew: no one can ever earn the love of God. God's love is a gift. All we can do is fling ourselves on the love and mercy of God in faith. And miracle or miracles, we are accepted, loved, and given life. Dunham, p. 21
Taken from The Preacher's Commentary Series Volume 31: Galatians, Ephesians, Philippians, Colossians, Philemon by Maxie Dunnam. Copyright © 1991 by Word, Inc. Used by permission of Thomas Nelson. www.thomasnelson.com

Gal 1:8: *But even if we or an angel from heaven should preach a gospel other than the one we preached to you, let him be eternally condemned!*
The popular view is that there are many different ways to God, that the gospel changes with the changing years, and that you must not condemn the gospel to fossilization in the first century AD. But Paul would not endorse these notions. He insists here that there is only one gospel and that this gospel does not change. As we hear of the multifarious views of men

and women today spoken, written, broadcast and televised, we must subject each of them to two rigorous tests. Is their opinion consistent with the free grace of God and with the plain teaching of the New Testament? If not, we must reject it, however august the teacher may be. Stott, p. 26, 28

"If you believe what you like in the Gospels, and reject what you don't like, it is not the gospel you believe, but yourself." Augustine of Hippo (AD 354–430)

Gal 3:3: *Are you so foolish? After beginning with the Spirit, are you now trying to attain your goal by human effort?*
The gospel is not good advice to men, but good news about Christ; not an invitation to us to do anything, but a declaration of what God has done; not a demand, but an offer….The law says 'Do this'; the gospel says 'Christ has done it all'. The law requires works of human achievement; the gospel requires faith in Christ's achievement. The law makes demands and bids us obey; the gospel brings promises and bids us believe….The gospel offers blessings; what must we do to receive them? The proper answer is 'nothing'! We do not have to *do* anything. We have only to *believe*.
Stott, p. 70, 71, 75

Gal 3:24: *So the law was put in charge to lead us to Christ that we might be justified by faith.*
In modern evangelism, we cast our pearls before swine [Mt 7:6]. People cannot see the beauty of the pearl because they have no conception of the filth of the pigsty [Lk 15:16]. It is only against the inky blackness of the night sky that the stars begin to appear [Phil 2:15], and it is only against the dark background of sin and judgment that the gospel shines forth. We cannot come to Christ to be justified until we have first been to Moses to be condemned. But once we have gone to Moses and acknowledged our sin, guilt, and condemnation, we must not stay there. We must let Moses send us to Christ [Mt 17:4–8]. Stott, p. 93, 102

Gal 5:22–23: *But the fruit of the Spirit is love, joy, peace, patience, kindness, goodness, faithfulness, gentleness and self-control. Against such things there is no law.*

Gal 5:22–23 Ὁ δὲ καρπὸς τοῦ πνεύματός ἐστιν ἀγάπη χαρά εἰρήνη μακροθυμία χρηστότης ἀγαθωσύνη πίστις πραότης, ἐγκράτεια κατὰ τῶν τοιούτων οὐκ ἔστιν (Textus Receptus)

How different it is when people live the life of the Spirit. In introducing this catalogue of the character traits of a Christian, Paul uses a singular word, καρπὸς (karpos), whereas he talked in the plural about the works of the flesh [5:19]. This leads us to see that the fruit of the spirit is love, and each fruit of the spirit which follows in the list is another expression of love. The distinction between the works of flesh and fruit of the Spirit grew out of Paul's experience. His life had been in chaos. His sinful nature in rebellion against God made him at war even with himself, and split his life into fragmentary deeds. Then came the reconciling love of Christ, integrating his life with God and with others and bringing him together inside. It all centered in the unifying love of Christ. Thus joy, peace, longsuffering, etc were simply love in another form.

The fruit of the Spirit is the outward expression of Christ dwelling within. The fruit grows and is expressed in any person that willingly dies to what Christ died to so that the Spirit may bring him or her to new life in Christ. Powerfully and surely the Spirit works—sometimes dramatically; sometimes slowly, almost imperceptibly—in our lives to repeat the miracle of a new creation in Christ Jesus. Dunnam, p 112

Taken from The Preacher's Commentary Series Volume 31: Galatians, Ephesians, Philippians, Colossians, Philemon by Maxie Dunnam. Copyright © 1991 by Word, Inc. Used by permission of Thomas Nelson. www.thomasnelson.com

Personal Note: Early in my Christian walk I was trying to internalize certain key scripture passages by memorizing them. I would be saying them over and over in my mind as I went about my business (eg, walking from a parking lot into a store). One day as I entered a discount department store, I was trying to memorize the Fruit of the Spirit verses (Gal 5:22-23). When I came to the checkout stand, there was a long line and several people in front of me had items for which the clerk could not find the price. I waited perhaps five minutes and by the time it was my turn I was steaming with impatience. Then as I exited the store, I slapped my forehead and realized I had totally violated the very verse I was trying to memorize. I believe the Lord wanted to teach me a lesson, because the very next day, I went to the same store, memorizing the same verse. As I came to the checkout stand, the clerk ran out of tape on her cash register and took some time changing it. She was very apologetic as she fumbled with the paper and I just patiently waited and said, "No problem, take your time." She gratefully gushed "most people get really upset when I have this problem. Thanks so much for your patience." I realized that the previous day, I was walking by the flesh, but the next day, I let the Spirit live through me.

Life often gives no warning on stressful situations. For example, someone doesn't say "Now brace yourself. I am going to say something really obnoxious to you, so be prepared with a Christian answer." The abuse just comes tumbling out and we as Christians can only respond appropriately by letting the Spirit live through us. Easy to say. But we (at least I) often still fail.

The Fruit of the Spirit
Personal Note, February 2009

Galatians 5:22–23 are justly considered among the most famous from the pen of the Apostle Paul. I pause here to admire this text and add my observations as a layman. Note the following general points:

- All nine fruits are perfectly modeled in Father, Son, and Holy Spirit.
- The source of the fruit is the Holy Spirit. We cannot conjure up these Spirit-led characteristics by self-effort, but can only produce momentary imitations of them. As Paul says in verse 17, the flesh and the Spirit are constantly at war, and the only way we can display the Fruit is to allow its power to flow through us.
- Notice the contrast Paul paints between the fruits of the flesh in verse 19 and the fruit of the Spirit in vv 22–23.
- Mysteriously we can quench the Spirit's power (1 Thes 5:19). We are not puppets on a string, but dearly loved children (cf Personal Note on Deut 30:19).
- This is the singular fruit of the spirit, not the plural fruits of the spirit. If you have one, you have all nine. They are nine facets on a single jewel.

Now with the risk of violating the second point above, I examine each of these nine characteristics of one possessed by the Holy Spirit.

Love

It is no surprise that **love** heads the list. Indeed, love is the glue which binds all nine "fruits" into one cohesive whole. If we love, we are patient[1] and if we are patient we are self-controlled[2]. If we love, we are filled with joy[3]. If we love we will be faithful just as the Lord is faithful[4]. The supremacy of love is asserted not only by Paul in this letter (5:6, 5:14) but also in his other letters (eg 1 Cor 13:13) and elsewhere in the gospel (Mt 22:39–40, 1Pet 4:8, 1 John 4:7–8). Our love for one another is evidence that we are Christians[5]. Moreover, our love should not be limited to those who are "loveable." Love springs from the heart of the lover, not the worthiness of the recipient. Christ raises the bar in Mt 5:44–48 as he asks us to love our enemies. And this teaching is not confined to the Sermon on the Mount. It is seen both in the Old Testament[6] and elsewhere in the NT[7]. In short, without love, we walk by the flesh. But with it, we walk by the spirit, shining our light into a dark world, and exhibiting the other eight fruits. A popular song calls for "a little more love." The gospel calls for the love which abides[8].

---

[1] 1 Cor 13:4 [2] Prov 19:11 [3] Phil 4:1, Philemon 1:7 [4] Lam 3:22–23, 1 Cor 13:8

[5] Jn 13:33–34 [6] Prov 25:21–22 [7] Lk 23:34, Rom 12:20–21, 1 Pet 2:23 [8] 1 Cor 13:13, Jn 15:9

Joy

The world often confuses **joy** with happiness. The earth's tinsel attractions bring fleeting happiness but the Spirit's indwelling presence produces lasting joy. The Spirit-filled Christian experiences joy that the flesh cannot produce. For example, though strong drink can produce momentary happiness, the Holy Spirit inspires a deeper, more lasting sense of contentment[1]. We rejoice at the abundant blessings of the Lord[2], and realize that even greater joy awaits us as we arrive at his celestial city and achieve our destiny according to his plan³. The spirit filled Christian also realizes true happiness cannot be manufactured. It instead 'overtakes us'⁴, and leaves us contented with any and all situations⁵. Happiness is shallow and fleeting. Joy is deep and eternal.

---

¹ Eph 5:18   ²Ps 65:11–12   ³Isa 25:6–8, 55:1–3, Rev 21:2–4   ⁴Isa 35:10   ⁵ Phil 4:12

Peace

The word translated **peace** in Scripture has a rich set of meanings which cannot be expressed in any one single English word. Much more than the mere absence of war or strife, peace denotes a wholeness and an inner sense of rest. It transcends all understanding⁶. Most of us can recognize peace by contrasting it with its opposite [Job 3:26]. Strife between people ratchets up stress in both parties. But all experience a restful spirit produced by the bond of peace⁷. Envy "rots the bones" but contentment brings peace⁸. Gossip and cantankerousness stir the fires of strife, but without wood the fire goes out⁹. Peace is pleasant and restful¹⁰. Peace is intertwined with joy¹¹. Our Lord blesses the peacemakers¹², and St. Francis of Assisi asks the Lord to make him 'An Instrument of your Peace' (see St. Francis Prayer after Mt 5:9). What a better world we would have if we all prayed the same prayer!

---

⁶Phil 4:7   ⁷Eph 4:3   ⁸Prov 14:30   ⁹Prov 26:20–21   ¹⁰Ps 4:8   ¹¹Ps 147:14, Prov 3:17, Isa 14:7
¹²Mt 5:9

Patience

Paul reminds us that love is patient¹³. He urges us to do all things without complaining or arguing so that we may be blameless and pure¹⁴. **Patience** is one of the fruits most easily quenched when we walk by the flesh. In our modern society with instant coffee, instant potatoes, and instant replays, we want every thing right now. Waiting requires the "long-suffering" (KJV) of the Spirit's fruit. The scriptures are filled with admonitions to do things on the Lord's timing¹⁵. Why do so many verses which basically say the same thing? Partly in answer to the many times the Psalmists and others ask "How Long?"[16]. But mostly because most of us need the spirit's repeated reminders[17] before we can allow him to penetrate and control us. And our patience must extend beyond waiting on the Lord. We must also be patient with one another[18] if we expect to experience the fruit of peace. Patience can only come through the gentle yet persistent prodding of the Spirit.

---

[13]1 Cor 13:4 [14]Phil 2:14 [15]Ps 37:7, Prov 8:34, Isa 30:18, Lam 3:24, Hos 12:6, Mic 7:7, Hab 2:3, Rom 8:25 [16]Ps 6:3, 13:1, 35:17, 119:84, Hab 1:2, Rev 6:10 [17]Jn 14:26 [18]Prov 19:11

Kindness

I vividly recall my mother repeatedly and vigorously urging us five kids with the admonition "Be ye kind, one to another!" (paraphrasing Eph 4:32). When we are kind to one another, a warm glow radiates both inward and outward. This fruit is the outward expression of the inner love and joy we feel as we gradually let the Spirit take hold of our lives. When we are kind to others, we wish them joy and try to be an instrument of that joy. We see **kindness** exhibited and recognized in many scriptural stories. In Genesis 24, the servant sent to find a wife for Isaac mentions the Lord's kindness four times[1]. Naomi recognizes the kindness with which Boaz favors Ruth[2] and then Boaz recognizes that same kindness in Ruth[3]. King David shows kindness to Jonathan's son Mephiphosheth[4]. May we clothe ourselves with kindness[5] as we let the Spirit work His will in our lives! May we add kindness[6] to the other fruits the Spirit imparts to us!

---

[1]vv12, 24, 27, 49 [2]Ru 2:20 [3]Ru 3:10 [4]2 Sam 9:7 [5]Col 3:12 [6]2 Pet 1:5–7

Goodness

The Bible's frequent unabashed presentation of absolutes (eg, good or evil) is jarring to modern humans who want to see nuanced shades of gray. But our maker is absolutely good[7]. And we, in our fallen state, are absolutely bad[8]. The Spirit, however, quickens us[9] and enables us to do good works[10], to exhibit the **goodness** of this fruit[11]. Goodness is the opposite of evil[12].

If we are good we do not want to harm people[13]. If we are good we do what is right[14]. If we are good we help others in need[15]. We do good not to gain applause or point to our own merit, but to bring positive results to those around us and bring glory to God[16]. The world often lampoons "do-gooders" as those who want to run the lives of others and toot their own horns. The Spirit-filled Christian instead does good to help others not to condemn them. Doing good requires effort, and Paul urges us not to become weary in that effort[17].

---

[7]Isa 6:3, Rev 4:8, Lk 18:19   [8]Eph 2:1, Rom 3:10, 3:23   [9] Eph 2:5   [10] Eph 2:10
[11]Gn 1:31   [12]Gn 3:5   [13]Gn 50:20   [14]Deut 6:18, 12:28   [15]Lk 10:33–34
[16]1 Pet 2:12   [17]Gal 6:9

Faithfulness

One can depend on a Spirit-Filled Christian to do what he/she says and to say what he/she does [cf discussion on Job 1:1]. The prophets praise the **faithfulness** of God[18] as do the psalmists[19], and the Lord expects us to show that same faithfulness to others[20]. The Spirit's fruits are intertwined[21], once again showing that they are all facets of a single jewel. Faithfulness is in it for the long haul[22]. We often encounter faithlessness in our encounters with others. How refreshing it is when we find someone we can depend on! The Spirit-Filled Christian perseveres for that prize[23].

---

[18]Isa 25:1, Lam 3:22–23   [19]Ps 36:5, 108:4, 119:90   [20]1Sam 26:23   [21]Ps 85:10, Prov 3:3   [22]Rev 13:10b   [23]Rom 5:3–4, Phil 3:14, James 1:12

Gentleness

All three persons of the trinity, Father[1] Son[2] and Holy Spirit[3] restrain their power and exhibit a gentle demeanor. Throughout the Scriptures, meekness[4], humility[5], and **gentleness**[6] are urged and praised. One of the paradoxes of the Spirit filled life is stated succinctly by Paul in 2 Cor 12:10: *when I am weak, then I am strong*. The gentle spirit patiently seeks peace in love[7] (note 4 of the fruits in one verse) rather than self-aggrandizement. When the Spirit's power is quenched, we become so full of ourselves and our own self-sufficiency that we fail to recognize that apart from the true vine we can do nothing[8]. The Spirit gives a quiet inner strength that does not need to blow its own horn to get attention[9]. Instead the Spirit reminds us that as we humble ourselves before the Lord He will lift us up[10].

---

[1]Isa 40:11   [2]Mt 11:29, 21:5   [3]1 Kings 19:12, Lk 3:22   [4]Ps 37:11, Zp 3:12, Mt 5:5
[5]Prov 11:2, 22:4, Zp 2:3, Phil 2:3, Col 3:12, Jas 3:13   [6]Prov 25:15, 1 Th 2:7, 1 Pet 3:4, 3:15   [7]Eph 4:2
[8]Jn 15:5, cf Dwight Moody quote after Ps 101:5   [9]Prov 18:2   [10]1 Pet 5:6

Self-Control

The final fruit of ***self-control*** is again intertwined with the previous eight. If we love, we are self-controlled because we seek the good of others. If we are patient, we are self-controlled: we control our impulses and wait to get the whole story before acting. Kindness and Gentleness place a holy restraint on our actions. From the point of view of human logic, we should be able to control ourselves. But in our fallen state, we often find it harder to control our own impulses than to control others[11]. We, like the Israelites during the exodus, chafe under the authority of others[12]. We long to be kings and control our own destiny. In doing so, we discover that what appears to be freedom ends up as bondage. In contrast, as we submit our will to the Spirit's guidance, we experience an exhilarating freedom. In the final analysis, we find that self-control is really submission to the Spirit's control. As we think on noble things[13], we find ourselves more in tune with the Spirit, and abler to walk in step with Him[14]. Lack of self-control results in avoidable calamities[15] while self-control leads to abiding joy.

---

[11]Prov 25:28   [12]Ex 16:2   [13]Phil 4:8   [14]Gal 5:25   [15]Prov14:17

Ephesians

Commentaries:
- *The Message of Ephesians*, by John Stott (1979)
- *Living Insights*, Vol 8, by Charles Swindoll (2015)
- *The Preacher's Commentary*, NT Vol 31, by Maxie Dunnam (1982)

Personal Note: While most consider Romans to be the summit of the New Testament, I believe this book of Ephesians may also lay claim to that title. It presents an extraordinarily densely packed presentation of the Gospel. Though Paul is in chains, he has "slipped the surly bonds of earth.*" From its soaring opening to its simple closing verse, this book challenges us to comprehend the glorious riches that await us as we live a life in gratitude for God's grace.

The epistle tells us that in Christ, God has transformed us and sealed us in the Holy Spirit. The apostle's expansive language lifts our minds into the heavenly realms (mentioned five times) as we contemplate where we once were (2:1) and where we are headed (2:6). The keynote verses of 2:8–10 sum up in a nutshell nearly the entire Christian faith. The prayer of 3:14–21 is perhaps one of the most finely crafted prayers ever written. Paul's words help us get our minds around a love that surpasses knowledge and fills every dimension completely. May our hearts be stirred as we read this clarion call to fulfill our destiny and live lives which bring honor to Father, Son, and Holy Spirit!   * from the poem *High Flight* by John Gillespie Magee

Eph 1:3: *Praise be to the God and Father of our Lord Jesus Christ, who has blessed us in the heavenly realms with every spiritual blessing in Christ.*

The first three chapters of Ephesians form an almost continuous prayer, giving the entire letter the sound of music. Though in prison, Paul's spirit is ecstatic. The first three chapters are doctrine set to music, truth that rings, theology from the knees and heart of prayer. Paul is not debating or answering ugly charges against him; he is not using all of his intellectual powers to make reasoned statements. Rather, he prays—and he shares his prayer. He breaks out into joyful praise, then moves into deep intercession. … His intention is to unify the entire cosmos in Christ Jesus. This is big thinking and big praying! Dunnam, p. 145

Taken from The Preacher's Commentary Series Volume 31: Galatians, Ephesians, Philippians, Colossians, Philemon by Maxie Dunnam. Copyright © 1991 by Word, Inc. Used by permission of Thomas Nelson. www.thomasnelson.com

Eph 1:18: *I pray also that the eyes of your heart may be enlightened in order that you may know the hope to which he has called you, the riches of his glorious inheritance in the saints*

Is there anything more exciting that the unfolding and blossoming of a life yielded to Christ and shaped by His indwelling Holy Spirit? A garden, dazzling with the radiant color of tulips and daffodils is beautiful; yet that beauty does not compare to the beauty of a courageous soul who has taken the rough and rugged soil of a stubborn will, a mean temper, and selfish impulses and, by God's grace, through the recreating power of the Spirit, transformed and landscaped it into the likeness of Jesus Christ. Moonlight is beautiful, especially as it reflects on the smooth silk calmness of a glistening lake—but not nearly so beautiful as the unselfish lovelight sparkling in the eyes on one who has been made loving by the Spirit of Christ. A mountain peak, robed in fresh fallen snow, is a magnificently glorious sight, but not half as glorious as a mountain peak personality—one who has been made a giant by the Spirit. Dunnam, p. 158

Taken from The Preacher's Commentary Series Volume 31: Galatians, Ephesians, Philippians, Colossians, Philemon by Maxie Dunnam. Copyright © 1991 by Word, Inc. Used by permission of Thomas Nelson. www.thomasnelson.com

Eph 2:1–2: *As for you, you were dead in your transgressions and sins, in which you used to live when you followed the ways of this world and of the ruler of the kingdom of the air, the spirit who is now at work in those who are disobedient.*

Man seems incapable of managing his own affairs or of creating a just, free, humane and tranquil society. For man himself is askew. Against the somber background of our world today, Ephesians 2:1–10 stands out in striking relevance. Paul first plumbs the depths of pessimism about man, and then rises to the heights of optimism about God. It is this combination of pessimism and optimism, of despair and faith, which constitutes the refreshing realism of the Bible. For what Paul does in this passage is to paint a vivid contrast between what man is by nature and what he can become by grace. Stott, p. 69

Taken from The Bible Speaks Today Series edited by J. Alec Motyer; John Stott. Copyright (c) 1983 edited by J. Alec Motyer; John Stott. Taken from *The Message of Ephesians* by John Stott. Copyright (c) 1984 by John Stott. Used by permission of InterVarsity Press, P.O. Box 1400, Downers Grove, IL 60515, USA. www.ivpress.com

Eph 2:6–7: *And God raised us up with Christ and seated us with him in the heavenly realms in Christ Jesus, in order that in the coming ages he might show the incomparable riches of his grace, expressed in his kindness to us in Christ Jesus.* [cf John 12:26, 32, 14:19b]

The verbs 'made alive', 'raised' and 'made to sit' refer to the three successive historical events in the saving career of Jesus, which are normally called the *resurrection*, the *ascension*, and the *session*. What excites our amazement, however, is that now Paul is not writing about Christ but about us. He is affirming not that God quickened, raised, and seated Christ, but that he quickened, raised and seated us with Christ. We were dead, but have been made spiritually alive and alert. We were in captivity, but have been enthroned [cf Ps 73:24, 2 Cor 4:14]. Stott, p. 81

Taken from The Bible Speaks Today Series edited by J. Alec Motyer; John Stott. Copyright (c) 1983 edited by J. Alec Motyer; John Stott. Taken from *The Message of Ephesians* by John Stott. Copyright (c) 1984 by John Stott. Used by permission of InterVarsity Press, P.O. Box 1400, Downers Grove, IL 60515, USA. www.ivpress.com

"There is a new wonder in heaven and on earth: God is on earth and man is in heaven."

Thalassios the Libyan (7th Century) Quoted in Ward and Wild

Eph 2:8–10: *For it is by grace you have been saved, through faith-and this not from yourselves, it is the gift of God- not by works, so that no one can boast. For we are God's workmanship, created in Christ Jesus to do good works, which God prepared in advance for us to do.*

We are exhibits of God's skill and trophies of his grace [1 Tim 1:16]. We are God's workmanship (ποίημα *poiema*, his 'work of art or his masterpiece').

Salvation is creation, re-creation, new creation. The paragraph ends as it began with our human walk, a Hebrew idiom for our manner of life. Formerly we walked in trespasses and sins in which the devil had trapped us; now we walk in good works which God has eternally planned for us to do. The contrast is complete. What could possibly have effected such a change? Just this: a new creation by the grace and power of God [2 Cor 5:17]. The key expressions of the paragraph are surely *but God* (vs 4) and *by grace* (vv 5,8). True, the only hope for dead people (2:1) lies in a resurrection. But then the living God is the God of resurrection. He is even more than that: he is the God of creation. Both metaphors indicate the indispensable necessity of divine grace. For resurrection is out of death, and creation is out of nothing [cf 1 Pet 1:23]. That is the true meaning of salvation. Stott, p. 85

Taken from *The Message of Ephesians* by John Stott. Copyright (c) 1984 by John Stott. Used by permission of InterVarsity Press, P.O. Box 1400, Downers Grove, IL 60515, USA. www.ivpress.com

"I do not want merely to possess faith; I want a faith that possesses me." Charles Kingsley (1819–1875)

Personal Note: These verses are perhaps the keynote of Ephesians and of the gospel. Other religions of the world (notably Judaism and Islam) say *do*. Christianity says *done*. Salvation is entirely a work of God, so no one can boast that he has achieved what only God can give. To use another Christian aphorism, "grace is the root and works are the fruit." In their book *Leadership by the Book*, Blanchard, Hybels and Hughes state it this way: "Jesus wants us to 'be' before he wants us to 'do' anything." We do not do good deeds to work ourselves into God's favor; he grants his favor and we do good works in gratitude for the rich inheritance he bestows.

Eph 3:17–19: *And I pray that you, being rooted and established in love, may have power, together with all the saints, to grasp how wide and long and high and deep is the love of Christ, and to know this love that surpasses knowledge-that you may be filled to the measure of all the fullness of God.*

As we now look back down the staircase which we have been climbing with Paul, we cannot fail to be struck by his audacity. He prays that his readers may be given the strength of the Spirit and the ruling presence of Christ, the rooting of their lives in love, the knowledge of Christ's love in all its dimensions, and the fullness of God himself. These are bold petitions. Climbers on this staircase become short of breath, even giddy.   Stott, p. 138, 139

Taken from *The Message of Ephesians* by John Stott. Copyright (c) 1984 by John Stott. Used by permission of InterVarsity Press, P.O. Box 1400, Downers Grove, IL 60515, USA. www.ivpress.com

So confounding, so unexpected, and so infinite is the love of the One who gave His life for our sins that Paul runs out of images with which to express it. Paul uses a spatial image to convey the inexpressible and incomprehensible nature of the love of Christ. Its breadth, length, height, and depth are immeasurable. His love extends boundlessly in every direction, like an infinite universe whose end can never be reached. I can't help but think of the cross when I read those words:

- *Broad* enough to cover anybody!
- *Long* enough to go beyond any barrier!
- *High* enough to take us all the way to glory and beyond!
- *Deep* enough to touch any need, any sin, or any hurt!

So, addressing the mental dimension of his readers' being, Paul prays that the believers would grow deeper in their knowledge of God, whose greatness can never be fully grasped, whose love can never be understood, and whose glory can never be fully experienced. Paul is not talking here about 'head knowledge.' Anybody can believe and confess that God's love is beyond anything we can imagine. But to experience it—to know it as a recipient of his mercy and grace—that's something that can't be understood in a merely intellectual sense.

It reminds me of the response by jazz great Louis Armstrong when he was asked to explain what jazz is. 'Man, if you gotta ask, you'll never know.' Jazz isn't something that's dissected, measured, described, and explained. It's something that's heard, felt, and experienced. The same is true of the love of Christ but in an infinitely greater sense. Swindoll, pp. 222–223

Eph 3:20–21: *Now to him who is able to do immeasurably more than all we ask or imagine, according to his power that is at work within us to him* *be glory in the church and in Christ Jesus throughout all generations, for ever and ever! Amen.*

A great prayer like this deserves a grand benediction—a magnificent conclusion. God's greatness overwhelmed Paul, just as it overwhelms you and me today. So he turned all of our attention from what we need to become to who God is and what God can do. Compared to what God is able to do for us, our thoughts and prayers appear to be mere musings and ramblings. Yet the inexhaustible power of the Holy Spirit works within us, as He mediates his miraculous abilities to us through the church. Such a God—and only such a God—is worthy of all glory and honor forever and ever. Swindoll, p. 224

Eph 4:15: *Instead, speaking the truth in love*
Thank God there are those in the contemporary church who are determined at all costs to defend and uphold God's revealed truth. But sometimes they are conspicuously lacking in love. When they think they smell heresy, their nose begins to twitch, their muscles ripple, and the light of battle enters their eye. Truth becomes hard if it is not softened by love; love becomes soft if not strengthened by truth. The apostle calls us to hold the two together [cf 1 John 5:1]. Stott, p. 172

Taken from *The Message of Ephesians* by John Stott. Copyright (c) 1984 by John Stott Used by permission of InterVarsity Press, P.O. Box 1400, Downers Grove, IL 60515, USA. www.ivpress.com

Eph 4:22–24: *put off your old self, which is being corrupted by its deceitful desires; to be made new in the attitude of your minds; and to put on the new self, created to be like God in true righteousness and holiness.*
In these verses, we see two solid doctrinal foundations for Christian holiness which Paul has laid. They are like two roots from which holiness sprouts and grows. First, we have experienced a new creation [2 Cor 5:17], and secondly, in consequence, we have received a new mind which is constantly being renewed [Rom 12:2]. Moreover, the two are organically related to one another. It is our new creation which has given us our new mind; and it is our new mind which understands our new creation and its implications. When a soldier leaves the army and becomes a civilian, he gets out of uniform into "civvies". Just so, since by a new creation we have put off the old humanity and put on the new, we must also put away the

old standards and adopt new ones. Our new role will mean new clothing [Gn 35:2, Isa 61:10, Zech 3:4, Rom 13:14, Col 3:9–10], our new life a new ethical lifestyle. Stott, p. 183

Taken from *The Message of Ephesians* by John Stott. Copyright (c) 1984 by John Stott. Used by permission of InterVarsity Press, P.O. Box 1400, Downers Grove, IL 60515, USA. www.ivpress.com

Eph 4:32: *And be ye kind one to another, tenderhearted, forgiving one another, even as God for Christ's sake hath forgiven you.* (KJV)

> *People are often unreasonable, irrational, and self-centered. Forgive them anyway.*
> *If you are kind, people may accuse you of selfish, ulterior motives. Be kind anyway.*
> *If you are successful, you will win some unfaithful friends and some genuine enemies. Succeed anyway*
> *If you are honest and sincere people may deceive you. Be honest and sincere anyway.*
> *What you spend years creating, others could destroy overnight. Create anyway.*
> *If you find serenity and happiness, some may be jealous. Be happy anyway.*
> *The good you do today, will often be forgotten. Do good anyway.*
> *Give the best you have, and it will never be enough. Give your best anyway.*
> *In the final analysis, it is between you and God. It was never between you and them anyway.*

Mother Teresa of Calcutta (1910-1997) (Catholic Nun)

Eph 5:18: *Do not get drunk on wine, which leads to debauchery. Instead, be filled with the Spirit.*

Personal Note: Pastor Joe Focht of *Calvary Chapel* Philadelphia had a striking observation about the concept of being filled with the spirit. He observed that we often pray for a fresh infilling of the holy spirit. If we are once filled, why do we need refills? Because we leak.

Eph 5:21: *Submit to one another out of reverence for Christ.*
The clearest and most challenging expression of the biblical meaning of submission is Mark 8:34–35: 'If any man would come after me let

him deny himself and take up his cross and follow me. For whoever would save his life will lose it; and whoever loses his life for my sake will save it.' We cower back from such a hard word. Self-fulfillment and self-actualization touch our ears gently. Self-denial cuts to the quick of our feeling and challenges us at the core of our being. No one need remind us that we are self-seeking, self-serving, self-indulging people. ... Self-denial is a way by which we realize that our happiness and fulfillment are not dependent upon having our own way or getting what we want. ... Self-denial, according to Jesus, is the only road to self-fulfillment. We save our lives by losing them for Christ's sake. Willingness to be last makes us first.

Dunnam, pp 228–229

Taken from The Preacher's Commentary Series Volume 31: Galatians, Ephesians, Philippians, Colossians, Philemon by Maxie Dunnam. Copyright © 1991 by Word, Inc. Used by permission of Thomas Nelson. www.thomasnelson.com

Personal Note: Verse 22 which follows this verse is often lifted out of its context and has become a source of needless controversy and strife. Many modern women bristle at the command for wives to submit to their husbands, but we must remember in the preceding verse, we are all told to submit to one another. Christ taught the same thing numerous times, particularly in Mark 10:45. In our modern world, we often hear strident claims about defending our rights. But Christ teaches us instead to submit to one another. This is hard teaching for the modern mind to grasp, but it is a central admonition of the Christian faith.

Perhaps the easiest way we may relate to this is to consider that we often submit without question in our daily lives. Most of us probably go to work where we submit to our supervisor. Does that mean we consider the supervisor superior to us? No, it means that we recognize the supervisor's role and our role. The business world would not run smoothly if everyone were grasping for their rights. The world in general does not work well under these circumstances either.

Eph 5:22: *Wives, submit to your husbands as to the Lord.*
Eph 5:25: *Husbands, love your wives, just as Christ loved the church and gave himself up for her*

The church's head is the church's bridegroom (Christ). He does not crush the church. Rather he sacrificed himself to serve her, in order that she might become everything he longs for her to be, namely herself in the fullness of her glory. Just so the husband should never use his headship to crush or stifle his wife, or frustrate herself from being herself. His love for her will lead him to an exactly opposite path. He will give himself for her, in order that she may develop her full potential under God and so become more completely herself. ... The apostle's instruction is not 'Wives submit, husbands boss'; it is 'wives submit, husbands love'. Submission and love are two aspects of the very same thing, namely of that selfless self-giving which is the foundation of an enduring and growing marriage. As the husband loves his wife and the wife submits to her husband, each is seeking to enable the other to become more fully himself or herself, within the harmonious complementarity of the sexes.   Stott, pp. 229, 234–236

Taken from *The Message of Ephesians* by John Stott. Copyright (c) 1984 by John Stott. Used by permission of InterVarsity Press, P.O. Box 1400, Downers Grove, IL 60515, USA. www.ivpress.com

Philippians

Commentaries:
- *Living Insights*, Vol 9, by Charles Swindoll (2017)
- *The Message of Philippians*, by J. Alec Motyer (1984)
- *The Preacher's Commentary*, NT Vol 31, by Maxie D. Dunnam (1982)

Phil 1:6: *being confident of this, that he who began a good work in you will carry it on to completion until the day of Christ Jesus.*
The Greek ἐναρξάμενος *enarchomai* means to inaugurate, and the tense points to decisive and deliberate act; both the impulsive and imperfect are ruled out. Here was something planned and executed to completion. Here the verb 'carry it on to completion' is intensive and can express a continuous sense. 'will evermore put his finishing touches on it.' God never gives up. Here is confidence indeed. Our salvation can no more be forfeited than the Father can break his pledged word to glorify his Son [Jn 17:1–2]. No wonder, then, that Paul uses the language of a man who has no doubts: *I am sure*. The perseverance of the saints rests on the perseverance of God with the saints [Rom 8:38–39]. But the great and true doctrine of Christian assurance is no friend to pride. The salvation we are assured of is wholly wrought by God for helpless, hopeless sinners. Assurance, biblically understood, keeps the saints on their toes. Motyer, p 43, 45, 50

Taken from *The Bible Speaks Today* Series edited by J. Alec Motyer; John Stott. Copyright ©1983 edited by J. Alec Motyer; John Stott. Used by permission of InterVarsity Press, P.O. Box 1400, Downers Grove, IL 60515, USA. www.ivpress.com Taken from *The Message of Philippians* by J. Alec Motyer. Copyright (c) 1984 by J. Alec Motyer. Used by permission of InterVarsity Press, P.O. Box 1400, Downers Grove, IL 60515, USA.

Phil 2:5–7: *Your attitude should be the same as that of Christ Jesus: Who, being in very nature God, did not consider equality with God something to be grasped, but made himself nothing,*
taking the very nature of a servant, being made in human likeness.
Though he could have clutched the heavenly glory He had with the Father before time and space came into being [Prov 8:30, John 1:2, Col 1:17]—and he had every right to do so—He didn't. Christ voluntarily acted with an attitude of selfless humility, not with an air of self-focused superiority. Think about this. God the Son—eternal, all powerful—didn't regard his exalted position as something to be grasped. Nothing within Him tempted Him to exploit his preeminent position as absolute Sovereign over all. Why not? Because of His perfect love for humanity manifested in selfless humility.
In a state of absolute perfection and full control, Jesus willingly stepped out of his rightful realm of glory for the sake of humanity. Though encompassed by an angelic chorus of perpetual praise [Rev 5:8–12], the Son unselfishly came to dwell among those who would curse and abuse Him. Though enwrapped in the radiant light [Heb 1:3] of his own divine glory God the Son put a veil of flesh over His glory—not diminishing it or extinguishing it, but concealing it—all on behalf of a cold, dark world that sought to plunge Him into the shadow of death. What an incomprehensible, unfathomable example of selfless humility! Swindoll, p. 42

"Mild he lays his glory by, born that man no more may die
Born to raise the sons of earth, born to give them second birth."

From *Hark the Herald Angels Sing*, by Charles Wesley (1739)

Phil 2:9–11: *Therefore God exalted him to the highest place and gave him the name that is above every name, that at the name of Jesus every knee should bow, in heaven and on earth and under the earth, and every tongue confess that Jesus Christ is Lord, to the glory of God the Father.*
He was not grasping in relation to his glory (v 6), defensive in relation to his deity, protective of his unique human experience: he emptied himself (v 7) and humbled himself (v 8). From the brightness of the glory [Jn 17:5] to the dust of death and the place of the curse [1 Pet 2:24], from the glory

of a true humanity down to the lowliest identification with our common clay, by his own self-humbling decision, Jesus showed both obedience and love to the uttermost. And the Father loves to see it so, for it is a principle with God that he who humbles himself will be exalted [Ps 149:4, Prov 3:34, Isa 66:2, Mt 23:12, James 4:6, 4:10, 1 Pet 5:5–6]. Motyer, p. 122

Motyer, J. Alec, *The Message of Philippians*, Taken from *The Bible Speaks Today* Series edited by J. Alec Motyer; John Stott. Copyright ©1984 edited by J. Alec Motyer; John Stott. Used by permission of InterVarsity Press, P.O. Box 1400, Downers Grove, IL 60515, USA. www.ivpress.com

Phil 2:14–16: *Do everything without complaining or arguing, so that you may become blameless and pure, children of God without fault in a crooked and depraved generation, in which you shine like stars in the universe as you hold out the word of life*

<u>**Personal Note**</u>: "Do all things without complaining or arguing" has been a tough verse for me over the years. I don't have to work to complain or argue, it just comes naturally. While I have improved in this area in recent years, it still keeps me humble. Like the grumbling Israelites, I more easily can enumerate my grievances than I can count my blessings (Num 10:10, 20:5). I think the key here is the verse which immediately precedes 2:14. Easy to say, but not easy to live out.

Phil 3:8 *What is more, I consider everything a loss compared to the surpassing greatness of knowing Christ Jesus my Lord, for whose sake I have lost all things. I consider them rubbish, that I may gain Christ and be found in him*

Man at his most privileged, his most moral, his most religious, his most zealous and devoted is yet not thereby made fit and acceptable to God [Isa 64:6]. Paul had no recourse but to add up his advantages and achievements one by one and admit that the total was zero. No-one had ever striven for righteousness as did Paul, and yet he does not see Christ as the prize standing just above the top rung of the ladder of self-advancement. He cannot have Christ until he has toted up all his works of righteousness and admitted the answer to be loss. Motyer, p. 158, 159

Motyer, J. Alec, *The Message of Philippians*, Taken from *The Bible Speaks Today* Series edited by J. Alec Motyer; John Stott. Copyright ©1984 edited by J. Alec Motyer;

John Stott. Used by permission of InterVarsity Press, P.O. Box 1400, Downers Grove, IL 60515, USA. www.ivpress.com

"He is no fool who gives what he cannot keep to gain what he cannot lose." Jim Elliott (1927–1946) American Missionary

Hymn: *When I Survey the Wondrous Cross*
(1707), Text: Isaac Watts, 1674–1748
, Music: Lowell Mason, 1792–1872

When I survey the wondrous cross	[Heb 12:2, Col 2:14]
On which the Prince of Glory died;	[Acts 5:31, Rom 6:10]
My richest gain I count but loss,	[Phil 3:8]
And pour contempt on all my pride.	[Ps 131:1]
Forbid it, Lord, that I should boast,	[Rom 3:27]
Save in the death of Christ, my God;	[Gal 6:14]
All the vain things that charm me most,	[Eccl 2:10–11]
I sacrifice them to his blood.	[Rom 12:1]
See, from his head, his hands, his feet,	[Jn 20:27]
Sorrow and love flow mingled down.	[Isa 53:4, Lk 23:34a]
Did e'er such love and sorrow meet,	[Jn 15:13, Mk 14:34]
Or thorns compose so rich a crown.	[Jn 19:5]
Were the whole realm of nature mine,	[Gen 1:28, Ps 8:6]
That were an offering far too small;	[Ps 116:12]
Love so amazing, so divine,	[Ps 108:4]
Demands my soul, my life, my all.	[Deut 6:5, Ps 103:1]

Personal Note: As a tenor in the eighty voice Cedar Springs Choir, it was my privilege to sing a wonderful arrangement of this classic hymn. The last line in particular was very memorable. Our director added a dramatic pause (Caesura or //) between *my life* and *my all*. In early rehearsals, several of us sang impromptu solos at this point until we got it right. As I think of that dramatic pause, I now realize that during that pause we should be thinking of the significance of that statement: *love so amazing so divine, demands my soul, my life, my all.* We all would do well to ponder this profound statement.

Phil 3:9: *and be found in him, not having a righteousness of my own that comes from the law, but that which is through faith in Christ-the righteousness that comes from God and is by faith.*
Faith is leaning heavily on Christ: not labor, but cessation of labor; not doing, but ceasing to do; simply leaning the whole weight of our needs upon him, and finding in him acceptance before the presence of God, and a righteousness which could never be ours by our own works. Paul's own intense, demanding and sacrificial labors [Col 1:29] had produced conformity to a legal code of behavior (3:6). Of what worth was this conformist righteousness? Just that and nothing more. A 'certificate of good behavior'. Such a righteousness is self-conferred. We have weighed our own merits. A certificate of good behavior which we have awarded to ourselves is not enough to give us confidence as we face the judgment of God   Motyer, p. 159, 165, 166
Motyer, J. Alec, *The Message of Philippians,* Taken from *The Bible Speaks Today* Series edited by J. Alec Motyer; John Stott. Copyright ©1984 edited by J, Alec Motyer; John Stott. Used by permission of InterVarsity Press, P.O. Box 1400, Downers Grove, IL 60515, USA. www.ivpress.com

"I will try to find an elevator by which I may be raised to God, for I am too small to climb the steep stairway to perfection." Therese of Lisieux (1873–1897)   Quoted in Ward and Wild

Phil 4:4: *Rejoice in the Lord always. I will say it again: Rejoice!*
Strangely, some seem to treat anxiety like a close friend they don't want to lose: they excuse it, make room for it, accommodate it, and coddle it. They treat it like a destructive, codependent relationship, and it eats away at their joy day after day. Think about what worry really is and does. When we worry, we're preoccupied with distressing fears—burdened by the past, nervous about the present, and tormented by the future. We live in a realm of 'what if's.' That kind of mental and emotional agitation can't be healthy. No wonder Jesus took worldly worry head on in his Sermon on the Mount.

Five times in that famous passage the Greek term μεριμνάω *merimnaō* meaning 'to worry' appears.

To combat this dangerous trajectory, Paul recenters our focus in Philippians 4:4. In a letter in which joy has been a central theme, it is no surprise that Paul reiterates that theme now, as he is about to discuss the threat of anxiety. By refocusing on the joy we have in the Lord, we already begin to pour water on the flames of worry. ... Instead of worrying about every jot and tittle of our lives—and the lives of others—we need to relax. Let things go. Yield to others. Extend a hand of grace to brothers and sisters in Christ. Let insignificant things slide. Accept differences. This kind of gentle spirit will rain on the uncontrolled fires of anxiety. Swindoll, pp. 87–88

Phil 4:6: *Do not be anxious about anything, but in everything, by prayer and petition, with thanksgiving, present your requests to God.* [Ps 94:19]
Anxiety, in the way Paul is using the term, and the way we most often experience it, is the futile, frustrating, debilitating attempt to bear the burdens of life and especially of the future, ourselves, alone. The Christian answer to anxiety is confident prayer which issues in 'the peace of God which surpasses all understanding (v 7)'. This is no glib word, no pious cliché, no easy moralizing about complex issues. Remember, Paul was in prison. Ponder for even a minute the immediate circumstances out of which this word came, and let the movement of his life be flashed, however quickly, upon the screen of your mind. At every step of his Christian journey, the hound of anxiety was snapping at his heels. Paul's word comes from the sweaty arena of life where his word needs to be heard, and from a person who has experienced the answer he is offering. Dunnam, p. 309
Taken from The Preacher's Commentary Series Volume 31: Galatians, Ephesians, Philippians, Colossians, Philemon by Maxie Dunnam. Copyright © 1991 by Word, Inc. Used by permission of Thomas Nelson. www.thomasnelson.com

Phil 4:7 And *the peace of God, which transcends all understanding, will guard your hearts and your minds in Christ Jesus.*
The opposite of anxiety is peace. Not numbness nor unconcern, not the absence of inner and outward struggle, but God's peace, the peace that is from Him, giving us hope and confidence, strengthening us to carry on with joy when the burdens are heavy and the pathway rough. The word

in Greek *phroureo* (φρουρήσει) for 'guard' or 'keep' was employed when speaking of a company of soldiers keeping watch over a city—a good metaphor. God's peace is an inward sentinel protecting us, keeping watch that we be not invaded by all the alien forces that would disrupt and ravage our minds and hearts, making us [impotent] by crushing us with anxiety. Dunnam, p. 310

Taken from The Preacher's Commentary Series Volume 31: Galatians, Ephesians, Philippians, Colossians, Philemon by Maxie Dunnam. Copyright © 1991 by Word, Inc. Used by permission of Thomas Nelson. www.thomasnelson.com

Phil 4:8: *Finally, brothers, whatever is true, whatever is noble, whatever is right, whatever is pure, whatever is lovely, whatever is admirable-if anything is excellent or praiseworthy-think about such things.* [Jer 4:14]
Τὸ λοιπόν ἀδελφοί ὅσα ἐστὶν ἀληθῆ ὅσα σεμνά ὅσα δίκαια ὅσα ἁγνά ὅσα προσφιλῆ ὅσα εὔφημα εἴ τις ἀρετὴ καὶ εἴ τις ἔπαινος ταῦτα λογίζεσθε (Textus Receptus)

The verb *think about* (λογίζεσθε *logizomai*) means to ponder, to give proper weight and value to, and to allow the resultant appraisal to influence the way life is to be lived. Just as a carnal mind is the surest passport to the downward path, so a mind drilled in the things of which God approves is the steadiest way to practical holiness. It is the will of God that by giving attention to things of which he approves we should shape our minds (Rom 12:2) to be like his: to those who do so, he pledges his guardian peace and his own presence as the God of peace. Motyer, p. 212

Motyer, J. Alec, *The Message of Philippians,* Taken from *The Bible Speaks Today* Series edited by J. Alec Motyer; John Stott. Copyright ©1984 edited by J. Alec Motyer; John Stott. Used by permission of InterVarsity Press, P.O. Box 1400, Downers Grove, IL 60515, USA. www.ivpress.com

"Occupy your minds with good thoughts, or the enemy will fill them with bad ones: unoccupied they cannot be." Thomas More (1478–1535)
Quoted in Ward and Wild

Personal Note: Verses 6–8 contain some practical advice for Christians. In Verse 6, Paul reminds us that anxiety is basically a choice we make. We can either present our requests to the Lord and await the providential outcome he grants or we can worry about circumstances that do not suit us. The scriptures remind us over and over (I count at least thirty times) that the Lord DOES hear our prayers (Gen 24:45, Ex 3:7, 2 Sam 22:7, 1 Chr 5:20,2 Chr 30:27, Ps 4:3, 5:3, 6:9,18:6, 28:6, 31:22, 34:1, 34:6, 15, 17, 40:1,55:17, 61:5, 65:2, 65:5,66:19, 86:7, 91:15, 94:9, 102:17, 102:19–20, 116:1, 120:1, 138:3, 145:19, Dan 10:12, Lam 3:56, Lk 1:13, Lk 11:9, Rom 8:26–32, 1 John 5:14) but we may at times think he is either too busy or too distracted to respond. In the rough and tumble of real life, it is easy for us to slide away from reliance on our all powerful and all loving Lord. Yet many a troubled soul has experienced the peace that transcends all understanding (v 7) when they rest their heads on the soft pillow of trust that the Lord knows what He is doing. Finally, in verse 8, Paul reminds us of what we already know. If we stuff our heads with bad thoughts, after gaining a foothold, these bad thoughts will just take over. So the antidote is to instead stuff our head with good thoughts. With noble thoughts. With lovely and excellent and praiseworthy thoughts. The next time you're worried, try what Paul suggests in these three golden verses. Memorize them. Apply them. The more you do, the more you just might experience the warm glow of tranquility and contentment. We can choose what we think about! So choose *these* things and not *those* things.

Colossians

Commentaries:
- *Colossians and Philemon for Pastors*, by John Kitchen (2012)
- *The Message of Colossians and Philemon*, by R.C. Lucas (1980)
- *The Preacher's Commentary*, NT Vol 31, by Maxie D. Dunnam (1982)
- *Colossians & Philemon: So Walk in Him*, by John Woodhouse (2011)

Col 1:3–5: *We always thank God, the Father of our Lord Jesus Christ, when we pray for you, because we have heard of your faith in Christ Jesus and of the love you have for all the saints- the faith and love that spring from the hope that is stored up for you in heaven and that you have already heard about in the word of truth*

Paul is the champion of justification by grace through faith. This was the heartbeat of his preaching. We will never plumb the depths of this great truth: we can only celebrate it and rejoice. Matthew Henry said "Faith opens the door of the soul to receive Christ; faith admits him, and submits to him." Pungent! Faith is the door; faith is the hinge on which the door swings; faith is the key that unlocks the door; faith is the impulse to open the door when the knock comes; faith is the willingness to invite the guest in; faith impels surrender which allows the guest to become master of the house. Dunnam, p. 330

Taken from The Preacher's Commentary Series Volume 31: Galatians, Ephesians, Philippians, Colossians, Philemon by Maxie Dunnam. Copyright © 1991 by Word, Inc. Used by permission of Thomas Nelson. www.thomasnelson.com

Col 1:7: *You learned it from Epaphras, our dear fellow servant, who is a faithful minister of Christ on our behalf*

Too often we fall into the snare of thinking that the gospel has moved across the face of the earth through the zeal, passion, and commitment of superstars like Paul. Not so! To be sure, there are occasional fiery beacons who light up the sky of history—Paul, Augustine, St. Francis, Luther, Wesley. But were they alone in their witness, the sky of history would be bereft of the luminous light of the gospel. The sky is lighted only because of thousands of "lesser" stars: Epaphras, Onemsimus, Eunice, Aquilla, Grandpa Lewis, Brother Grissom, Murdoc and Cora, Clara Mae Sells, Nettle Beeson. You can extend the list to include those through whom the gospel came to you as lively experience that set you on the path to and in Christ. Dunnam, p. 331

Taken from The Preacher's Commentary Series Volume 31: Galatians, Ephesians, Philippians, Colossians, Philemon by Maxie Dunnam. Copyright © 1991 by Word, Inc. Used by permission of Thomas Nelson. www.thomasnelson.com

My Comment: My list would include Pastors John Wood, John Batusic, Ben Phillips, Dee Hammond; Tom Richey, Walt and Carolyn Bigney, Joe Foy, and Larry DeHeer. I think my wife Laurie's would include Aunt Dee and Uncle Jerry, Beth Moore, Karen Matevich, and others. These "lesser stars" as Dunnam puts it, quietly but passionately work to spread the gospel personally and powerfully.

Col 1:11–12: *being strengthened with all power according to his glorious might so that you may have great endurance and patience, and joyfully giving thanks to the Father, who has qualified you to share in the inheritance of the saints in the kingdom of light.*

Two very important lessons are here. One, there are two kingdoms: light and darkness [Ps 18:28, Isa 5:20, 9:2 Isa 45:7], flesh and spirit [Mt 26:41, John 3:6, Rom 8:5], good and evil [Ps 34:14, Prov 14:22, Amos 5:14, Mt 12:35, Rom 12:21]. We have been rescued from the darkness and brought into the kingdom of light [1 Pet 2:9]. If Paul's terminology is archaic, or if his understanding of the system of angelic powers that rule in the elements seems outdated, the truth of his message is not less relevant, or the power of the promised deliverance any less needed.

How impotent we feel in a technological society—how helpless in the clutches of mechanical law, scientific determinism! How often do we give in to the overwhelming feeling that we have no control—that everything is determined by heredity, environment, natural powers, economic and social forces. How ominous the power of sin! We move along as best we can, propelled by forces around us, bobbing erratically along the torrential river of life as though we were ping pong balls in a mountain stream. Paul says no! We have been delivered into the kingdom of light, of freedom.... No darkness can overcome us, no power can overwhelm us, no experience can completely devastate us. Sin cannot hold sway in our lives. We belong to Christ; His is the kingdom, the power, and the glory. We have been *qualified to be partakers of the inheritance of the saints in the kingdom of light.*

Dunnam, pp. 333–334

Taken from The Preacher's Commentary Series Volume 31: Galatians, Ephesians, Philippians, Colossians, Philemon by Maxie Dunnam. Copyright © 1991 by Word, Inc. Used by permission of Thomas Nelson. www.thomasnelson.com

Col 1:15–17: *He is the image of the invisible God, the firstborn over all creation. For by him all things were created: things in heaven and on earth, visible and invisible, whether thrones or powers or rulers or authorities; all things were created by him and for him. He is before all things, and in him all things hold together.*

Though some of the details may be elusive, the main thrust of this section is not difficult to grasp—once the reader has recovered his breath! The whole created order, in time and space, owes its existence to Christ [cf John 1:2–3, Prov 8:22–23]. He is its true origin. He sustains it in being. Without him it would have no ultimate meaning. All this, and much besides, is included in these brief overwhelming affirmations. Lucas, p. 49

Hymn: *Fairest Lord Jesus*, Text: Munster Gesangbuch (1677); trans. by Joseph August Seiss (1873)   Music: Schlesische Volkslieder; arr. by Richard Storrs Willis

Fairest Lord Jesus, ruler of all nature,	[Eph 1:21–22]
O thou of God and man the Son,	[John 1:1, 1 Tim 2:5]
Thee will I cherish, Thee will I honor,	[Mk 1:11, Rev 5:12]
Thou, my soul's glory, joy, and crown.	[2 Tim 4:8, 1 Pet 5:4]
Fair are the meadows, fairer still the woodlands,	[Ps 65:13, 96:12]
Robed in the blooming garb of spring:	[Mt 6:28–29]

Jesus is fairer, Jesus is purer	[Heb 1:3, 1 Jn 1:9]
Who makes the woeful heart to sing.	[Ps 42:5, 40:3a]
Fair is the sunshine, fairer still the moonlight,	[Song 6:10]
And all the twinkling starry host:	[Neh 9:6]
Jesus shines brighter, Jesus shines purer	[Mk 9:3, Rev 1:16b]
Than all the angels heaven can boast.	[Heb 1:4]
Beautiful Savior! Lord of all the nations!	[Eph 1:10, Rev 19:16]
Son of God and Son of Man!	[Rom 1:3–4]
Glory and honor, praise, adoration,	[Eph 3:21]
Now and forevermore be thine.	[Phil 2:9–11, Rev 22:13]

Personal Note: It was my great personal privilege and joy to sing the tenor part to a wonderful arrangement of this classic hymn on a mission trip to Peru. About half of the Cedar Springs Church choir traveled to Lima and sang about twenty concerts, most of them ending with this anthem by Derek Hakes and arranged by Craig Courtney. We sang it in a variety of settings, from a large stage at the National Academy of Music to a small classroom in a missionary school. But wherever we sang it, chill bumps were guaranteed. This arrangement has the men singing the first verse, the ladies the second, and then the whole choir singing the last two verses with some of the most magnificent harmony imaginable, along with a poignant violin accompaniment. The drama builds and reaches its climax in the words *Glory and honor, praise, adoration, now and forevermore be thine.* I will never forget the look on our choir director's face as we performed this piece. She was lit up from within and, though she was directing us, she was being carried along by the song's sacred atmosphere. What an experience!

Col 2:13–14: *When you were dead in your sins and in the uncircumcision of your sinful nature, God made you alive with Christ. He forgave us all our sins, having canceled the written code, with its regulations, that was against us and that stood opposed to us; he took it away, nailing it to the cross.*

Consider a document that records all of our indebtedness to God. What a disturbing document that would be! It would not be a certificate you would want to frame and put on your wall for all to see! This is a document

you would want hidden in a secret place, where no one would find it. The trouble is that hiding it would not change the facts that were recorded on it. The forgiveness of all our trespasses was accomplished by canceling the record of debt. The debt was ἐξαλείψας 'canceled'. The word is strong. It means 'obliterated'. The record of debt no longer exists. The slate has been wiped clean. The record has been completely expunged.
Woodhouse, pp. 139, 140

Col 2:20–22: *Since you died with Christ to the basic principles of this world, why, as though you still belonged to it, do you submit to its rules: "Do not handle! Do not taste! Do not touch!"? These are all destined to perish with use, because they are based on human commands and teachings.*
Paul now gives three examples of the kind of decrees the false teachers in Colossae were handing down. The abrupt, staccato expressions make it probable that Paul implies a mocking tone. It is not so much that he is quoting directly from the false teachers, but that he is paraphrasing in a derisive tone the general nature of the kind of things they teach. ... It is irrational to base one's eternal, spiritual destiny upon the use of things that are inherently so temporal. Food and drink were designed by God as 'consumables,' things provided to assist us along our earthly, temporal sojourn on this earth (Mk 7:18–19). They exist for this temporary function. They cease to exist when that fleeting, momentary, time bound purpose is fulfilled in their eating and drinking of them. ... The false teachers had inexplicably made eternal things dependent upon temporal, earthbound things. A ministry maxim is: 'Never hang matters of eternal weight upon temporal hooks.' Kitchen, p. 222, 223

Col 3:2 *Set your minds on things above, not on earthly things.*
Paul repeats the 'things above' (τα ἄνω *ta anō*) verbatim from verse 1. Now he connects it to one of his favorite verbs φρονέω *phroneō* ('set your mind'). Paul makes use of it in 23 of its 26 NT usages (10 in Philippians). It describes the realm of the mind: to think, to have an attitude, to form an opinion. Paul's frequent use of it underscores the high place he affords the Christian mind. 'You must not only *seek* heaven; you must also *think* heaven.' The things of earth belong to the realm of fleshly indulgence. While the believer resides on earth, his home and center and source of his

life is from above (3:3, 4). To move a boulder requires a solid, stable point of leverage outside the rock itself. To achieve real life-change requires a leverage point outside of ourselves and outside of this world. The things of earth can only be moved by leveraging them against the things above. ... Paul sets heavenly realities ('the things above') in contrast to earthly realities. In doing so he tells us that reality upon earth is defined by the reality of heaven, not the other way around. Spiritual truth defines tangible reality. We are on dangerous ground when we weigh spiritual matters by what appears to be the facts based on limited, earthly evidence. He who sees only the earthly sees only partial reality; he misses the most vital pieces of evidence for interpreting reality in its fullness. Kitchen, pp. 232–233

"The main object of religion is not to get a man into heaven, but to get heaven into him."
Thomas Hardy (1840–1928)

Col 4:5–6: *Be wise in the way you act toward outsiders; make the most of every opportunity. Let your conversation be always full of grace, seasoned with salt, so that you may know how to answer everyone.*
Paul is not calling for a cookie-cutter approach to evangelism. He is calling for real-time, Spirit-born wisdom and grace to be applied in the specifics of each encounter with each person. The emphasis here is not on learning a method of gospel presentation, but upon personal dependence upon the Holy Spirit to produce in one's heart and mind the wisdom and grace essential to making the most effective use of each and every encounter with an unbeliever. It considers people as individuals, not as a category ('unbelievers'). It recognizes that we must listen carefully to each person God sovereignly puts before us. It also reminds us that each encounter demands fresh grace coming down from God, flowing through us to the person. Kitchen, p. 312

1 Thessalonians

Commentaries:
- *The Message of 1 and 2 Thessalonians*, by John R.W. Stott (BST Series) (1991)
- *1 and 2 Thessalonians*, by David J. Williams (1992)
- *The Preacher's Commentary*, NT Vol 32, by Gary W. Demarest (1984)

1 Th 2:19: *For what is our hope, our joy, or the crown in which we will glory in the presence of our Lord Jesus when he comes? Is it not you?*
If we ask how we may develop this double commitment to Word and Church, this balanced combination of truth and love, there is only one possible answer, namely the power of the Holy Spirit, since he is the source of both. He is the spirit of truth (John 14:17) and the fruit of the spirit is love (Gal 5:22). Pastoral leaders, therefore, have no greater need than the fullness of the spirit who alone can lead us in the single path of truth and love. Stott, p. 71

1 Th 4:1: *Finally, brothers, we instructed you how to live in order to please God, as in fact you are living. Now we ask you and urge you in the Lord Jesus to do this more and more.*
A weakness of contemporary evangelical Christianity is our neglect of Christian ethics, both in our teaching and in our practice. In consequence, we have become known rather as people who preach the gospel rather than as those who live and adorn it. ... It is a wonderfully liberating experience when the desire to please God overtakes the desire to please ourselves, and when love for others displaces self-love. True freedom is not freedom from responsibility to God and others in order to live for ourselves, but freedom from ourselves in order to live for God and others. Stott, p. 76, 91

1 Th 4:3 *It is God's will that you should be sanctified: that you should avoid sexual immorality*
The call to sanctification is not a call to stuffiness or drabness. It is a call to usefulness, to availability, and to fidelity. It is a call to an adventure of discovering what life is really intended to be. Color it bright and warm, the way God colored His world. ... It needs to be said loudly, lovingly, and clearly that sexual loving apart from marriage is out of bounds, not because sex is bad, but because it is so good. Sex is holy. It is set apart for special use. That this view is countercultural and regarded as antiquarian to many does not in the least invalidate its truth. The principles by which God's creation operates are neither determined nor discovered by the majority of the people surveyed, no matter how accurate the poll. The law of gravity is a description of the way things really are. We may decide to defy it and jump off the cliff together, but we will all hit the bottom at the same time. We may achieve by consensus a rewrite of sexual standards in our generation, but the way God made things is the way things really are. If Jesus is right, it's not for us to write new rules. ... The Christian standard confining sexual loving exclusively to marriage may appear to be bondage, but in reality it is a way to freedom—the freedom to enjoy one's sexuality in the way intended by God. Demarest, pp. 74–75

1 Th 5:23: *May God himself, the God of peace, sanctify you through and through. May your whole spirit, soul and body be kept blameless at the coming of our Lord Jesus Christ.*
May God himself, the God who makes everything holy and whole, make you holy and whole, put you together—spirit, soul, and body—and keep you fit for the coming of our Master, Jesus Christ. The One who called you is completely dependable. If he said it, he'll do it!
The Message, by Gene Peterson

Here he stresses that the consecration must be total. ... Peace, as we have seen (1:1), signifies well-being in the widest sense, but Paul has in mind spiritual well-being, peace with God. That peace originates with God himself, not the person concerned. God takes the initiative in salvation. The point is reinforced by the conjunction *de*, ('but', not shown in NIV), which sets this prayer over against the injunctions of the preceding verses. They speak of what we must do; this prayer concerns what God has done and will do on our behalf. God could not acquiesce in a state of affairs in which sinners were at enmity with himself. In Christ, therefore, he took the initiative to put them at peace (Rom 5:6 ff, Eph 2:13ff). To those who respond to his initiative, he gives a new status, a new start; and now Paul prays, in effect, that he who began a good work in them might 'carry it on to completion until the day of Christ Jesus (Phil 1:6).' That is, he prays that God might *sanctify* them *through and through*. The later expression renders the word ὁλοτελής *holotelēs*, unique to this passage in the NT. It is comprised of two words, the one signifying wholeness, the other completion. Paul was never afraid to aim high in his prayers. His prayer for the Thessalonians was for their total sanctification. We have seen there is a human role in this process, hence the exhortations above; but even that is largely a matter of letting God do the work, and this prayer focuses on that work of God in shaping their lives. Williams, pp. 102–103

Personal Note: As I read this verse in August 2014, I am thrilled at the thought that I will be sanctified through and through. It seems so far from happening right now as I stumble and bumble my way through life. But God finishes what he started. Praise his Name!

2 Thessalonians

Commentary:
- *The Message of 1 and 2 Thessalonians*, by John R.W. Stott (1991)
- *Thessalonians* (Pillar NT Commentary), by Gene L. Green (2002)

2 Th 1:10 *on the day he comes to be glorified in his holy people and to be marveled at among all those who have believed.*
So how will the coming Lord Jesus be glorified in relation to his people? Not 'among' them, as if they will be the theatre or stadium in which he appears; nor 'by' them, as if they will be the spectators, the audience who watch and worship; nor 'through' them or 'by means of' them, as if they will be mirrors which reflect his image and glory; but rather 'in' them, as if they will be a filament, which itself glows with light and heat when the electric current passes through it.
So when Jesus is revealed in his glory, he will be glorified in his people. We will not only see, but share, in his glory. We will be more than a filament which glows temporarily, only to become dark and cold again when the current is switched off. We will be radically and permanently changed, being transformed into his likeness. And in our transformation his glory will be seen in us, for we will glow forever with the glory of Christ as he indeed glowed with the glory of his father. Stott, p. 149–150

2 Th 3:1–2: *Finally, brothers, pray for us that the message of the Lord may spread rapidly and be honored, just as it was with you. And pray that we may be delivered from wicked and evil men, for not everyone has faith.*
Paul's repeated commands, with their expectation of obedience, condemn those churches whose attitude to the Word of God appears to be subjective and selective. They wander at random through Scripture, choosing a verse here and discarding a verse there, like a gardener picking flowers in a

herbaceous border. They have no concept of a thorough study of the Bible, or of a conscientious submission to its teaching. Let not such a church imagine that it will receive the blessing of the Lord! For to despise the Word of the Lord is to despise the Lord of the Word.
Stott, p. 185, 199

2 Th 3:10: *For even when we were with you, we gave you this rule: "If a man will not work, he shall not eat."*
The necessity of working formed part of the ethical tradition of the church (Eph 4:28; 1 Thes 4:11-12), finding its roots both in the OT (Gen 3:17-19; Ps 128:2; Prov 10:4; 12:11; 19:15). The same idea appears in Greek literature (Phaedrus: 'You don't work? For this reason you don't have anything when you need it.') as well as in later Christian instruction. The *Didache* says that if a traveler comes, the church may help him for a few days. ... The apostle reminds the congregation that they were not under any obligation to sustain such people, and even commended them not to feed them. He shall not eat is a third person singular imperative in the Greek that embraces the responsibility of the church not to feed the person. With these words, Paul liberates the patrons of their patronal responsibility, which under normal circumstances was considered to be a perpetual obligation if the client responded to the patron with thanks and honors.   Green, Gene L., *Thessalonians* (Pillar NT Commentary), Grand Rapids, MI: Eerdmans, 2002, p. 350

1 Timothy

Commentaries:
- *The Message of 1 Timothy and Titus,* by John Stott (1996)
- *Living Insights,* Vol 11, by Charles Swindoll (2014)

1 Tim 1:3: *As I urged you when I went into Macedonia, stay there in Ephesus so that you may command certain men not to teach false doctrines any longer*
One of the chief tenets of post-modernism is that there is no such thing as objective truth, let alone universal and eternal truth. On the contrary, everybody has his or her own truth. You have yours, and I have mine, and they may diverge widely from each other, even contradict each other. In consequence, the most prized virtue is tolerance. It tolerates everything except the intolerance of those who insist that certain ideas are true and others are false, while certain practices are good and others are evil. No follower of Jesus Christ can possibly embrace this complete subjectivism. For he said that he was the truth, that he had come to bear witness to the truth, that the Holy Spirit is the Spirit of truth, and that the truth will set us free. So truth matters, the truth which God has revealed through Christ and by the Spirit.

Stott, p. 42

Taken from *The Bible Speaks Today* Series edited by J. Alec Motyer; John Stott. Copyright ©1983 edited by J. Alec Motyer; John Stott. Used by permission of InterVarsity Press, P.O. Box 1400, Downers Grove, IL 60515, USA. www.ivpress.com
Taken from The Message of *1 Timothy & Titus* by John Stott. Copyright (c) 2001 by John Stott. Used by permission of InterVarsity Press, P.O. Box 1400, Downers Grove, IL 60515, USA. www.ivpress.com

"I have seen gross intolerance shown in support of tolerance."
Samuel Taylor Coleridge (1772–1834)   Quoted in Ward and Wild

1 Tim 1:14: *The grace of our Lord was poured out on me abundantly, along with the faith and love that are in Christ Jesus.*
Grace overflowed like a river in spate, which cannot be contained but bursts its banks and carries everything before it, sweeping irresistibly on. What the river of grace brought with it, however, was not devastation, but blessing, in particular the 'faith' and the 'love' to which Paul has already assigned a primacy. The Nile overflows, the crops abound. Grace overflowed, and faith and love sprang up. Grace flooded with faith a heart previously filled with unbelief, and flooded with love a heart previously polluted with hatred. Stott, p. 52

Taken from The Message of *1 Timothy & Titus* by John Stott. Copyright (c) 2001 by John Stott. Used by permission of InterVarsity Press, P.O. Box 1400, Downers Grove, IL 60515, USA. www.ivpress.com

Personal Note: Pastor Joshua Knott of EPC Newark (Delaware) presented a moving message about this passage. Paul is awestruck at this flood of grace: "Can you believe that God chose *me* to serve him?" It's a question we all should ask. There is a God who loves us and calls our name. Before the foundation of the world, he looked down and said "I'm going to save *that one*" (Eph 1:4). The Lord knew every mis-step we would take (Ps 139:16) and yet in spite of this intimate knowledge of who we really are, he chose us for his service! Are we awestruck? Have we ever experienced this flood of grace? When we begin to see the boundaries of our sin, Jesus comes in and fills every nook and cranny with his grace. And he who calls is he who strengthens us for that call (v 12). Where do we find this flood of grace? It's right here in our Bible. Let God tell you what is wrong with your life (Ps 139:24). Experience the inrush of grace at firehose strength each day as you surrender to God's Word. And at the end of our wayward zig-zags through life, and after many dismal failures, Jesus stands to welcome us to his eternal kingdom (2 Pt 1:11). What an extraordinary, mind-boggling concept is this amazing grace that saved a wretch like Paul (1:16) and like me!

1 Tim 1:16: *But for that very reason I was shown mercy so that in me, the worst of sinners, Christ Jesus might display his unlimited patience as an example for those who would believe on him and receive eternal life.*

Are we to understand Paul literally? Common sense tells us not to take his statement as a precise, scientific fact. For he had not investigated the sinful and criminal records of all the inhabitants of the world, carefully compared himself to them, and concluded that he was worse than them all. The truth is rather that when we are convicted of sin by the Holy Spirit, an immediate result is that we give up such comparisons. Paul was so vividly aware of his own sins that he could not conceive that anybody could be worse. It is the language of every sinner whose conscience [1:5, 1:19, 3:9] has been awakened and disturbed by the Holy Spirit....Paul seems to speak to us across the centuries: 'Don't despair. Christ had mercy even on me, the worst of sinners; he can also have mercy on you!' Stott, p. 53, 55

Taken from The Message of *1 Timothy & Titus* by John Stott. Copyright (c) 2001 by John Stott. Used by permission of InterVarsity Press, P.O. Box 1400, Downers Grove, IL 60515, USA. www.ivpress.com

"Although my memory's fading, I remember two things very clearly: I am a great sinner and Christ is a great Savior."   John Newton (1725–1807)

1 Tim 2:5–6: *For there is one God and one mediator between God and men, the man Christ Jesus, who gave himself as a ransom for all men*

The juxtaposition of words in the Greek sentence is striking. An intermediary must be able to represent both sides equally. Christ is both God and man, and therefore able to mediate between us. He is God from the beginning [Jn 1:1], deriving his divine being from his Father eternally [Col 1:19], and he became human in the womb of his mother Mary, deriving his human being from her in time [cf Jn 14:20]. Here, then, is the double uniqueness of Jesus Christ, which qualifies him to be the only mediator. First, there is the uniqueness of his divine-human person, and secondly the uniqueness of his substitutionary, redeeming death. The one mediator is the man Jesus Christ who gave himself as a ransom. We must keep these three nouns together, the man, the ransom, and the mediator....There is no other. No-one else possesses, or has ever possessed, the necessary qualifications to mediate between God and sinners [cf Gal 3:19–20, Heb 4:15, 7:25].
Stott, p.69, 71

Taken from The Message of *1 Timothy & Titus* by John Stott. Copyright (c) 2001 by John Stott. Used by permission of InterVarsity Press, P.O. Box 1400, Downers Grove, IL 60515, USA. www.ivpress.com

1 Tim 4:4: *For everything God created is good, and nothing is to be rejected if it is received with thanksgiving*
Personal Note: Here the Apostle declares that happiness and even fun are OK! The Christian should overflow with joy, but all too many believers have a dour Puritanical demeanor, so preoccupied with exposing the sin of others that we ruin the joy not only of others, but also of ourselves. These modern-day Pharisees [cf Lk 5:30–32] embody curmudgeon H.L. Mencken's definition of Puritanism: "The haunting fear that someone, somewhere may be happy." But the Lord has blessed us with things that should make us sing, and our song should be a hymn of praise, not a dirge. Christ came to give us abundant lives both in eternity (Isa 35:10, Rev 21:4) and here and now (John 10:10).

1 Tim 6:11–12: *But you, man of God, flee from all this, and pursue righteousness, godliness, faith, love, endurance and gentleness. Fight the good fight of the faith. Take hold of the eternal life to which you were called when you made your good confession in the presence of many witnesses.*
Generally speaking, the Bible offers two kinds of instruction: principles and precepts. Principles are nonspecific and require wisdom to apply. The Lord gives us principles to prepare us for the ever-changing landscape of culture and a variety of circumstances. Principles equip us to behave wisely in a broad spectrum of situations. Precepts, on the other hand, are very specific and require little if any thinking to apply. God expects us to obey precepts, no questions asked. ... Throughout this section, Paul gave Timothy several principles to apply concerning authority, false teachers, and contentment. Then, suddenly, his tone changed. He aimed his pen directly at Timothy and fired off several precepts. The Greek verbs change from the more common indicative mood to the less common imperative mood.
While Paul issued these precepts specifically for Timothy, the Holy Spirit intended them for all believers in all circumstances and especially for all ministers of the gospel. Whatever your circumstance, wherever you serve in God's kingdom, read the passage again slowly. Only this time, imagine your shoulders gripped by Paul's battle scarred hands—gnarled from beatings and hardened by weather. Imagine his eyes, flashing with keen intellect yet softened by suffering, staring intently into yours. These commands—these precepts—are for you and me.
Swindoll, p. 141

2 Timothy

Commentary:
- *The Message of 2 Timothy*, by John Stott (1973)

2 Tim 1:9–10: *This grace was given us in Christ Jesus before the beginning of time, but it has now been revealed through the appearing of our Savior, Christ Jesus, who has destroyed death and has brought life and immortality to light through the gospel.*

To appreciate the full force of this Christian affirmation, we need to call to mind who it is who is making it. Any day now he expects to receive the death sentence. Already he can see in his imagination the flash of the executioner's sword. And yet, in the very presence of death, he can shout aloud: 'Christ has abolished death'. This is Christian faith triumphant! It is not truly wonderful that, although Paul's body is confined within the narrow limits of an underground cell, his heart and mind can thus soar into eternity?
Stott, p. 39.

2 Tim 3:16–17: *All Scripture is God-breathed and is useful for teaching, rebuking, correcting and training in righteousness, so that the man of God may be thoroughly equipped for every good work.*

The single Greek word (θεόπνευστος *theopneustos*) would be literally translated 'God-breathed' (so NIV) and indicates not that Scripture itself or its human authors were breathed into by God, but that Scripture was breathed out by God. 'Inspiration' is doubtless a convenient term to use, but 'spiration' or even 'expiration' would convey the meaning of the Greek adjective more accurately. It originated in God's mind and was communicated from God's mouth by God's breath or Spirit. It is therefore rightly termed 'the Word of God', for God spoke it. ... The Bible is essentially a handbook of salvation. Its over-arching purpose is to teach not the facts of science (eg, the nature of moon rock) which men can discover by their own empirical investigation, but facts of salvation, which no space exploration can discover but only God can reveal.   Stott, p. 101, 102

"Apply yourself wholly to the scriptures, and apply the scriptures wholly to yourself."
Johannes Albrecht Bengel (1687–1752)   Quoted in Ward and Wild

The Bible in a Nutshell

Personal Note, November 2007

In November, 2007, I conclude my latest journey through the Bible with Paul's letter to the Romans. What an enriching experience this has been! The Scriptures in their entirety tell an awesome story, a story with divine direction and purpose. From the initial chapters of Genesis where God created the heavens and the earth to the final chapters where He creates the new heavens and the new earth, his purpose has been to bless his people both here and now through His Indwelling Spirit and ultimately as our hopes are fulfilled at the final consummation when every tear will be wiped away. In his sovereign grace, he elected Abraham[1] to be a vehicle of blessing to the whole earth. He redeemed the people of Israel out of the hands of their slave-masters[2], brought them through the wilderness of their own sin[3], gave them the direction of his law[4], and brought them into the promised land flowing with milk and honey[5]. He stuck with them through the dark period of the Judges and anointed a king who gave them peace and rest on all sides[6]. He revealed his divine wisdom in the Psalms and Proverbs[7] and reaffirmed his covenants through the Prophets. If the people would but listen[8], they would partake in a rich feast[9]. Joy would overtake them as they traveled the highway to his glorious holy city[10].

Then, at the hinge of history, God so loved the world that He gave his only Son that whosoever believed in him would have everlasting life[11] and boundless bliss in spite of rebellion and sin[12]. Christ's ministry began in a humble stable[13] and culminated in exaltation to the highest place[14]. He and his holy apostles preached a new kind of love[15], one which springs from a heart enriched by the Holy Spirit[16].

Christ was there from the beginning[17]. Through his death and resurrection, he reconciled us to the Father[18], gave us his indwelling spirit[19], prepared a secure place for us[20] sealed by the Holy Spirit[21], seated us in the heavenly realms[22], and will one day say with great finality "It is done!"[23]. What better way to give thanks for his glorious grace than to reaffirm that great hymn:

Beautiful Savior! Lord of all the nations!
Son of God and Son of Man!
Glory and honor, praise, adoration,
Now and forevermore be thine!

from *Fairest Lord Jesus* Text: Munster Gesangbuch; trans. by Joseph August Seiss

---

[1] Gen 12:3 [2] Ex 3:8 [3] Jer 2:6, Numbers [4] Ex 20, Deut 5
[5] Deut 31:20, Josh 5:12 [6] 2 Sam 7:1, 1K 4:20, 25 [7] Ps 119:105, Prov 3:5–6
[8] Isa 55:2 [9] Isa 25:6–8, 55:1–3 [10] Isa 35:8–10

[11] John 3:16 [12] Rom 3:10, 3:23 [13] Luke 2:7 [14] Phil 2:6–11
[15] Mt 5:44–48, 1 Cor 13, Eph 3:18, Col 3:14, 1 Pet 4:8, 1 John 4:7–11 [16] Gal 5:22–23
[17] John 1:1–14, Col 1:15–20 [18] Rom 5:1–3 [19] John 20:22, Mt 28:20
[20] John 14:2, Rom 8:38–39, 1 Pet 1:3–4 [21] Eph 1:13–14 [22] Eph 2:6
[23] Rev 21:6

2 Tim 4:6–8: *For I am already being poured out like a drink offering, and the time has come for my departure. I have fought the good fight, I have finished the race, I have kept the faith.*

Already the anchor is weighed, the ropes are slipped, and the boat is about to set sail for another shore. Now, before the great adventure of his new voyage begins, he looks back over his ministry of about 30 years. The

work of the apostle, and to a lesser extent of every gospel preacher and teacher, is pictured as fighting a fight [Col 4:12], running a race [Heb 12:1], guarding a treasure [Job 23:12, Mt 13:44]. Each involves labor, sacrifice and even danger. In all three Paul has been faithful to the end. Now nothing remains for him but the prize [cf Acts 20:24, Phil 3:14]. ... Our God is the God of History. God is working his purpose out as year succeeds year. He buries his workmen but carries on his work. The torch of the gospel is handed down by each generation to the next. As the leaders of the former generation die, it is all the more urgent for those of the next generation to step forward bravely to take their place.
Stott, excerpts from pages 113, 114, 115, 116

2 Tim 4:18: *To him be glory for ever and ever. Amen.*
2 Tim 4:22: *The Lord be with your spirit. Grace be with you.*
It would be difficult to find a better summary than these two sentences of the Apostle's life and ambition. First he received grace from Christ. Then he returned glory to Christ. 'From him, grace; to him, glory.' In all our Christian life and service we should desire no other philosophy than this.

Stott, p. 127

Lord, be thy word my rule, in it I may rejoice;
Thy glory be my aim, thy holy will my choice.
Thy promises my hope, thy providence my guard
Thine arm my strong support, thyself my great reward.

Christopher Wordsworth (1807–1885)

Titus

Commentaries:
- *The Message of 1 Timothy and Titus*, by John Stott (BST Series) (1996)
- *Cornerstone Biblical Commentary*, Vol 17, by Jon C. Laansma (2009)
- *The Preacher's Commentary*, NT Vol. 32, by Gary W. Demarest (1984)

Titus 1:1-3: *Paul, a servant of God and an apostle of Jesus Christ for the faith of God's elect and the knowledge of the truth that leads to godliness-a faith and knowledge resting on the hope of eternal life, which God, who does not lie, promised before the beginning of time, and at his appointed season he brought his word to light through the preaching entrusted to me*

This letter to Paul's coworker Titus–brief, blunt, and thick with teaching and exhortation–opens with a richly packed greeting, teased out to a much greater degree than those in the letters to Timothy and infused with the teaching to come. As we read the letter through, we should picture an apostle energetically executing his mission of founding churches sometime following his release from the Roman imprisonment of Acts 28 and prior to his later arrest and imprisonment in Rome, where we find him writing 2 Timothy. Though Paul may have sensed that he was in the final phase of his life's work–that perspective emerges more clearly in the letters to Timothy with which this one generally coincides–there is no particular air of emergency in this letter beyond what we see in Paul's earlier letters. . . . The voice we hear in this letter emanates from an apostle on the go, driving ahead with the mission, remaining thoroughly in touch with the world of his churches as with the truth he preached, and balancing equally the desires to move ahead and sustain what was behind, both to plant and to nurture.

The message in relation to the false teachers is clear and uncompromising. They were upstarts, charlatans, pretenders. Paul's implicit argument is no mere trumping of reason with authority, but it does operate with a belief that, in what we like to call the "marketplace of ideas," not all ideas are of equal weight, and their weight is ultimately a matter of their source. The Good News is ultimately reason itself, but in the fog of half-truths and human perspectives, it is necessary to assert that here the transcendent God has spoken, precisely through the true apostles of Jesus Christ. Here is truth.Laansma, Jon C., *Cornerstone Biblical Commentary*, Vol 17, Carol Stream, IL: Tyndale, 2009, excerpts, pp. 222,223, 225

Titus 2:10: *so that in every way they will make the teaching about God our Savior attractive.*
Christian doctrine is salvation doctrine, a jewel called 'the teaching about God our Savior.' So either we give no evidence of salvation (1:16) in which case the gospel-jewel is tarnished, or we give good evidence of salvation by living a manifestly saved life, in which case the gospel-jewel shines with extra luster. Our lives can bring either adornment or discredit to the gospel. Stott, p. 191
Stott, John R.W., *The Message of 1 Timothy and Titus,* Taken from *The Bible Speaks Today* Series edited by J. Alec Motyer; John Stott. Copyright ©1996 edited by J. Alec Motyer; John Stott. Used by permission of InterVarsity Press, P.O. Box 1400, Downers Grove, IL 60515, USA. www.ivpress.com

Titus 2:12: *It teaches us to say "No" to ungodliness and worldly passions, and to live self-controlled, upright and godly lives in this present age*
Grace disciplines us to renounce our old life and to live a new one, to turn from ungodliness, from self-centeredness to self-control, from the world's devious ways to fair dealing with each other. It is not only that grace makes good works possible, but that grace makes them necessary (challenging us to live accordingly). He who appeared briefly on the stage of history, and disappeared, will one day reappear. He appeared in grace, he will one day reappear in glory [cf comment on Mk 8:24]. Thus the apostle, in this short paragraph of only four verses, brings together the two termini of the Christian era, that is, the first and second comings of Christ. He bids us look back to the one and on to the other. For we live 'in between times' suspended rather uncomfortably between the 'already' and the 'not yet.'

The best way to live now is to learn to do spiritually what is impossible physically—namely to look in opposite directions at the same time. We need both to look back and remember the epiphany of grace [v 11] and also to look forward and anticipate the epiphany of glory [v 13].   Stott, p. 193–196

Stott, John R.W., *The Message of 1 Timothy and Titus,* Taken from *The Bible Speaks Today* Series edited by J. Alec Motyer; John Stott. Copyright ©1996 edited by J. Alec Motyer; John Stott. Used by permission of InterVarsity Press, P.O. Box 1400, Downers Grove, IL 60515, USA. www.ivpress.com

Personal Note: Pastor John Batusic of Chestnut Mountain Presbyterian Church in Georgia preached on Titus 2:11–14 in August 2015. He emphasized what the passage teaches about grace:

- Grace: The soil in which we are saved and in which we grow as Christians
- The Grace-Full Church: a church full of people who are full of saving grace
- The Grace-Fueled Church: a church fueled by grace to become like Jesus
- Grace-Fooled: Fooled by misunderstandings of grace which substitutes license for grace.
- Grace blasts away the darkness

Titus 2:13–14: *while we wait for the blessed hope—the glorious appearing of our great God and Savior, Jesus Christ, who gave himself for us to redeem us from all wickedness and to purify for himself a people that are his very own, eager to do what is good.*

While our faith both lends itself to and requires doctrinal formulation, we must never lose sight of the fact that Christianity is Jesus Himself. It is a person, not a set of ideas. God didn't drop a scroll of theology out of heaven; He came Himself! His coming is His grace that brings us salvation. Out of the profound mystery of the incarnation has come the teaching about what we know about the meaning of life. In a day when so many messages are being beamed at us, purporting to tell us how to find the good life, this one may appear to be deceptively simple. ... The third great theme of this doctrinal statement is 'hope.' We move from the Incarnation, through the style of our lives, to the hope that keeps us going. The doctrine of Christ's return is vital to our staying power in the tough issues of Christian obedience and discipleship. ... I hope you agree with me that this chapter in Titus is a beautiful summary of everything in the Pastoral Epistles. How it whets our appetite for active goodness in all of the stages and relationships of our lives—goodness grounded in grace and redemption that is in Jesus Himself—our great God and Savior. Demarest, excerpts, pp 329, 330

Titus 3:3: *At one time we too were foolish, disobedient, deceived and enslaved by all kinds of passions and pleasures. We lived in malice and envy, being hated and hating one another.*
Ultimately every honest heart will breath a sigh of deep relief when the lies of our claims to merit are unmasked for what they are. Knowing that God saved us purely because of his mercy puts us on granite footing. There is no more self-deception, no more need of pretense, no longer any cause for despair and doubt. God, who was never fooled by our masquerades, has done it because he wanted to, simply because of his mercy, and he doesn't change. It's all over but the worshipful shouting. ... Plainly salvation here is more than the flat concept of a spiritual, legal grant waiting to be cashed in at the time of the final judgment. It is already in the present unfolding of the new creation. Laansma, pp. 287, 288

Personal Note: Pastor Ben Phillips of Chestnut Mountain Presbyterian in Georgia commented that verse 3 is our "resume before God." In spite of such a bad resume, he nevertheless elects us into his family. What a wonder that "He should give his only Son to make a wretch his treasure" as the song says! We would not vote for a candidate with a resume like verse 3, yet we are elected in spite of it. (June 21, 2015)

Philemon

Commentaries:
- *The Preacher's Commentary,* NT Vol. 31, by Maxie D. Dunnam (1982)
- *The Message of Colossians and Philemon*, by R.C. Lucas (1980)

Phm 9: *yet I appeal to you on the basis of love. I then, as Paul—an old man and now also a prisoner of Christ Jesus— I appeal to you for my son Onesimus, who became my son while I was in chains.*
Paul now makes his plea for Onesimus. His words are artful, tender, sensitive, brilliant, understanding, convincing. There is a balance of conviction and compassion—conviction about the worth of Onesimus, a slave become a Christian; and tender compassion for Philemon, and the dilemma of a slave-master become a Christian. The power of the gospel shines through with a rare brilliance. The markings, faint and obvious, of the redeeming love of Christ transforming persons, relationships and circumstances, can be noted throughout the letter. Rehearse the story. Philemon, a wealthy man of Colossae, hears Paul, probably on one of his business trips to Ephesus. Captured by the message, he eventually becomes a Christian, along with his son and wife. He emerges as a leader in the church that grows up in Colossae and his house becomes one of the meeting places for this new Christian community.   Dunnam, p. 404

Phm 14: *But I did not want to do anything without your consent, so that any favor you do will be spontaneous and not forced.*
On examining the text, we are immediately impressed by the tact and care with which it has been composed. Evidently Paul felt the delicate nature of his task. Yet there is nothing 'sticky' or awkward about it. In fact, having gently prepared the way, Paul is extraordinarily bold in his request. It is no

grudging forgiveness that is asked for, but that Onesimus should be given a royal welcome, such as might be expected if the apostle were the one arriving. ... Once we grasp something of the miraculous transformation of human affairs brought about by the gospel in these young churches of the New Testament, we are better able to appreciate the patterns and priorities of apostolic involvement in society's problems. What was being achieved everywhere was the establishment of little oases where an alternative way of life was being practiced and could be observed. This powerful leaven must do its work. Yet it is absurd to speak as though eighteen long centuries must elapse before the leaven did its predestined work through Wilberforce's triumph. In Paul's time a new day was already dawning for slaves in a multitude of households as the Word of God advanced in its triumphant progress. The narrowness of Paul's aim becomes of fascinating significance. A burning appeal to an unknown house-church in Phrygia is his way to begin to change the world! It is decidedly less impressive than a grand pronouncement of an ideal to a wider audience. But long after such rhetoric would be forgotten, the influence of a letter like this would spread from life to life and from group to group, in the Lycus valley, and wherever its inhabitants journeyed. Lucas, p. 186, 188, 189

Hebrews

Commentaries:
- *The Message of Hebrews*, by Raymond Brown (1982)
- *The Preacher's Commentary*, NT Vol 33, by Louis H. Evans (1985)
- *Hebrews*, by Donald A. Hagner (1990)

Heb 1:2–4: *but in these last days he has spoken to us by his Son, whom he appointed heir of all things, and through whom he made the universe. The Son is the radiance of God's glory and the exact representation of his being, sustaining all things by his powerful word. After he had provided purification for sins, he sat down at the right hand of the Majesty in heaven.*

Without him the Old Testament revelation is partial, fragmentary, preparatory, and incomplete. God spoke at different times, by different means. But in Christ, he spoke fully, decisively, finally, and perfectly.
Brown, p. 28, 32

The Son is set forth as the embodiment of the three main offices of the OT: prophet (speaking for God); priest (accomplishing forgiveness of sins); and king (reigning with God at his right hand). But he is even more than this marvelous combination of traits can express. He is the one through whom and for whom everything exists that has been created, the one who sustains the universe, and who is the very expression of God's glory and essence. He is the one with whom not even the angels can compare. The person of Christ is the key to understanding this epistle.
Hagner, excerpts, pp. 22–27

Heb 4:12: *For the word of God is living and active. Sharper than any double-edged sword, it penetrates even to dividing soul and spirit, joints and marrow; it judges the thoughts and attitudes of the heart.*

The word not only lives [Isa 40:8], it works. It is an effective as well as a perpetually relevant word [Ps 119:89]. Its activity is such that it cannot return void, it must accomplish its sovereign purposes (Isa 55:11). The word is energetic. It is like a sharp sword cutting its way through this substance or that without any difficulty. This sword of the word (Isa 49:2, Eph 6:17, Rev 1:16, 2:12) can penetrate deeply into the human heart and mind [1 Cor 4:5]. It can scrutinize the unspoken thoughts and hidden conceptions of the heart of man [Ps 139:4]. It can reach deep down where, because of earth's bewildering and preoccupying noises [Mt 13:22], no other voice can easily be heard [somewhat like a "bunker busting" bomb]. Brown, p. 92

Heb 6:1: *Therefore let us leave the elementary teachings about Christ and go on to maturity*
Endeavor, practice, sweat, agony of perseverance, and experience through involvement are the components that make for maturity, and he sees little or none of these [5:11–14]. They are yet where they began—at the starting gate, still in the blocks at the starting line while others are well into the race; babies needing to be suckled by a wet-nurse. Such a condition is unacceptable to him; he is stirred, agitated, angry and concerned. The exhortation is clear: go on to maturity! ... There is no room for either languid lolling nor individualism that denies the body (the church) and its interdependent functions. The world is out there, hurting, blind, ignorant, oppressed, imprisoned, sick, alienated, in spiritual darkness, and without God or hope. Our author exhorts, 'Get on with it; grow to your ministry potential; touch that world with the redeeming love of Jesus Christ in every facet of its agonizing need!' Evans, excerpts, pp 127, 130

Heb 7:25: *Therefore he is able to save completely those who come to God through him, because he always lives to intercede for them.*
The name of Jesus gives my prayers royal access. They get through. Jesus isn't just the Savior of my soul. He's also the Savior of my prayers. My prayers come before the throne of God as the prayers of Jesus. "Asking in Jesus' name" isn't another thing I have to get right so my prayers are perfect. It is one more gift of God because my prayers are so imperfect. Paul Miller, *A Praying Life: Connecting with God in a Distracting World*

"If I could hear Christ praying for me in the next room, I would not fear a million enemies. Yet distance makes no difference. He is praying for me."   [Rom 8:34, Job 16:19–21 Isa 53:12]
Robert Murray M'Cheyne (1813–1843)   Quoted in Ward and Wild

Heb 8:1–2: *We do have such a high priest, who sat down at the right hand of the throne of the Majesty in heaven, and who serves in the sanctuary, the true tabernacle set up by the Lord, not by man.*
The ascension idea recurs throughout this letter [1:3, 8:1, 10:12, 12:2] like the main theme of a great symphony; variations are introduced, but only to give further expression to the rich cadences and majestic tones of the most memorable music ever heard. Here is a clear word to any Christian in despondency or despair. We may feel crushed, dejected, bewildered, broken [2 Cor 4:8–9], but our eternal salvation has never depended on our vacillating moods or changing circumstances. Christ has entered the heavenly sanctuary; 'once for all' he offered his blood for us. There he has appeared for us and now he is praying for us. We are ever remembered at the throne and our names are enrolled in heaven [Luke 10:20, Phil 4:3, Heb 12:22, Rev 21:27]. This is our confidence. Our faith is grounded not on what we have done but ever and always in what he is, God's perfect Son, and what he has done through his perfect, eternal sacrifice.   Brown, p. 142, 146

Heb 11:1 *Now faith is being sure of what we hope for and certain of what we do not see.*
<u>**Personal Note**</u>: Pastor John Wood of Cedar Springs Church in Knoxville Tennessee once preached on Heb 11:1, eloquently showing how faith is usually the beginning point to knowledge. He illustrated this with a hypothetical example of a young man standing outside a college Physics classroom. He buttonholes the professor and says "Prove to me that force equals mass times acceleration! Prove to me that gravitational forces are inversely proportional to the square of the distance! Prove to me that quarks exist (I can't see them with a microscope)! If you cannot prove these to me here and now, forget it—I'm not coming into your classroom." The professor would rightly brush aside this brash young man. He may offer him some advice that would go something like this. "Physics is a complicated subject. Before you can question it, you must learn the basics.

You have to suspend your disbelief for a time and accept some of the things I teach on faith. After you have learned the basics, you will be progressively equipped to challenge my teaching. But you don't have the knowledge to do so here in this hallway."

Many outside the Christian faith are like this young student. They insist on proofs before they are willing to even consider whether the Bible might be telling the truth. Like Physics, the Bible is complex. It is an intricate book which has been studied by scholars and theologians over the centuries and still contains surprises and new insights. Surely it is worthy of at least a cursory examination before it is to be declared irrelevant.

"Anybody who has been seriously engaged in scientific work of any kind realizes that over the entrance to the gates of the temple of science are written the words: 'Ye must have faith.'"
Max Planck (1858–1947)   German Scientist and Nobel Prize Winner

Excursus: Engineer's Perspective on Scripture
Personal Note, May 2009

I have been a chemical engineer for over thirty years, so I often look at things from a technical perspective. For about twenty years, I worked in a manufacturing plant that did Emulsion Polymerization, where water is combined with an organic monomer layer and a surfactant or "soap" to emulsify the mixture into a single phase. A polymerization reaction converts the liquid raw materials into a milky emulsion of plastic particles in water. These emulsion polymers are used in a wide variety of consumer applications including water-based paints, paper coatings, and textile binders.

Over the years, I have designed systems to analyze millions of data records from factory floor instruments such as temperature probes, flow meters, and vessel load cells. I also have interacted extensively with pH D scientists who specialized in emulsion polymerization. With all this data, and with all these brilliant scientific minds, many problems proved to be intractable. As I consulted the scientists, I discovered that the laboratory often bounded their knowledge. They could make excellent predictions and conclusions in a controlled laboratory environment, but when the process was scaled up to production, new factors intruded into the process. By controlling confounding factors in the lab, the scientists could explain nearly everything. But in the rough and tumble "real" world of production when many factors such as raw material quality, heat transfer, agitation, and instrument precision impacted in combinations that were too numerous to predict, the scientists had reached their limits.

As I reflect on the limits of science and human reason in my experience as an engineer, I realize that if I can't even understand things in the limited, controlled, and minutely observed production environment described above, I wonder whether we may be missing something in our observations of more complex issues such as evolution, psychology, and the origins of the universe. I begin to see the wisdom of the 17th century mathematician Blaise Pascal's statement that "Reason's last step is the recognition that there are an infinite number of things which are beyond it. It is merely feeble if it does not go as far as to realize that."

A British columnist named Gerard Baker recently wrote: "the biggest difference between Americans and Europeans is religion: ignorant Americans cling to faith; enlightened Europeans long ago embraced the liberating power of reason." My experience as an engineer has shown that the power of reason may not be as liberating as Mr. Baker suggests. It may put blinders on our eyes and may limit our peripheral vision. We are so focused on what we can plainly see that we miss the worlds beyond.

As much as I respect and admire science (after all, it puts bread on my table!), I have seen its limits "up close and personal." Human reason only goes so far, and yet some have put reason and science on a pedestal it does not deserve and has not earned. There is something more—a divine dimension which I cannot see, taste, touch, or measure, but which is nevertheless just as real as the computer in front of me. I urge others of a scientific and technical bent to get past their perhaps dogmatic insistence in the supremacy of science and reason and open up to the wonder of the "other world" revealed in the pages of Scripture.

Charles Swindoll states it well in his commentary on the gospel of Mark:

> God has much to teach us, but we often miss precious truths because we are preoccupied, or we live in denial, or we're simply not open to receiving what He has to show us. I'm not referring to knowledge, however. There's a difference between being educated—having knowledge—and being wise. I have known some well-educated fools. They're smart, but they're not wise. Conversely, many godly people have little or no academic training, but they're brimming with wisdom. The difference between these two types has almost nothing to do with coursework or degrees; the difference is their relationship with God. He is full of wisdom, and His plan is marked by wisdom. His desire is to help us rise above mere intelligence to appreciate a realm that is deeper and more profound than we're able to comprehend on our own.
> Quoted from Charles Swindoll, *Insights for Living*, Vol 2, Tyndale House, 2016.

Heb: 11:16: *Instead, they were longing for a better country-a heavenly one. Therefore God is not ashamed to be called their God, for he has prepared a city for them.*
They did not merely anticipate heaven, they evaluated the things of earth. Looking at the things that were 'seen', they quickly discerned that all the marks of transience, impermanence and perishability were upon them. They looked away from such material gains to something which was 'better,' the heavenly home of the people of God. Once again, the key word 'better' has made a dramatic appearance in the letter [eg, 1:4, 7:19, 7:22, 8:6, 9:23, 10:34]. The man or woman of faith has the ability to distinguish [Prov 1:1–2] between good and evil [Rom 12:21], eternal and temporal [2 Cor 4:18], permanent and perishable [1 Pet 1:23]. Brown, p. 207

"Paradise is our native country, and we in this world be as exiles and strangers."
Richard Greenham (1535–1594)   Quoted in Ward and Wild

Heb 12:1: *Therefore, since we are surrounded by such a great cloud of witnesses, let us throw off everything that hinders and the sin that so easily entangles, and let us run with perseverance the race marked out for us.*
The setting is a great stadium of spiritual athletics. The stands are filled with the great athletes of the past who have run their races and completed their events and are now eager to encourage the new contestants. Notice, they are alive, aware, and present. The picture is of an active, watching throng shouting encouragement to those now struggling in their own events. … Our writer encourages those who read his exhortation to 'lay aside every weight.' For spiritual athletes that can be the case of too many irons in the fire, too many dissipating interests, too many branches of good things that suck the energy from the very best. … In order to win, every ounce of human and divine energy must be directed to the race.   Evans, pp 210–211

Heb 12:11 *No discipline seems pleasant at the time, but painful. Later on, however, it produces a harvest of righteousness and peace for those who have been trained by it.*
At the time, all discipline is painful. The believer, however, does not think solely of his present reaction, but considers its ultimate usefulness. It all takes time. Fruit does not appear immediately after the tree is planted. If life's adversities, and God's use of them in discipline, produce in the end both inward peace and moral uprightness, we cannot possibly have suffered in vain [cf Ps 119:71, Prov 3:11–12, Job 5:17, Jer 31:18].   Brown, p. 235

"Discipline puts back in its place that something in us which should serve but wants to rule."
Carthusian Monks (anonymous)   Quoted in Ward and Wild

James

Commentaries:
- *Living Insights*, Vol 13, by Charles Swindoll (2014)
- *The Message of James*, by J. Alec Motyer (1985)
- *James*, by Peter H. Davids (1989)
- *The Preacher's Commentary*, NT Vol 34, by Paul A. Cedar (1984)

James 1:5: *If any of you lacks wisdom, he should ask God, who gives generously to all without finding fault, and it will be given to him.*
What better gift could they request than the wisdom needed to withstand the trials they face. God gives it, for God is a good giver; God gives generously, which means that he gives without mental reservations, that he gives simply, with a single heart. He is not looking for some hidden return from believers; he does not have mixed motives or grudging feelings. In fact, he gives not just generously but without finding fault. That is, he does not complain about the gift or the cost. ... No, God gives true gifts, no complaining, no criticizing. (What? You need help *again*?), no mixed motives, no reluctance. Free, generous, even spendthrift giving characterizes the Christian's God. Davids, p. 29

James 1:18: *He chose to give us birth through the word of truth, that we might be a kind of firstfruits of all he created.*
Just as God said 'Let there be light' (Gen 1:3), so also he said 'Let there be life', thus bringing us to the new birth [2 Cor 4:6]. Turning to 1 Pet 1:23, we read that 'you have been born anew through the living and abiding word of God.' Peter thus matches what James says: the word is the agent in the new birth. The father uses the powerful word of the gospel in two ways: first, he speaks it, inwardly, to our dead souls, imparting life, bringing us to new birth; secondly, he presents the same word of truth to

us in the preached gospel, to which the new life within makes a personal and believing response. This is one of the most glorious truths of the whole Bible [cf Jn 5:21]. Motyer, p. 59

Motyer, J. Alec, *The Message of James*, Taken from *The Bible Speaks Today* Series edited by J. Alec Motyer; John Stott. Copyright ©1983 edited by J. Alec Motyer; John Stott. Used by permission of InterVarsity Press, P.O. Box 1400, Downers Grove, IL 60515, USA. www.ivpress.com Taken from *The Message of James* by J. Alec Motyer. Copyright (c) 1985 by J. Alec Motyer. Used by permission of InterVarsity Press, P.O. Box 1400, Downers Grove, IL 60515, USA. www.ivpress.com

James 1:19: *This you know, my beloved brethren. But everyone must be quick to hear, slow to speak and slow to anger* [NASB]
One of the most marvelous characteristics of God is that He listens to us. He is available at all times to hear our prayers, to listen to our concerns and even to be touched with the nonverbal communications of our feelings. God does not keep office hours, nor does He require appointments. He hears us (Ps 66:16–20). ... Jesus traveled the same roads and village streets as His contemporaries. Yet He heard and saw needs which no one seemed to notice. His authentic love for people motivated Him to listen not only to words but to nonverbal communication. He was constantly meeting people at a point of need, whether it was the Samaritan woman at the well or Zaccheaeus who was up a tree. He listened. ... And so our Lord invites us to the ministry of listening. Most of us would be amazed at how much more effective we would be in our witnessing if we stopped talking and began to listen. The more effective means of ministry, for example, is responding to need, not dumping our load. Cedar, p. 42

James 3:2: *We all stumble in many ways. If anyone is never at fault in what he says, he is a perfect man, able to keep his whole body in check.*
Sin remains our universal experience and it takes all sorts of forms. Among them, as every self-aware believer will admit, sins of speech are prominent – the hasty word, the untruthful statement, the sly suggestion, harmful gossip, innuendo, impurity. Control of the tongue leads to a master-control of ourselves and our lives [Judg 11:34, Ps 141:3, Prov 13:3, Eph 4:29].
We ask ourselves how we are to control the powerful forces within us that drive us into sin, and James replies by talking about something we never considered—do we control our tongues? Are we the masters of the

master-key? Circumstances vary. There are the pressures of adversity and the (often greater) pressures of prosperity; there are sudden and unexpected shocks—the blows which life administers to us. Can we hold our course? James' marine illustration (3:4) is not all wide of the mark as a description of life with its tides, currents, and storms. Once again, there is a rudder to hold the ship on course, and the tongue is that rudder. ... Would not this be a marvelous display of the glory of the Lord Jesus Christ in our lives if our tongues were as his: 'No man ever spoke like this man!' (John 7:46) Motyer, p. 120, 125

Motyer, J. Alec, *The Message of James*, Taken from *The Bible Speaks Today* Series edited by J. Alec Motyer; John Stott. Copyright ©1985 edited by J. Alec Motyer; John Stott. Used by permission of InterVarsity Press, P.O. Box 1400, Downers Grove, IL 60515, USA. www.ivpress.com

James 3:17: *But the wisdom that comes from heaven is first of all pure; then peace-loving, considerate, submissive, full of mercy and good fruit, impartial and sincere.*

Personal Note: Notice that James does not say "the wisdom that comes from above is logical and intellectual"; instead it is full of the fruit of the spirit (Gal 5:22–23). James thus draws a distinction between mere knowledge and true wisdom. British philosopher Bertrand Russell observes that "So far as I can remember, there is not one word in the Gospels in praise of intelligence." This secular thinker is correct here but for all his "intelligence" he fails to see the distinction between knowledge and wisdom. Wisdom from heaven knows that relationships are important, and relationships cannot thrive, indeed they wither, if they are not seasoned with the fruits listed here.

James 4:2: *You want something but don't get it. You kill and covet, but you cannot have what you want. You quarrel and fight. You do not have, because you do not ask God.*

What exactly is envy? It is a painful and resentful awareness of an advantage enjoyed by another, accompanied by a strong desire to possess the same advantage. Envy sheepishly wants to have what someone else possesses. Envy is sneaky and subtle. It is forever reaching, longing, squinting, pondering, and saying sinister things. ... Envy's fangs may be hidden, but take care when the creature coils. No matter how cultured and dignified it may appear, the green-eyed monster's venom can leave a whole community in chaos. … Are you struggling with envy? Ask yourself these questions. When somebody at work gets a commendation or promotion that you were hoping for, how do you respond? Do you share the news with a 'but' attached? Do you try to discern wrong motives that might be driving the recognition? Do you try to 'put it in perspective' by comparison? If so, you've been bitten by the green-eyed monster. Feeling sick yet? … What's the cure? *Contentment.* Feeling comfortable and secure with who you are and where you are. Contentment means surrendering your frustrated hopes and missed goals to God. … Having some struggles with envy? Eating your heart out because somebody's a step or two ahead of you in the race and gaining momentum? *Relax.* You are you—not him or her. And you're responsible to do the best you can with what you've got for as long as you are able. The choice is yours: *contentiousness* or *contentment*. If you want the peace that comes with contentment, why don't you spend some time committing Philippians 4:11–13 to memory? Then turn to God and ask for strength to slay the green-eyed monster. Swindoll, pp. 94–95

James 4:8: *Draw nigh to God, and he will draw nigh to you.* (KJV)
Fellowship with God, and its consequent blessing of his fellowship with us, does not just 'happen'; we cannot drift into it any more than we can drift into holiness. It is our first obedience [cf Deut 30:14, Lam 3:57, Phil 4:4, Isa 30:21, Heb 10:22]. Motyer, p. 152
Motyer, J. Alec, *The Message of James*, Taken from *The Bible Speaks Today* Series edited by J. Alec Motyer; John Stott. Copyright ©1985 edited by J. Alec Motyer; John Stott. Used by permission of InterVarsity Press, P.O. Box 1400, Downers Grove, IL 60515, USA. www.ivpress.com

What a wonderful invitation and what an incredible promise. It takes risk to reach out to another or to attempt to draw near to someone else. God has promised not to 'back off'. He is always ready to respond appropriately to us with His love and grace. As we draw near to Him and allow Him to draw near to us, a marvelous thing takes place. Jesus refers to this phenomenon as 'abiding' in Him and He is us (Jn 15:4–5). As we are possessed more and more by Christ Himself, His character increasingly supplants ours. We become more and more like Him. As we die to self and are filled with the Holy Spirit, the fruit of the Spirit flows from our lives.

We become more and more like Jesus—including being more and more humble. His humility becomes ours. Cedar, pp. 83–84

James 4:10: *Humble yourselves before the Lord, and he will lift you up.*

"Lord, enfold me in the depths of your heart; and there, hold me, refine, purge, and set me on fire, raise me aloft, until my own self knows utter annihilation."

Pierre Teilhard de Chardin (French Theologian) (1881–1955) Quoted in Ward and Wild

James 4:17: *Anyone, then, who knows the good he ought to do and doesn't do it, sins.*
Verse 17 finds James at his abrupt best! He moves without preparatory warning from the particular of verse 16 to the general of verse 17, from the evil of the sin of arrogance to a searching statement of the principle of the sin of omission. In fact, the whole idea of sinning by default has never been given so pointed an expression. It is a principle which exposes the insufficiency of even our best accomplishments, and makes us realize we are never more than unprofitable servants. "We may be able', says C.L. Mitton, 'to avoid committing forbidden evil; but who can ever seize positively every opportunity of doing good?' Motyer, p. 162–163
Motyer, J. Alec, *The Message of James,* Taken from *The Bible Speaks Today* Series edited by J. Alec Motyer; John Stott. Copyright ©1985 edited by J. Alec Motyer; John Stott. Used by permission of InterVarsity Press, P.O. Box 1400, Downers Grove, IL 60515, USA. www.ivpress.com

Personal Note: James knocks us all down a peg elsewhere in his letter (eg, 1:22, 2:10) but especially here. A smug Christian walk is an oxymoron, yet there are some who believe they can play it safe and simply avoid bad things to please God (Mt 25:25). But the upward call (Phil 3:14) is more demanding than that. We must not just avoid the bad, but positively seize the good (cf discussions of Mt 7:12, Lk 19:20). We are all "busted" on James 4:17.

James 5:16: *The effectual fervent prayer of a righteous man availeth much* (KJV)

James 5:16: *The prayer of a righteous man is powerful and effective.* (NIV)
Prayer involves the patience which awaits the divine response [Ps 66:19–20]. It is part of the simplicity of prayer to act in simple faith—faith that the Lord's moment will come, and that he will do 'far more abundantly than we can ask or think' (Eph 3:20). Motyer, p. 208

Motyer, J. Alec, *The Message of James,* Taken from *The Bible Speaks Today* Series edited by J. Alec Motyer; John Stott. Copyright ©1985 edited by J. Alec Motyer; John Stott. Used by permission of InterVarsity Press, P.O. Box 1400, Downers Grove, IL 60515, USA. www.ivpress.com

1 Peter

Commentaries:
- *The Message of 1 Peter*, by Edmund Clowney (1988)
- *ESV Expository Commentary*, Vol. 12, by Sam Storms (2018)
- Charles Haddon Spurgeon Sermons On line http://www.romans45.org/spurgeon/spsrmns.htm

1 Pet 1:1-2 *Peter, an apostle of Jesus Christ, To God's elect, exiles scattered throughout the provinces of Pontus, Galatia, Cappadocia, Asia and Bithynia who have been chosen according to the foreknowledge of God the Father, through the sanctifying work of the Spirit, to be obedient to Jesus Christ and sprinkled with his blood: Grace and peace be yours in abundance.*

Yes, we are aliens and sojourners on this earth; the language and values and customs of this world feel foreign to us. But we are more than exiles. We are elect exiles, the chosen people of God. Our core identity is as God's elect, members of his spiritual family, the church. This truth must be established in our hearts. God wants us to know that none of the hardships or disappointments we face as exiles in the earth are a surprise to him. Dwell on this majestic truth. Let it sink deeply into your soul. God has chosen you. The Spirit has set you apart for his unique and beloved possession. And your life has been designed for obedience to Jesus.

Storms, Sam, *ESV Expository Commentary* (1 Peter), Vol. XII, Wheaton, IL: Crossway, 2018, p. 303

1 Pet 1:3–4: *Blessed be the God and Father of our Lord Jesus Christ! According to his great mercy, he has caused us to be born again to a living hope through the resurrection of Jesus Christ from the dead, to an inheritance that is imperishable, undefiled, and unfading, kept in heaven for you* [ESV]

What a vast mass of meaning is packed away in these words! Men's books, even when they are good, are like gold-leaf; a little precious metal is very thinly hammered out so as to cover a wide surface, but almost every word in the Bible seems to contain a whole mine of heavenly wealth.

Joy, my brethren, in the glorious inheritance which is prepared for you, unstained, uncorrupted, perfectly pure, and therefore to last for ever, because the elements which produce decay are not in it. It is without sin, and therefore it shall be without end. What a mercy it is to be "kept by the power of God"! See, heaven is kept for us, and we are kept for heaven; heaven is prepared for us, and we are prepared for heaven. There is a double action of God's grace thus working in us, and working for us, unto bliss eternal. Charles Haddon Spurgeon

1 Pet 1:13: *Therefore, prepare your minds for action; be self-controlled; set your hope fully on the grace to be given you when Jesus Christ is revealed.*

In the first twelve verses of 1 Peter (which in the Greek text is one long sentence), there is not a single command: no imperatives, admonitions, or exhortations. There is nothing but glorious affirmations and declarations of the saving grace of God in Christ. Thus to this point Peter has focused exclusively on what God has done. But in verses 13-16 he turns his attention to the moral and ethical responsibilities we must embrace as children of God.

The transitional conjunction "therefore" that begins verse 13 is crucial. This word tells us that all of Peter's forthcoming exhortations depend on the grace he has been expounding in verses 1-12. The call to obedience and holiness is thus rooted in the realities of grace. The imperative is always based on the indicative. We must never revers the order. Otherwise, we fall into legalism and works-righteousness. Storms, pp. 308-309

1 Pet 2:9: *But you are a chosen people, a royal priesthood, a holy nation, a people belonging to God, that you may declare the praises of him who called you out of darkness into his wonderful light.*

If God does not choose his people for their worth or their serviceability [Ex 4:10], why does he choose them? The answer is clear (Deut 7:7). The Lord loves...because he loves! Nothing can explain the love of God for sinners. God's 'good pleasure' [Ps 51:18, Mt 11:26] is the movement of his own will, springing from his own nature. How the language of love is lavished upon God's people in the Old Testament! They are God's inheritance, his personal and prized possession [Dt 14:2], his treasure[1]. God bears them upon his shoulders[2], carries them in his arms[3], holds them in his hands, seats them at his feet[4]. He loves them with a jealous love; they are to be his alone to the exclusion of all other gods; they bear his name[5]. The love of a father for a son[6], of a husband for a wife[7], is used to describe God's love for his people. Worship finds its burning focus to lifting the name of God in adoration. Nothing can be put above worship. We adore God not to gain his favor, but because adoration is our response to his grace. Peter reminds us that the inestimable privilege of entering the presence of the Lord contains yet a greater privilege: to lift his name in praise. He lifts us up so that we may lift him up. Clowney, pp. 92, 96

---

[1] Dt 32:9 [2] Lk 15:5 [3] Isa 40:11 [4] Dt 33:3, 12, 27; Lv 9:5; Isa 49:16
[5] Ex 20:5, Nu 6:22–27 [6] Ps 103:13 [7] Rev 21:2

1 Pet 4:8: *Above all, love each other deeply, because love covers over a multitude of sins.*
The word translated 'deeply' describes something which is stretched and extended (1 Pet 1:22). The love of the saints keeps stretching, in both depth and endurance [1 Cor 13:7, Eph 3:17–19]. It is the reach of God's love that stretches our love [Ps 36:5, Jn 13:34]. Our love, kindled by God's love, is stretched by exercise. If love collapses at its first test, it is not worthy of the name that never fails (1 Cor 13:8). Love does not keep score [1 Cor 13:5], but grants forgiveness freely to every brother or sister who seeks it [cf Prov 10:12]. Clowney, p. 179, 180

2 Peter

Commentaries:
- *Living Insights*, Vol 13, by Charles Swindoll (2014)
- *1 and 2 Peter and Jude*, by Norman Hillyer (1990)

2 Pet 1:5–8: *For this very reason, make every effort to add to your faith goodness; and to goodness, knowledge; and to knowledge, self-control; and to self-control, perseverance; and to perseverance, godliness; and to godliness, brotherly kindness; and to brotherly kindness, love. For if you possess these qualities in increasing measure, they will keep you from being ineffective and unproductive in your knowledge of our Lord Jesus Christ.*

Faith is the foundation, the taproot of the Christian life. It means relying on what Peter has described as the provision and promises for spiritual growth. It means abandoning ourselves to our God—to His will, His strength, His wisdom. Upon this foundation of faith—focused on Christ and established by the Holy Spirit—we are able to build. So to 'supply' to this foundation means to add to it, to build upon it. Peter then lists seven qualities we should add to this foundation of faith. … What a list! If Peter hadn't prefaced these steps from faith to love with a reminder that God provides the power (1:3), these seven tiers might appear as insurmountable as Mt. Everest, even though they are built upon the foundation of faith. But accompanied by God's promises and presence through the Spirit, we can take Peter's instruction seriously and begin to apply diligence, having a firm hope that God will work in us and with us as we grow more like Christ. Swindoll, pp. 297–298

2 Pet 1:20–21: *Above all, you must understand that no prophecy of Scripture came about by the prophet's own interpretation. For prophecy never had its* *origin in the will of man, but men spoke from God as they were carried along by the Holy Spirit.*

True prophecy never came about as a result of some individual's personal ideas it never had its origin in the will of man. The impulse came from the Holy Spirit of God. When OT prophets spoke they were jot passing on some understanding or view of their own. They were revealing a message from the Spirit; they spoke from God. It was for this reason that their words must be closely heeded.

It follows, therefore, that readers of the Scriptures must look to the same divine Spirit to inspire their understanding of the text (Ps 119:18). It is the Spirit who must interpret and apply his own message in his own way. The translators of KJV were very conscious of this fact, as is shown by their frequent prayer during their work: 'more light, Lord!'   Hillyer, p. 180

"The right way of interpreting scripture is to take it as we find it, without any attempt to force it into any particular system."

        Richard Cecil (1748–1810)   Quoted in Ward and Wild

1 John

Commentaries:
- *The Message of John's Letters*, by David Jackman (1988)
- *The Preacher's Commentary*, NT Vol 35, by Earl F. Palmer (1982)

1 John 1:5: *God is light; in him there is no darkness at all.*
We are like the character in one of G.B. Shaw's plays, whom the playwright describes as 'a self-made man who worships his creator.' You see the symptoms every time someone says 'But I like to think of God as …' Usually what follows is a picture of a benevolent, avuncular figure, whose main purpose is to satisfy the whims of his creatures; or some other distortion of the God revealed to us in the Scriptures. But if our view of God is distorted, everything else is bound to be out of joint.…A foundation stone of right Christian believing and living, then, is that intellectually, morally, and spiritually, God is light, unsullied and undiluted. It speaks of holiness and purity; of truth and integrity; but also of illumination and guidance, warmth and comfort. Jackman, p. 26, 28

Taken from *The Bible Speaks Today* Series edited by J. Alec Motyer; John Stott. Copyright ©1983 edited by J. Alec Motyer; John Stott. Used by permission of InterVarsity Press, P.O. Box 1400, Downers Grove, IL 60515, USA. www.ivpress.com
Taken from *The Message of John's Letters* by David Jackman. Copyright (c) 1988 by David Jackman. Used by permission of InterVarsity Press, P.O. Box 1400, Downers Grove, IL 60515, USA. www.ivpress.com

John throws another great stone upon the clear lake: God is light and in Him is no darkness at all. What a sentence! It is bold and electrifying. … John announces to his readers the liberating news that God is not only the source of life, but also of light, of truth. John dares to commit God to the way of light. God never deceives, misleads, and distorts. There can be no strategy of 'heavenly deception' on God's part, because God

is Light and His own Character, His own essential nature, rejects such a stratagem. God is not the prince of lies but the One who reveals and shows the way. Darkness hides and confuses pathways, but light makes the faces recognizable and the outline of the roadway discernible.
Palmer, pp. 23, 25
Taken from The Preacher's Commentary Series Volume 35: 1, 2, 3, John, Revelation by Earl F. Palmer Copyright © 1991 by Word, Inc. Used by permission of Thomas Nelson. www.thomasnelson.com

1 John 1:9: *If we confess our sins, he is faithful and just and will forgive us our sins and purify us from all unrighteousness*
We are told by John that our responsibility is to agree with God about the nature of our crises.
This openness and vulnerability on our part is what firmly plants our feet upon the pathway of light. There are no special code words to learn or special incense formulas to master, or elaborate rituals to perform! How unlike the mysticism and religiosity of the first century and our own day are John's words. They are simple, direct, and real. Come into the light where Jesus Christ is; here you will meet yourself and here you will meet Him. Then stand in the open position and admit who you are, agree with God and receive cleansing and forgiveness.
Palmer, p. 29
Taken from The Preacher's Commentary Series Volume 35: 1, 2, 3, John, Revelation by Earl F. Palmer Copyright © 1991 by Word, Inc. Used by permission of Thomas Nelson. www.thomasnelson.com

1 John 2:4–5: *The man who says, "I know him" but does not do what he commands is a liar, and the truth is not in him. But if anyone obeys his word, God's love is truly made complete in him.*
When John Wesley left home, his mother Susannah is said to have written these words in the flyleaf of his Bible: 'Sin will keep you from this book, but this book will keep you from sin.' Grace does not abolish God's law; it internalizes it by writing it on our hearts [Jer 31:33–35, Ezek 36:26–28].
Jackman, p. 43, 48
Jackman, David, *The Message of John's Letters*, Taken from *The Bible Speaks Today* Series edited by J. Alec Motyer; John Stott. Copyright ©1988 edited by J. Alec Motyer; John Stott. Used by permission of InterVarsity Press, P.O. Box 1400, Downers Grove, IL 60515, USA. www.ivpress.com

"Oh most merciful Redeemer, Friend, and Brother, may I know thee more clearly, love thee more dearly, follow thee more nearly, day by day."
Richard of Chichester (1197–1253)   Quoted in Ward and Wild

1 John 2:20: *But you have an anointing from the Holy One, and all of you know the truth.*
Mere recognition of error is not enough. We have to counteract it by firmly holding to and living out the truth—not just giving it intellectual credence—but embracing and making it the very heartbeat of our lives. It was said of John Bunyan, author of *Pilgrim's Progress*, that his blood was 'Bibline'; if you cut him, the Bible would flow out of his veins. Jackman, p. 71
Jackman, David, *The Message of John's Letters,* Taken from *The Bible Speaks Today* Series edited by J. Alec Motyer; John Stott. Copyright ©1988 edited by J. Alec Motyer; John Stott. Used by permission of InterVarsity Press, P.O. Box 1400, Downers Grove, IL 60515, USA. www.ivpress.com

1 John 4:8: *God is love*   Θεὸς ἀγάπη ἐστίν
The last 3 words of verse 8 form one of the most profound statements of the whole Bible and perhaps for many people today one of the hardest to believe. God is love. When we think of this 'grubby tennis ball' of a planet, set in the vast infinity of space, our own lives as just moments in the onward surge of time, and our individuality among countless millions, can we really talk meaningfully about God loving us? And when we look at the world with all its evil and suffering, so many damaged and broken lives, how can there be a God who really loves? Yet, John insists, this is the very nature of God. And if we are not to empty the word 'God' of all its meaning, we must realize that such an infinite yet personal Creator is not too great to be bothered with my tiny life. He is so great he can be bothered with each of us individually.
Our study of the last few paragraphs has been like a progression through the ante-rooms in a great palace, each one more breathtaking as we move closer to the throne room. We have seen the splendor of the King's magnificent provision for his children in the revolutionary difference of their attitudes and actions when compared to those of the world. We have marveled at his detailed love and care for each one of us, accepting us in our weakness and producing confidence in our lives as we reflect his love. But now the

magnificence becomes overwhelming as the throne-room doors are flung open and we are introduced to the glorious person who has done all this—the God who is Love. Everything else in the splendor of these verses circles around this one supreme reality: 'God is Love.' Jackman, p. 117–118

Jackman, David, *The Message of John's Letters,* Taken from *The Bible Speaks Today* Series edited by J. Alec Motyer; John Stott. Copyright ©1988 edited by J. Alec Motyer; John Stott. Used by permission of InterVarsity Press, P.O. Box 1400, Downers Grove, IL 60515, USA. www.ivpress.com

1 John 4:9–10: *This is how God showed his love among us: He sent his one and only Son into the world that we might live through him. This is love: not that we loved God, but that he loved us and sent his Son as an atoning sacrifice for our sins.*

God loved us enough to send the Lord Jesus to die for our sins, so the punishment has already been met in full; there is nothing left to pay. He did it for me! And when that grips me in the depths of my being, how can I but respond in love? What we discover is that the more we love him, and demonstrate that reality by loving our fellow Christians, however weakly and faintly, the less we are a prey to fear. Fear is the child of bondage. Love is the child of freedom. 'So if the son sets you free, you will be free indeed.' (John 8:36) Jackman, p. 130

Jackman, David, *The Message of John's Letters,* Taken from *The Bible Speaks Today* Series edited by J. Alec Motyer; John Stott. Copyright ©1988 edited by J. Alec Motyer; John Stott. Used by permission of InterVarsity Press, P.O. Box 1400, Downers Grove, IL 60515, USA. www.ivpress.com

Hymn: *Love Divine, All Loves Excelling*, Charles Wesley, 1747, John Zundel 1870

Love divine, all loves excelling,	[Ps 36:5]
Joy of heav'n to earth come down.	[Jn 3:16]
Fix in us, thy humble dwelling,	[Eph 2:22]
all thy faithful mercies crown	[Isa 35:10]
Jesus, thou art all compassion,	[Mt 14:14]
pure, unbounded love thou art;	[Eph 3:18–19]
Visit us with thy salvation,	[Lk 19:9]
enter ev'ry trembling heart.	[Lk 8:15]

Breathe, O breathe thy loving spirit	[Jn 20:22]
into every troubled breast	[Gal 4:6]
Let us all in thee inherit,	[1 Pet 3:9]
let us find the promised rest.	[Mt 11:28]
Take away the love of sinning,	[Rom 6:14]
Alpha and Omega be.	[Rev 22:13]
End of faith, as its beginning,	[Rev 1:5–6]
set our hearts at liberty.	[Jn 8:36]
Come, Almighty, to deliver,	[Ps 40:2–3]
let us all thy life receive.	[1 Pet 1:3]
Suddenly return and never,	[1Cor 15:52]
nevermore thy temples leave.	[Ezek 43:4, 7]
Thee we would be always blessing,	[Ps 34:1]
serve thee as thy hosts above.	[Ps 103:20–22]
Pray, and praise thee, without ceasing,	[1 Th 5:17, Rev 4:8]
glory in thy perfect love.	[1 John 4:18]
Finish, then, thy new creation,	[Phil 1:6]
pure and spotless let us be	[Eph 1:4]
Let us see thy great salvation,	[Isa 12:3]
perfectly restored in thee.	[Rom 5:1–2]
Changed from glory into glory,	[2 Cor 3:18]
till in heav'n we take our place.	[Eph 2:6]
Till we cast our crowns before thee,	[Rev 4:10]
lost in wonder, love, and praise.	[Rom 11:33–36]

2 John

2 John 6: *And this is love: that we walk in obedience to his commands. As you have heard from the beginning, his command is that you walk in love.*
Sometimes we separate obedience from love, so that it hardens into a grinding duty, a ritualistic keeping of the rules. It is hardly surprising that we eventually lose heart and give up the struggle. But if we are in a right relationship to God, if our Christianity is primarily a matter of love for God, we shall find, as John did, that 'his commands are not burdensome' (1 John 5:3). Love for the Father and the Son is the great incentive to obedience and to moving on in the narrow way [Mt 7:13] of the truth.

Jackman, p. 179

Jackman, David, *The Message of John's Letters,* Taken from *The Bible Speaks Today* Series edited by J. Alec Motyer; John Stott. Copyright ©1988 edited by J. Alec Motyer; John Stott. Used by permission of InterVarsity Press, P.O. Box 1400, Downers Grove, IL 60515, USA. www.ivpress.com

"How many observe Christ's birthday! How few, his precepts! O! 'tis easier to keep Holidays than Commandments." Benjamin Franklin (1706 – 1790)

Personal Note: The commentaries on this verse are short and sweet, but that doesn't make it easy to live out! Pastor John Wood of Cedar Springs Church once told a story of his relationship with his earthly father. When he was very young, he obeyed out of fear (of punishment). When he got a little older, he obeyed out of respect. But as he matured further, he obeyed out of love. May we obey our heavenly father not out of fear or even respect, but out of love! May we, with David, say "I desire to do your will, O my God; your law is within my heart" (Ps 40:8).

3 John

3 John 9: *I wrote to the church, but Diotrephes, who loves to be first, will have nothing to do with us*

Diotrephes has had his followers throughout the history of the church, and the species is by no means extinct today. Too many congregations have been held in the grip of petty tyrants for us to regard this sad phenomenon as extraordinary. Destroying unity, flaunting authority, making up his own rules to safeguard his position, spreading lies about those whom he had designated his enemies—the catalogue is appalling. This is what happens when someone who loves to be first decides to use the church to satisfy his inner longing for a position of pre-eminence, for his own personal aggrandizement. … There is only one who can have pre-eminence in the church and that is its Head, the Lord Jesus Christ [Eph 1:22, Col 1:18]. The true Christian leader is one whose life reflects John the Baptist's desire: 'He must increase, I must decrease' (John 3:30). Diotrephes clearly knew nothing of that, or of what it meant to be crucified with Christ, so his life was a fraud. … Whenever we start to serve ourselves rather than Christ, or to use our fellow Christians for an ego trip, or to become concerned about our status within the church, we need to recognize the Diotrephes syndrome and take whatever strong action is needed to eliminate it.

The challenge to us now is how much we are prepared to let Jesus Christ change us. Is it to be my will or his? On this will depend the ultimate verdict, whether we proved to be frauds or followers. Who is at the center of our lives? Is it 'self' with its longing to be first, to be number one? Or is it Christ, enabling us to keep faithful and to continue walking in the truth? There is still no issue with greater or more far-reaching implications for the church or for the Christian.

Jackman, excerpts pp 198, 199, 202 Jackman, David, *The Message of John's Letters*, Taken from *The Bible Speaks Today* Series edited by J. Alec Motyer; John Stott. Copyright ©1988 edited by J. Alec Motyer; John Stott. Used by permission of InterVarsity Press, P.O. Box 1400, Downers Grove, IL 60515, USA. www.ivpress.com

Jude

Commentary:
- *The Message of 2 Peter and Jude*, Dick Lucas and Christopher Green (1995)
- *Living Insights*, Vol 14, by Charles Swindoll (2018)

If we were first-century believers immersed in the theological and moral crisis of Jude's day, his words would strike like a hammer blow on the anvil of our hearts, fashioning our attitudes and sharpening our actions. This book was profoundly relevant and practical. … and it can just as relevant and practical for us when we understand its vibrant language and imagery. …, Jude's brevity shouldn't be confused with lack of concern. Instead of dancing around the issues, Jude waste no pen strokes getting to his point. So obvious and egregious were the errors of the false teachers that Jude instantly called out their wicked deeds and passed judgment on them, even from afar. … After an abrupt, cut-to-the-chase greeting and statement of his purpose (1-4), Jude barrels headlong into an exposure of the false teachers (5-16). From there he engages his readers directly with urgent warnings and commands (17-23), closing the short but powerful message with an encouraging benediction (24-25).
Charles Swindoll, *Living Insights*, Vol 14, Carol Stream, IL: Tyndale, 2018, excerpts, pp. 161-167

Jude 24–25: *To him who is able to keep you from falling and to present you before his glorious presence without fault and with great joy- to the only God our Savior be glory, majesty, power and authority, through Jesus Christ our Lord, before all ages, now and forevermore! Amen.*

Malachi asks "who can stand when he appears?" (Mal 3:2). The correct answer is that no one is able to stand on the basis of the lives we have lived. Yet Jude has seen that a wonderful transformation will have occurred, enabling Christians to face that holiness without flinching.

This wonderful heaping up of praise is due to God [Rom 11:33–36] for one great reason, the reason that has shone through Jude's letter from start to finish, and the only beam of bright light that can offer any glimmer of hope to those who live in a world with a grim present and an even grimmer future under God's judgment. The reason is that he is *the only God our Savior*. When the mighty day of God comes, more terrible than we can imagine—when we see for the first time who it is we rebel against; how perfect his standards are; how ghastly our sin is; how seriously he meant all the Old Testament warnings of judgment on the grumbling Israelites, the mutinous angels, and Sodom and Gomorrah—then we shall see with fear and wonder what a mighty work the cross of Christ was, and is, and shall be forever. The fact that God himself has acted on our behalf to rescue us from a judgment which we so thoroughly deserve means that the heavens will echo forever with our shout of praise. *Amen.* Green, p. 232, 234

Revelation

Commentaries:
- *The Preacher's Commentary*, NT Vol. 35, by Earl F. Palmer (1982)
- *The Message of Revelation*, by Michael Wilcock (1975)
- *Cornerstone Biblical Commentary*, Vol. 18, by M. Robert Mulholland, Jr. (2011)
- *Reversed Thunder*, by Eugene H. Peterson (1988)

Rev 1:1: *The revelation of Jesus Christ, which God gave him to show his servants what must soon take place.*
'Come up hither,' says the mysterious voice (4:1); and John is transported into regions so strange and remote that many Christians hesitate to explore them with him. The Gospels and Letters are territory which is more familiar and more accessible; can this extraordinary book at the end of the Bible belonging to a different world, have anything to do with the practicalities of life in the twenty-first century? As comprehensive as Romans, as lofty as Ephesians, as practical as James or Philemon, this 'Letter to the Asians' is as relevant to the modern world as any of them.

Revelation is addressed to all his servants without distinction. Its chief value must therefore be of such a kind that Christians with no special academic resources can nevertheless appreciate it. For the majority of those who have set out to explore John's book, that Word and that Witness have had to be the only illumination: the Bible in their hands, and the Spirit in their hearts. It is by focusing of a beam down the center of our path, rather than by the sidelights which critical study sheds on its dark corners that wayfaring men, though fools, shall not err therein.

Wilcock, excerpts, p. 27–31

Taken from *The Bible Speaks Today* Series edited by J. Alec Motyer; John Stott. Copyright ©1983 edited by J. Alec Motyer; John Stott. Used by permission of InterVarsity Press, P.O. Box 1400, Downers Grove, IL 60515, USA. www.ivpress.com

Scripture Commentary Sampler

Taken from *The Message of Revelation* by Michael Wilcock. Copyright (c) 1984 by Michael Wilcock. Used by permission of InterVarsity Press, P.O. Box 1400, Downers Grove, IL 60515, USA. www.ivpress.com

The Revelation has 404 verses. In those 404 verses, there are 518 references to earlier scripture. The statistics post a warning: no one has any business reading the last book who has not read the previous sixty-five. In the 518 references to earlier scripture, there is not a single direct quotation. This means that though St. John is immersed in scripture and submits himself to it, he does not merely repeat it—it is recreated in him. Peterson, pp 7, 22, 23

Rev 1:4–5: *To the seven churches in the province of Asia: Grace and peace to you from him who is, and who was, and who is to come, and from the seven spirits before his throne, and from Jesus Christ, who is the faithful witness, the firstborn from the dead, and the ruler of the kings of the earth. To him who loves us and has freed us from our sins by his blood, and has made us to be a kingdom and priests to serve his God and Father-to him be glory and power for ever and ever! Amen.*

Much of what we see in this book we have seen before in Scripture. Repetition is one means by which the psalmists 'rhyme' their poetry; what is echoed from line to line is not the sound but the sense. To say a thing twice is to intensify it. To repeat means to underline. And this is what God is doing constantly. He has basically just one message for men, the good news of salvation. But in his concern to get it across, he knows that one statement of it will not be enough. The purpose of hitting the same nail several times is obvious: to drive it home. God is plainly teaching by this method throughout the rest of Scripture. And with good reason. The mind of man is incurably centrifugal, forever flying off at a tangent. He must be brought back to the great central truths, made, literally, to concentrate. Those truths God outlines for him again and again, sometimes by a pencil sketch, sometimes by a more detailed pen drawing, sometimes by brushfulls of paint. Wilcock, p. 38–39

Wilcock, Michael, *The Message of Revelation* Taken from *The Bible Speaks Today* Series edited by J. Alec Motyer; John Stott. Copyright ©1975 edited by J. Alec Motyer; John Stott. Used by permission of InterVarsity Press, P.O. Box 1400, Downers Grove, IL 60515, USA. www.ivpress.com

Rev 2:4: *Yet I hold this against you: You have forsaken your first love.*
The Ephesus problem happens quietly and by gradual, imperceptible shifts of focus. The Christian becomes totally preoccupied, fascinated by themes and goals which would have never won him or her in the first place to have joined the church; arguments over fine doctrinal points, distinctives of polity, esoteric giftedness, etc. How can it happen to us? It happens to marriages; it happens to human friendships; it happens to the life of discipleship. The stern and good letter to the Christians at Ephesus is a letter to all persons who have drifted into the loss of first love. There is no easy solution for Ephesus. They must vigorously repent and rediscover the true center. When such wanderlust takes over our lives [Lk 15:13] what we need to hear is the sharp prophetic command of a loving adversary—Stop! [3:19] Palmer, excerpts p. 123–125

Taken from The Preacher's Commentary Series Volume 35: 1, 2, 3, John, Revelation by Earl F. Palmer Copyright © 1991 by Word, Inc. Used by permission of Thomas Nelson. www.thomasnelson.com

Rev 3:15–16: *I know your deeds, that you are neither cold nor hot. I wish you were either one or the other! So, because you are lukewarm-neither hot nor cold-I am about to spit you out of my mouth.*
What is their problem at Laodicea? These Christians have become lukewarm because they perceived virtues within themselves, and because of that confident self-understanding they were blinded to the steady deterioration that had already turned them into hollow shells reaching out to hollow shells. Here is the tragedy of a person who has gone soft and indolent by overestimating his or her wealth for too long. Lukewarmness as a spiritual, emotional disorder is so insidious and so self-deceptive that it takes the kind of vigorous shock we witness in this letter to clear the air. Lukewarmness, when it becomes a way of life, so completely blurs and dulls the colors that it becomes almost impossible to tell differences when they occur. Lukewarmness is low-grade paranoia, low-grade cynicism, low-grade immorality. The result is fatigue, and finally despair. Palmer, excerpts, p 145–148

Taken from The Preacher's Commentary Series Volume 35: 1, 2, 3, John, Revelation by Earl F. Palmer Copyright © 1991 by Word, Inc. Used by permission of Thomas Nelson. www.thomasnelson.com

Rev 3:20: *Here I am! I stand at the door and knock. If anyone hears my voice and opens the door, I will come in and eat with him, and he with me.*
Jesus stands at the door and knocks. What happens when we open the door? Revelation 4 and 5 answers the question and gives the last word on worship in five parts: worship centers, gathers, reveals, sings, and affirms. People who do not worship live in a vast shopping mall where they go from shop to shop, expending enormous sums of energy and making endless trips to meet first this need and then that appetite, this whim and that fancy. Life lurches from one partial satisfaction to another, interrupted by ditches of disappointment. ... For persons and congregations who have been bombarded with tedious, footnoted, complaining analyses for these many years, the seven succinct letters of St. John are a relief. The churches of the Revelation show us that churches are not Victorian parlors where everything is picked up and ready for guests. A corrupt church still functions as a church. Dirty lampstands do not extinguish Christ's light. A prettified church, still, despite itself, functions as a church: polished gold does not outshine Christ's light. Peterson, p. 54, 55, 60

Rev 4:10-11: *The four and twenty elders fall down before him that sat on the throne, and worship him that liveth for ever and ever, and cast their crowns before the throne, saying, Thou art worthy, O Lord, to receive glory and honour and power: for thou hast created all things, and for thy pleasure they are and were created.* (KJV)
The crown represents authority, rule, control. Here we see the elders yielding the control of their lives to God. They are allowing God to be God in their life on God's terms, not theirs.
It is possible for us to acknowledge God to be God and to allow God to be God in our lives–but on our terms! We define God for ourselves in ways that allow us to cling to many attitudes, habits, and relationships that are precious to us but actually damaging. We set the boundaries with respect to what God can and cannot do in our life. We attempt to appease God or manipulate him for our own purposes. We want a God who will fit more or less comfortably into our agendas, not upset our status quo, not impact the structures of our relationships, not question our values, and not turn our world upside down. This kind of relationship with God will never lead us out of our brokenness into the wholeness of being in God's image; it

will never heal our woundedness and bring light to our darkness. Only the radical abandonment of ourselves to God–casting the crown–will lead us into such transformation.

The holy life is a life whose steady habit is saying "yes" to God–casting the crown–in each and every situation and relationship even though there is always the possibility to say "no" in that situation or relationship.

Mulholland, Jr, M. Robert, *Cornerstone Biblical Commentary*, Vol. 18, Carol Stream IL: Tyndale, 2011, excerpts, pp. 462-463

Rev 5:1 *Then I saw in the right hand of him who sat on the throne a scroll with writing on both sides and sealed with seven seals.*

It is reasonable to see this amazing scroll with its seven seals as the narratives and meanings of the whole created order. No one in the whole of creation from heaven to hell is able to open the seals. The one who must open them cannot be found within creation. John tells us that he wept loudly because no one was found to take authoritative hold of the scroll and claim its seals as their rightful owner. John weeps because he senses the profound significance of the scroll and of the great question. This is a question that has haunted mankind from the opening of the story of life. What is the meaning of my life, my name, my past, my present, my future? Palmer, p. 160

Taken from The Preacher's Commentary Series Volume 35: 1, 2, 3, John, Revelation by Earl F. Palmer Copyright © 1991 by Word, Inc. Used by permission of Thomas Nelson. www.thomasnelson.com

Rev 7:4: *Then I heard the number of those who were sealed: 144,000 from all the tribes of Israel.*

Rev 7:9: *After this I looked and there before me was a great multitude that no one could count, from every nation, tribe, people and language, standing before the throne and in front of the Lamb.*

There are parallel visions in Revelation 7, the 144,000 (Rev 7:4–8) and the 'multitude than no one could number' (Rev 7:9). They are all the same people. Rhymed repetition is a favorite device among poets to achieve emphasis. St. John *hears* the number of the sealed as 144,000. When he looks he *sees* a multitude that no man can number. Sound is 'rhymed' with sight. Peterson, pp 83, 84

Personal Note: Pastor John Wood of Cedar Springs Church made a similar point. He likened it to hiking through the woods towards a mighty waterfall. Before you arrive, you hear its thundering waters. But then when you arrive at the waterfall, you see it and finally comprehend the totality of its glory.

Rev 8:4–5: *The smoke of the incense, together with the prayers of the saints, went up before God from the angel's hand. Then the angel took the censer, filled it with fire from the altar, and hurled it on the earth; and there came peals of thunder, rumblings, flashes of lightning and an earthquake.*
He mixed the prayers of the Christians with incense (which cleansed them from impurities) and combined them with fire (God's Spirit) from the altar. Then he put it all in the censer and threw it over heaven's ramparts. The censer, plummeting through the air, landed on earth. On impact there were "peals of thunder, voices, flashes of lightning, and an earthquake". The prayers which had ascended, unremarked by the journalists of the day, return with immense force—in George Herbert's phrase as 'reversed thunder'. Prayer re-enters history with incalculable effects.
Peterson, excerpts, pp. 88, 90

Rev 11:15: *The seventh angel sounded his trumpet, and there were loud voices in heaven, which said: "The kingdom of the world has become the kingdom of our Lord and of his Christ, and he will reign for ever and ever."* [cf Dan 7:14]
Following the song there is an over-whelming shower of fireworks and sound. Notice that this display of sheer power does not come at first as if to intimidate the senses and destroy thought. The words of the chorale are first; then there is the celebration of sound. The music and sounds of celebration are the major ingredients in the Old Testament Psalms, and indeed many of the Psalms contain instructions to the instrumentalists. The Book of Revelation is the musical book of the New Testament, and very large parts of chapters 4 through 22 are pure celebration. But, as with the Psalms, the celebration in the Revelation is the result of the people's discovery of God's grace and justice. Celebration in this biblical sense is not a superficial or contrived production; it is the acceleration of joy. John is caught up by the vision of the ark [11:19], the very presence of Almighty God, and then the sights and sounds that are beyond imagination. The end

of the first movement. ... [My comment: If this verse sounds familiar, it should: it was used by Handel in his famous Hallelujah Chorus].

Palmer, excerpts, pp. 187–188

Taken from The Preacher's Commentary Series Volume 35: 1, 2, 3, John, Revelation by Earl F. Palmer Copyright © 1991 by Word, Inc. Used by permission of Thomas Nelson. www.thomasnelson.com

Rev 12:7: *And there was war in heaven. Michael and his angels fought against the dragon, and the dragon and his angels fought back.*
The central theme of this second symphonic movement is quite clear, but many details of the vision are more difficult to interpret precisely. In biblical interpretation there is a natural instinct in an interpreter to want to fasten down as many of the details within a text as possible. The Book of Revelation is a book that defies that instinct [cf Roberts on Est 9:28]. In fact, this book has its richest impact in the life of the Christian and the church when the great broad strokes of the book are allowed to make their mark without being artificially interpreted or over read.
Palmer, pp. 189–190
Taken from The Preacher's Commentary Series Volume 35: 1, 2, 3, John, Revelation by Earl F. Palmer Copyright © 1991 by Word, Inc. Used by permission of Thomas Nelson. www.thomasnelson.com

I do not sit down to a perusal of Scripture in order to impose a sense on the inspired writers, but to receive one, as they gave it to me. I pretend not to teach them, I wish like a child to be taught by them
Charles Simeon (1759–1836) Quoted in Ward and Wild

Rev 13:11 *Then I saw a second beast, coming out of the earth. It had two horns like a lamb, but it spoke like a dragon.*
Following this, John saw a vision of another beast. This, again, modulates Daniel's vision. In Daniel, the four beasts that come forth from the sea are subsequently interpreted as four kings who arise from the earth (Dan 7:17). John's vision of a single beast that comes up out of the earth suggests that John was seeing the deeper reality that stood behind Daniel's four kings. ... This beast masquerades as a savior of humanity, a "messiah" who will restore all things and establish God's rule over the earth. But as soon as the beast opens its mouth, it gives itself away; "it speaks with

the voice of the dragon." ... The second beast did "astounding miracles" (13:13). ... All sorts of charlatans abounded in John's day who, through various stratagems, did what appeared to be miraculous things, purporting to be representatives of the gods. ... Almost always, they induced their gullible audience to give them lavish gifts as an act of worship toward the god. ... Anyone refusing to worship the image must die. Fallen Babylon is remarkably intolerant of anyone who does not play by its rules. Anyone whose values, structures, and dynamics contradict those of the prevailing culture must be silenced. Mulholland, p. 523-524

Personal Note: As I read Mulholland's commentary in November 2020, I am struck with how well the second beast seems to describe Big Tech: Google, Twitter, Facebook, Amazon, Apple. Like this second beast, Big Tech seems to have an almost almighty aura. Nearly all knowledge is contained in it, and it is a gatekeeper. Sometimes, Google almost appears to be doing miracles. Google suggests search refinements as you type the first word and recognizes what you really mean even if the search text is misspelled. They give their services "free of charge" when in fact each user surrenders personal information in exchange for convenience. It is intolerant of anyone who does not play by its rules. In some cases, it even places a mark on a user ("de-listing" or fact check cautions). Is Big Tech the "second beast"? Too early to tell and we don't want to over-press seeming coincidences, but the situation is striking.

Rev 13:18: *This calls for wisdom. If anyone has insight, let him calculate the number of the beast, for it is man's number. His number is 666.*
What does the number of the beast mean? Any amount of ink has been spilt over this fascinating, and misleading, question. The number is said to stand for Nero, or Caligula, or Domitian, or the Caesars in general, or the Roman Empire, or any one of several solutions, mostly based on the fact that in the Greek and Hebrew as well as in Latin, numerals were indicated by letters of the alphabet, so that the letters of various names had numerical values which could be added together to obtain the total 666. For example, *qsr nrôn* (a Hebrew spelling of 'Caesar Nero') adds up to this—100+60+200 and 50+200+6+50. It is our contention that the number does not stand for any particular person or institution. The number simply stands for the beast (and the beast is a symbol of false

religion). ... The number 666 does not mean Nero or Caligula or Rome. It simply means the beast, false religion. Wilcock, excerpts, pp. 128–31

Wilcock, Michael, *The Message of Revelation* Taken from *The Bible Speaks Today* Series edited by J. Alec Motyer; John Stott. Copyright ©1975 edited by J. Alec Motyer; John Stott. Used by permission of InterVarsity Press, P.O. Box 1400, Downers Grove, IL 60515, USA. www.ivpress.com

Personal Note: Ironic that I read this verse on June 6, 2006—6/6/6 ! I did not plan it.

Another somewhat amusing event occurred in my workplace. There was a storage tank number 666. It kept springing leaks and no matter what we did we could not plug the leaks. It was finally decommissioned after repeated repair attempts.

Rev 20:12: *And I saw the dead, great and small, standing before the throne, and books were opened. Another book was opened, which is the book of life. The dead were judged according to what they had done as recorded in the books.*

There is no evasion of divine justice. The judgment is still according to work, but whose works? The book of life belongs to the Lamb (13:8), and all whose names are in it belong to him; his obedience covers their sin, and his power within them produces holiness. They are therefore accounted righteous because of his righteousness, both imputed and imparted to them. Those, however, who have not accepted the shame of their sin and the glory of salvation and have never had their names written in the book of life, have nothing to plead but their own righteousness, and this is woefully inadequate [Isa 64:6]. Wilcock, p. 196–197

Wilcock, Michael, *The Message of Revelation* Taken from *The Bible Speaks Today* Series edited by J. Alec Motyer; John Stott. Copyright ©1975 edited by J. Alec Motyer; John Stott. Used by permission of InterVarsity Press, P.O. Box 1400, Downers Grove, IL 60515, USA. www.ivpress.com

Personal Note: As we stand on the threshold of the grand finale of this magnificent book I pause to reflect and add my thoughts as a layman. It is with some trepidation that I intrude here to say what the book of Revelation means to me. Many learned scholars have rendered their thoughts, so what can I possible have to add? Just this.

I do not believe we have to map out every detail of this book to appreciate its grandeur. There have been heated debates on the meaning of the rich symbolism and the exact timing of the events portrayed in John's vision.

The Apostle is trying to describe the indescribable. Does it really matter precisely when the elect are raptured? Does it really matter what 666 means? Does it really matter whether the thousand year reign is literally one thousand years? I suspect these questions will pale into insignificance as we stand in glory and finally take in the meaning of the Almighty's plan of redemption. The hymn that closes this *Sampler* expresses my reaction to Revelation very well: the book, like the mighty Potentate of Time, is ineffably sublime. I am lost in wonder, love, and praise.

Rev 21:1–2: *Then I saw a new heaven and a new earth, for the first heaven and the first earth had passed away, and there was no longer any sea. I saw the Holy City, the new Jerusalem, coming down out of heaven from God, prepared as a bride beautifully dressed for her husband.*

When we first read the seven letters we thought that the divine Physician was diagnosing the church's 'real' condition. And on one level, that of the Christian community's day-to-day life in the actual world, the letters were indeed an exhaustive diagnosis. But that was drama in black and white on the flat small screen, compared with the full-color, three dimensional, wide-screen epic that has unrolled since. Our minds have been stretched to take in something of what the apostle calls the 'breadth and length and height and depth' [Eph 3:18]; our vision has been enlarged to see, as the prophet puts it, 'a land of far distances' (Isa 33:17). Wilcock, p. 204

Wilcock, Michael, *The Message of Revelation* Taken from *The Bible Speaks Today* Series edited by J. Alec Motyer; John Stott. Copyright ©1975 edited by J. Alec Motyer; John Stott. Used by permission of InterVarsity Press, P.O. Box 1400, Downers Grove, IL 60515, USA. www.ivpress.com

Rev 21:5: *He who was seated on the throne said, "I am making everything new!"*

The language of the fourth movement is fulfillment language which means that the old orders have been fulfilled by the new. God promises all things new, and yet the first new we meet is the new city with the old name. Jerusalem is the city that David first founded; it now becomes the new. The vision of Jerusalem is fulfilled and now made into the city that it was originally intended. The same shall happen for the earth, heaven, and the seas; they pass away not toward oblivion but toward this new completion of God's fulfilled design. Palmer, p. 227

Taken from The Preacher's Commentary Series Volume 35: 1, 2, 3, John, Revelation by Earl F. Palmer Copyright © 1991 by Word, Inc. Used by permission of Thomas Nelson. www.thomasnelson.com

"Christ came when all things were growing old. He made them new."
Augustine of Hippo (AD 354–430) Quoted in Ward and Wild

Rev 21:6: *He said to me: "It is done."*
In Eden the work of creation was finished (Gn 2:1,2); at Calvary the work of redemption was finished (Jn 19:30); in Paradise the voice of God will finally say, concerning the whole of his work, "It is done!" Wilcock, p. 215
Wilcock, Michael, *The Message of Revelation* Taken from *The Bible Speaks Today* Series edited by J. Alec Motyer; John Stott. Copyright ©1975 edited by J. Alec Motyer; John Stott. Used by permission of InterVarsity Press, P.O. Box 1400, Downers Grove, IL 60515, USA. www.ivpress.com

Personal Note: Rev 21:1-7 are the culmination of the Bible and show the ending we all long for. I am surprised that none of the commentators has adequately addressed this passage (in my humble opinion), possibly because the passage is gloriously self-explained, so I fill the gap with my own observations today in November 2020. Our story begins in Genesis with the Lord God creating a world which he deemed to be be very good (Gen 1:31). But then Adam and Eve messed up the creation by disobeying the one restriction they were given. They chose to eat from the Tree of the Knowledge of Good and Evil, thus usurping the Lord's role. Instead of consulting God, they formed their own theories. They were locked out of the Garden of Eden (Gen 3:24) and lost the fellowship they formerly had with the Lord. But God had not given up on humanity. He saved Noah and his family from a devastating flood and made the first of many covenants he made with humanity. He chose Abram as a vehicle of his blessing to the entire world. He elevated David to a never ending throne (2 Sam 7:11) and empowered his son Solomon to build the temple. Solomon indicated that he built a temple for the Lord (1 Kings 8:13), but later confessed the temple could not contain the immensity of God (1 Kings 8:27). The Lord promised to live with his people when the temple was dedicated (1 Kings 6:13), but it was conditioned on obedience (1 Kings 6:12). Now, at the end of the process, the problem of sin has finally been "corrected" as each believer becomes a resident of the New Jerusalem. Each believer is fit to be in God's presence as their sins have been washed in the blood of the lamb and they have been sanctified through and through (1 Thes 5:23). The promise Jesus made to be with us to the end of time is finally fulfilled. This process, though often painful and circuitous is now finally "done." Really done. Amazingly done. The Lord has made all things new. He can now truly say, "Behold. It was very good." Praise the Lord!

Rev 21:22–23: *I did not see a temple in the city, because the Lord God Almighty and the Lamb are its temple. The city does not need the sun or the moon to shine on it, for the glory of God gives it light, and the Lamb is its lamp.* [cf Isa 60:19]
In the heavenly Jerusalem there is no need of a temple, because merely to be in the city is to be with him. His glory pervades every nook and cranny of it. Such total interpenetration between man and his God, the light in the city, the city in the light—is the aim and object of the gospel.
Wilcock, p. 210
Wilcock, Michael, *The Message of Revelation* Taken from *The Bible Speaks Today* Series edited by J. Alec Motyer; John Stott. Copyright ©1975 edited by J. Alec Motyer; John Stott. Used by permission of InterVarsity Press, P.O. Box 1400, Downers Grove, IL 60515, USA. www.ivpress.com

Rev 22:20: *He who testifies to these things says, "Yes, I am coming soon." Amen. Come, Lord Jesus.*
A question that inevitably emerges in the study of the New Testament second coming expectation is this: how soon is soon? To answer this question, we must be careful not to measure the eschaton of God by an earthly, chronological measuring rod. We have witnessed in these passages, on the one hand, the prophetic shortening of time; but also, we have been introduced to the prophetic / apocalyptic mystery of time. Time itself is a baffling mystery, and the vision of John has borne witness to that mystery, but not in a way that confuses or distorts reality. All of time, as all of creation, belongs to its Lord.
This is the New Testament conviction about time. 'Soon' is the best word, the most accurate word, to describe the return of Christ as Lord because we have already received the companionship here and now of the Lord of the beginning and the end. The central importance of the second coming

of Christ is that Jesus Christ stands at the end of history 'writ large.' He holds in His hand the destiny of the whole. Jesus Christ also stands at the end of history 'writ small'—the destiny of my own life. History does not trail off into emptiness, nor does it endlessly repeat its themes, like a vast confined circle. History moves toward the decisive fulfillment. The same Jesus Christ who stands at its beginning [Jn 1:1–3, Col 1:16–17, Prov 8:22–23] and at its center [Mk 1:11, Jn 14:2–3, 15:5] also stands to greet us at its end [Rev 22:13]. The book ends where it began—with the first love that comes from the Lord Jesus Christ [2:4]. Amen! Here is the rock upon which to build your life: the faithfulness and love of Jesus Christ. It will last [Rom 8:38–39].

Palmer, excerpts, pp 239–241

Taken from The Preacher's Commentary Series Volume 35: 1, 2, 3, John, Revelation by Earl F. Palmer Copyright © 1991 by Word, Inc. Used by permission of Thomas Nelson. www.thomasnelson.com

As Christ comes to us, there is always an element of surprise that will cause us to cry out in delight, "So *that* is what he meant." The unexpected puts a keen edge on our expectations. No longer do we face the future with anxious questions on chronology, but with the welcoming, *kairotic* "Come!"

Peterson, p. 194

Hymn: *Crown Him with Many Crowns* (1851)
Text: Matthew Bridges, 1800–1894, and Godfrey Thring, 1823–1903 Music: George J. Elvey, 1816–1893

Crown him with many crowns,	[Rev 19:12]
The Lamb upon his throne,	[Rev 7:17a]
Hark! how the heavenly anthem drowns all music but its own.	[Job 38:7, Ps 148:2]
Awake, my soul, and sing	[Ps 57:8]
Of him who died for thee,	[1 Pet 3:18a]
And hail him as thy matchless King through all eternity.	[1 Tim 1:17]
Crown him the Lord of life,	[John 1:4]
Who triumphed o'er the grave,	[Acts 2:31, 1 Cor 15:54]
And rose victorious in the strife	[1 Cor 15:55]

For those he came to save.	[Lk 19:10]
His glories now we sing,	[Isa 12:5]
Who died, and rose on high,	[1 Th 4:14]
Who died, eternal life to bring, and lives that death may die.	[1 Th 5:10, Rev 20:14]
Crown him the Lord of peace,	[Eph 2:14]
Whose power a scepter sways	[Heb 1:8]
From pole to pole, that wars may cease,	[Isa 2:4b]
And all be prayer and praise.	[Ps 66:20]
His reign shall know no end,	[Rev 11:15]
And round his pierced feet	[Rev 1:7]
Fair flowers of paradise extend their fragrance ever sweet.	[Isa 51:3, 2 Cor 2:14]
Crown him the Lord of love;	[Ps 36:5]
Behold his hands and side,	[John 20:27]
Those wounds, yet visible above,	[Isa 53:5]
in beauty glorified.	[Phil 3:21]
All hail, Redeemer, hail!	[Isa 54:5b]
For thou hast died for me;	[Rom 5:8]
Thy praise and glory shall not fail throughout eternity.	[Dan 4:34b]
Crown Him the Lord of years,	[Rev 15:3]
the Potentate of time,	[Ps 90:2]
Creator of the rolling spheres,	[Isa 40:26, Amos 9:6]
ineffably sublime.	[Rom 11:33, 36]
All hail, Redeemer, hail!	[Job 19:25]
For Thou has died for me;	[2 Cor 5:15]
Thy praise and glory shall not fail throughout eternity.	[Ps 145:1, Dan 7:14b]

Epilogue

What God's Word Says to Me

*"Accept, O LORD, the willing praise of my mouth,
and teach me your laws."* (Ps 119:108)
Personal Note Written May 2010, updated Aug 2018

After presenting highlights from learned Bible Scholars, I now add my own postscript as a layman. As I have repeatedly admitted, I have no seminary training and present my thoughts only as I have gleaned them over the last couple of decades from a variety of sources. You, gentle reader, will be excused if you wish to skip this perhaps too wordy essay from a rank amateur.

If you are reading this book cover to cover, you've just experienced the consummation of all things in all its majesty and glory. I thus hesitate to bring you down from this ineffably sublime experience. But life here under the sun is often like that. As noted by Christopher Wright in his commentary on Daniel, we experience a triumphant pinnacle moment but then go in to the office the next day almost like Daniel did in 8:27: "I, Daniel, was worn out. I lay exhausted for several days. Then I got up and went about the king's business. I was appalled by the vision; it was beyond understanding."

We too must go on with life as we struggle to comprehend the incomprehensible. If we are to profit by what we learn on this side of glory, we must think about what we have learned and apply it to our daily routines as we go to work, interact with family and friends and do the mundane tasks we need to do. One of the most exciting things about Scripture is how relevant it is to our lives centuries after it was written. Scripture is not sealed off in a water-tight compartment or put on a shelf only to be consulted in emergencies. Is serves us in the crush and press of everyday life. It should be hidden in our hearts (Ps 119:11).

After reading and re-reading the Bible since 1994, I began putting this sampler together in 2005 and expect to be updating it continually in the coming years as I go through the Bible again and again. This has been an exciting, exhilarating effort, and I pause at the five-year mark to reflect on the Scriptures and what they mean to me.

I approach this task with trepidation. The Bible is so comprehensive that I run the risk of grossly oversimplifying it and choosing only the parts that I particularly like. I also realize that many much wiser scholars have already contributed their thoughts, so what can this modest layman add? Yet in spite of these cautions, I invoke the reformed principle of priesthood of all believers and boldly plow ahead. One of the wonders of the Word of God is that it speaks not only to everyone, but to specific people. It has spoken to me. This is what I have heard.

The Transcendent God

In his justly famous doxology in Romans 11, the Apostle Paul can scarcely contain himself as he ponders the magnificence of the Transcendent God: "O the depth of the riches both of the wisdom and knowledge of God! how unsearchable his judgments, and his ways past finding out!" (Rom 11:33). As we observe God's world and his word, we, like Paul, cannot help but be struck with the majesty and splendor that surrounds us. Other classic verses such as Job 26:14 and 1 Chronicles 29:10–13 cause us to gasp as we consider the overwhelming wonder of our God of glory. When we gaze into the night sky, we are in awe of the millions of stars and galaxies. Closer to home, we marvel at the regularity of the seasons and days marked by sunrise and sunset. And when we ponder life, we, with the psalmist, see that we are "fearfully and wonderfully made" (Ps 139:14). All of this points us back to the sovereign creator of all we see. He created *ex nihilo* (out of nothing), and all we can do is stand back and worship any power large enough to do that.

Perhaps even more amazing than his awesome power in creation is his love and faithfulness to his people. The famous hymn says it all: "Great is Thy Faithfulness. Morning by morning new mercies I see." (Lam 3:22–23) In a world where everything changes, we can rely on a God who changes not. In his power, he could squash all of us like a bug, but fortunately his love and holiness restrain his power. He chooses to be faithful to his promises. And he is persistent. He finishes what he starts (Phil 1:6).

Our God is also omniscient. He knows and sees all. He knows us better than we know ourselves (Ps 139:1–5). We humans can't understand this amazing God. It is like asking a grasshopper to understand a human. His ways and thoughts are far above our ways and thoughts (Isa 55:8–9), and any attempt to subject him to our examination and scientific instruments is bound to fail. Try as we might, our logic, reason, and science will never enable us to comprehend his glory.

While our world appears to be chaotic and cyclical, our Sovereign Lord has a plan and a purpose. World War II concentration camp survivor Corrie Ten Boom uses the lovely metaphor of a tapestry that we are viewing from the underside. Its light and dark threads hang down and it appears rather bland and odd. Our failure to see the rich tapestry the Lord is weaving is caused by our "ground level" approach. Like the writer of Ecclesiastes, we can only see the things that happen 'under the sun' (Eccl 1:7). But in the end, we will see the tapestry from above and finally comprehend the beauty and significance of our lives in God's plan.

The only way we can grasp even a tiny fraction of the Lord's purpose is to lift our eyes to him and listen to his voice. What little we can understand before he concludes his grand plan is given to us in the pages of his Holy Word. As we probe its pages, the eyes of our hearts are enlightened (Eph 1:18) and we catch at least a "whiff of heaven." Our lives as believers take on new meaning as we contemplate the riches of the glorious inheritance that awaits us (Eph 1:18, Col 1:12).

The scriptures also portray God's sovereignty and His wrath. These two characteristics of God often make us queasy. We chafe at His sovereignty because we want to rule our lives. We don't like to talk about his wrath, because it shines the light on our unworthiness. But the Bible does not pull punches as it portrays the Lord's wrath. He alone is God and He will tolerate no rivals. Again, we have to be thankful that God's wrath is restrained by his holiness and love. He is not some petulant potentate, looking for a way to zap us when we disobey. His wrath guides us to his light. And his wrath helps us to see the wonder of his grace.

Humanity's Rebellion against God

Given the holy, faithful, loving, powerful God we see in his word, one would think we would fall down and worship him, adore him, obey him. But that's now how things turned out. From the very beginning, humans have not merely rebelled against his holy restraints (Dan 9:5), they have wanted to rule in his place (Gen 3:5, Isa 14:14). Adam and Eve were given a paradise, and there was just one restriction (Gen 3:3). But that was the very restriction they chose to break. King David had power and wealth and the prophet Nathan told him could have asked God for even more (2 Sam 12:8). Yet he wanted Bathsheba, so he took her and killed her husband. The pattern has been repeated over and over not only in the pages of scripture, but also in every life since Adam and Eve were expelled from Eden (with one exception).

One of the most amusing things we do is to try to reverse roles with God. He made us in his image (Gen 1:27), but all too often we attempt to make God in *our* image. In fact, many prominent atheists such as Richard Dawkins correctly point to this behavior in Christians. But the Lord is so high above our level that it is absurd to think we can put him in our back pocket. He is not a cruise ship director there to serve our every whim. He is our Lord. Many of the authors in the *Sampler* paint eloquent portraits of this ridiculous yet persistent human tendency. But as Solomon said at the dedication of the temple, "The heavens, even the highest heaven, cannot contain you. How much less this temple I have built!" (1 Kings 8:27). Try as we might, we cannot contain or control God.

We humans think we have things "figured out." We think we can run our lives better than God can, so we try to do things on our own, setting out for the distant country of the prodigal son (Lk 15:13). We then find out that the distant country is not all it is cracked up to be. Time and again, our lives are shipwrecked on the shoals of our pride. Some of us require more painful experiences than others before we realize that our way doesn't work. God's gentle whisper (Isa 30:21) sometimes has to be backed up with a two by four.

The Christian is painfully aware that he/she sins just as much as the atheist. And one way we attempt to atone for our sins is to go through rituals and rote religion. We think that by going to church, singing hymns, and praying prayers, we are somehow "better" in God's eyes. But he sees through the ritual and is not impressed at all. In fact, he is downright disgusted (Amos 5:23–24). The Lord wants us to live godly lives, not go through the motions of religion. In fact, our most righteous acts are as "filthy rags" (Isa 64:6) when we try to use them to justify ourselves.

God Reaches Down

The builders of the Tower of Babel tried to reach up to God (Gen 11:4), but they could never accomplish their goal. Instead, God reaches down and condescends to dwell among his people. From the very beginning, the Lord has delighted in being with his people (Gen 3:8). He is not some far off emperor making lofty speeches about how much he empathizes. He comes to dwell among his people and establishes covenants with them. He chose Abraham as a special friend and blessed him with wealth and progeny (Gen 22:17). He saw the suffering of his people in Egypt and brought them out, leading and protecting them all the way. He lived in the midst of their camps as they wandered in the desert and led them into a land flowing with milk and honey.

Given the depravity of his people, one would think the Lord would be so totally disgusted that he would just "drop" his plan of redemption. That is what we humans would do if our loved ones acted the same way to us. But his love restrains his wrath. Scripture tells us that God not only forgives our sins, he delights in us (Zp 3:17). He is our refuge and strength. He will never leave us nor forsake us. In fact, he sent his Son to live among us and his Spirit to dwell within us.

Some in our modern world scoff at this talk of "God with Us" as a thing of the past. God only came among his people thousands of years ago, but doesn't do so today. But that sort of thinking has been proven wrong in millions of lives. God's providence operates today just as it did in ancient times. A person whose heart has been quickened by the Spirit perceives God's work. "Coincidence or Providence? Our answer depends on seeing with the eyes of faith" (cf Roberts on Est 6:1–3).

God Pardons the Rebellion

From our human perspective, it appears that God is confronted with a divine dilemma. His sovereignty and wrath make it impossible for him to excuse sin. If he excuses sin, won't that just encourage more sin? But his love and holiness tell him to excuse it. If he metes out a punishment for it, won't that grieve his heart and compromise his love? What to do? From our human perspective, there is nothing God can do to untie this knot.

Yet this is where the mystery of grace makes its dramatic entrance. We humans like to think we can earn our way into God's favor. Many world religions teach this. But God's word tells us that all of our efforts to alleviate his wrath are futile. All have sinned and fall short of God's glory (Rom 3:23). All deserve his righteous judgment. None of us bring anything to God. He can't be bribed (Deut 10:17). He can't be bought.

The Lord solves his dilemma by an incomprehensible yet symmetric transaction (described in detail in Romans 5). All have sinned. So the Lord sends his Son to earth to live a perfect life for us. He alone did not sin. Since he is totally innocent, he is able to absorb the Father's wrath by taking the punishment that should be given to you and me. In his little book *More than a Carpenter*, Josh McDowell uses the metaphor of a driver in traffic court. The driver was caught speeding. There is no doubt about the driver's guilt. The judge must pronounce guilt. But then the judge does something surprising. He takes off his robe, comes out from behind the bench, and writes a check to pay for the speeding violation.

The red ribbon of redemption (Isa 43:1) runs though the Scriptures from Genesis to Revelation. We were hopelessly lost. Our guilt and sin was piled up to the sky. We could do nothing about it. Then the glorious "But God" (Eph 2:4–6) breaks through and lifts us from the muck and mire in which we are trapped (Ps 40:2, 69:1–3). He sets our feet on firm ground and puts a new song in our heart (Ps 40:3). Our account has a balance of trillions of dollars worth of sins, but he forgives the debt (Mt 18:27). Christ has paid the price (1 Cor 6:20). No wonder the hymnist John Newton enthuses, "Amazing grace that saved a wretch like me." God's grace is truly amazing.

God the Son

It is impossible to overstate the importance of the Lord Jesus Christ. He was with God and was God from the beginning (John 1:1). All things were created through him (John 1:3, Col 1:16) and in him all things hold together (Col 1:17). He alone was sufficient to solve the Father's apparent divine dilemma. And he alone enables us to not just escape punishment, but be crowned with joy and gladness as we enter the celestial city (Isa 35:10). He will triumph over death and banish all tears (Isa 25:8) and will seat us at a joyous banquet celebrating his glorious victory (Isa 25:6, Rev 19:9).

Many Old Testament prophecies point to a Messiah. The four 'Servant Songs' of Isaiah (Chapters 42, 49, 50, and 53) have many details that strikingly correspond to fulfillment in Christ. Psalm 22 sounds like it could have been written by Christ on the cross. These and other OT prophecies substantiate Augustine's observation that "The New (Testament) is in the Old concealed, the Old is in the New revealed."

Christ's earthly life began in a humble stable in an obscure backwater of the Roman Empire. Yet the location of his birth does not diminish its glory. The angel Gabriel announced the birth to a terrified teenager named Mary. She justly feared reprisals both from her betrothed and from her contemporary society that condemned adultery. Who could believe her claim that she was with child of the Holy Spirit? But Mary submitted to the angel's words. "I am the Lord's servant," Mary answered. "May it be to me as you have said." (Lk 1:38).

The mystery of the incarnation has baffled scholars for centuries. How can one be both God and man at the same time? Yet that is what scripture teaches. Though Jesus was fully God, he also walked in our steps. He experienced joy (John 15:11) and grief (Mt 23:37, John 11:35). He became weary (John 4:6). He was tempted in every way we are, and yet did not sin (Heb 4:15). Because he is both fully God and fully flesh and blood, he alone is qualified as a mediator (1 Tim 2:5) to reconcile us to God.

His earthly life showed examples of both parts of his nature. As God, he healed and performed miracles. As man, he associated with "sinners" and condemned the pride of the Pharisees. He taught using familiar but riveting examples in parables. He brought the good news of the Gospel to one and all. Though he was fully God, he did not cling to his divinity or use it for his own advancement, but instead laid aside his glory (Phil 2:6–11) and became a ransom for many (Mk 10:45).

His most important accomplishment was his atoning sacrifice on the cross. What we were unable to do for ourselves he did by taking God's wrath at sin upon his own innocent shoulders. He suffered shame and enormous pain as he was tortured for the sins of others. And then for several hours on the cross, he was abandoned by the Father (Mt 27:46). Yet even as he was tortured and killed, he prayed for those who had punished him so unjustly (Lk 23:34).

One would have thought that the cross was the end of the story. One more great religious guru had met his fate. But God had other plans. He raised Jesus from the dead (Eph 1:20), and the world has never been the same.

The authorities at the time tried to cover the resurrection up (Mt 28:12–15), and since that time even to the present day, many have tried to explain it away. Yet after two thousand years of attempts to extinguish the light, billions of people believe in Christ's resurrection. The empty tomb mocks the vain attempts to silence the gospel (Col 2:15). He is risen! Hallelujah!

God the Spirit

The mystery of the trinity is another topic we humans find difficult to grasp. How can there be one God (Deut 6:4) and yet be Father, Son, and Holy Spirit (Mt 28:19)? Many scholars have attempted to formulate metaphors to help us grasp this concept. One such model uses water as an example: it can be solid, liquid, or gas, but it is still water. Another model uses mathematics: $1 \times 1 \times 1 = 1$. But all of the models fall short. Father, Son, and Spirit coexist as separate yet coequal and united.

The Holy Spirit is given to all believers. Salvation is not just a transaction: it is the beginning of a process. The Spirit indwells believers to sanctify them. Humans are caught in a tension of the "already" but "not yet." We have a split personality. Our spiritual side wants to please God, but our flesh continues to be tempted. The two sides are constantly at war (Romans 7).

As soon as a person is saved, he/she is sealed for redemption by the Holy Spirit (Eph 1:13). From that day forward, the Spirit provides counsel to the believer. He pricks our conscience and convicts us of sin. At the same time, He reveals divine wisdom at just the right rate we can absorb. The indwelling Spirit captivates our minds, but still yields to our desires to run our own lives. As we yield to His promptings, however, we bear fruit (Gal 5:22–23). The process of sanctification is a gradual one, and it only becomes complete after death.

The wisdom that comes from the Spirit is different from that which we absorb from the world around us. It's as if there is another dimension that cannot be detected by our five senses. We need a "sixth sense" to perceive it. Those who have not been enlightened by the Spirit find its wisdom to be foolish (1 Cor 2:14). But once enlightened, a believer begins to see things that were once invisible. The Spirit's work transforms lives one at a time. Through his work, we are born again (1 Pet 1:23) and adopted into the family of God (Gal 4:6) to a glorious inheritance that can never spoil or fade (1 Pet 1:4).

Human Foibles: Fruits of the Flesh

We now come to a topic I *am* an expert on: human foibles. The sins and faults brought to light in the pages of the Bible reverberate in my soul because I seem to be looking in the mirror. I am just as much as schemer as Jacob. I am sometimes a big talker like Peter. I let anger and bitterness take over my emotions. And as for arrogance, complaining, and carping: oh, please!

One of the wonders of the Bible is its realism. It doesn't portray plaster saints with painted on smiles. It shows humanity warts and all. As mentioned previously, we live in a world of betwixt and between. Although the Spirit indwells the believer and pricks our conscience, he also stands back to let us learn from the mistakes we make when we submit to the desires of the flesh. The authors of the scripture commentaries in this *Sampler* have many piercing and vivid portrayals of the faults of the flesh. I mention just a few of them here.

The Catholic Church of the 14th century listed what it called the *Seven Deadly Sins*, depicted in a 1485 painting by Hieronymus Bosch. Topping the list is pride. The reason this one tops the list is that it usually is at the root of other sins. We humans are so proud of what we accomplish. We think we don't need God. We are so full of ourselves. We forget that our wealth and skills come not from ourselves but from the Father of heavenly lights (James 1:17). The *Torah* gives an eloquent statement of this error: "You may say to yourself, 'My power and the strength of my hands have produced this wealth for me.' But remember the Lord your God, for it is he who gives you the ability to produce wealth, and so confirms his covenant, which he swore to your forefathers, as it is today" (Deut 8:17). Our pride not only is incorrect, it is destructive. Proverbs puts it well: "Pride goes before destruction, a haughty spirit before a fall" (Prov 16:18).

Envy is another ugly sin that rears its head in our flesh. This tendency basically ruined King Saul's life (1 Sam 18:7-8). In the parable of the prodigal son (Luke 15), the older brother envied the banquet given to the returning younger brother. King Ahab envied Naboth's vineyard (1 Kings 21:4). These are but a few examples. This sin is not only destructive–it is illogical. Why should we be angry when something good happens to someone else? This can only come from the flesh.

Finally, complaining and arguing come to mind. We often are better at enumerating our grievances than we are at counting our blessings. We (I) gripe and moan, thinking "why me?" We rarely thank our creator for the abundant life we have been given. The more we are aware of his grace, the less we should be complaining. All we have is a gift.

Human Virtues: Fruits of the Spirit

In Galatians 5, the Apostle Paul paints a dramatic contrast between the flesh and the Spirit. In verses 19–21 he gives an ugly list of the "works of the flesh." But then in verses 22-23, he pens one of his most famous thoughts: "But the fruit of the Spirit is love, joy, peace, patience, kindness, goodness, faithfulness, gentleness, and self control."

Many stories in scripture illustrate active faith. While believers should be careful to tread where the Spirit is not leading, an opposite tendency can sometimes develop as well: playing it safe. The folly of this approach is depicted in the parable of the talents in Matthew 25. Believers are called not to merely refrain from doing bad things. No, the inspired writers challenge us to positively do good things (James 4:17). We must seize opportunities to do good (Gal 6:9, Rom 12:21) as gifts from God. The book of Ruth demonstrates the active faiths of both Naomi and Ruth who were sensitive to the Lord's leading, but nevertheless stepped out in faith to move events along.

There is a fine line, however. Many in the secular world seek boilerplate cookbooks to guide their lives, but the more one reads the scriptures, the more one realizes that simple answers are unrealistic. While active faith is applauded in some scriptures, many other Bible stories show the folly of trying to rush ahead of the Lord's leading. For example, Abraham had been promised a son, but after waiting for many years, he became impatient with Sarah's inability to conceive, so he, with Sarah's agreement, went in to his servant Hagar. This one little decision turned out to be disastrous not only for Abraham's family life, but for millions of others thousands of years into the future.

For the most part, scriptures teach that obedience to God will result in blessing. Ironically, atheist Friedrich Nietzsche expressed this well:

The essential thing in heaven and earth is…that there should be a long obedience in the same direction; there thereby results, and has always resulted in the long run, something which has made life worth living.

I suspect many a believer has experienced the truth of this statement in his/her life. The more I'm in step with God (Gal 5:25), and the longer I'm in step with God, the more joyful my life becomes.

But even this last statement can lead to mystification, puzzlement, and even ridicule from those outside the faith. The Bible calls believers to be different, but we often commit the same sins as non-believers. Worse still, many Christians get on their moral high horse with their angry condemnation of sins like adultery, abortion, drinking, drugs, and other vices. They justify their efforts to force their lifestyle on an unwilling secular public by claiming to have zeal for the Lord. When we are tempted to judge the secular world, we must remember the example of our Lord Jesus Christ. He mixed with "sinners" and did not condemn them (eg John 8:11). In fact, he saved his anger for the religious people of the day (the Pharisees) and scolded them relentlessly for their hypocrisy (eg Mt 23). The apostle Paul also wrote extensively that we should avoid judging the secular world (1 Cor 5:12, Rom 2:1). He pointedly asks: "you, then, who teach others, do you not teach yourself?" (Rom 2:21). We are to leave room for God to do the judging (Rom 12:19) since he alone knows the human heart (1 Cor 4:5, 1 Sam 16:7). While believers must take seriously their role as ambassadors for Christ (2 Cor 5:20), we must avoid a pharisaical spirit that condemns others in an attempt to shift blame from ourselves. Ours should be a winsome witness (Col 4:6) where we influence by example (Mt 5:16) and not from a perch of pride.

But there is another side to this topic as well. Just as believers are not always virtuous, so the secular world is not always evil. Far from it. Though the Bible teaches that all have sinned and fall short of the glory of God (Rom 3:23), we all can name examples of people we know that couldn't care less for the Bible or Christian faith and yet lead decent, even admirable lives. Looking from the outside in, it appears that they have integrity and honesty. They are loving toward their neighbors and generous with their time and resources. They often exhibit all nine Fruits of the Spirit. How is this possible?

I believe the reason is "common grace" (cf Mt 5:45). All of God's creatures have "wired into their mother board" a force C.S. Lewis called the "natural law". Whether our heart has been quickened by the Holy Spirit or not, we all have a sense of right and wrong. I think the big difference between Christians and seculars is that genuine Christians are sickened and saddened by the many ways they fall short of God's perfect plan for them (Mt 5:48). The longer one experiences the indwelling of the Spirit, the more one realizes just how badly one has disappointed God. Believers long for the sanctifying work to be complete, but that never happens this side of glory.

The Abundant Life

As I sit in my home in Maryland this day, April 30, 2010, I pause to reflect just how blessed I am. I have a healthy body, comfortable home, a wonderful wife, two happy healthy grown children, a well paying and fascinating job, and many comforts that amply demonstrate God's more than sufficient provision. As Michael Wilcock notes in his commentary on the Psalms, it is significant that the very first word of the Psalter is "Blessed." This, blessing humanity, has been the Lord's plan from Genesis 1 (Gen 1:28) to Revelation 22 (Rev 22:7, 22:17). Even as Adam and Eve were ruining the Garden of Eden, God had in mind the holy city in heaven where the curse would be lifted and life-giving water would flow in abundance (Rev 22:17, Ps 36:8–9, Ezek 47:12).

The Christian looks forward to the glorious consummation of all things with a longing we call *hope*. This is not some airy-fairy "pie in the sky bye and bye" concept. The Christian hope is instead a tiptoe expectation that knows God's gracious outcome is certain even though the timing is uncertain. The early 20th Century Swiss theologian Emil Brunner encapsulated the importance of hope: "Hope is the positive as anxiety is the negative mode of awaiting the future. What oxygen is for the lungs, such is hope for the meaning of life. Take away hope and humanity is constricted for lack of breath. We wheeze; we cannot survive without hope."

But we don't have to wait till the end of time to enjoy the Lord's blessing. The glorious immediacy of the gospel is that Christ came to give us joy and to live life to the full (John 10:10). The secular world often misses the distinction between joy and happiness. Even in the most tragic, troubled life, happy times occur. But happiness apart from the Lord is fleeting and ultimately non satisfying. Each happy moment is accompanied by a longing for more, and this longing often is not satisfied. In contrast the joy that comes from the Lord is profound and permanent (Ps 30:5). In addition, we find that the more we pursue happiness, the more it eludes us. But as we focus our attentions on the noble thoughts (Phil 4:8), joy follows us (Ps 23:6). Isaiah's beautiful picture of the blessed of the Lord traveling his Holy Highway (Isa 35:8–10) captures some of the bliss we experience as we follow the Lord's leading and joy overtakes us.

The key to lasting joy is the transformation we receive in being born again. The Holy Spirit's transforming power radically re-orients our walk. I can attest to this dramatic transformation in my own life. The first two verses of Psalm 40 describes how the Lord made me 'do a 180' on the long detour I had taken from His path. I had made a mess of my life before I discovered the saving grace of the Lord Jesus Christ. My eyes still glisten as I recall just how badly I had messed up. Here nearly two decades after my conversion experience, I sing the hymn *Amazing Grace* with an intensity I could not have predicted when I was in my twenties and thirties. If the Lord can save a wretch like me, he can save anyone.

Though the new birth in Christ is an important turning point, it is not a culmination, but a new beginning. Now that I know where I should go, how do I get there? By following the light. The Word of God is a "lamp to my feet and a light to my path" (Ps 119:105). The apostle John tells us that God is light (1 John 1:5). In the final consummation, that light will illuminate the new heavens and the new earth with such brilliance that the sun and moon will no longer be necessary (Rev 21:23). And one day the Lord's light will lead me to his holy mountain (Ps 43:3, Prov 4:18).

Hardship / Adversity

While we long to arrive at the place where death will be swallowed up in victory and all tears will be wiped away (Isa 25:8), we are far from that place today. Hardship and adversity seem to tumble into our lives at the most inopportune times. And the suffering happens not just to those who are in active rebellion against God, it happens to good people, to virtuous people, to people who have walked in obedience to God. Here too, the Bible offers guidance to the struggling soul.

The book of Job is all about suffering. The man Job, one commended by God Himself (Job 1:8), suffers the loss of his children, the loss of all his wealth, and the loss of his health as his body is covered with boils. After his devastating losses he and his friends debate the meaning of it all. His three friends are convinced that Job is suffering for some secret sin. They make the same mistake Christ's disciples make in John 9:2 when they ask Jesus who sinned to cause a man's blindness. Once again, the Bible puzzles us because it provides no easy answers that follow a boilerplate pattern. While suffering often is caused by sin, it sometimes is not. The reader of Job is privy to the council of heaven and knows why Job's suffering has occurred. But we humans at ground level are often mystified. David McKenna's commentary on the book of Job treats this subject brilliantly, and I can't do it justice here.

One of the reasons we encounter hardship is to teach us the hard lesson that we draw our strength not from ourselves, but from God. This goes against the grain of modern culture's message of self-help, self-fulfillment, and self-love. But the Bible teaches just the opposite.

P.T. Forsyth in *The Soul of Prayer* states that God's final purpose in trouble is to drive us closer to himself: "The joiner, when he glues together two boards, keeps them tightly clamped till the cement sets. So with calamities, depressions, and disappointments that crush us into closer contact with God. The pressure on us is kept up till the soul's union with God is set."

Over and again, the Scriptures teach us that the Lord delights in strengthening his people. When Moses protests that he is not qualified to lead the people out of Egypt, God in effect replies, "of course you're not qualified. But what about me?" (cf Alec Motyer on Ex 3:11). The disciples of Jesus were common fishermen and tradesmen with no theological training. Yet they were tasked to bring Christ's redemption to the world. Christ emptied himself and became lowly but was exalted to the highest place (Phil 2:6–11). Scriptures speak with a unanimous and clear voice that the way up is down (Isa 14:14–15) and the way down is up (1 Pet 5:6, Mt 23:12). The apostle Paul puts it succinctly: "When I am weak, then I am strong." (2 Cor 12:10)

Community of Believers

The early chapters of the book of Acts depict the ideal community of faith. Believers break bread together. They study God's word together. They pray for one another. And they care for one another deeply regardless of ethnicity, gender or status (Gal 3:28). Those in the faith are to model the Lord's love (John 13:35). And it can't be a shallow love. No, they are to love one another deeply from the heart (1 Pet 4:8). They are to often meet together (Heb 10:25). Without this frequent meeting, their love muscle atrophies.

Christians form a colony in the midst of a secular world. Jesus called believers to be "salt and light" (Mt 5:13–14): salt to provide flavor and preserve the culture and light to bring praise to the Lord who is the father of the heavenly lights (Jas 1:17). We are to reflect the Lord's glory by loving one another and by leading godly lives (1 Pet 2:12). Not surprisingly, the Christian witness often is not pleasing either to the world or to God. Christians frequently are so focused on exposing the sin of those around them that they forget the fact that they are every bit as corrupt. John Stott puts it well in his commentary on Thessalonians: "A weakness of contemporary evangelical Christianity is our neglect of Christian ethics, both in our teaching and in our practice. In consequence, we have become known rather as people who preach the gospel rather than as those who live and adorn it."

A cornerstone of Christian community is discipleship. The gospels lay out an example of a perfect life. Christ submitted to the Father's will in all aspects and so should we. When we are concerned about our rights we tend to forget about our wrongs. Instead we should be listening to the master's voice (John 10:4). He is leading us on a highway to a glorious celestial city. The important concept is *he is leading*. That means we are following. He will sometimes lead us through rough patches, but we must have confidence that he knows what he is doing. We can only do that by submitting to his leadership. We must echo John the Baptist: "He must increase, I must decrease" (John 3:30).

Communicating with God

"The heavens declare the glory of God, the skies proclaim the work of his hands. Day after day they pour forth speech; night after night they display knowledge," states Psalm 19:1–2. The Scriptures proclaim that God desires communication with his creatures. He speaks, we listen. But even more amazing is that *we* speak and *he* listens (Ps 5:3). He knows every language (Ps 19:3). He can hear millions of prayers at once because he is not bound by time but stands above time.

All too often, we complain about God's silence. But we nearly always find that he is in fact speaking; we are just not listening. "Why do you complain to him that he answers none of man's words?" says Elihu, "For God does speak—now one way, now another— though man may not perceive it. In a dream, in a vision of the night, when deep sleep falls on men as they slumber in their bed." (Job 33:13–15). Jesus said "He who has ears to hear, let him hear" (Mk 4:9). The transmitter is sending, but we have not tuned our receiver to detect the signal clearly.

So how can we tune our receiver? One way is to soak our minds in God's written word (Rom 12:2). Humans often are awkward communicating with each other when they first meet. But as they get to know one another after a long acquaintance, communication becomes easier. It's the same with the Lord. The more familiar we are with him, the easier it becomes to both hear his voice and formulate words that we know reach him (Eph 1:17–18). And we're not left to our own resources. The Holy Spirit is right there at our side on both sides of the communication. He enlightens us with the truth (John 16:13) and also serves as an intermediary or interpreter for us. He amplifies and polishes our prayers (Rom 8:26).

As we come before the throne, we should not just give a laundry list of wishes. Yes, the Lord does listen to our petitions and graciously grants us many of them. But a redeemed people who have been blessed by God should be filled with gratitude. They should be bursting with praise, adoration, and worship. As Augustine put it "A Christian should be an alleluia from head to foot." There are no cut and dried formulas for a good prayer, but one guiding principle should be that we first thank him for what he has already given us before we ask for more. And when we remember his past blessing, we are reassured that he will hear us again.

The Holy Scriptures

The apostle Paul states that all scripture is "God breathed" (2 Tim 3:16). Just as God breathed into Adam the breath of life (Gen 2:7), so the Lord breathed into the authors of Scripture the breath of his truth. The human writers were not just inspired by God. The Holy Spirit filled their lungs, hearts, and minds as they wrote down the precious truths that were revealed to them. No other book, however eloquent, can match the Bible because no other book contains God's own thoughts.

As one might expect, a divine Author produces divine literature. Not only is the Bible magnificent in its truths and revelations about God, it is no less impressive in its literary artistry. The scriptures abound in artistic touches such as *inclusio* (see Psalm 84), *chiasm* (see Gen 6, Luke 15), and strategic word repetition ("rhyming" words – see Isa 53). This *Sampler* contains many examples. These poetic devices not only make the scriptures more beautiful, enjoyable to read, and easier to memorize, they point to the artist who made us (Ps 139:13–14).

Even though the Bible was compiled by dozens of authors over more than a thousand years, it is amazingly consistent in its message. While many through the ages have contended that the Bible is inconsistent, their arguments always fail. When you ask for a specific example of where it is inconsistent, the examples given are shallow and easy to refute. The Bible has withstood the test of time and relentless attacks of those who don't want to believe its truth. I suspect these attacks will continue, but they will be fruitless. "The grass withers and the flowers fall, but the word of our God stands forever" (Isa 40:8).

Mysteries and Paradoxes

God's word can be understood at a variety of levels. Some of it is pretty straightforward and can be understood even by a child. But the pages of Scripture also present many profound issues that are not so easily comprehended. This is not surprising since God's ways and thoughts are so much higher than our ways and thoughts (Isa 55:8–9). Nevertheless, in creating humanity, he gave us brains, and in speaking His word, he gave us instructions. On this side of glory, however, we only see through a glass darkly (1 Cor 13:12), so many questions we ask find no pat answers in scripture.

One of the most troubling questions humanity asks is "Why do the wicked prosper and why do the righteous suffer?" A smug and cynical world declares "A good God would not allow such suffering and pain." The reality of life appears to fly in the face of Psalm 1's simple message that the good prosper and the wicked are condemned and we object that the Psalm just doesn't match our experience. In his comments at the end of the Psalter, Michael Wilcock brilliantly states that Psalms 2–149 answer all the "yes, buts" we offer in protest. The Psalms passionately work through the rough and tumble of real life and then end on a note of praise. The Psalms thus form a microcosm of scripture in general. The story begins in Eden, works through the fall, and then climaxes in the final destiny of humanity, in a new and better paradise.

Although the book of Job contains the most comprehensive treatment of this mystery, Psalm 73 is also instructive. The psalmist spends the first half of the psalm bemoaning his fate: "For I envied the arrogant when I saw the prosperity of the wicked. They have no struggles; their bodies are healthy and strong" (Ps 73:3–4). He goes on itemizing all the injustice he sees, but finally reaches a turning point at the midpoint of the psalm when he enters the "sanctuary of the Lord." He then sees that the assertions he made at the beginning of the psalm are ultimately proven wrong. The wicked may prosper for a season, but they will ultimately hit a dead end because they live outside the blessing of God.

The contrast between transitory and eternal is also prominent in scripture. The apostle Paul paints a vivid picture: "Though outwardly we are wasting away, yet inwardly we are being renewed day by day" (2 Cor 4:16). He then contrasts what is seen with what is unseen: "So we fix our eyes not on what is seen, but on what is unseen. For what is seen is temporary, but what is unseen is eternal" (2 Cor 4:18). Our few decades of life are but a pinprick in eternity, and one day the veil will be lifted and we will see and experience a glorious eternity. 17th century English Archbishop John Tillotson observes, "He who provides for this life but takes no care for eternity, is wise for a moment but a fool forever." May we not be so preoccupied with our earthly life that we neglect our eternal destiny!

Human Pilgrimage on the Divine Path

Life is a journey. We travel along a divinely lit path. We have a tour guide who knows the road and knows how to get to the destination. But as we travel along the path, we see little side roads that look good. We want to explore these and see where they lead. So we leave the path, abandon our tour guide, and end up in darkness. Fortunately, however, we have taken our road map (the Bible) with us and can find our way back. The closer we get to the main road, the more it is illuminated.

As we travel the pilgrim path, we come to many forks in the road. Each time we can either go one way or the other. There are no nuanced shades of gray. We either take this road or that. Each decision we make either gets us closer to final destination or takes us farther away. Each decision is not necessarily critical. But the cumulative impact of all these decisions may well be.

Voices beckon at each fork in the road, and according to the book of Proverbs, we hear two main voices: wisdom and folly. Folly gives us only one side of the story and it is often false. For example, a gang of thieves beckons us to join them and reap the benefits of theft. "We will get all sorts of valuable things and fill our houses with plunder; throw in your lot with us, and we will share a common purse" (Prov 1:13–14). The fool doesn't see through their deception, but just a little thought will expose the stupidity of the gang's claim. How naïve to think that a gang that specializes in theft will be honest with its own members. The old saw that "there is no honor among thieves" has been proven over and over.

So how can we make sure we stay on the right road and make the right choices? "Whether you turn to the right or to the left, your ears will hear a voice behind you, saying, 'This is the way; walk in it'" (Isa 30:21). Listen to your tour guide. Hide his word in your heart (Ps 119:11), for he has your best interest at heart. "Direct me in the path of your commands, for there I find delight" (Ps 119:35).

The Final Destination

And so I come to the end of the *Sampler* and contemplate the glorious future that awaits us in heaven. Paradoxically, the end of the Bible is also a beginning. The apostle John sees the creation of a new heavens and a new earth (Rev 21:1). "He who was seated on the throne said, 'I am making everything new!'" (Rev 21:5). Our life in heaven completes the Lord's plan which basically had three phases, each punctuated by a declaration of completion:

- Creation (Gen 2:1–3)
- Redemption (John 19:30)
- Consummation (Rev 21:6)

Although we cannot imagine the splendor of the new heavens and the new earth (1 Cor 2:9), we are given glimpses of it all throughout the Bible. The most vivid images of the final destination are, appropriately, 'revealed' in the book of Revelation. But commentator Eugene Peterson points out that in 404 total verses, the book of Revelation refers to 518 other verses scattered throughout the Bible. The biblical authors, by inspiration of the Holy Spirit, have begun with the end in mind, and so should we.

The glimpses we see are staggering in their beauty and majesty. The apostle Peter tells us of "an inheritance that can never perish, spoil or fade" (1 Pet 1:4). Paul declares that we will be seated in the heavenly realms (Eph 2:6). The prophet Isaiah describes a banquet of rich foods (Isa 25:6). Christ himself tells of the "many mansions" prepared for his disciples (John 14:2, KJV). All these glorious riches await the arrival of the saints at the kingdom of light (Col 1:12).

The scriptures reject the gloomy assessment of the early chapters of Ecclesiastes that echo a popular secular notion that all is meaningless and a striving after the wind (eg, Eccl 1:14). Many cynics see life as a pointless treadmill with no significance, but God gives us the answer (Isa 55:2). Our problem is that like the author of Ecclesiastes, we only see things at ground level ("under the sun"), but God's word gives us a bird's eye view. Like the observer in Prov 7:6, when we examine our lives from God's vantage point, we see that life, indeed our individual life, has profound meaning and purpose. Our choices do matter. Our pilgrim road doesn't go round and round. It doesn't peter out in a ditch. It advances to the celestial city (Heb 11:10), where every tear will be wiped away (Rev 21:4).

May we praise our God who lavishes such glory on such unworthy people as we! May we rejoice as we boldly approach his throne of grace! And may we joyfully anticipate the day when with a united voice, God's people give him the adoration, laud, and honor He and He alone so richly deserves!

Quotations

Name	Dates	Ref	Name	Dates	Ref
Adams, Henry Brooks	1838-1918	Prov 1:7	Cowper, William	1731-1800	Gen 41:40
Addison, Joseph	1672-1719	Prov 12:16			Judg 3:15
Athanasius	296-373	Psalms			1 Cor 8:1
		2 Cor 5:21			Prov 5:12
Augustine of Hippo	354-430	Mt 11:28			Zech 13:1
		Ps 122:4	Crashaw, Richard	1613-1649	Mt 1:23
		Nah 3:1	de Chardin, Pierre T	1881-1955	Jas 4:10
		Mt 22:21	de l'Incarnation, Marie	1599-1672	Jas 4:8
		Gal 1:8	DeHeer, Larry		Lk 19:9
		Heb 13:14	Dickens, Charles	1812-1870	Ps 134:2
		Rev 21:5	Eckhart, Meister	1260-1327	Amos 5:23
Ausonius	310-394	Prov 13:3	Elizabeth I	1533-1603	Deut 8:17
Bacon, Francis	1561-1626	Acts 17:11	Elliott, Jim	1927-1946	Phil 3:8
		Prov 10:19	Erasmus, Desiderius	1467-1536	Acts 2:2
Barth, Karl	1886-1968	John 14:6	Evagrius of Pontus	305-400	Rom 11:33
Beecher, Henry Ward	1813-1887	John	Faulkner, William	1897-1962	Ps 120
Bengel, Johannes A	1687-1752	2 Tim 3:16	Focht, Joe		Lk 15:12
Benson, Richard M	1824-1915	Isa 55:8-9	Forsyth, P.T.	1848-1921	Num 21:7
Blanchard, Ken	1939-	Eph 2:8	Francis of Assisi	1182-1226	Mt 5:9
Bonhoeffer, Dietrich	1905-1945	Mt 13:45	Francis of Paola	1416-1507	Prov 19:11
		Rev 22:20	Franklin, Benjamin	1706-1790	2 Cor 4:16
Boreham, F.W.	1871-1959	Acts 24:25			2 John 6
Bradley, Omar	1893-1981	Mt 7:24	Fuller, Thomas	1608-1661	Rom 10:2
Brooks, Phillips	1835-1893	Introduction	Gailei, Galileo	1564-1642	Ps 104:19
Browne, Thomas	1605-1682	Prov 17:9	Godet, Frederic	1812-1900	Rom 11:33
Brunner, Emil	1889-1966	Num 24:17	Greenham, Richard	1535-1594	Heb 11:16
		Rom 12:1	Hardy, Thomas	1840-1928	Col 3:1
Bunyan, John	1628-1688	Mt 7:13	Hart, Joseph	1712-1768	Lk 18:10
Burns, Robert	1759-1796	Prov Intro	Hawthorne, Nathaniel	1804-1864	Isa 35:10
Calvin, John	1509-1564	Mt 20:12	Henry, Matthew	1662-1714	Gen 2:18
Carlyle, Thomas	1795-1881	Ex 1:11	Hodges, Phil		Eph 2:8
Carthusian Monks	11th-13th c	Heb 12:11	Hybels, Bill	1951-	Eph 2:8
Carver, George W	1864-1943	Ps 19	Inge, William Ralph	1860-1954	Mt 6:34
Cervantes, Miguel De	1547-1616	Prov Intro	Jefferson, Thomas	1743-1826	Prov 17:14
Chapin, Edwin H.	1814-1880	Job 23:10			Prov 25:16
Coleridge, Samuel T	1772-1834	1 Tim 1:3			

Herrick, Robert	1591-1674	Jas 5:16	Phillips, Ben		Titus 3:3
Hodges, Phil		Eph 2:8	Planck, Max	1858-1947	Heb 11:1
Hugh of St. Victor	1096-1141	Prov 3:13	Plato	428-348 BC	Prov 19:11
Hybels, Bill	1951-	Eph 2:8	Plummer, Alfred A.	1841-1926	Lk 15:17
Inge, William Ralph	1860-1954	Mt 6:34			Mt 5:43
Jefferson, Thomas	1743-1826	Prov 17:14	Quoist, Michael	1921-1997	Phil 2:14
		Prov 25:16	Reichel, Carl Rudolph	1718-1794	Isa 43:1
Jerome	331-420	Ezek 3:1	Richard of Chichester	1197-1253	1 John 2:4
John of Avila	1500-1569	Hab 3:17	Rosetti, Christina	1830-1894	Mt 7:5
		Gal 3:3	Ross, Hugh	1945-	Jonah 2:1
John of the Cross	1542-1591	Ps 122:4	Russell, Bertrand	1872-1970	Jas 3:17
		Prov 26:20	Rutherford, Ernest	1871-1937	1 Chr 29:14
Johnson, Samuel	1709-1786	1 Sam 24:4	Ryle, John Charles	1816-1900	Rom 8:5
Keller, Tim	1950-	John 1:14	Sangster, William E.	1900-1960	Neh 5:9
Kierkegaard, Soren	1813-1855	Ruth 3:1	Simeon, Charles	1759-1836	Rev 12:7
Kingsley, Charles	1819-1875	Eph 2:8	Spurgeon, Charles H	1834-1892	Num 20:5
Knott, Joshua		Neh 9:5			1 Chr 29:10
Latimer, Hugh	1485-1555	Judg 16:16			Zech 12:10
Lewis, C.S.	1898-1963	Ps 19	Steyn, Mark	1959 -	Isa 5:20
Lincoln, Abraham	1809-1865	2 Chr 7:14	Swift, Jonathan	1667-1745	Gen 1:1
Lotz, Ann Graham	1948-	Zp 1:4	Swindoll, Charles	1934-	Ex 2:24
			Talmud	c 200ad	Prov 3:13
Luther, Martin	1483-1546	Psalms	Temple, William	1881-1944	Rom 3:24
		Ps 73:3	Tennyson, Alfred	1809-1892	Prov 2:1
		Mk 10:45	Teresa, Mother	1910-1997	1 Cor 13:6
		Rom 1:1			Eph 4:32
		Rin 5:1	Tertullian	155-240	Jn 13:34
M'Cheyne, Robert M	1813-1843	Heb 7:25	Thalassios the Libyan	7th C	Eph 2:6
MacDonald, George	1824-1905	2 Cor 4:16	Threse of Liseux	1873-1897	Phil 3:9
Magee, John Gillespie	1922-1941	Eph	Tillotson, John	1630-1694	Ps 39:3
Margaret of Cortona	1247-1297	1 Kings 8:27	Twain, Mark	1803-1890	Lev 19:18
Mencken, H.L.	1880-1956	1 Tim 4:4	Washington, George	1732-1799	Deut 11:14
Merton, Thomas	1915-1968	Psalms	Watts, Isaac	1674-1748	Zech 9:9
Miller, Paul		Prov 8:1	Wayne, John	1907-1979	Ps 30:5
More, Thomas	1478-1535	Phil 4:8	Wesley, Charles	1707-1788	Phil 2:5
Moule, Handley	1824-1920	Rom 3:23			Phil 2:5
Morris, Leon	1914-2006	1 Cor 12:31	Wesley, Susannah	1669-1742	1 Jn 2:4
Murray, Andrew	1828-1917	Eph 3:20	Whitman, Walt	1819-1892	Num 13:1
Newton, Isaac	1643-1727	Gen 1:1	Wilkerson, David	1930-2011	Ps 27:13
Newton, John	1725-1807	1 Tim 1:16	Wilson, Thomas	1663-1755	Lev 19:18
			Wood, John M.		2 John 6
Pascal, Blaise	1623-1662	Ps 139:6			Rev 7:4
Patrick of Ireland	389-461	Ps 40:1	Wordsworth, Christopher	1807-1885	2 Tim 4:22
			Yancey, Philip	1949-	Jonah 2:1

Author Index

Adam, Peter	Mal 2:17, 3:14
Allen, Leslie C.	1 Chr 10:13, 13:10, 16:36, 2 Chr 7:14, 21:6, Joel 2:24, Obad 21, Jonah 1:5, 4:9, Mic 7:18
Atkinson, David	Gen 2:16
Augsberger, Myron S.	Mt 10:32
Augustine of Hippo	Heb 13:14
Baldwin, Joyce	Gen 13:12, 19:12
Baker, William	1 Cor 1:18
Barnett, Paul	2 Cor 3:18, 4:16, 12:7
Batusic, John	Gen 4:7, Ps 19:7, Dan 5:6, 11:35, Titus 2:12
Boice, James Montgomery	Gen 1:1, 4:7, Gen 6:9
Bridger, Gordon	Zp 1:4, 1:5, 3:17
Briscoe, Stuart	Gen 1:27, 22:1, 32:24, Rom 1:18, 3:27
Brown, Raymond	Num 6:24, 16:48, 20:5, 21:7, 24:17, 36:13, Deut 4:28, Neh 5:9, 9:5, Heb 1:2, 4:12, 8:1, 11:16, 12:11
Bruckner, James K	Ex 34:6
Cedar, Paul A.	Jas 1:19, 4:8
Chafin, Kenneth L.	1 Sam 28:15
Clarke, Adam	Prov 3:6
Clowney, Edmund	1 Pet 2:9, 4:8
Davids, Peter H.	Jas 1:5
Davis, Dale Ralph	Josh 5:12, 11:20, 15:20, 21:44, 24:19, 1 Sam 4:3, 16:7, 20:31, 22:17, 24:4, 25:11, 25:32, 30:3, 30:18, 2 Sam 2:4, 4:8, 6:6, 12:7, 16:23, 17:14, 18:14, 1 Kings 4:32, 8:27, 11:4, 16:23 18:21, 2 Kings 1:3, 17:33, 19:15, 25:27
Demarest, Gary W.	Lev 1:4, 11:44, 1 Th 4:3, 2 Tim 1:8, Titus 2:13

Diehl, Judith A.	2 Cor 4:7, 5:1
Dilday, Russell H.	1 Kings 3:3, 11:4, 2 Kings 4:5
Dunnam, Maxie	Ex 9:27, 12:11, 20:17, Gal 1:6, 2:16, 5:22, Eph 1:3, 1:18, 5:21, Phil 2:5, 4:6, 4:7, Col 1:3, 1:7, Phm 9
Edward, James R	Rom 3:23, 6:23, 7:25, 8:1, 8:18, 8:30, 12:1, Mk 2:16, 4:26, 7:26, 10:43, 12:29, 14:11, 14:68 Lk 1:46, 2:11, 4:18, 5:5, 6:35, 9:20, 9:34, 11:52, 14:11, 15:12, 15:17, 18:10, 19:9
Evans, Mary J.	1 Sam 14:1, 2 Sam 3:14, 2 Sam 7:22
Evans, Louis H.	Heb 6:1, 12:1
Firth, David G.	Est 4:14, 4:16
Ferguson, Sinclair	Dan 2:1
Fredrikson, Roger L.	John 1:1, 20:22
Fyall, Robert	Ezra 1:11, 4:24, 7:6
Green, Christopher	2 Pet 3:11, Jude 24
Green, Michael	Mt 1:23, 5:16, 5:48, 6:10, 7:13, 11:28, 13:45, 18:21, 18:26, 20:12, 22:12, 22:21, 23:24, 26:10, 27:21, 28:19
Grogan, Geoffrey	Mark 1:20, 14:3, 15:30
Guest, John	Lam 1:9, 3:7
Hagner, Donald A.	Heb 1:2
Hartley, John E.	Gen 12:2
Harvey, Jay	Ps 86:11, Dan 3:25
Henry, Matthew	Gen 1:1, 2:16, 3:6, 9:13, 22:9, 45:7, Ex 16:2, 25:9, Deut 6:4, 11:13, Psalms, Ps 19:1, 36:8, 107:7, Prov 12:16, 13:3, 15:23, 16:16, 16:18 Isa 6:3, Mt 6:19, 18:21, 27:3, Lk 23:42 Eph 2:6, Heb 6:19, Jas 3:17, Rev 21:3
Hillyer, Norman	2 Pet 1:5, 1:20–21, 2 Pet 3:18
Hubbard, David A.	Eccl 2:9, 8:17, Song 1:1, 4:7, 8:6–7, Prov 1:2, 1:7, 8:22, 13:1, 15:28, 31:10
Hubbard, Robert	Ruth 1:11, 1:15, 4:6, 4:17
Huffman, John A.	Josh 3:1
Jackman, David	Judg 3:15, 16:16, 21:25, Ruth 2:3, 3:1, 4:1, 4:17, 1 John 1:5, 2:4, 4:8, 4:9, 2 John 6, 3 John 9
Jacobson, Rolf A.	Ps 1:1
Jennings, F.C.	Isa 35:8, 43:1–2, 52:13, 55:1, 55:10

Kaiser, Walter	Hab 2:3, Hag 1:5, 2:7, Zech 1:3, 3:3, 9:9, Mal 1:2, 3:2
Keller, Phillip	Ps 23:3
Keller, Timothy	Gal 3:27, 4:23, Lk 15:29
Kidner, Derek	Eccl 8:17, 4:7, 8:6
Kitchen, John A.	Prov 1:1, 1:21, 3:5, 4:18, 4:23, 5:12, 8:1, 8:22, 10:13, 10:19, 14:12, 15:23, 17:14. 18:2, 18:22, 21:24, 22:3, 22:4, 23:17, 26:11, 27:17, 29:18, 31:10, 31:28, Col 1:27, 2:2, 2:20, 3:2, 4:5
Konkel, August H.	Job 28:12
Knott, Joshua	Judg 17:13, 19:25, Hag 1:5, 1 Tim 1:14
Laansma, Jon C.	Titus 1:1-3, 3:5
Larkin, William J.	Acts 10:19
Larniac, Timothy S.	Est 7:5
Larson, Bruce	Lk 2:13, 7:43
Lucas, Dick	1 Pet 2:18, Jude 24
Lucas, R.C.	Col 1:15, Phm 14
MacArthur, John	1 Cor 13:4
Mackay, John L.	Mal 2:16
Maxwell, John C.	Deut 1:28, 4:2
McKenna, David L.	Job 1:1, 8:18, 9:33, 19:25, 23:10, 31:26, 32:20, 33:14, 35:11, 38:4, 38:33, 42:6, 42:17, Mk 1:41, 7:37, 10:45
Millar, Gary	1 Kings 4:20, 2 Kings 16:10
Miller, Paul	Heb 7:25
Milne, Bruce	John 1:1, 1:14, 3:3, 3:16, 3:30, 8:58, 10:28, 11:37, 13:34, 16:8, 17:3, 18:39, 19:30
Missler, Chuck	Gen 5
Motyer, J. Alec	Ex 1:11, 2:24, 3:11, 19:5, 40:34, Isa 6:3, 30:10, 40:28, Amos 4:7, 5:23, 8:2, Phil 1:6, 1:20, 2:9, 3:8, 3:9, 4:8, Jas 1:18, 3:2, 4:8, 5:16
Mullholland, M. Robert	Rev 4:10-11, 13:11
Nixon, Rosemary	Jonah 1, 2:1, 4:10
Nouwen, Henri J.M.	Lk 15:13, 15:29
Ogilvie, Lloyd	Hos 3:1, 4:6, Amos 1:11, Obad 3, Obad 21, Acts 2:2, 10:34, 15:11, 24:25, 28:30
Olley, John W.	1 Kings 16:23

Oswalt, John N.	Ex 3:2, Isa 6:5, 9:6, 14:14, 24:5, 29:16, 30:18, 30:21, 35:10, 36:20, 40:9, 53:2, 53:6, 53:12, 55:1, 60:9, 66:22
Palmer, Earl F.	1 John 1:5, 1:9, Rev 2:4, 3:15, 5:1, 7:17, 11:15, 12:7, 21:5, 21:18, 22:20
Peterson, Eugene	2 Sam 6:6, 12:7, Ps 10:13, 19:1, 19:7, 36:5, 40:17, 51:1, 73:3, 77:8, 84:1, 98:4, 121:8, 123:1, 124:1, 124:8, 126:5, 131:1, 134:2, 139:23, Eph 1:18, 1Th 5:23, Rev 1:1, 3:20, 7:4, 8:4, 13:8, 13:18, 19:9, 21:6, 21:10, 21:22, 22:20
Patterson, Richard D.	Hos 7:13-14
Philip, James	Num 9:17, 11:1
Phillips, Ben	John 3:4, 18:11, Titus 3:3
Phillips, John	Gen 6:14, 12:1, 22:13, 25:12, 32:24, 41:40
Phillips, Richard D.	Zech 12:10, 13:1
Prior, David	Joel 3:16, 3:18, Mic 6:8, Hab 1:5, 3:17, 1 Cor 3:19, 4:5, 8:1, 12:31, 13:4, 15:42
Roberts, Mark D.	Ezra 10:11, Est 6:1, 8:2, 9:28
Robertson, O. Palmer	Nah 3:1, 3:19
Ruckman, Peter S.	2 Cor 5:1
Scott, James M.	2 Cor 13:14
Slick, Matt	Lk 15:12
Smedes, Lewis	1 Cor 13:4
Smith, Chuck	Acts 2:37, 10:5, 17:6
Storms, Sam	1 Pet 1:1, 1:13
Spurgeon, Charles Haddon	Ps 3:2, 4:6, 8:1, 16:11, 23, 25:1, 25:4, 42:1, 63:1, 90:4, 104:19, 119, 119:105, 139:6, 141:3, 150:6, Mt 5:9, 6:34, 7:5, 7:12, 7:24, Mk 8:36, 2 Cor 5:17, 5:21, 1 Pet 1:3
Stott, John	Mt 5:43, Acts 9:17, 12:23, 28:30, Rom 2:1, 3:24, 5:1, 8:5, 8:28, 8:38, 10:2, 11:33, 12:2 Gal 1:8, 3:3, 3:24, Eph 2:1, 2:6, 2:8, 3:17, 3:20, 4:15, 4:22, 5:18, 5:22, 1 Th 2:19, 4:1, 2 Th 1:10, 1 Tim 1:3, 1:14, 1:16, 2:5, 2Tim 1:9, 3:16, 4:6, 4:18, Titus 2:10, 2:12
Stuart, Douglas	Ezek 1:28, 33:11
Swindoll, Charles	Job 15:13, Mt 15:31, Lk 6:35, 24:5, 27:52, John 5:10, Acts 1:8 Eph 3:17, 3:20, Phil 2:5, 4:4, 1 Tim 6:11, Jas 4:2, 2 Pet 1:5, Jude

Tanner, Beth LaNeel	Ps 22:1
Tidball, Derek	Lev 5:18, 6:9, 11:2, 19:18
Thompson, David L.	Ezek 18:32
Trites, Allison	Lk 13:24
Wallace, Ronald	Dan 4:5, 7:13, 8:8, 12:1
Waltke, Bruce K	Gen 6–8, 11:7, Prov 3:13, 8:5
Ward, Hannah and Wild, Jennifer	Gen 1:1, Ex 1:11, 14:14, lev 19:18, Deut 8:17, Judg 16:16, 1 Sam 24:4, 1 Kings 8:27, Ps 40:1, 122:4, Prov 1:7, 2:10, 3:5, 5:12,12:16,16:18, 17:9, 17:14, Amos 5:23, Mt 1:23, 5:43, 6:34,7:13, 18:21, Mk 10:45, Rom 10:2,11:33, 12:1, 1 Cor 8:1, 13:6, 2 Cor 4:16, Eph 2:6, Phil 3:9, 4:8, 1 Tim 1:3, 2 Tim 3:16, Heb 7:25, 11:16,12:11, Jas 4:8, 4:10, 1 John 2:4, Rev 12:7, 21:5
Webb, Barry	Zech 3:3
Widder, Wendy L.	Dan 1:17
Wilcock, Michael	Judg 21:25, 1 Chr 29:14, Ps 1:1, 13:1, 23:6, 27:13, 30:5, 36:5, 40:1, 43:3, 51:1, 57, 64, 65:9, 73:16, 77:8, 84:1, 91:10, 93:1, 98:4, 103:12, 103:19, 104:1, 107:28, 119:19, 119:175, 126:5, 135:13, 139:1, 139:23, 145:9, 150:6, Rev 1:1, 1:4, 4:1, 13:18, 20:12, 21:1, 21:6
Williams, David J.	1 Th 5:23
Williams, Donald M.	Ps 19:1
Williams, Donald T.	Job 38:7
Winslow, Octavius	John 15:13
Wood, John	Introduction, Gen 1:1, Mt 26:10, Mk 8:24, Heb 11:1, 2 John 6
Woodhouse, John	Col 2:13, 3:1
Wright, Christopher J. H.	Ex 19:4, Deut 5:6, 6:4, 10:12, 30:19, Jer 8:4, 12:1 13:11, 23:3, 29:11, 31:1, 31:12,31:33, Lam, Lam 2:8,3:22, 3:25, 3:31, 5:21, Ezek 3:1, 16:14, 16:25, 18:2, 18:21, 33:21, 37:9, 43:7, 43:27, 47:12, 48:35

www.ingramcontent.com/pod-product-compliance
Lightning Source LLC
Chambersburg PA
CBHW071425070526
44578CB00001B/7